Nature of the Miracle Years

Studies in German History
Published in Association with the German Historical Institute, Washington, DC

General Editor: **Christof Mauch**, Director of the German Historical Institute, Washington, DC, and Professor of North American History at the University of Munich

NATURE OF THE MIRACLE YEARS

Conservation in West Germany, 1945–1975

Sandra Chaney

Berghahn Books
NEW YORK • OXFORD

Published in 2008 by
Berghahn Books
www.berghahnbooks.com

Library of Congress Cataloging-in-Publication Data

Chaney, Sandra.
    Nature of the miracle years: conservation in West Germany, 1945–1975 /
Sandra Chaney.
        p.   cm.
    Includes bibliographical references and index.
    ISBN 978-1-84545-430-2 (hardback : alk. paper)
    1. Nature conservation—Germany—History—20th century. I. Title.
QH77.G3C43   2008
333.720943'09045—dc22   2008007619

British Library Cataloguing in Publication Data

A catalogue record for this book is available from the British Library.
Printed in the United States on acid-free paper

ISBN 978-1-84545-430-2   hardback

CONTENTS

LIST OF MAPS

LIST OF ABBREVIATIONS

AA	Auswärtiges Amt
ABN	Arbeitsgemeinschaft Deutscher Beauftragter für Naturschutz und Landschaftspflege
AID	Auswertungs- und Informationsdienst für Ernährung, Landwirtschaft und Forsten e.V.
APO	Außerparlamentarische Opposition
BAK	Bundesarchiv, Koblenz
BAN	Bundesamt für Naturschutz
BANL	Bundesanstalt für Naturschutz und Landschaftspflege
BAStA	Bundesarchiv-Zwischenarchiv, St. Augustin-Hangelar
BAVNL	Bundesanstalt für Vegetationskunde, Naturschutz und Landschaftspflege
BBU	Bundesverband Bürgerinitiativen Umweltschutz
BDI	Bundesverband der Deutschen Industrie
BFANL	Bundesforschungsanstalt für Naturschutz und Landschaftsökologie
BHStA MK	Bayerisches Hauptstaatsarchiv, Staatsministerium für Unterricht und Kultus
BHStA MWi	Bayerisches Hauptstaatsarchiv, Staatsministerium für Wirtschaft und Verkehr
BHStA StK	Bayerisches Hauptstaatsarchiv, Staatskanzlei
BMI	Bundesministerium des Innern
BML	Bundesministerium für Ernährung, Landwirtschaft und Forsten
BUND	Bund für Umwelt- und Naturschutz in Deutschland
CDU	Christlich-Demokratische Union
CSU	Christlich-Soziale Union
DBB	Deutsche Bundesbahn
DIHT	Deutscher Industrie und Handelstag
DNR	Deutscher Naturschutzring

DRL	Deutscher Rat für Landespflege
ECY	European Conservation Year
EEC	European Economic Community
FAO	Food and Agriculture Organization of the United Nations
FDP	Freie Demokratische Partei
HStA S	Landesarchiv Baden-Württemberg, Hauptstaatsarchiv Stuttgart
IPA	Interparlamentarische Arbeitsgemeinschaft für eine naturgemäße Wirtschaft
JfNL	*Jahrbuch für Naturschutz und Landschaftspflege*
LH K	Rheinland-Pfalz, Landeshauptarchiv Koblenz
N & L	*Natur und Landschaft*
NDP	Nationaldemokratische Partei
RKFDV	Reichskommissariat für die Festigung Deutschen Volkstums
RNG	Reichsnaturschutzgesetz
SDW	Schutzgemeinschaft Deutscher Wald
SPD	Sozialdemokratische Partei Deutschlands
SWV-B	Schwarzwaldverein, Bonndorf
VDN	Verband Deutscher Naturparkträger
VNP	Verein Naturschutzpark
WVESI	Wirtschaftsvereinigung der Eisen- und Stahlindustrien

ACKNOWLEDGEMENTS

In working on this project, I have benefited from the support of many institutions and people. Research for the study was made possible by a grant from the German Academic Exchange Service and from funds approved by the Faculty Development Committee of Erskine College. I am grateful to the helpful and accommodating staff at the Bundesarchiv in Koblenz and St. Augustin-Hangelar, the Politisches Archiv of the Auswärtiges Amt in Bonn, the Bayerisches Hauptstaatsarchiv in Munich, the Hauptstaatsarchiv in Stuttgart, and the Landeshauptarchiv in Koblenz. The librarians at the Bundesamt für Naturschutz went out of their way to assist me. At the film archive in the Auswertungs- und Informationsdienst für Ernährung, Landwirtschaft und Forsten, Mr. Meyer made numerous films available for me to view. Mrs. Inden-Heinrich took time away from her other duties to assist me in using the Deutscher Naturschutzring archives, and Mr. Jens Tönnießen and Mrs. Maria Stadler steered me in appropriate directions in the archives of the Verein Naturschutzpark and the Verband Deutscher Naturparkträger. Mr. Oskar Stritt and Mr. Thomas Heidegger, members of the Schwarzwaldverein, were most helpful in arranging for me to use the society's archives. The staff in the Inter-Library Loan Department in Davis Library at the University of North Carolina at Chapel Hill and Sara Morrison in McCain Library at Erskine College provided valuable support for the project with their resourcefulness in obtaining research materials.

A number of individuals who agreed to talk with me in the 1990s about their experiences in conservation in West Germany enriched my perspective and reinforced that others can benefit from hearing their stories. Dr. Hans Bibelriether, Professor Dr. Wolfgang Haber, Mr. Fritz Hockenjos, the late Dr. h.c. Erich Hornsmann, Professor Dr. Wolfram Pflug, and Dr. Ernst Preising were generous with their time and responded to my questions with patience and frankness. I am especially indebted to the late Professor Dr. Wolfgang Erz for his constructive criticisms of, and support for, my work.

My colleagues in the Department of History at Erskine College—Nancy Erickson, Jim Gettys, David Grier, and the late Bill Kuykendall—have been a constant source of encouragement and good humor. Erskine's Academic Dean, Dr. Donald Weatherman, instituted a sabbatical program that helped immeasurably in completing this study. For their constructive comments on parts or all of the study and their exchange of ideas that made the research and writing intellectually rewarding, I would like to thank Doris Bergen, David Blackbourn, Jane Carruthers, Hans Engler, David Grier, Rita Gudermann, John Headley, Lloyd Kramer, Thomas Lekan, Christof Mauch, Joachim Radkau, Donald Reid, David Ritland, Nathan Stoltzfus, Jens and Margaret Tönnießen, Gerhard Weinberg, Douglas Weiner, and Thomas Zeller. Jens Ivo Engels deserves a special word of thanks for reading the manuscript in full, raising challenging questions, and offering helpful comments that improved the study in numerous ways. I owe Konrad Jarausch a debt of gratitude beyond measure for being a constant source of encouragement, pragmatic advice, and wisdom over the years. An anonymous reviewer of an early version of the manuscript provided detailed comments that encouraged me to make needed revisions from a fresh perspective. Two anonymous reviewers of the revised manuscript offered immensely helpful comments in the final stages of the project and challenged me to open the study to a wider audience. I am grateful to Christopher Robinson for his painstaking work in producing the maps that accompany the text.

I am indebted to the Friends of the German Historical Institute in Washington, DC for encouraging research in German history, including by establishing the Fritz Stern Dissertation Prize. It was a special honor for the dissertation version of this study to have been the first corecipient of the award. Sincere thanks goes to the members of the selection committee, Kathleen Conzen, Vernon Lidtke, and Jonathan Petropoulos, for reading the study and finding it worthy of the prize. I am especially grateful to Christof Mauch, Director of the German Historical Institute, for taking an interest in the manuscript and supporting its publication. David Lazar, Senior Editor at the German Historical Institute, has my thanks for his patience, humor, and advice. I am grateful to Marion Berghahn at Berghahn Books for accepting the manuscript for publication. Many thanks to Melissa Spinelli, Production Manager at Berghahn Books, for patiently responding to my lists of questions and for attending to the details involved in the production process. For her careful editing of the manuscript I thank Cassandra Caswell.

I am especially appreciative of my family. For their constant loving presence, I thank my mother, Jane Chaney, and my late father, Richard Chaney. They made a good living on the land in southwestern Montana, and I cannot help but think that it was their choice of livelihoods that shaped my views of nature and eventually inspired my search for it in a country half a world away. While I was working on the project, my dearest friend and spouse, David Grier, patiently offered support and read countless revisions, and our daughter, Anna Mei, constantly kept me amused and amazed. It is to her and David that this study is dedicated.

Introduction

As he traveled east across north central Germany in mid April 1945 in the comfort of a sedan, Major Charles Kindleberger, an intelligence officer with the US Twelfth Army Group and later one of the most influential economists and economic historians of his time, marveled at the "beautiful view of a beautiful countryside that the autobahn affords." True, there were signs of war everywhere: en route from Frankfurt to Dora Mittelbau, the elaborate underground factory near Nordhausen where the Nazi regime manufactured V-weapons using forced labor, Kindleberger took in scenes of fuel dumps and destroyed bridges, of "Germans moving in all directions, possessions piled high on carts," of "roads strewn with foreigners . . . in every ditch . . . resting, thinking, waiting, worrying." But there also was much attractive, orderly countryside that had escaped the ravages of war. "This is a lovely time of year at most places in the northern hemisphere," he wrote in a letter home to his wife, "But the well-cultivated fields of German farmers who put prodigious amounts of work into the preparation of the land . . . the lack of any waste land, the trimness of cultivated forests free from underbrush and with spaced trees growing straight and tall, make the scenery viewed from the autobahn, skirting all cities, something quite magical and apart."[1]
As Kindleberger glided along the highway over the rolling hills of central Germany, he recalled the parkways that meandered through the hilly landscapes of the American Northeast. The images he took in of carefully tended countryside were reminiscent of places back home, and yet they seemed uniquely German to him, shaped by that people's supposed penchant for hard work, thrift, and order. Viewed from the window of a car, the German countryside was lovely scenery suspended in time in an otherly realm, one that remained unmarked by the harsh realities of the present and untainted by the cruelties of the recent past. But the manicured fields and timber plantations that Kindleberger found "magical" in their visual effect were physical spaces that had been shaped continuously over centuries, influenced by changing visions of nature and by shifting political, social, and economic contexts.

Notes for this chapter begin on page 12.

Kindleberger was not unique in using the physical appearance of landscapes to make judgments about the cultural values and temperament of the people who inhabited them. Influenced by the legacy of Romanticism and the movement to protect local or homeland landscapes (*Heimatschutzbewegung*) that emerged at the end of the nineteenth century, German conservationists long had assumed that the strength and character of people were reflected in and dependent upon the beauty and health of the landscapes they occupied. At the end of the most destructive war in modern history, they, like Kindleberger, viewed their managed forests and ordered farms as politically neutral places offering sanctuary from the chaos and despair of the present. Unsullied by the recent past, but displaying the indelible mark of human uses in better, more distant times, nature seemed to be a source of "spiritual strength for clearing away the rubble in the cities and in souls" and a fount of hope for healing society and rebuilding a stable economy and polity.[2]

That was in 1945. What happened to nature, and to the practice of conservation, after Germany was divided and became even more industrialized, urban, and prosperous within a generation? This study seeks to answer this question by focusing on developments in conservation in West Germany after the collapse of National Socialism and before the emergence of the ecology movement and the Green Party. The chapters that follow show how a predominantly conservative, often nationalistic cause (and for some in the interwar years, a racially justified one) gradually became associated more clearly with the political left and the international movement to protect the global environment, though without losing its traditional base of support among social conservatives and without completely abandoning its critique of modern civilization. By situating conservation in the mainstream of West German political and cultural history, the study refutes the assumption that protecting nature (*Naturschutz*) was ineffective after 1945 because of too close an association with National Socialism. *Naturschutz* emerged from the war somewhat tainted, but no more so than other activities that had been unevenly coordinated by the Nazis.[3] Admittedly, postwar conservationists never commanded a mass following. And they lost many battles during the so-called Miracle Years when economic growth and western European integration were commanding priorities of state and society. Yet conservationists were resilient. Forced by necessity to change, those involved in state-sponsored conservation institutionalized and professionalized their efforts, while several private groups adopted a more confrontational message and style and broadened their membership base. Such changes assured conservationists a strong position of transitioning, rather than vanishing, during the shift to left-leaning environmental protection (*Umweltschutz*) in the 1970s.

There is no book length account in English that focuses exclusively on the thought, goals, and day-to-day activities of conservationists during the critical years between 1945 and 1975. A study that examines continuity and change in Germany's long tradition of protecting nature after the Nazis and before the Greens has been made more important with the recent publication of numerous books and edited collections on nature and environmental protection under National Socialism. These studies emphasize that the Nazi regime implemented some "green" reforms (sometimes in the service of racial ideology), but rarely was it done consistently. In addition, the regime did not co-opt preservationists fully or uniformly, especially because of the persistence of regional identities.[4] Precisely because of these realities, conservationists resumed their work after the war with little interruption, as recent research on the post–1945 era by German scholars has shown.[5] These studies, as well as others that address the postwar years in their long range view of nature and environmental protection, also make clear that the 1950s and 1960s did not lack people with an environmental awareness or an ecological consciousness according to today's understanding of those phrases. What conservationists lacked during the boom years was a political climate and mass following that would allow them to transform their awareness into policies that provided better protection for nature and people.[6]

Despite acknowledging increased activity to protect nature and the environment, some accounts of the postwar years imply that "old" conservation, with its undeniable elitism and social conservatism was not only distinct from, but also far less effective than, the "new" left-leaning, anti-nuclear, grassroots environmentalism that emerged in the 1970s.[7] Without a doubt, the emphasis that activists of the 1970s placed on participatory democracy and deep social reform was distinct and set the modern environmental movement apart from the conservation tradition. But viewing activists of the late 1960s and 1970s as the norm against which conservationists of the 1950s and 1960s are measured leads to the predictable conclusion that these latter people—most of them, anyway—failed to measure up most of the time. In addition, highlighting the rebellious rhetoric and sensational protests associated with modern environmentalism overshadows more subtle shifts in language, thought, and daily activity that occurred within the conservation tradition prior to the 1970s.

Another tendency in the writing of conservation history involves adopting the story line of conservationists themselves, depicting their efforts to protect nature as an heroic, moral struggle by a marginalized minority against formidable, unprincipled foes—typically industrial capitalism or technology.[8] Although conservationists were a minority, they were not as marginalized as they claimed. But if they lacked support (and they often did), it was partly their own fault. Convinced that they knew how to defend nature better than most people, they resisted forming alliances with groups that did not share their conservative world view.[9] Yet as historian Michael Bess has argued in his study of postwar France, conflicts over the use of nature in development projects typically ended in compromises in which defenders of nature and proponents of technology had partial gains and losses.

"[E]ither through political compromise or through the sheer inertia of decision-making processes in a mass democracy," he writes, "an outcome emerged that borrowed elements from both visions. . . ." Over many years, the two seemingly opposing perspectives—the pro-nature and the pro-technology—intermingled, contributing to "the *partial* greening of the mainstream, in which neither side emerged wholly satisfied nor utterly dismayed, but in which a whole new complex of discourses and institutions nonetheless came into being." Such an assessment is relevant also in the West German context. Bess's findings for postwar France invite historians of Germany to examine the Miracle Years with an eye toward discovering how conservationists and their real and perceived opponents participated in creating what Bess calls "the light-green society," i.e., a society that aspires to be "traditional *and* modern, green *and* mass-consumerist" simultaneously.[10]

The challenge of reconciling these seemingly opposing goals was not entirely new. Yet the need to harmonize them appeared increasingly urgent in the postwar era. Beginning in the 1950s, industrialized nations around the world experienced an accelerated increase in gross domestic product, energy consumption, land use, trash accumulation, and pollution of water, soil, and air, a complex of problems that European environmental historians have dubbed the "1950s Syndrome." The convergence of these developments marked the beginning of the shift from an industrial to a mass consumer society, with significant changes in lifestyle and consumption that exacerbated environmental deterioration and caused irreversible harm in some cases.[11] Earlier periods in history had experienced similar upheavals, for example after 1870 and 1920, but the pace of change was more rapid after 1945, and the invasiveness of development projects greater.[12]

Demographics also deepened their impact. Between the late 1940s and the early 1970s, the population of West Germany climbed from 49 million to over 60 million. With an average of 247 people per square kilometer in 1970, West Germany ranked seventh among the world's most densely populated nations. By 1970, one-third of the country's inhabitants lived in cities of over 100,000 and roughly 90 percent of the population earned a living in industry or the service sector. Only 8.5 percent of West Germans made a living from agriculture, down from 23 percent two decades earlier. Commerce and industry contributed most to the Federal Republic's powerful economic position behind only the United States and Japan.[13] But there was a price to pay for this prosperity and economic influence.

Already in the early 1960s, West German conservationists warned that 260 square kilometers of countryside were lost annually to support the expansion of industry, housing, transportation, and the military. More of the country was adversely affected by the "garbage of civilization" in the form of noise, dust, and harmful pollutants. And there was no indication that the pace of these negative changes would slow.[14] As West Germany became more densely populated, urbanized, industrialized, and polluted, people involved in preservation broadened the range of their activities, getting more involved in land use and spatial planning (*Raumordnung*) in the 1960s before finding their work subsumed under, and transformed by, the government's program to protect the human environment (*Umweltschutz*) in the early 1970s. Using the shift in public discourse from *Naturschutz* to *Umweltschutz* as a broad framework, this study identifies continuities and incremental changes in conservationists' views and treatment of nature as they sought to modernize their movement in the challenging postwar context.

In describing the activities of those involved in protecting nature this study faces something of a challenge because the German terms are more precise than those in English and because the meanings given to even the most basic concepts fluctuated over time and depended on the context in which they were used. In general, the study avoids using "environmental protection" until the term becomes a part of public discourse around 1970. The text assumes that the term "conservation" is appropriate only when activities include preservation *and* stewardship of land and natural resources. Applying this latter term is problematic because there is no German word that directly translates as "conservation," or resource management, as it was defined by Anglo-Americans. Those involved in protecting and caring for nature in West Germany initially employed the cumbersome pairing, "nature preservation" (*Naturschutz*) and "landscape care" (*Landschaftspflege*), as the German equivalent. However awkward the phrasing, it captured the coming together of two approaches toward tending nature in Germany, one emphasizing the preservation of species and small spaces in the interest of historic preservation and scientific research, the other focusing on shaping rural landscapes in their entirety to accommodate economic modernization. With no wilderness to speak of, conservationists in Germany and elsewhere in Europe had long focused on protecting nature in the form of "cultural landscapes," i.e., aesthetically pleasing parts of the countryside that seemed to exhibit the harmonious interplay of natural forces and centuries of traditional human uses.[15]

In the first decades of the twentieth century, some German preservationists had advocated landscape care as a way to reform traditional nature protection, broadening its scope beyond the preservation of individual natural objects, species, and small reserves to include the protection and planned use of entire landscapes, including their urban, industrial features. Germans and other Europeans sought to protect what many environmental historians today would call "hybrid landscapes," a phrase that refers to areas displaying varying combinations of the natural and the human engineered.[16] In industrial nations during the twentieth century, the natural and the engineered intersected more frequently, and at an accelerated pace after the 1950s, resulting in landscapes that seemed increasingly artificial. Thus, West German conservationists faced a significant challenge during the Miracle Years in trying to preserve or restore varying degrees of naturalness to landscapes that ranged from predominantly rural to primarily urban and industrial.

The pairing of the terms *Naturschutz* and *Landschaftspflege* more intentionally after World War II reflected the continued influence of landscape architects, who occupied an important place in early twentieth century preservation and whose small profession rose to prominence under National Socialism.[17] Yet the conjoining of these familiar concepts also expressed the attempt to develop a more flexible response to the challenge of protecting nature and natural resources when the times required their temporary exploitation. After 1945, resource conservation came to be associated with what Germans referred to as *Naturschutz* and *Landschaftspflege*, because of critical shortages of food, fuel, and raw materials that accompanied the country's economic and political collapse, but also because of the role that North America played in addressing the global scarcity of resources in the aftermath of war.

In view of these developments, the study applies the label "conservationist" to those people most actively involved in debates over nature's protection and use in the postwar era. It does so, however, without losing sight of the diversity of occupations (especially forestry, landscape architecture, engineering, and civil service, including pedagogy) and fields of study (most commonly biology, botany, horticulture, zoology, and later, ecology) these people represented. It uses the designation also while remaining sensitive to their sometimes conflicting priorities (such as species preservation, resource conservation, recreation, and land use planning) and to their different levels of commitment to the cause (avocation versus career).

This discussion of terminology is not simply quibbling over concepts. Influenced by the "linguistic turn" in history several years ago, environmental historians acknowledge that the language available to people at a given time to talk about nature does not merely reflect material reality. Nature, the "real thing," cannot be separated from the meanings people have assigned to it over time. Words used in reference to nature communicate mental images of the shape that nature is supposed to take (e.g., a "healthy landscape," a "green environment," or a protected "fragile biotope") and express perceptions of nature's reality based on the current state of knowledge ("a living river" in 1950s' parlance became "a river ecosystem" a decade later, for example). Furthermore, the terms employed in relation to nature's treatment communicate what is being done or what people think ought to be done to shape it according to agreed upon standards (such as "preservation," which implies non-use or "landscape care," which suggests guided use). But when accepted terms no longer capture changing material realities, there is a shift in discourse, one that not only reflects those changes, but also simultaneously facilitates the development of new ways of thinking and acting.[18] When West German conservationists talked about protecting "primeval landscapes of the homeland," about improving the "health and productivity of landscapes where people lived, worked, and relaxed," about protecting humans' "endangered living space," about "rationally managing ecosystems of the biosphere," and finally, about securing a "healthy environment," they communicated the shift away from an aesthetic and provincial strategy in caring for nature toward an approach that was presumably more scientific, objective, and universal. This process of modernization was neither even nor without conflict, but it was underway before the emergence of the modern environmental movement.

Although scholars have scrutinized the concept "nature" and the meanings associated with "landscape"[19] and "ecology,"[20] they have been less critical of the term "environment." But as historian Douglas Weiner has observed, "Because 'the environment' is a term that has a universal ring to it and pretends to embrace the general good, it serves as an excellent mask for particular interests."[21] Moreover, as another scholar has written, the environment (*Umwelt*) is "a highly anthropocentric term that encourages the notion that nature is strictly 'ours'—i.e., 'our environment.' Furthermore, since *environment* literally means *surroundings,* it is obviously a rather bland and inadequate term to use in reference to nature."[22]

In 1970, West German conservationists came to some of the same conclusions, but they could not prevent the adoption of "environmental protection," a slogan that captured the new concern to protect human beings in their increasingly imperiled surroundings. As worsening pollution gave tangibility to the surroundings that people heretofore had little noticed, the idea of "protecting the environment" (more so than "protecting nature") seemed urgently necessary. And to the inhabitants of urban areas that were perceived to be unhealthy—and highly engineered—the notion of protecting the environment seemed directly relevant and personal in a way that protecting nature probably never could or would be. But what was the role of nature—as an idea and the thing in and of itself—within the newly invented environment? This study concludes that the invention of the environment in West Germany and elsewhere expressed the widespread realization that humans had become the primary architects of their surroundings. As such, they were responsible for keeping the environment healthy and "natural" to varying degrees. Although there was not one shared ideal of what nature ought to look like, there was broad consensus that it had become something finite and in need of protection.[23]

As the West German case illustrates, at its core, protecting the natural world involves a contest for power among groups and institutions who want their subjective views of nature and their ideals about the relationship that humans ought to have with it to prevail. But in democratic societies like West Germany, people must make compromises in deciding what objects, species, spaces, and uses of nature to protect. This study shows that these ongoing compromises contributed to the gradual and partial greening of the mainstream of society even before the emergence of modern environmentalism. It illustrates, too, how these compromises reflected not only thoughts and ideas about nature, but laws and institutions. Thus, this study seeks to navigate between the "envisioned" and the material, between conservationists' thoughts and words on the one hand, and their actions as determined by legal and administrative arrangements, on the other. As Joachim Radkau has stressed in an appeal for more attention to institutions in environmental history, "it is important to distinguish between the history of the imagination, on the one hand, and the history of the real, effective relations between man and nature, on the other." David Blackbourn, too, has cautioned that "in the era after the 'linguistic turn' it is important to defend the legitimacy of a materialist history" while continuing to take into account the "mental geographies and constructs that humans place on the natural world."[24]

The mental geographies that shaped conservationists' actions after 1945 were marked more by constancy than by change. Those responsible for conservation resumed their work after the war with a high degree of continuity in terms of laws, personnel, and ideology. The Reich Nature Protection Law of 1935 remained in effect and the administrative arrangement it provided for survived in modified form until the 1970s. Under the Federal Republic, however, the states resumed their traditional hold over conservation, reversing the centralization that had occurred under National Socialism. Despite opposition from some, postwar refederalization sometimes worked to the advantage of conservationists. In West Germany, and traditionally in Central Europe, parties wanting to use natural resources must secure approval through local licensing hearings in which those affected have the opportunity to raise objections, including conservation officials. But when a distant authority makes decisions about use, often with limited knowledge of local conditions, locals have fewer means to shape the outcome.[25]

Continuity, more so than change, was also evident in the profile of conservationists. Many of the men (there were few women) who shaped postwar conservation into the 1960s came from the generation born around 1900, in the latter years of the Wilhelmine Empire, and had been responsible for nature's care since the 1920s and 1930s. They tended to be solidly middle class and conservative in their politics. Many of them, but by no means all, were guided by an aesthetic of nature that had been shaped by the homeland preservation movement and by their shared experiences in the back-to-nature youth movement of the 1910s and 1920s. Their ideal of nature most often took the form of carefully tended agrarian landscapes dating from before 1850 and displaying a harmonious blending of meadows, fields and hedgerows, orchards and patches of forest, and tidy villages made quaint by regional architecture. Walking regularly in the solitude of nature, they believed, fostered introspection and aided in cultivating self-reliant individuals capable of combating the alienation associated with modernity and urban mass society. So, too, would a lifestyle of temperance and moderation. Into the 1960s, leading conservationists, Social Democrats among them, embraced this set of assumptions, promoting them as a way to strengthen individual moral character, and by extension, foster patriotic citizens loyal to the state—now a democratic one. In general, however, conservationists tended to be wary of mass democracy, preferring to work behind the scenes to lobby officials and political leaders. They continued to sound elitist in assuming that "rootless" urbanites living in "denatured" cities needed to spend time in the presumably purer realm of nature to regain their sense of well-being. And they never tired of echoing their predecessors in demanding better instruction in the natural sciences to cultivate among the majority of people an appreciation for nature and an understanding of how they should conduct themselves in the outdoors.[26]

Continuity also was apparent in the lingering popularity among conservationists to protect nature-as-*Heimat,* to use David Blackbourn's apt phrasing. Although some historians have asserted that homeland preservation lacked influence after the war because of its anti-modern outlook and its supposed corruption by National Socialism, this is not supported by the evidence. During the first postwar decade in West Germany, and for an even longer period in East Germany, conservationists expressed some of their goals in terms of *Heimatschutz,* embracing its inclusiveness, its emphasis on moderation, and its qualified acceptance of modernity.[27] As one historian has written, *Heimat* emerged from the "Nazi Reich as a victim, not a perpetrator" and "embod[ied] the political and social community that could be salvaged from the Nazi ruins."[28] Like "women of the rubble," who for some symbolized German victimhood and reconstruction, nature of the homeland was viewed as a victim of Nazi and Allied exploitation as well as the source of natural resources essential for rebuilding the nation.[29] Whether depicted as idyllic rural settings in popular *Heimat* films of the 1950s, defined as a welcoming home for expellees and returning POWs, reclaimed as the city of origin of wartime evacuees awaiting return, or envisioned as a harmonious blend of fertile landscapes and ordered economic development in the writings of conservationists, "the homeland" represented something good in Germany's past and offered hope for its future.[30] In a time when overt nationalism was taboo, and when few West Germans felt an attachment to their new political boundaries that were presumed to be temporary, the language of *Heimat* provided a familiar and acceptable way to express loyalty to the national community as well as affection for one's locality or region. For conservationists, protecting nature-as-local-homeland also was a practical goal because the base of support for *Naturschutz* historically had been at the provincial level.

In no way, however, did postwar conservationists want their activities to be viewed merely as an extension of homeland preservation with its broad cultural agenda that only sometimes overlapped with nature's care. Over the course of the 1950s, protecting nature-as-*Heimat* faded in importance as a goal, replaced by the more scientific-sounding concern to protect the health of landscapes—and by extension, the health of people and the economy. Such a shift reflected the prioritization of scientific and economic considerations in political discourse, as well as the Federal Republic's integration into Western Europe, a development that made the nativist-sounding aims of *Heimatschutz* less convincing.

Despite striking continuities with early twentieth century preservation, postwar conservationists had little choice but to modify their views and practices in direct response to larger political and economic events and social and environmental conditions. Chapter periodizations in this book help to capture shifts in conservationists' goals and practices as they asserted the value of their work first for economic recovery and democratic renewal, then for public health and spatial planning, and finally, for cleaning up the environment. The study begins with a background chapter that outlines the mixed legacy conservationists inherited in 1945, one that bore the imprint of three different political systems, the Second Empire (1871–1918), the Weimar Republic (1919–1933), and the Nazi Dictatorship (1933–1945). The core of the study is divided into three chronological sections, which include an overarching chapter that examines dominant trends in conservation, and a narrowly focused case study that illustrates these tendencies in greater depth. (Though all three case studies focus on Catholic regions, they can be viewed as representative of general trends.) Each section covers roughly a ten year period that corresponds to political and economic developments shaping West German society as a whole. This periodization is not meant to imply a one-to-one causal relationship between cultural changes and political events or economic cycles. Trends in culture often do not correspond with political or economic ones, though developments in all of these areas affect each other mutually, if unevenly.

The first section of the book examines conservation during the occupation years between 1945 and 1955, when West Germany gained full sovereignty and joined NATO. Chapter 2 examines the reconstruction of state-sponsored and private nature protection, as both resumed their activities with limited interruption. It describes how conservationists continued to view their work in nationalistic and nativist terms, yet also as acts of patriotism that supported the restoration of a comforting homeland, a strong economy, and a stable polity. However conservative conservationists' rhetoric and conduct, the emergence of several new local, regional, and national alliances strengthened the base of support for *Naturschutz* and contributed to the revival of civic life in the conservative political climate of the 1950s. Despite efforts to broaden the scope of conservation to confront the intensified exploitation of water, soil, and forests, the most tangible successes in these years involved traditional preservation at the regional and local levels.

This is illustrated in chapter 3, a case study of the successful effort to protect the Wutach River and gorge near Freiburg im Breisgau from being dammed and drained by a utility company intent on expanding its operations to meet rising demand for electricity. At a time when many West Germans said "no thanks" to politics, conservationists united thousands of supporters in an alliance to protect nature-as-local-*Heimat,* relying on restored democratic institutions to force the company to beat a small retreat. Yet in this and many other conflicts, both sides were forced to reach a "partially green" compromise, to borrow historian Michael Bess's phrasing.

The second section of the book focuses on the economic boom years between 1956 and 1966, when conservationists took steps to modernize and professionalize their efforts in order to guide the country's rapid economic growth in directions less harmful to nature and people. Chapter 4 examines conservationists' concern about the irreversible loss of healthy landscapes (i.e., areas scenic, fertile, and pollution free) at an alarming rate as urban sprawl and pollution blurred the distinction between city and country, and as the ideal of the small farm faded in the reality of industrialized agriculture. Concerned that the country's entire "living space" was at risk, conservationists participated in establishing dozens of nature parks and sought a partnership role in spatial planning (*Raumordnung*), a promising policy tool of the 1960s. Although they did not exert as much influence on territorial planning as they desired, their involvement in decisions over land use often resulted in compromises that benefited nature to some degree.

This is evident in chapter 5, the second case study on canalizing the Mosel River, an engineering project that facilitated Chancellor Konrad Adenauer's foreign policy objective to integrate the Federal Republic into Western Europe. Unlike West Germans embroiled in the regional Wutach conflict, citizens involved in the national debate over the Mosel canal had limited means to shape the decision because it was the chancellor's to make. Although their nativist-sounding appeals to protect the Mosel—a "jewel of the German *Heimat*"—had little impact on federal officials, their warnings about protecting the regional water supply did. Once Adenauer agreed to transform the Mosel into an international shipping lane, conservationists in the profession of landscape planning hoped to guide engineers in restoring a more natural appearance and healthier condition to the mechanized river, but their vision was only partially fulfilled.

The final section of the study examines the turbulent years between 1967 and 1975, a period that began with student unrest and ended after a global energy crisis. Chapter 6 discusses the scientification of conservation (evident in the new concern to manage "ecological systems of the biosphere"), and describes the creation of "the environment" as a legitimate sphere for political action through the environmental program introduced by Chancellor Willy Brandt's social-liberal (SPD/FDP) coalition government. With the invention of "the environment" as a political issue and a tangible object of reform between 1970 and 1971, diverse groups—from officials and scientists to revitalized conservation organizations and new citizens' initiatives—claimed the right to participate in shaping it according to their values and ideas about society and nature. According to a vocal minority of pioneering conservationists, because so many pressures were at work making the environment "artificial," they needed to ensure that parts of it were restored to a presumably more natural state.

The working out of this argument is illustrated in chapter 7, the third case study on establishing West Germany's first national park in the Bavarian Forest, a remote area located along the Iron Curtain. Initially approved of in the context of regional planning, the national park eventually became a space where preservation and economic development acquired near equal status. After more than a decade of ecological design that restored a supposedly more natural condition to the landscape, a new aesthetic of nature became operable. In the national park, officials eventually adopted a policy of limited interference, protecting the ecological processes at work in order to "let nature be nature," even if the results were not economically productive or aesthetically pleasing. The decision to let nature go "wild" in a remote corner of this densely populated nation stemmed from an aesthetic of nature that was nurtured by affluence and made acceptable by the perceived loss of nature and the natural.[31]

The study emphasizes that conservationists in the first three decades of the Federal Republic were not marginalized or entirely ineffective. Although they lost many battles and made repeated compromises, they diversified, modernized, and institutionalized their efforts in the challenging postwar context. By participating in the democratic process, they were forced to take a long tradition of protecting nature in more democratic and socially oriented directions, sometimes reluctantly. Yet in doing so, they assured themselves a role in actively shaping the contours of the land in West Germany, whether by establishing nature parks or the country's first national park. With their steady, often conservative, presence within the mainstream of society, they ensured that at least some of the increasingly mechanized landscapes of the Miracle Years retained, or were restored to, varying degrees of naturalness.

Notes

1. Major C. P. Kindleberger to Sarah Kindleberger, 19 April 1945, letter #170, in Charles P. Kindleberger, *The German Economy, 1945–1947: Charles P. Kindleberger's Letters from the Field* (Westport, CT: Meckler, 1989), 200–201. On the state's role in transforming "chaotic" forests into productive timber plantations lacking ecological diversity see James C. Scott, *Seeing Like a State. How Certain Schemes to Improve the Human Condition Have Failed* (New Haven: Yale University Press, 1998), 11–22.

2. Wilhelm Lienenkämper, "Gedanken zur Tätigkeit der Naturschutzbeauftragten," *Verhandlungen Deutscher Beauftragter für Naturschutz und Landschaftspflege* (1949): 35 (hereafter *Verhandlungen*). Because not all of the proceedings of conservation commissioners' annual meeting were published in the same year of the conference, citations will refer to the year of the meeting, not the year of publication. Beginning with the 1968 conference (published in 1970), the proceedings were entitled *Jahrbuch für Naturschutz und Landschaftspflege* (*JfNL*) Until then they will be referred to as *Verhandlungen*.

3. For arguments that nature and homeland preservation was discredited see Stefan Körner, "Kontinuum und Bruch: Die Transformation des naturschützerischen Aufgabenverständnisses nach dem Zweiten Weltkrieg," in *Naturschutz und Nationalsozialismus*, ed. Joachim Radkau and Frank Uekötter (Frankfurt am Main: Campus, 2003), 422; Arne Andersen,

"Heimatschutz. Die bürgerliche Naturschutzbewegung," in *Besiegte Natur: Geschichte der Umwelt im 19. und 20 Jahrhundert*, ed. Franz-Josef Brüggemeier and Thomas Rommelspacher (Munich: C.H. Beck, 1989), 156–57; Rolf Peter Sieferle, *Fortschrittsfeinde? Opposition gegen Technik und Industrie von der Romantik bis zur Gegenwart* (Munich: C.H. Beck, 1984), 227. For a view challenging the assumption that conservation was discredited after 1945 see Burkhardt Riechers, "Nature Protection during National Socialism," *Historical Social Research* 29, no. 3 (1996): 52.

4. Frank Uekötter, *The Green and the Brown. A History of Conservation in Nazi Germany* (New York: Cambridge University Press, 2006); Franz-Josef Brüggemeier, Mark Cioc, and Thomas Zeller, eds., *How Green Were the Nazis?: Nature, Environment, and Nation in the Third Reich* (Athens: Ohio University Press, 2005); and Radkau and Uekötter, eds., *Naturschutz und Nationalsozialismus*. On the unevenness of co-opting preservationists in the Rhineland see Thomas Lekan, *Imagining the Nation in Nature. Landscape Preservation and German Identity, 1885–1945* (Cambridge: Harvard University Press, 2004).

5. See especially Jens Ivo Engels, *Naturpolitik in der Bundesrepublik. Ideenwelt und politische Verhaltensstile in Naturschutz und Umweltbewegung 1950–1980* (Paderborn: Schöningh, 2006). Willi Oberkrome's *"Deutsche Heimat." Nationale Konzeption und regionale Praxis von Naturschutz, Landschaftsgestaltung und Kulturpolitik in Westfalen-Lippe und Thüringen (1900–1960)* (Paderborn: Schöningh, 2004), is one of the few studies that focuses on both Germanys. Essays on continuity and change during the postwar years include those in the volume edited by Franz-Josef Brüggemeier and Jens Ivo Engels, *Natur- und Umweltschutz nach 1945. Konzepte, Konflikte, Kompetenzen* (Frankfurt am Main: Campus, 2005); and several included in the volume edited by Hans-Werner Frohn and Friedemann Schmoll, *Natur und Staat. Staatlicher Naturschutz in Deutschland 1906–2006* (Bonn: Bundesamt für Naturschutz, 2006). See also Sandra Chaney, "For Nation and Prosperity, Health and a Green Environment: Protecting Nature in West Germany, 1945–70," in *Nature in German History*, ed. Christof Mauch (New York: Berghahn, 2004), 93–118; Jens Ivo Engels, "'Hohe Zeit' und 'dicker Strich': Vergangenheitsdeutung und-bewahrung im westdeutschen Naturschutz nach dem Zweiten Weltkrieg," in Radkau and Uekötter, *Naturschutz und Nationalsozialismus*, 363–404; Körner, "Kontinuum und Bruch," in Radkau and Uekötter, *Naturschutz und Nationalsozialismus*, 405–34; Thomas Rohkrämer, "Contemporary Environmentalism and its Links with the German Past," in *The Culture of German Environmentalism: Anxieties, Visions, Realities*, ed. Axel Goodbody (New York: Berghahn, 2002), 47–62; Thomas Rommelspacher, "Zwischen Heimatschutz und Umweltprotest. Konflikte um Natur, Umwelt und Technik in der BRD 1945–1965," in *Soziologie als Krisenwissenschaft*, ed. Hans Uske, Hermann Völlings, Jochen Zimmer, and Christof Stracke (Münster: Lit, 1998), 74–95. For an historiographical overview of the postwar years see Frank Uekötter, "Umweltbewegung zwischen dem Ende der nationalsozialistischen Herrschaft und der 'ökologischen Wende': Ein Literaturbericht," *Historical Social Research* 28 (2003): 270–89.

6. Monika Bergmeier, *Umweltgeschichte der Boomjahre. Das Beispiel Bayern* (Münster: Waxmann, 2002); Kai F. Hünemörder, *Die Frühgeschichte der globalen Umweltkrise und die Formierung der deutschen Umweltpolitik (1950–1973)* (Stuttgart: Steiner, 2004); Frank Uekötter, *Naturschutz im Aufbruch. Eine Geschichte des Naturschutzes in Nordrhein-Westfalen 1945–1980* (Frankfurt am Main: Campus, 2004). Several books that examine nature and environmental issues over the long term devote attention to pollution control, conservation, ecological thought, and environmental policy in the postwar period. See David Blackbourn, *The Conquest of Nature. Water, Landscape, and the Making of Modern Germany* (New York: Norton, 2006); Franz-Josef Brüggemeier and Thomas Rommelspacher, *Blauer Himmel über der Ruhr. Geschichte der Umwelt im Ruhrgebiet 1840–1990* (Essen: Klartext-Verlag, 1992); Brüggemeier, *Tschernobyl, 26. April 1986. Die ökologische Herausforderung* (Munich: Deutscher Taschenbuch Verlag, 1998); Mark Cioc, *The Rhine. An Eco-Biography, 1815–2000* (Seattle: University of Washington Press,

2002); Raymond Dominick, *The Environmental Movement in Germany. Prophets and Pioneers, 1871–1971* (Bloomington: University of Indiana Press, 1992); Jost Hermand, *Grüne Utopien in Deutschland. Zur Geschichte des ökologischen Bewußtseins* (Frankfurt am Main: Fischer, 1991); Hansjörg Küster, *Geschichte des Waldes: von der Urzeit bis zur Gegenwart* (Munich: C. H. Beck, 1998); Frank Uekötter, *Von der Rauchplage zur ökologischen Revolution. Eine Geschichte der Luftverschmutzung in Deutschland und den USA 1880–1970* (Essen: Klartext-Verlag, 2003); Klaus-Georg Wey, *Umweltpolitik in Deutschland. Kurze Geschichte des Umweltschutzes in Deutschland seit 1900* (Opladen: Westdeutscher Verlag, 1982). Essay-length surveys that mention the postwar years include Colin Riordan, "Green Ideas in Germany: A Historical Survey," in *Green Thought in German Culture. Historical and Contemporary Perspectives,* ed. Riordan (Cardiff: University of Wales Press, 1997), 3–41; Karl Ditt, "Nature Conservation in England and Germany 1900–70: Forerunner of Environmental Protection?" translated by Jane Rafferty, *Contemporary European History* 5, no. 1 (1996): 1–28.

7. Rommelspacher, "Zwischen Heimatschutz und Umweltprotest"; Karl Ditt, "Die Anfänge der Umweltpolitik in der Bundesrepublik Deutschland während der 1960er und frühen 1970er Jahre," in *Demokratisierung und gesellschaftlicher Aufbruch. Die sechziger Jahre als Wendezeit der Bundesrepublik,* ed. Matthias Frese, Julia Paulus, and Karl Teppe (Paderborn: Schöningh, 2003), 305–48.

8. For a critique of this tendency see Frank Uekötter, "The Old Conservation History—and the New: An Argument for Fresh Perspectives on an Established Topic," *Historical Social Research* 29, no. 3 (2004): 172; Michael Bess, *The Light-Green Society. Ecology and Technological Modernity in France, 1960–2000* (Chicago: University of Chicago Press, 2003), 4.

9. Engels, *Naturpolitik,* chap. 1.

10. Bess, *Light-Green Society,* 4.

11. Christian Pfister, "'Das 1950er Syndrom': Zusammenfassung und Synthese," in *Das 1950er Syndrom. Der Weg in die Konsumgesellschaft,* ed. Pfister (Bern: Paul Haupt, 1995), 23. See also the following publications by Arne Andersen: *Der Traum vom guten Leben. Alltags- und Konsumgeschichte vom Wirtschaftswunder bis heute* (Frankfurt am Main: Campus, 1997); "Mentalitätenwechsel und ökologische Konsequenzen des Konsumismus. Die Durchsetzung der Konsumgesellschaft in den fünfziger Jahren," in *Europäische Konsumgeschichte: Zur Gesellschafts- und Kulturgeschichte des Konsums (18. bis 20. Jahrhundert),* ed. Hannes Siegrist, Hartmut Kaelble, and Jürgen Kocka (Frankfurt am Main: Campus, 1997), 763–91; "Das 50er-Jahre-Syndrom. Umweltfragen in der Demokratisierung des Technikkonsums," *Technikgeschichte* 65, no. 4 (1998): 329–44. For a view skeptical of the "1950s Syndrome" see Joachim Radkau, *Natur und Macht. Eine Weltgeschichte der Umwelt* (Munich: C.H. Beck, 2000).

12. John R. McNeill, *Something New Under the Sun. An Environmental History of the Twentieth Century World* (New York: Norton, 2000), 4–5; Bess, *The Light-Green Society,* 16; Blackbourn, *Conquest,* 327.

13. Federal Republic of Germany, *Report of the Federal Republic of Germany on the Human Environment Prepared for the United Nations Conference on the Human Environment June 1972, Stockholm, Sweden* (Lüdenscheid: Druckhaus Maack KG, 1972), 118, 120, 124; Volker Berghahn, *Modern Germany: Society, Economy and Politics in the Twentieth Century,* 2d ed. (Cambridge: Cambridge University Press, 1982), 226, 253; Hermann Glaser, *Kleine Kulturgeschichte der Bundesrepublik Deutschland 1945–1989* (Munich: Carl Hanser, 1991; Bonn: Bundeszentrale für politische Bildung, 1991), 175.

14. Konrad Buchwald, "Landschaftspflege und Naturschutz in der industriellen Gesellschaft," in *Naturschutz—eine politische Aufgabe?,* ed. Georg Fahrbach (Stuttgart: Fink, 1965), 70.

15. Mark Cioc, "The Impact of the Coal Age on the German Environment: A Review of the Historical Literature," *Environment and History* 4, no. 1 (1998): 105–24, here 106; Körner, "Kontinuum und Bruch," in Radkau and Uekötter, *Naturschutz und Nationalsozialismus,* 418.

16. See, for example, William Cronon's introduction and essay, "The Trouble with Wilderness; or, Getting Back to the Wrong Nature," in *Uncommon Ground: Toward Reinventing Nature,* ed. Cronon (New York: Norton, 1995); Richard White, "From Wilderness to Hybrid Landscapes: The Cultural Turn in Environmental History," *The Historian* 66, no. 3 (Fall 2004): 557–64.

17. On landscape architects and their influence on protecting and shaping nature in the twentieth century see Gert Gröning und Joachim Wolschke-Bulmahn, *Die Liebe zur Landschaft,* vol. 1, *Natur in Bewegung. Zur Bedeutung natur- und freiraumorientierter Bewegungen der ersten Hälfte der 20. Jahrhunderts für die Entwicklung der Freiraumplanung* (Munich: Minerva, 1986); Gröning and Wolschke-Bulmahn, *Die Liebe zur Landschaft,* vol. 3, *Der Drang nach Osten. Zur Entwicklung der Landespflege im Nationalsozialismus in den 'eingegliederten Ostgebieten' während des Zweiten Weltkriegs* (Munich: Minerva, 1987); Thomas Zeller, *Straße, Bahn, Panorama. Verkehrswege und Landschaftsveränderung in Deutschland von 1930 bis 1990* (Frankfurt am Main: Campus, 2002); Stefan Körner, *Theorie und Methodologie der Landschaftsplanung, Landschaftsarchitektur und sozialwissenschaftlichen Freiraumplanung vom Nationalsozialismus bis zur Gegenwart* (Berlin: Technische Universität Berlin, 2002).

18. Literature on the social construction of nature is vast. See Elizabeth Ann R. Bird, "The Social Construction of Nature: Theoretical Approaches to the History of Environmental Problems," *Environmental Review* (Winter 1987): 255–64; Neil Evernden, *The Social Creation of Nature* (Baltimore: The Johns Hopkins University Press, 1992); Ian G. Simmons, *Interpreting Nature. Cultural Constructions of the Environment* (London: Routledge, 1993); Cronon, "Trouble with Wilderness," and other contributors' essays in Cronon, *Uncommon Ground;* Michale E. Soulé and Gary Lease, eds., *Reinventing Nature?: Responses to Postmodern Deconstruction* (Washington, DC: Island Press, 1995); White, "From Wilderness to Hybrid Landscapes"; Douglas Weiner, "A Death-defying Attempt to Articulate a Coherent Definition of Environmental History," *Environmental History* 10, no. 3 (July 2005): 404–20. For a radical position that proposes eliminating the idea of "nature," see Timothy Morton, *Ecology Without Nature: Rethinking Environmental Aesthetics* (Cambridge: Harvard University Press, 2007). Discussions relevant in the German context include Götz Großklaus and Ernst Oldemeyer, eds., *Natur als Gegenwelt. Beiträge zur Kulturgeschichte der Natur* (Karlsruhe: Loeper, 1983); Gernot Böhme, *Natürlich Natur. Über Natur im Zeitalter ihrer technischen Reproduzierbarkeit* (Frankfurt am Main: Suhrkamp, 1992); Sandra Schulze Hannöver and Martin Becker, "Natur im Sinn," in *Natur im Sinn. Beiträge zur Geschichte des Naturschutzes,* ed. Stiftung Naturschutzgeschichte (Essen: Klartext-Verlag, 2001), 9–30; Uta Eser, *Der Naturschutz und das Fremde. Ökologische und normative Grundlagen der Umweltethik* (Frankfurt am Main: Campus, 1999).

19. Among many studies of the meanings assigned to "landscape" see Gerhard Hard, "'Landschaft'—Folgerungen aus einigen Ergebnissen einer semantischen Analyse," *Landschaft + Stadt* 4, no. 2 (1972): 77–89; Anne Whiston Spirn, *The Language of Landscape* (New Haven: Yale University Press, 2000); Denis Cosgrove and Stephen Daniels, eds., *The Iconography of Landscape: Essays on the Symbolic Representation, Design and Use of Past Environments* (Cambridge: Cambridge University Press, 1988); Stephen Daniels, *Fields of Vision: Landscape Imagery and National Identity in England and the United States* (Princeton: Princeton University Press, 1993); Simon Schama, *Landscape and Memory* (New York: Knopf, 1995); Norbert Fischer, "Der neue Blick auf die Landschaft: Die Geschichte der Landschaft im Schnittpunkt von Sozial-, Geistes- und Umweltgeschichte," *Archiv für Sozialgeschichte* 36 (1996): 434–42; W.J.T. Mitchell, *Landscape and Power,* 2d ed. (Chicago: University of Chicago Press, 2002).

20. Among the critical explorations of ecology as a science and as a tool of politics see Stephen Bocking's books, *Nature's Experts. Science, Politics, and the Environment* (New Brunswick: Rutgers University Press, 2004); and *Ecologists and Environmental Politics. A History of Contemporary Ecology* (New Haven: Yale University Press, 1997) for the North American and British contexts.

In the German context see Thomas Potthast, *Die Evolution und der Naturschutz. Zum Verhältnis von Evolutionsbiologie, Ökologie und Naturethik* (Frankfurt am Main: Campus, 1999); Potthast, "Wissenschaftliche Ökologie und Naturschutz: Szenen einer Annäherung," in Radkau and Uekötter, *Naturschutz und Nationalsozialismus,* 225–34; Gert Gröning and Joachim Wolschke, "Naturschutz und Ökologie im Nationalsozialismus," *Die Alte Stadt,* 10 (1983): 1–17; Jonathan Olsen, *Nature and Nationalism: Right-Wing Ecology and the Politics of Identity in Contemporary Germany* (New York: St. Martin's, 1999); Ludwig Trepl, "Ökologie—eine grüne Leitwissenschaft?" *Kursbuch,* no. 74 (December 1983): 6–27; Trepl, *Geschichte der Ökologie. Vom 17. Jahrhundert bis zur Gegenwart* (Frankfurt am Main: Atheneum, 1987). In a more general context refer to Donald Worster, *Nature's Economy: A History of Ecological Ideas* (Sierra Club Books, 1977; reprint, New York: Cambridge University Press, 1985); Worster, "The Ecology of Order and Chaos," in *The Wealth of Nature: Environmental History and the Ecological Imagination,* ed. Worster (New York: Oxford University Press, 1993), 156–70.

21. Weiner, "Definition of Environmental History," 409.

22. Evernden, *Social Creation of Nature,* 136, n. 2.

23. Bess, *Light-Green Society,* 5.

24. Joachim Radkau, "Germany as a Focus of European 'Particularities' in Environmental History," in *Germany's Nature. Cultural Landscapes and Environmental History,* ed. Thomas Lekan and Thomas Zeller (New Brunswick: Rutgers University Press, 2005), 18; David Blackbourn, "'Conquests From Barbarism': Taming Nature in Frederick the Great's Prussia," in Mauch, *Nature in German History,* 26.

25. Radkau, "Germany as a Focus of European 'Particularities,'" in Lekan and Zeller, *Germany's Nature,* 18–21.

26. Eser, *Der Naturschutz und das Fremde,* 126; Engels, *Naturpolitik,* chap. 1; Engels, "Vergangenheitsdeutung im westdeutschen Naturschutz," in Radkau and Uekötter, *Naturschutz und Nationalsozialismus,* 370–71; Lekan, *Imagining,* 219.

27. On *Heimatschutz* after World War II compare Arne Andersen, "Heimatschutz. Die bürgerliche Naturschutzbewegung," in *Besiegte Natur,* 156–57; and Sieferle, *Fortschrittsfeinde?,* 227, who contend it was discredited, with Oberkrome, *"Deutsche Heimat";* and Uekötter, *Green and the Brown,* 195, 205–6, who demonstrate its powerful lure. On its continued use in East Germany see Sandra Chaney, "Protecting Nature in a Divided Nation: Conservation in the Two Germanys, 1945–1972," in Lekan and Zeller, *Germany's Nature,* 220–43; Oberkrome, *"Deutsche Heimat,"* 289–389; Jan Palmowski, "Building an East German Nation: The Construction of a Socialist *Heimat,* 1945–1961," *Central European History* 37, no. 3 (September 2004): 365–99.

28. Quote from Celia Applegate, *A Nation of Provincials: the German Idea of Heimat* (Berkeley: University of California Press, 1990), 229, 242–43.

29. Elizabeth Heineman, "The Hour of the Woman: Memories of Germany's 'Crisis Years' and West German National Identity," *American Historical Review* 101, no. 2 (April 1996): 354–95.

30. On postwar uses of *Heimat* in West Germany see Applegate, *Nation of Provincials,* chap. 8; Robert G. Moeller, *War Stories: The Search for a Usable Past in the Federal Republic of Germany* (Berkeley: University of California Press, 2001), 128–34; Heide Fehrenbach, *Cinema in Democratizing Germany: Reconstructing National Identity after Hitler* (Chapel Hill: University of North Carolina Press, 1995); Gregory F. Schroeder, "Ties of Urban *Heimat:* West German Cities and Their Wartime Evacuees in the 1950s," *German Studies Review* 27, no. 2 (May 2004): 307–24.

31. Schulze Hannöver and Becker, "Natur im Sinn," 29.

Chapter 1

THE INHERITANCE
A Mixed Legacy for Postwar Conservation

When leading conservationists sat down in the 1950s to write a history of efforts to protect nature in Germany, they were selective in interpreting events of the past. They acknowledged their intellectual debt to Romanticism, but dwelled on the enduring influence of the homeland preservation movement that emerged in the late nineteenth century. Reflecting their humanist education, these authors praised the idealism, dedicated volunteerism, and pedagogical mission of early preservationists. They recalled the years between 1935 and 1938 as a "high point," when the legal and administrative foundations of preservation were centralized and strengthened, but remembered the years of total war as a time when they made repeated sacrifices.[1]

By the 1960s, accounts by a younger generation stressed the importance of landscape care (*Landschaftspflege*), a tradition that dated back to the Enlightenment, when garden design and landscape beautification became popular. Frustrated by the defensive posture of classical preservation, which limited practitioners' ability to influence decisions about land use, these men drew inspiration from an older tradition shaped not by amateurs, but by professionals who envisioned a more flexible approach in caring for nature. In tracing the trajectory of landscape beautification, these writers, too, reflected uncritically on the Nazi years. They acknowledged gains made by landscape architects who guided engineering projects like the Autobahn, but expressed regret that the war prevented landscape care from evolving into comprehensive land use planning.[2]

Notes for this chapter begin on page 38.

It is not surprising that these insider histories from the 1950s and 1960s failed to problematize the authoritarian nature of the Nazi state, which made possible some noteworthy improvements in conservation, however temporary and uneven those gains may have been. Nor is it a surprise that these accounts ignored the complicity of some landscape architects in the regime's genocidal aims. Only in the 1980s did two individuals trained in the field, Gert Gröning and Joachim Wolschke-Bulmahn, break the silence of their profession and expose the sins of their teachers. Their investigation of the fortunes of landscape architects working in the occupied territories of Poland had a significant impact on the writing of history about the treatment of nature under National Socialism. Their research forced scholars to scrutinize the extent to which racial ideology had perverted understandings of nature and its proper care, and also highlighted the need for more information about the contexts in which not only landscape architects operated, but conservationists in general. Their work also underscored the need for more research into what happened to these people and their activities after 1945.[3]

After World War II, conservationists picked up where they had left off with very little interruption. But what alternative did they have? They preserved the practical gains made in conservation prior to and during the era of National Socialism and purged their rhetoric of phrasings that ranged from opportunistic to overtly racist. Their actions before, during, and after the Third Reich showed that *Naturschutz* was neither inherently good nor thoroughly nazified. Those involved in nature's care under the Nazi regime used the system in place to achieve what goals they could, but in the process they supported the dictatorship and some of its unethical policies. Preservationists' activities during the Third Reich, and their continued influence after the war, demonstrated the troubling ease with which they could adapt to changing political systems. Although the years between 1933 and 1945 were among the most formative and problematic for conservationists who remained active under the Federal Republic, the tradition they inherited and transformed after World War II was older, its legacy decidedly mixed.

The Romantic Bequest

When postwar conservationists acknowledged their debt to Romanticism, they were seeking to deflect attention away from their nation's shameful recent political past by focusing on a respected part of their cultural heritage. But they also appreciated the romantic legacy, particularly its belief in the spiritual essence of the natural world and its ability, according to Friedrich von Schiller, to shape individual moral character and inspire contemplation of higher truths that might improve the human condition. Romantics left to conservationists an appreciation for the mystery of nature, for its gentleness as well as its unpredictable wildness. They depicted humanity living in harmony with nature and awed by its powerful forces, yet comforted by its seeming innocence. In their poetry, art, and philosophy, Romantics celebrated images of nature, which they thought would inspire people to overcome the alienation they felt in the modern world by embarking on a noble quest for wholeness and timeless truths.[4] In idealizing nature, however, Romantics passed on to preservationists—and to people in our own time who ignore the instability and flux observed in nature by ecologists—the tendency to long for a golden age when humanity's relationship with nature was supposedly more harmonious.[5]

The Romantic writer Johann Gottfried von Herder (1744–1803) occupied a place of particular importance for later preservationists. Writing at the time of the Napoleonic Wars, which strengthened the Germans' sense of national identity, Herder hoped to remind people of the value of community and local traditions. Not opposed to the individualism and cosmopolitanism of the Enlightenment, he nonetheless emphasized the role of geography, climate, and natural features of a particular place in shaping the uniqueness of a people, or *Volk,* including its customs. According to his implicitly conservative views, not only did the *Volk* evolve organically in relationship with its natural surroundings, so, too, did the "natural" social order.[6]

The Mixed Legacy of Homeland Preservation

As industrialization spread inexorably in the nineteenth century, the organic evolution of society and nature appeared to be threatened, inspiring some middle class reformers to take steps to protect the nature and cultural traditions that made their local and regional homelands distinct. Translating *Heimat* as "homeland" does not convey its diffuse meaning adequately. As Celia Applegate has explained, "[t]o talk of one's '*Heimat*' implied a belief in the influence of place on personality, of climate on custom, and of nature on national character. It was, moreover, a highly flexible term, capable of referring to places as specific as the village and as general as the nation."[7] Prior to the eighteenth century, *Heimat* referred primarily to the land a person owned. But with agricultural modernization, the concept came to express the loss of a familiar harmonious order, one that supposedly had prevailed in the pre-industrial past. *Heimat,* Andreas Knaut has written, became a "metaphor for the time and the place where the apparent lost harmony [between humans and nature] was restored."[8]

In the decades prior to German unification (1870–1871), the journalist-turned-ethnographer, Wilhelm Heinrich Riehl (1823–1897), introduced the idea of protecting Germany's diverse homeland landscapes to preserve the source of the nation's moral strength and to thwart the homogenizing and democratizing forces of modernity. Riehl maintained that nations formed organically through people's deep attachments to the nature and culture of a particular place, a view that contrasted sharply with assumptions from the Enlightenment which held that nations could be created through written documents and a commitment to shared ideals. When Riehl wrote of landscapes, he had in mind scenic rural areas that had been shaped over the ages by Germany's peasantry, the people he valorized as the source of strength and character of the national community, or *Volk*. Of course, it was not only the peasantry that had influenced the appearance of the land. In Prussia, an indelible mark was left by eighteenth– and nineteenth–century hydraulic engineers and foresters in the state's employ who transformed "marginal" marshlands into fertile farms and chaotic woods into scientifically managed forests, imposing order and efficiency—with mixed results—on landscapes that had seemed barbaric and dangerously wild.[9] For Riehl, however, it was the peasants, who through their daily toil stood rooted in the land and in tune with the cycles and rhythms of nature. Firmly bound to the native soil, they could and would resist the destabilizing social and economic changes associated with Germany's swelling cities. According to Riehl, preserving cultural landscapes that displayed the historical interaction between people and their natural surroundings (especially through farming) would strengthen urbanites' feelings of attachment to their locality. Cultivating strong ties to the regional homeland, he believed, would in turn foster loyalty to a national German homeland.[10]

Because Riehl's conservative ideas influenced the middle and upper middle class founders of the homeland preservation movement that emerged at the end of the nineteenth century, scholars have, until rather recently, viewed *Heimatschutz* as primarily an expression of anti-urban, anti-modern cultural pessimism.[11] Such interpretations are understandable because of commentaries by the founder of the homeland preservation movement, Ernst Rudorff (1840–1916), a little-known composer who went public with his critique of modern life in the late 1870s. In an often quoted essay from 1880, Rudorff attacked agrarian reforms that consolidated quaint pastures into rationalized fields with far fewer hedges and that straightened streams, hastening the flow of water from the land and lowering the water table. From Rudorff's perspective, the destruction of the "picturesque" quality of nature for rational economic ends and its "prostitution" for tourism reflected a lack of appreciation for the moral value of nature in its "unspoiled" state. Although Rudorff often spoke of protecting "natural, untouched landscapes," he had in mind rural areas that looked as if the farms, roads, bridges, canals, and architecture formed an organic unity. According to Rudorff, the urban masses insensitive to nature needed to spend time in these landscapes to cultivate a love for the homeland, for "in the inner and deep feelings for nature reside the very roots of the Germanic essence."[12]

This belief in an organic connection between nature and national identity remained a part of homeland preservation after Rudorff and others founded the

German League for Homeland Preservation (*Deutscher Bund Heimatschutz*) in Dresden in 1904 and offered the chairmanship to the architect and cultural reformer, Paul Schultze-Naumburg (1869–1949).[13] There is no denying that the movement's critique of modernity, its elevation of peasant life as the source of national strength, its tendency to associate city life with degenerate behavior, and its insistence on preserving local landscapes that supposedly shaped the character of the German people made the movement susceptible to *völkisch* ideology in times of crisis, particularly during the 1920s and 1930s. But the sense of loss that some homeland preservationists expressed about their rapidly changing natural surroundings in the latter nineteenth century was part of a broader cultural phenomenon, evident also in the works of prominent writers like Theodor Storm and Theodor Fontane, and in the art of Worpswede painters.[14]

Homeland preservation was not inherently anti-modern or reactionary. Not long after unification, when Germans' sense of nationhood remained uncertain, homeland preservationists offered a way of seeing scenic local and regional landscapes, native plants and animals, and unique natural objects as "'natural monuments' that anchored the organic foundation of national identity," in Thomas Lekan's words. In the late nineteenth century in Germany and other countries such as the United States where the national park movement was gaining momentum, preserving nature afforded a way to express and shape national identity. Through organized outdoor activities, educational reform initiatives, and mass produced postcards, middle and upper class Germans assigned national significance to natural landscapes and monuments, hoping to convince people irrespective of class that they had a common natural heritage and a shared national identity. Unlike today's environmentalists who pursue a local and global agenda simultaneously, nineteenth century preservationists were intentionally local, regional, and nationalistic.[15]

Yet by appealing to popular notions of nationalism, William Rollins has argued, homeland preservationists urged contemporaries to imagine an alternative to the exploitative relationship between society and nature that had become common with advancing capitalism. At a time when few criticized urbanization and industrialization, and when little scientific data on environmental decline was available, homeland preservationists' attention to the aesthetic and historical value of nature registered the visible, negative consequences of industrialism. Moreover, attempts by homeland preservationists to protect cultural landscapes conveyed ecological insight by envisioning a harmonious integration of natural features, cultural traditions, regional architecture, *and* guided economic development. As part of its critique of economic growth, the modernist wing of the homeland preservation movement advocated city planning, urban parks, housing reform, and the protection of rural landscapes in their entirety. True, the civil servants, entrepreneurs, and urban professionals—from architects, lawyers, and doctors to schoolteachers—who dominated the movement promoted these reforms out of concern for shaping the moral character of people of all social classes. But this paternalistic, middle class reform agenda was similar to that of its Anglo-American counterparts, such as the British National Trust and the US Sierra Club. Yet Germany's preservationists were led by a vision that was perhaps more sustainable ecologically than the wilderness preservation movement in Progressive Era America in making room for people and modernization.[16]

But one should be careful not to assign too much intentionality to homeland preservationists' ecological sensitivities, even in the land of Ernst Haeckel, the zoologist who coined the term "ecology" in 1866. In general, the holistic views of homeland preservationists owed more to the tradition of descriptive natural history shaped by the naturalist and statesman Alexander von Humboldt (1769–1859) than to the emerging science of ecology, whose few practitioners had limited interaction with preservationists. Generally speaking, ecologists also lacked the respect of other scientists, especially biologists, who viewed ecologists' methodology as too descriptive and non-experimental.[17] Despite the implicitly ecological goals of homeland preservationists, the movement was primarily an expression of cultural politics. At a time when loyalty to one's region was stronger than loyalty to the new nation-state, protecting landscapes of the local homeland appeared to be one way of strengthening regional pride while building ties to a new German homeland, one that was a reflection of and strengthened by regional diversity.[18]

Government-sponsored Preservation

During the Second Empire (1871–1918), homeland preservation activities frequently overlapped with the state-supported practice of protecting natural monuments such as waterfalls, groves of old trees, unique geological formations, and areas with rare animals and plants. At the time, the care of historic monuments (*Denkmalpflege*) was a popular activity carried out by officials and citizens. It thus was logical to attach "nature" to the concept of "monument" to express the new interest in preserving natural features that were a source of local, regional, and national pride.[19]

As the nineteenth century came to a close, Hugo Conwentz (1855–1922), an active homeland preservationist and director of the West Prussian Provincial Museum in Danzig, convinced the political leaders of Prussia, Germany's most powerful state, to protect the nation's unique natural objects, landscapes, and flora and fauna. The supportive parliamentarian and schoolmaster, Wilhelm Wetekamp (1859–1945), announced that this task would involve preserving "part of our fatherland in the original, natural form" as "state parks," an idea that intentionally resembled the plan for national parks in the United States.

In administrative deliberations, however, Conwentz's proposal was scaled back. Aware that Germany could not set aside large tracts of land as in the US, and concerned about the prohibitive cost of purchasing land for reserves and parks and of compensating property owners, preservationists settled for protecting natural monuments to serve as landmarks of the nation's diverse natural history. Although Conwentz defined "natural monument" broadly, extending it to include areas such as Saxon Switzerland (*Sächsische Schweiz*) near Dresden, it came to be narrowly focused on protecting natural monuments, rare flora and fauna, and small reserves for scientific research.[20]

Conwentz was instrumental in establishing the State Agency for the Care of Monuments of Nature under the Prussian Ministry of Culture in 1906, a body that coordinated efforts to identify natural monuments and to ensure that protection ordinances were enforced. But the agency had no legal authority. It operated with limited funds and depended on the support of a few public officials, willing volunteers, and private organizations. In contrast to Prussia, where the initiative for a state-supported body had come from the government, in Bavaria the idea originated with the Munich section of the Alpine Society. Here the interior ministry reluctantly agreed to establish and provide small subsidies for an advisory State Committee for the Care of Nature (*Landesausschuß für Naturpflege*) in 1904. The committee was headed by the chairman of the Alpine Society, but its membership reflected the variety of organizations involved in preservation at the turn of the century. When the state committee failed to have much of an impact on government decisions and was denied the right to raise money, its members set up the Bavarian League for Nature Protection in 1913. During World War I, the league and the state committee managed to prevent the government from emblazoning an image of the Bavarian lion on the cliffs that tower above Königsee, Germany's most pristine lake near Berchtesgaden. When the war was over, they successfully lobbied to protect the lake as a reserve. In the 1970s, conservationists made it the core of West Germany's second national park.[21]

By World War I, several German states had established offices similar to the Bavarian State Committee and the Prussian Agency, marking the beginnings of government-sponsored preservation and the assumption that the state ought to accept some responsibility for nature's care, although with little financial outlay. Because these official bodies lacked funding and professionals with expertise, their political influence was limited. And they depended on networks of volunteers at the state and local levels to perform a variety of functions, from preserving species to weighing in on controversial development projects. This collaborative relationship between private groups (armed with idealism and moral conviction, and supported by socially prominent patrons) and official bodies (possessing limited personnel and funding and little expertise to deal with preservation adequately) outlined the strategy for protecting nature in Germany into the 1970s.[22]

Private Organizations and Nature's Protection

At the same time that official bodies and homeland preservation organizations formed in response to the loss of plant and animal life and scenic parts of rural areas, existing scientific societies expanded their goals to include preservation. Several new groups emerged expressly for this purpose.[23] Among the most influential new organizations was the German League for Bird Protection (*Deutscher Bund für Vogelschutz,* or DBV), founded in Stuttgart in 1899 by Lina Hähnle, the wife of the prominent textile manufacturer and parliamentarian Hans Hähnle. By 1914, the DBV claimed a national membership of over 41,000 (including the kings of Württemberg and Saxony). The league established fifty sanctuaries in several German states and convinced the *Reichstag* to expand existing legislation for protecting birds. It also campaigned against threats to birds, be it from women's fashions, gastronomic fads, uninsulated electricity lines, or habitat loss due to river regulation and hedge removal that accompanied agricultural modernization.[24]

In Bavaria, botanists and outdoor enthusiasts in the Alpine Society founded the Society for the Protection and Care of Alpine Flowers in 1900 to preserve the diversity of mountain vegetation in designed gardens. Within a decade, the society shifted its focus toward protecting flora from tourists and preventing the commercialization of nature. Some scholars view this and other efforts to protect nature from people as a regressive tendency which prevented preservationists from focusing on providing better managed access to the natural world.[25] But this alternative would have required more legal, administrative, and financial support from the state than was available or likely at the time. However self-limiting the defensive strategy of protecting nature from people, it reveals preservationists' understandable ambivalence about modernity. They were acutely aware of the negative impact that industrialization, agricultural modernization, and concentrated tourism could have on nature in a short period of time. Convinced of their moral responsibility to protect vanishing nature for present and future generations, and yet not opposed to the benefits of the industrial age, most pursued a middle course, protecting nature in a few places while allowing economic development to continue elsewhere.

As part of this strategy, several organizations relied on land purchases or leases to establish reserves that were larger than natural monuments yet smaller than national parks being erected abroad. This was the case with the DBV as well as the Isar Valley Society, the latter established in 1902 by a Munich architect and supported by a number of the city's prominent residents. The Isar Society bought up land along the shores of the Isar River to keep it off limits to development. Working with the State Committee for Care of Nature, the society temporarily obstructed plans by a utility company to direct water from the Isar to replenish Walchensee, a pristine alpine lake that was to be harnessed for hydroelectricity. After WWI, however, the project went through, critically lowering the flow of water in the Isar.[26]

The Nature Park Society (*Verein Naturschutzpark,* or VNP), established in Munich in 1909 by the ornithologist, Dr. Kurt Floericke, with support from the editors of the popular science journal, *Kosmos,* raised money from state-supported lotteries and its 12,000 members from across the empire to purchase land in the Lüneburg Heath and in the Hohe Tauern near Salzburg. In the VNP's public parks, several motives for protecting nature converged, illustrating the range of justifications for preservation at the time. While Floericke stressed the importance of these spaces for scientific study and protecting nature "for its own sake," VNP members emphasized their recreational value. True to form, Rudorff viewed them as a place where urbanites could satisfy the "deeper needs of the human soul" through rest and introspection.[27]

Germany's numerous hiking and outing clubs advocated preservation only after they saw the impact that unguided tourism could have on the spaces they initially wanted to make more accessible. One of the oldest hiking groups, the Baden Black Forest Society, was established in Freiburg in 1864 by innkeepers and entrepreneurs who hoped to attract tourists to the region. There also was the German Alpine Society (1869), the Taunus Club (1868), and the Oden Forest Club (1882), among others. In 1883, many of these groups formed the precursor of today's League of German Mountaineering and Hiking Societies, an alliance that played an important part in conservation in West Germany during the Miracle Years. To make the "beauties of nature" more accessible, members prepared maps, marked trails, and built benches and lookout towers. Later they shared preservationists' pedagogical mission to instruct "the masses" in appreciating the scientific and aesthetic value of local flora, fauna, and geology.[28]

Around the turn of the century, organizations emerged to encourage hiking among the youth. The middle class *Wandervogel* wing of the youth movement was formed in 1901 as a hiking club for boys, but it soon spread beyond the suburbs of Berlin to attract male and female members across Germany. By 1911, it claimed 15,000 members. This movement, which grew more nationalistic after World War I, exerted a powerful influence on several youth who went on to pursue careers in landscape architecture or play leadership roles in private conservation organizations. Journals of the back-to-nature youth movement featured images of young ramblers with rucksacks and walking sticks, gazing out over rolling hills of an idealized rural landscape where people live in harmony with the land. In romanticizing these pre-industrial landscapes, some scholars argue, young observers aestheticized what they saw and ignored the people and social inequalities that prevailed there. Moreover, they carried these conservative, paternalistic views of the natural and social order with them in their later careers.[29] Veterans of the back-to-nature youth movement who figured prominently in West German conservation through the 1960s dispute these charges, arguing instead that their outdoor rambling encouraged introspection and self-reliance as well as a lifestyle of moderation and self-discipline.[30] As later chapters illustrate, these assumptions about the "proper" way to experience nature contributed to conservationists' elitist reputation.

Although most hiking organizations were dominated by the middle and upper classes, the Friends of Nature was largely working class and socialist. Founded in 1895 in Vienna, the Friends of Nature had local chapters in Germany beginning in 1905. The intent of the organization was to strengthen class solidarity, escape the city temporarily, and foster a scientific appreciation for nature through organized outings, or "social hiking." Chapters also campaigned to keep parts of the countryside and the outskirts of cities clean and open to the public. Despite having goals similar to those of bourgeois organizations, the Friends of Nature faulted capitalism and its middle class benefactors for harming workers' natural surroundings. During the politically divisive years of the Weimar Republic, the organization resisted efforts by middle class preservationists to create a unified community, one supposedly strengthened by a deep attachment to the landscapes of the German homeland.[31]

By the 1920s, an impressive diversity of private organizations and semi-official bodies had formed to protect flora and fauna, natural monuments, and scenic areas, primarily at the local, regional, and state levels. Yet these groups' concerns remained parochial and they were too disparate to form a movement. In addition, those attracted to the cause tended to be social and economic elites who felt obliged to protect nature from people they thought lacked their education and moral cultivation to appreciate nature properly—a concern hardly unique to Germany.[32] Irrespective of their motives or emphases, a majority of Germans involved in preservation expressed concern about protecting an image of nature that was frozen in time. Their ideal was not a wilderness, but a cultural landscape shaped by pre-industrial economic uses; it was a hybrid landscape dating from before 1850 and contrasting sharply with the modern world.[33]

Preservationists from Conwentz to Schultze-Naumburg did not oppose industrial development. Schultze-Naumburg, in particular, advocated the creation of a new aesthetic of nature that made room for the modern world. Since the early 1900s, his artistic sensibilities convinced him that power lines, roads, dams, and canals could and should be installed to blend in with their natural surroundings, and areas defaced by mining or quarrying should be renatured. Harmonizing nature and technology would create not only a modern landscape, but a new work of art. Such strategies were also favored in the 1920s by preservationists like the architect Werner Lindner and Württemberg commissioner for nature protection, Hans Schwenkel.[34] Their aesthetic recommendations reveal preservationists' guarded acceptance of modernity and their desire to see that the country's seemingly inevitable economic growth proceed in more orderly and less invasive ways. During the Second Empire, however, the imperial and state governments and the general population were most concerned with promoting industrial expansion and the protection of property rights.[35]

Protecting Nature and the Homeland
during the Weimar Republic, 1919–1933

These priories continued to obstruct preservation during the difficult years of the Weimar Republic, Germany's first parliamentary democracy. Between 1920 and 1934, every state but Thuringia passed laws for protecting nature, yet they were neither comprehensive nor uniform. Article 150 of the Weimar Constitution established that "the monuments of art, history and nature, as well as the landscape enjoy the protection and cultivation of the state." But preservationists' repeated appeals for a national law went unheeded. Officials feared that effective nature protection would involve expropriating property and prohibitive compensation payments to owners. Although by 1931 Germany had over 400 nature reserves, two-thirds of them in Prussia, this defensive strategy was powerless against urban, industrial growth.[36]

In search of a practical strategy for harmonizing preservation and economic development, prominent landscape architects in the modernist wing of the homeland preservation movement advocated more attention to the tradition of landscape care (*Landschaftspflege*).[37] Landscape care had its beginnings in the eighteenth century. Through patronage of the nobility, landscape architects and gardeners hoped to improve society by beautifying cities and the countryside and by boosting commerce and agricultural production. That these grand designs, like those of hydraulic engineers and foresters mentioned earlier, seemed possible reflected an increase in the power of absolutist rulers to conduct land surveys, gather statistics, and make maps—powers that aided in subduing nature and rationalizing its use to promote human settlement and commerce.[38] During the nineteenth century, the broad vision for embellishing entire regions under royal patronage narrowed to a focus on planning public parks, a responsibility that fell to city governments.[39]

Only around the turn of the century did landscape and garden architects call for a mutli-pronged approach to land use, which included preservation, the greening of cities, and the recultivation of areas harmed by industry and agricultural reform. Eugen Gradmann, state curator in Württemberg and enthusiastic protector of his Swabian homeland, promoted the concept "landscape care" (*Landschaftspflege*) in 1910, challenging those homeland preservationists who continued to insist that nature could only be protected, but not embellished. Nature was not a static relic of the past, he argued, but the product of ongoing interaction with human society. By constantly tending landscapes that resulted from the historical interplay of nature and culture, it was possible to preserve natural beauty and accommodate industrial development, ensuring prosperity for the *Heimat.*[40]

In turning to landscape care in the early 1900s, but most clearly in the 1920s, preservationists not only helped keep the tradition alive, they also used it to reform *Naturschutz.* With the advantage of hindsight, it is apparent that well into the 1960s, landscape care was viewed as the primary vehicle for modernizing efforts to protect nature in an urban industrial society. In taking on concerns associated with *Landschaftspflege,* especially the need to set aside recreational spaces in and near cities in the interest of public health, preservationists of the Weimar era gave their work a clear social orientation that had been less evident in earlier efforts aimed at protecting nature from people, however sensible that approach had seemed at the time. Furthermore, in accepting the challenge to constantly tend landscapes (e.g., by insisting that areas damaged by exploitative use be repaired), preservationists developed a flexible and more practical approach to nature's care. Yet too frequently this strategy meant that preservationists accommodated intrusive development projects, settling for cosmetic measures (like embedding structures into landscapes for a more pleasing visual effect). Nonetheless, the tradition of landscape care encouraged preservationists to view the countryside and the city as inseparable parts of a whole. A holistic vision and an ambitious one, the nascent planning discipline of *Landschaftspflege* presupposed a professional class of landscape architects who had the expertise to naturalize technology and industry and who had political clout to influence decisions about land use. But in the 1920s, professional landscape architects were limited to "a few dozen men" employed primarily by elites to lay out gardens; they could point to few tangible successes.[41]

More than preservationists, it was spatial planners of the Weimar years who set their sights on renaturing urban industrial landscapes degraded by exploitative uses. Spatial planning (*Raumordnung*), sometimes translated as "territorial" planning, was a professional field of growing importance in an era that prized rationalization, efficiency, and productivity. Planners perceived a need to guide the advance of industrial capitalism, ultimately to prevent a waste of space and resources. Many of these goals were influenced by the garden city movement, which emerged at the turn of the century first in England to improve living conditions and contain urban sprawl. More encompassing visions for developing entire regions evolved as a result of state planning during World War I. Government control over the distribution of scarce resources during the conflict convinced Germany's postwar planners of the need for the state to regulate the use of land and resources over large areas. During the 1920s, however, planning was limited to densely populated industrial regions like the Ruhr and Upper Silesia or major cities such as Hamburg and Berlin. Here, planners tried to ensure a more orderly use of territory to settle competing claims on space. Influenced by this new attention to rational planning, preservationists, too, called for order, urging the protection of natural spaces where a growing urban population apparently alienated from nature might be rejuvenated and "plant[ed] . . . more firmly in the homeland soil."[42] Such appeals would be revived by preservationists in the 1930s and 1940s, and again in modified form during the 1950s.

During the Weimar years, preservationists hoped they might attract broader support by tapping into the new enthusiasm among urban dwellers to spend increased leisure time outdoors. While some, such as Walther Schoenichen (1876–1956), Conwentz's successor as director of the Prussian Agency for the Care of Natural Monuments, were encouraged by this apparent appreciation for the restorative powers of nature, they insisted that potentially unruly urbanites needed instruction in how to behave properly in nature. Only then would spending time outdoors combat the pessimism that followed the Great War and help heal social divisions that prevailed in Weimar Germany. Previously, preservationists had aimed their "social healing message" at the working classes, the group they traditionally associated with social rebellion. But in the 1920s, they also looked to contain young adults who had more freedom in Weimar society. Through supervised hiking and collaboration with teachers of local history and culture (*Heimatkunde*), preservationists hoped to cultivate among workers and youth an appreciation for nature and *Heimat,* the foundations, they believed, of a strong national community. But their conservative agenda could not compete with Weimar's vibrant urban culture. When support for protecting nature and *Heimat* declined in the turbulent later years of Weimar (1928–1933), prominent preservationists blamed the destabilizing forces of modernity and foreign influences that "corrupted" Germany with "degenerate" forms of mass culture.[43]

Some like Schoenichen, Schwenkel, and Schultze-Naumburg found an explanation for waning support in theories of racial hygiene in vogue in Germany, Western Europe, and the US. In the US, Progressive Era conservationists such as Theodore Roosevelt, Gifford Pinchot, and Henry Fairfield Osborn, Sr. endorsed eugenics, and some preservationists linked the protection of America's natural heritage to the protection of the white race against foreign "contamination."[44] In Germany, where preservationists had long viewed the native "soil" as the organic source of strength of national character, some came to argue that national strength now also depended upon racial purity, or "blood." Like other conservatives of the era, Schoenichen and Schwenkel were openly anti-Semitic.[45] Interestingly, they, Schultze-Naumburg, and several others also looked to technology to strengthen *Heimat, Volk,* and nation, maintaining that a uniquely German approach to building cities, roads, dams, and other structures would create modern landscapes that pointed to a promising future while reflecting traditions of the past. Under National Socialism, race and technology merged, creating new visions for shaping the "Germanic landscape."[46] Yet Weimar preservationists were not a uniform group that the National Socialists co-opted fully or uniformly.

Protecting Landscapes and Living Space under National Socialism, 1933–1945

After the National Socialists came to power in 1933, many preservationists accepted the dictatorship for pragmatic reasons. They hoped that a strong central government might pass a nation-wide preservation law, a long-standing goal that repeatedly ran aground in the partisan struggles of Weimar democracy. Generally speaking, middle class preservation groups did not resist National Socialist coordination (*Gleichschaltung*), though the degree to which they responded to Nazification ranged from outward conformity to outright support. Groups based in predominantly Catholic areas were less compliant, such as Bavaria's Isar Valley Society and the Rhineland's Eifel Society. While these organizations were left alone to pursue their traditional agenda, the socialist Friends of Nature was dissolved in March 1933, an indication of the fate that awaited high-profile groups ideologically at odds with the regime. Although several powerful Nazis vied for control over preservation groups, the competition ended in favor of Hermann Göring in 1935. But Göring paid little attention to these organizations because of his more pressing duties as Commander-in-Chief of the Air Force and head of the Four Year Plan (1936–1940) to revive the economy.[47]

Leading preservationists' level of participation in the Nazi Party was comparable to other professional groups until 1939, after which their numbers appeared to have been higher. Yet it is difficult to determine the extent to which individual preservationists supported National Socialist ideology because of the perceived and real pressure to express goals in Nazi language.[48] Yet several ideas associated with Nazism offered preservationists hope that the state would elevate the cause of protecting nature. The regime's call for a return to Germanic cultural traditions sounded familiar to preservationists who shared with the Nazis the desire to see Germany rise to national greatness again by overcoming the forces that supposedly had contributed to the crisis of Weimar: liberal parliamentary democracy, Marxism, selfish individualism, crass materialism, and deviation from tradition in art and architecture.[49] At least in rhetoric, some Nazi ideologues echoed the ambivalence toward modernity and scorn for mass culture expressed by many preservationists with greater or less emphasis since the late nineteenth century. Nazis and some preservationists also shared the view that national revival depended on firmly anchoring Germans in their native land and traditions—sources, they contended, of spiritual strength that united people in a national *Volksgemeinschaft*. But preservationists were a rather elitist lot and had difficulty imagining camaraderie with the majority of Germans who lacked their idealism and devotion to the green cause. In terms of practical, modernist-sounding measures, the regime's concern to implement centralized planning (*Raumordnung*) appealed to preservationists who hoped to participate more in decisions over land use. But only some approved of the racism and anti-Semitism that were central to Nazi ideology.[50] In general, attention to ideology provides only a partial explanation for the instances when preservation and Nazism converged. Also at work, Frank Uekötter emphasizes, was opportunism and preservationists' willingness to look to party officials to achieve what goals they could, even if doing so in some cases implicated them in the regime's ruthless policies.[51]

After initial uncertainty about the fate of nature protection, preservationists found reason to be hopeful when Göring, as Reich Master of the Forest, personally ensured passage of the Reich Nature Protection Law (RNG) in 1935, bringing about long-awaited legal uniformity in protecting nature. The RNG has been examined in several studies, but a brief overview of its important provisions is in order here because the law remained in effect after 1945.[52] The RNG must be seen in the context of the regime's efforts to centralize the laws of the Reich and as part of Göring's effort to implement conservation-related legislation between 1933 and 1935, which included the protection of animals and the promotion of ecologically sound forestry. Yet, conservationists quickly learned that enforcement of these laws was uneven and often lax.[53]

The RNG created a uniform, nationwide bureaucracy for preservation, establishing offices for nature protection at the national, provincial, and local levels. It also built on the practice started by Conwentz in creating advisory boards (*Naturschutzstellen*) that existed parallel to preservation offices. Heading up the advisory boards were honorary commissioners (*Beauftragter*), some of them active in nature protection already. The RNG elevated the former Prussian Agency for the Care of Natural Monuments to the Reich Agency for Nature Protection, which was housed under the Reich Forest Office. Schoenichen stayed on as the agency's director until he fell from grace in 1938. He was replaced by his long time rival, Hans Klose (1880–1963), whom scholars characterize as "a consummate opportunist" and "a skillful tactician" with a pragmatic view of what preservationists could accomplish.[54] After 1945, the bureaucratic apparatus established by the RNG remained in place, though primary responsibility for *Naturschutz* devolved to the new West German states.

When it was passed in the 1930s, the RNG was a model preservation law. The RNG extended protection to rare or endangered plants and nongame animals, natural monuments and their surroundings, nature reserves, and "other landscape areas in open nature." Although the first three categories had been the subject of previous legislation in various states, the provision for protecting parts of the countryside was new and broadly defined, extending the possibility of protection to "groups of trees," ravines, hedges, parks, and cemeteries. The

RNG continued to emphasize aesthetics in determining what merited protection, but also acknowledged the importance of scientific, historical, and cultural criteria.[55]

In the postwar era, some preservationists heralded the RNG as a "decisive turn" for conservation, while a younger cohort viewed it as an unfortunate obstruction to the development of a more effective strategy for managing nature in an urban, industrial society.[56] The latter group had not had a hand in drafting or lobbying for national legislation in the 1920s and 1930s, and thus had difficulty viewing the RNG as an achievement. Those who were involved in nature protection before the law's passage, however, were enthusiastic about the portions that created the possibility for broader planning responsibilities: paragraphs 5, 19, and 20. Paragraph 5 enabled officials to protect the countryside from intrusions that would despoil its scenic beauty or threaten flora and fauna, while paragraph 19 allowed officials to remove "disfiguring changes" that harmed nature or detracted from its "full enjoyment." Paragraph 20 required authorities to consult preservation officials before approving construction projects that might significantly alter "the open landscape," a measure with a precedent in state laws passed before WWI to prevent the "disfigurement" (*Verunstaltung*) of "outstanding landscapes."[57] Frank Uekötter illustrates that preservationists were at least sometimes consulted as per paragraph 20, and their involvement resulted in the occurrence of less intrusive actions.[58] Yet examples at the regional and local levels also show that preservationists' recommendations often were ignored.[59] Also disappointing was paragraph 6, which exempted from the law those areas vital to the armed forces, transportation, river navigation, and the economy. An attempt in 1942 to amend the RNG to protect "the entire German landscape as the living space of the German *Volk*," and to give preservation officials more authority in guiding development failed.[60]

Another weakness in the RNG that handicapped conservation after 1945 was the reliance on honorary commissioners to conduct the daily work of *Naturschutz*. In their volunteer posts, commissioners continued the pedagogical emphasis traditionally associated with nature protection, working with party officials, the Hitler Youth, the Labor Service, foresters, teachers, community leaders, and police to encourage public support for preservation. This educational activity was familiar to many commissioners who came from the teaching profession and typically had training in biology, botany, or geography. In general, commissioners lacked sufficient time, training, and funding to handle the volume of administrative work now associated with their honorary position. As a result, they struggled to limit damage caused by the regime's development initiatives—a steady refrain for postwar conservationists as well.[61]

West German conservationists understandably argued that the RNG was not a Nazi law, but the culmination of years of work. And yet passage of the RNG was facilitated by the dictatorship, which enabled influential Nazis like Göring to pursue matters of personal interest as state policy—until preparing for and fighting war made it inconvenient. The bill became law not after parliamentary deliberations but after Göring intervened personally to approve it and to claim responsibility for preservation. By centralizing the administration of *Naturschutz* under the Reich Forest Office, the RNG promised greater uniformity in efforts to protect nature. Yet central control weakened state governments' traditional hold on preservation and potentially limited locals' ability to influence bureaucratic decision making. The law reflected a significant increase in the power of the state. It sanctioned the expropriation of property without compensation (paragraph 24), an authority that enabled preservationists to establish an unprecedented number of nature reserves in the late 1930s and early 1940s. In general, however, they preferred to work out amicable settlements with property owners, invoking the power they might wield with paragraph 24 when they encountered resistance. The RNG also allowed for dispossession in order to establish "Reich nature reserves" (which Göring sometimes claimed for his personal use), and it created an office to oversee expropriation and resettlement (paragraph 18). In short, dictatorship made it easier and cheaper to put land in state hands, ostensibly to protect nature for the benefit of the mythical *Volk*. Most troubling of all, in trying to implement the RNG in conquered territories, preservationists linked the law and their activities to the regime's racial and genocidal policies.[62]

Encouraged by the RNG, preservationists sought broader planning responsibilities as they watched the Reich Labor Service implement "inner colonization" by building dams, draining wetlands, and straightening streams—all part of the regime's battle for economic production and rural modernization.[63] But their influence remained limited when compared with landscape and garden architects whose professional standing improved through involvement in land reclamation and major engineering projects like the Autobahn.[64] In the mid 1930s, the garden architect Alwin Seifert (1890–1972),[65] a strong-willed and dedicated conservationist with *völkisch* views, was able to publicly attack the Labor Service, due to the client-patron relationship he had with high-ranking Nazis and fellow Bavarians, Deputy Führer Rudolf Hess, and Inspector General of German Roads, Fritz Todt. Nor did it hurt that Seifert's criticisms were expressed in racial terms: reckless reclamation, he claimed, threatened to degrade Germany's landscapes into "Asiatic steppes," a term he used to evoke images of an infertile landscape presumably suited only for Slavs, whom he viewed as racially inferior.[66]

Garden and landscape architects such as Seifert tried to make themselves useful to the regime by pledging to make land use practices less environmentally destructive and by promising to heal Germany's "sick landscape," as they said in the language of racial hygiene.[67] Toward this end, landscape and garden architects borrowed methods from plant geography to make their work more scientific and to strengthen their small, but growing profession. Specifically, they accepted the climax theory of plant succession, which was developed in the 1930s by the American Frederic Clements, but also was evident in the research of Professor

Reinhold Tüxen, the internationally respected German botanist who remained influential after 1945. According to this theory, the most natural landscapes were those in which "native" vegetation (i.e., species that had been found in an area for centuries) existed in a "climax state" of equilibrium and would remain in such a state over the long term if climate, soil, and other environmental conditions were left undisturbed by humans. Botanists and plant geographers, or "plant sociologists" as they were then called in Germany, considered "native" species to be "more natural" than "foreign" ones because the former were considered hardier and capable of existing in a steady state for centuries under the right conditions. In their struggle for influence with high-ranking Nazis, Seifert and other landscape architects infused these contemporary ecological views with racial meanings, demonstrating ideological correctness by pledging, in Lekan's words to "restore the primordial *Lebensraum* of Germany, the unique habitat in which the race was formed and from which it drew its strength."[68]

Confident in their work and effective in using the support of Hess (until he fled to England in 1941) and Todt (until he died in a plane crash in 1942), Seifert and other landscape architects lessened the invasiveness of some river regulation measures and hydroprojects in southern Germany and Austria. They also hoped to extend their influence in the eastern conquered territories, taking over duties that belonged to preservationists. From their heightened social position, they looked down upon honorary commissioners whom they regarded as amateurs with little to contribute to planning decisions.[69] This competition between landscape architects and preservationists persisted into the 1960s, though in less dramatic form. Moreover, it resulted in the long term administrative separation of two potentially complementary endeavors, creating yet another hindrance to effective conservation after 1945.[70]

Like landscape architects, preservationists were opportunistic. But even the Reich Agency Director Hans Klose admitted during the war that his political ties with Nazi higher-ups were weaker than Seifert's.[71] Nonetheless, preservationists hoped to benefit from Germany's eastward expansion. Württemberg's Hans Schwenkel and Bavaria's Otto Kraus concluded that access to more territory in the east would reduce the need to drain wetlands within Germany. But they were wrong; land reclamation in the Old Reich (Germany's borders as of 1937) continued at a rapid pace. Others anticipated that the additional space might improve the chances of establishing more reserves in the Wartheland in Poland and in the Caucasus. Lutz Heck, Berlin Zoo director and head of preservation in the Reich Forest Office, initiated planning for several national parks, including in annexed Austria and Bohemia. Schoenichen, an ardent supporter of racial ideology, considered creating a national park in Bialowieza Forest—after Polish inhabitants had been removed. For his part, Klose proposed erecting national parks in Germany's former colonial possessions.[72] Such visions, motivated by opportunism, and in cases like Schoenichen and Schwenkel, by fanatical racism, further illustrate how preservationists worked within the system to take advantage of chances that came their way. But by tolerating and sometimes actively supporting the Nazi regime, they condoned conquest and genocide, compromising the moral principles they had vaunted for decades.

Preservationists experienced a degree of normalcy in their largely bureaucratic work in the early years of war. But as the conflict wore on, their influence weakened, despite the RNG, despite 400 new nature reserves to add to the 400 or more in existence before 1935, despite the 1,100 local, sixty-eight regional, and fifteen higher-level nature protection agencies throughout the Reich and annexed areas. Preservationists were crippled by limited funding, their perceived amateurism, and a series of decrees issued by Göring between 1942 and 1944, which restricted preservation and prioritized the war.[73] After such disappointing results, it is not surprising that preservationists after 1945 depicted themselves as victims of the regime, particularly when their experiences contrasted with the career advancements of landscape architects, who carved out a niche for themselves designing living space in the East.

Although Seifert's team of landscape architects hoped to have influence in the East, they had less leverage than their colleagues working with Seifert's rival, the Berlin Professor Heinrich Wiepking-Jürgensmann, a non-party member who served under Heinrich Himmler, head of the Reich Commissariat for the Strengthening of Germandom (*Reichskommissariat für die Festigung deutschen Volkstums*, or RKFDV), an organization responsible for ethnic cleansing in the annexed territories of western Poland.[74] The RKFDV's aim was to strengthen the Reich by repatriating people of German ancestry to the newly incorporated lands, but only after expelling those of an "alien race" who threatened the "German *Volksgemeinschaft*." Nearly ten million people lived in the 90,000 square kilometer area, most of them Catholic or Jewish Poles. Between 1939 and 1940, one million of them were brutally expelled and either deposited further east in the General Government of Poland or, if Jewish, placed in ghettos. Their forced removal eventually "made room" for an estimated 300,000 ethnic Germans, who, on average, received land confiscated from two or three Polish families. This racial resettlement project was viewed as only the beginning of a much larger, constantly evolving plan—General Plan East—which envisioned transforming vast "empty" space further east into an agrarian *Volksgemeinschaft* for Aryan settlers, though only after evicting the current occupants.[75]

Eastward expansion opened up new possibilities for spatial planning, a government competency that became more institutionalized in the 1930s, not only in Germany, but in other industrialized nations as well. In the face of public works programs that consumed resources and visibly disfigured large areas, and intent on expanding Germany's "living space" in the East, the Nazi Regime established research institutes and offices to carry out comprehensive territorial planning. The Reich Agency for Spatial Planning, established in 1935, oversaw twenty-two regional associations throughout the Old Reich. Here, planning was implemented in a pragmatic way, though with increasing support for the Four Year Plan and war. In the eastern conquered territories, however, Himmler's RKFDV pursued a racialized variant of spatial planning that was guided by General Plan East.[76]

Himmler appointed the leading agronomist and SS member Konrad Meyer to oversee the design of landscapes and settlements within the RKFDV planning office. Other influential individuals were Erhard Mäding, officer for landscape care in the RKFDV, and Wiepking-Jürgensmann, chair of the Institute for Landscape Design at the University of Berlin as of 1934, and special commissioner to Himmler in questions of landscape design.[77] The image of the "Germanic landscape" that informed their experimental plans was orderly, garden-like, and modern in contrast to the supposedly "degraded," "neglected" "wilderness" of the East. In their ideal landscape, fertile fields lined with hedgerows alternated with open meadows, orchards, and woodlands, while dunes, moors, and old-growth forest remained as remnants of "primeval" nature. Tidy farms and quaint villages built in regional architectural styles blended into surrounding countryside. Attractively designed structures for small-scale industry were contained; clean, ordered cities of between 20,000 and 30,000 inhabitants were surrounded by small gardens, forming a seamless organic link with the countryside.[78] Hydroplants, dikes, and irrigation ditches using the latest technology would, according to Mäding, reveal German planners' unique ability to "follow nature and harvest the reward of a greater mastery over it."[79]

To transform these racially driven visions into reality, the RKFDV issued comprehensive guidelines in 1942 for use by lower level officials. Drafted by Wiepking-Jürgensmann, Mäding, and Meyer, among others, the recommendations relied on research of several individuals, not all of whom embraced Nazi ideology. The guidelines contain suggestions that continue to hold relevance from the standpoint of ecology.[80] However practical these comprehensive measures were, they cannot be divorced from their historical context. As Robert Proctor has shown in his study of the Nazi campaign against cancer, advanced scientific research yielded useful insights, yet was motivated by the desire to protect Germans' racial health.[81] Similarly, landscape architects' vision for elevating landscape care to an all-encompassing planning discipline was justified in terms of Nazi racial policy and contingent upon territorial conquest and ethnic cleansing. In cultivating a healthy living space that would endure for all time, these particular landscape architects contended, they were strengthening the racial health of the *Volk* and sustaining it for eternity. Furthermore, if resettled Germans felt at home in their new surroundings, their innate love of nature would enable them to form strong ties to the land, making them willing to die in its defense.[82]

The conquest of territory in the east and the centralized authority made possible by dictatorship enabled landscape architects to strengthen their profession, making it central to spatial planning. Mäding proposed the adoption of the vague concept *"Landespflege,"* directly translated as "land cultivation," to leave no doubt that the field was going beyond aesthetic landscape design to take on comprehensive planning duties. In the occupied Eastern territories, Mäding believed that landscape architects would have total freedom to transform conquered space into a "perfect community," a work of art.[83] Yet one of the few model towns they built in Kreis Saybusch in Upper Silesia required the brutal expulsion in 1940 of over 17,000 Poles. Beyond this, war prevented landscape architects from doing little more than planting shelterbelts and establishing nurseries for use when the fighting ended.[84] Such a dismal performance made it easier for them to distance themselves from the genocidal policies of the regime they actively supported and to eventually continue their professional careers in the Federal Republic.

National Socialists' goal of building up a racially pure *Volk* that would be self-sufficient had required industrial expansion, environmental degradation, war, conquest, and genocide. Yet the Nazis' exploitation of forests, soil, water, and other resources did not put an end to the illusion that Germans had a unique attachment to nature. On the contrary, the claim continued to be made in more subtle ways during the occupation and early years of the Federal Republic by conservationists and prominent political figures who found it useful in setting themselves apart from a rapacious dictatorship and in justifying opposition to occupation policies that seemed designed to exploit the German landscape, and by extension, to weaken the German people.

During the Third Reich, the synchronization of nature preservation and landscape care had been uneven. As the experiences of preservationists and landscape architects make clear, ideas considered ecologically valuable by today's standards are neither inherently Nazi nor inherently good. They can be adapted to conform to the political system in place and manipulated by social groups to increase their influence. After 1945, conservationists tried to preserve the sound ideas and practices developed before and under National Socialism, and pledged to promote them in conformity with democracy. In the new democratic order, they proved to be ideologically flexible on the surface and yet remained conservative in their understandings of state and society. Racialized definitions of "landscape" disappeared, and not only because such views had been discredited: at war's end, Eastern Europeans expelled Germans from their populations, forcing them back into a country that would be 75 percent of its prewar size but far more homogeneous ethnically.[85]

Nationalistic understandings of landscapes continued to be used well into the 1950s. For an even longer period, the view persisted that restoring health to landscapes would strengthen the physical and psychological health of the people. Only in the 1960s did conservationists begin to revise this view, acknowledging that the country's unhealthy landscapes were the result of economic inequalities and disorderly land use. In response, influential conservationists once again sought greater involvement in spatial planning. Unlike in the 1930s and 1940s, however, they supported officials' goals to use this technocratic policy tool to promote constitutional guarantees of freedom, social equality, and security.

In resuming their work in the trying years of the Allied occupation, conservationists had a troubled legacy with which to work. They hoped to preserve the legal and administrative foundations for protecting nature that had been set forth in the RNG and subsequent ordinances, and were determined to strengthen their involvement in decisions about land and resource use, a goal that largely failed under National Socialism because of the regime's Four Year Plan and war of conquest. In the wake of total defeat, the most active conservationists worked immediately to implement the practices associated with landscape care. Rather than break with this tradition because some of its most prominent representatives had used its competencies to support the regime's genocidal aims, conservationists suppressed its association with conflict on the Eastern Front and promoted its scientifically based practices as the most effective means to prevent "terrible chaos" on the devastated home front.

Notes

1. Walter Schoenichen, *Naturschutz, Heimatschutz. Ihre Begründung durch Ernst Rudorff, Hugo Conwentz und ihre Vorläufer* (Stuttgart: Wissenschaftliche Verlagsgesellschaft, 1954), glosses over the Nazi years. Hans Klose, *Fünfzig Jahre staatlicher Naturschutz* (Giessen: Brühlscher, 1957), recalls the early years of National Socialism as a high water mark. Walter Hellmich, *Natur- und Heimatschutz* (Stuttgart: Franckh'sche, 1954); and Werner Siebold, *Geschützte Natur* (Mannheim: Bibliographisches Institut AG, 1958), are slim volumes that repeat information appearing in Schoenichen and Klose.
2. Walter Mrass, *Die Organisation des staatlichen Naturschutzes und der Landschaftspflege im deutschen Reich und in der BRD seit 1935 gemessen an der Aufgabenstellung in einer modernen Industriegesellschaft* (Stuttgart: Eugen Ulmer, 1970); Wolfram Pflug, "200 Jahre Landespflege in Deutschland. Eine Übersicht," in *Stadt und Landschaft, Raum und Zeit. Festschrift für Erich Kühn zur Vollendung seines 65. Lebensjahres,* ed. Alfred C. Boettger and Pflug (Cologne: Städtebau-Verlag, 1969).
3. See Frank Uekötter, "Die Beiträge Gert Grönings und Joachim Wolschke-Bulmahns," in Radkau and Uekötter, *Naturschutz und Nationalsozialismus,*" 454–59.
4. Meyer Howard Abrams, *Natural Supernaturalism: Tradition and Revolution in Romantic Literature* (New York: Norton, 1971), 88–94, 97–117, 143–95; Götz Großklaus, "Der Naturtraum des Kulturbürgers," in Großklaus and Oldemeyer, *Natur als Gegenwelt,* 190–95; Alfred Barthelmeß, *Landschaft—Lebensraum des Menschen: Probleme von Landschaftsschutz und Landschaftspflege* (Freiburg im Breisgau: Alber, 1988), 28–30; Schoenichen, *Naturschutz, Heimatschutz,* 20–34; Dominick, *Environmental Movement,* 25.
5. Hermand, *Grüne Utopien,* 42–44; Blackbourn, "'Conquests From Barbarism,'" in Mauch, *Nature in Germany History,* 24.
6. Andreas Knaut, *Zurück zur Natur! Die Wurzeln der Ökologiebewegung* (Greven: Kilda, 1993), 11–13; Rolf Peter Sieferle, "Heimatschutz und das Ende der Romantischen Utopie," *Arch + 81* (August 1985): 38.

7. Celia Applegate, "Localism and the German Bourgeoisie: the 'Heimat' Movement in the Rhenish Palatinate before 1914," in *The German Bourgeoisie: Essays on the Social History of the German Middle Class from the Late Eighteenth to the Early Twentieth Century*, ed. David Blackbourn and Richard J. Evans (New York: Routledge, 1991), 229.

8. Knaut, *Zurück zur Natur!*, 11–13, quote on p. 13.

9. Scott, *Seeing Like a State*, 11–22; Blackbourn, *Conquest*, chap. 1. More extensive on wetlands reclamation in Prussia is Rita Gudermann, *Morastwelt und Paradies: Ökonomie und Ökologie in der Landwirtschaft am Beispiel der Meliorationen in Westfalen und Brandenburg (1830–1880)* (Paderborn: Schöningh, 2000).

10. Woodruff Smith, *Politics and the Sciences of Culture in Germany, 1840–1920* (New York: Oxford University Press, 1991), 40–44, 133–35; George L. Mosse, *The Crisis of German Ideology: Intellectual Origins of the Third Reich* (New York: Grosset & Dunlap, 1964), 19–22; Lekan, *Imagining*, 6–7; Dominick, *Environmental Movement*, 22–23; Knaut, *Zurück zur Natur!*, 13–14; Schoenichen, *Naturschutz, Heimatschutz*, 16; Schama, *Landscape and Memory*, 113; Friedemann Schmoll, *Erinnerungen an die Natur. Die Geschichte des Naturschutzes im deutschen Kaiserreich* (Frankfurt am Main: Campus, 2004), 111–12.

11. Klaus Bergmann, *Agrarromantik und Großstadtfeindschaft* (Meisenheim am Glan: Anton Hain, 1970); Sieferle, *Fortschrittsfeinde?*; Gröning and Wolschke-Bulmahn, *Natur in Bewegung*.

12. Ernst Rudorff, "Über das Verhältnis des modernen Lebens zur Natur," *Preußische Jahrbücher* 45, no. 3 (1880): 261–76; Knaut, *Zurück zur Natur!*, 28, 30, 31–35; Schmoll, *Erinnerung*, 391–97.

13. On the evolution of Schultze-Naumburg's political views, including his support for National Socialism, see Matthew Jefferies, "Heimatschutz: Environmental Activism in Wilhelmine Germany," in Riordan, *Green Thought in German Culture*, 42–54; Lekan, *Imagining*, 64–67, 162–65; Dominick, *Environmental Movement*, 96-97; William Rollins, *A Greener Vision of Home. Cultural Politics and Environmental Reform in the German Heimatschutz Movement, 1904–1918* (Ann Arbor: University of Michigan Press, 1997), 83–84, 261–63.

14. Blackbourn, *Conquest*, 184–87.

15. Lekan, *Imagining*, 4–6, quote on p. 4; Rollins, *Greener Vision*, chap. 3; Brüggemeier, Cioc, and Zeller, "Introduction," *How Green*, 5; Schmoll, *Erinnerung*, 193–95; Uekötter, *Green and the Brown*, 19–21.

16. These views are summarized from Rollins, *Greener Vision;* Lekan, *Imagining;* and Knaut, *Zurück zur Natur!* In the context of German environmental history, Rollins and Knaut offer the most revisionist interpretations of homeland preservation. A nuanced but less revisionist interpretation is provided by Lekan, *Imagining*. See also Schmoll, *Erinnerung*, 435–39; John Alexander Williams, "'The Chords of the German Soul Are Tuned to Nature': The Movement to Preserve the Natural Heimat from the Kaiserreich to the Third Reich," *Central European History* 29, no. 3 (1996): 339–84. On the National Trust see John Sheail, *Nature in Trust. The History of Nature Conservation in Britain* (Glasgow and London: Blackie, 1976), 58–60.

17. Günter Küppers, Peter Lundgreen, and Peter Weingart, *Umweltforschung—die gesteuerte Wissenschaft? Eine empirische Studie zum Verhältnis von Wissenschaftsentwicklung und Wissenschaftspolitik* (Frankfurt am Main: Suhrkamp, 1978), 51–79; Potthast, "Wissenschaftliche Ökologie und Naturschutz," in Radkau and Uekötter, *Naturschutz und Nationalsozialismus*, 225–34.

18. See Thomas Lekan, "Regionalism and the Politics of Landscape Preservation in the Third Reich," *Environmental History* 4, no. 3 (July 1999): 384–404; Alon Confino, "The Nation as a Local Metaphor: Heimat, National Memory, and the German Empire, 1871–1918," *History and Memory* 5 (Spring/Summer 1993): 42–86; Applegate, *Nation of Provincials*.

19. On the evolution of the concept "natural monument" see Sieferle, *Fortschrittsfeinde?*, 60–61; Alfred Barthelmeß, *Wald—Umwelt des Menschen. Dokumente zu einer Problemgeschichte*

von Naturschutz, Landschaftspflege und Humanökologie (Freiburg im Breisgau: Alber, 1972), 118–21; Schoenichen, *Naturschutz, Heimatschutz,* 35–43, 214–15. See also Rudy Koshar, *Germany's Transient Pasts. Preservation and National Memory in the Twentieth Century* (Chapel Hill: University of North Carolina Press, 1998).

20. Schoenichen, *Naturschutz, Heimatschutz,* 103–10, 211–13; Barthelmeß, *Landschaft,* 179–80; Knaut, *Zurück zur Natur!,* 40–50; Schmoll, *Erinnerung,* 113–54; Hans-Werner Frohn, "Naturschutz macht Staat—Staat macht Naturschutz. Von der Staatlichen Stelle für Naturdenkmalpflege in Preußen bis zum Bundesamt für Naturschutz 1906 bis 2006—eine Institutionengeschichte," in Frohn and Schmoll, *Natur und Staat,* 85–122.

21. Andreas Knaut, "Die Anfänge des staatlichen Naturschutzes. Die frühe regierungsamtliche Organisation des Natur- und Landschaftsschutzes in Preußen, Bayern and Württemberg," in *Umweltgeschichte: Umweltverträgliches Wirtschaften in historischer Perspektive,* ed. Werner Abelshauser (Göttingen: Vandenhoeck & Ruprecht, 1994), 143–62; Dominick, *Environmental Movement,* 49–56; Williams, "Chords," 351–52.

22. Frohn, "Naturschutz macht Staat," in Frohn and Schmoll, *Natur und Staat,* 122; Edda Müller, "Die Beziehung von Umwelt- und Naturschutz in den 1970er Jahren," in Stiftung Naturschutzgeschichte, *Natur im Sinn,* 34–37.

23. Dominick, *Environmental Movement,* chap. 2; Barthelmeß, *Wald,* 91–96, 197–207.

24. Dominick, *Environmental Movement,* 53–54. For a discussion of the evolution of bird protection efforts, including the development of cultural taboos against hunting and eating songbirds, see Schmoll, *Erinnerung,* 249–379.

25. Dieter Kramer, *Der sanfte Tourismus: Umwelt- und sozialverträglicher Tourismus in den Alpen* (Vienna: Österreichischer Bundesverlag, 1983), 87; Dominick, *Environmental Movement,* 46–47; Schmoll, *Erinnerung,* 208–12. Gröning and Wolschke-Bulmahn, *Natur in Bewegung,* 130, find the approach regressive.

26. Reinhard Falter, "Achtzig Jahre 'Wasserkrieg': Das Walchenseekraftwerk," in *Von der Bittschrift zur Platzbesetzung. Konflikte um technische Großprojekte,* ed. Ulrich Linse, Reinhard Falter, Dieter Rucht, and Winfried Kretschmer (Bonn: Dietz, 1988), 63–105; Dominick, *Environmental Movement,* 45–48, 125.

27. Manfred Lütkepohl and Jens Tönnießen, *Naturschutzpark Lüneburger Heide* (Hamburg: Ellert & Richter, 1992), 28–36; Knaut, *Zurück zur Natur!,* 378–82, quote on p. 381; Dominick, *Environmental Movement,* 54–55; Gröning and Wolschke-Bulmahn, *Natur in Bewegung,* 180.

28. "125 Jahre Schwarzwaldverein e.V.," *Der Schwarzwald,* special edition (1989): 43, 58–63; Kramer, *sanfte Tourismus,* 26–55, 87–89; Gröning and Wolschke-Bulmahn, *Natur in Bewegung,* 124–30.

29. Joachim Wolschke-Bulmahn, "Die Ästhetisierung der Landschaft—Zum Einfluß der bürgerlichen Jugendbewegung auf die Landespflege," *N & L* 66, no. 10 (1991): 496–99; more extensive, Wolschke-Bulmahn, *Auf der Suche nach Arkadien: Zu Landschaftsidealen und Formen der Naturaneignung in der Jugendbewegung und ihrer Bedeutung für die Landespflege* (Munich: Minerva, 1990).

30. Konrad Buchwald, "Frühe Prägung und die Bussauer Zeit," *N & L* 61, no. 9 (1986): 319; Theodor Sonnemann, *Jahrgang 1900. Auf und ab im Strom der Zeit* (Würzburg: Wilhelm Naumann, 1980), 385; and Alfred Toepfer, *Erinnerungen aus meinem Leben 1894–1991* (Hamburg: Christians, 1991). See also Engels, *Naturpolitik,* chap. 2.

31. Jochen Zimmer, "Soziales Wandern. Zur proletarischen Naturaneignung," in Brüggemeier and Rommelspacher, *Besiegte Natur,* 158–67; Ulrich Linse, *Ökopax und Anarchie. Eine Geschichte der ökologischen Bewegungen in Deutschland* (Munich: Deutscher Taschenbuch Verlag, 1986), 43–56; Dominick, *Environmental Movement,* 61–62; Lekan, *Imagining,* 131, 143.

32. Raymond Williams, *The Country and the City* (New York: Oxford University Press, 1975).

33. Brüggemeier, Cioc, and Zeller, "Introduction," in *How Green,* 2; Lekan, *Imagining,* 103, 122; Friedemann Schmoll, "Schönheit, Vielfalt, Eigenart. Die Formierung des Natur-schutzes um 1900, seine Leitbilder und ihre Geschichte," in Frohn and Schmoll, *Natur und Staat,* 29–31, 65–69.

34. Williams, "Chords," 373–74; Linse, *Ökopax,* 26–34; Knaut, *Zurück zur Natur!,* 397–409; Lekan, *Imagining,* 122–27; Schmoll, *Erinnerung,* 406–9.

35. Rohkrämer, "Contemporary Environmentalism," in Goodbody, *Culture of German Environmentalism,* 54–57; Lekan, *Imagining,* 60.

36. Klose, *Fünfzig Jahre,* 19–20; Dominick, *Environmental Movement,* 85; Williams, "Chords," 354, 375; Lekan, *Imagining,* 121; Uekötter, *Green and the Brown,* 46–51.

37. Lekan, *Imagining,* 125.

38. Wolfram Pflug, "200 Jahre Landespflege," 239–240; Dorothee Nehring, *Geschichte des Stadtgrüns: Stadtparkanlagen in der ersten Hälfte des 19. Jahrhunderts* (Hanover: Patzer, 1979), 19–22, 161–68; Blackbourn, *Conquest,* chap. 1.

39. Pflug, "200 Jahre Landespflege," 243–44; Nehring, *Geschichte des Stadtgrüns,* 114–15, 156–59; Mrass, *Organisation,* 5.

40. Mrass, *Organisation,* 5–6; Knaut, *Zurück zur Natur!,* 400–402; Schmoll, *Erinnerung,* 409–11; Rollins, "Whose Landscape? Technology, Fascism, and Environmentalism on the National Socialist Autobahn," *Annals of the Association of American Geographers* 85, no. 3 (September 1995): 498–500.

41. On landscape architects' numbers see Thomas Zeller, "Molding the Landscape of Nazi Environmentalism: Alwin Seifert and the Third Reich," in Brüggemeier, Cioc, and Zeller, *How Green,* 150.

42. On regional planning during World War I and the 1920s see Scott, *Seeing Like a State,* chap. 3; Mechtild Rössler, "'Area Research' and 'Spatial Planning' from the Weimar Republic to the German Federal Republic: Creating a Society with a Spatial Order under National Socialism," in *Science, Technology and National Socialism,* ed. Monika Renneberg and Mark Walker (Cambridge: Cambridge University Press, 1994), 126–29; Gerd Spelsberg, *Rauchplage: Hundert Jahre saurer Regen* (Aachen: Alano, 1984), 119–35. On preservationists and planning see Lekan, *Imagining,* 121–29, quote on p. 127; Williams, "Chords," 368–74; Oberkrome, *"Deutsche Heimat,"* 129–40.

43. Lekan, *Imagining,* 136–41; Williams, "Chords," 356–61, 369–71; Frohn, "Naturschutz macht Staat," in Frohn and Schmoll, *Natur und Staat,* 130–43.

44. Gröning and Wolschke-Bulmahn, *Natur in Bewegung,* 142–43; Lekan, *Imagining,* 144–47, 164–65; Williams, "Chords," 364–65. On the US see Gregg Mitman, "In Search of Health: Landscape and Disease in American Environmental History," *Environmental History* 10, no. 2 (April 2005): 200–201.

45. Dominick, *Environmental Movement,* 85–95; Blackbourn, *Conquest,* 279; Uekötter, *Green and the Brown,* 23–28; Friedemann Schmoll, "Die Verteidigung organischer Ordnungen. Naturschutz und Anti-Semitismus zwischen Kaiserreich und Nationalsozialismus," in Radkau and Uekötter, *Naturschutz und Nationalsozialismus,* 169; Gröning and Wolschke-Bulmahn, *Natur in Bewegung,* 135–57. See also Thomas Rohkrämer, *Eine andere Moderne? Zivilisationskritik, Natur und Technik in Deutschland 1880–1933* (Paderborn: Schöningh, 1999).

46. Brüggemeier, Cioc, and Zeller, "Introduction," in *How Green,* 8.

47. Dominick, *Environmental Movement,* 98, 102–5; Uekötter, *Green and the Brown,* 58–61; Lekan, *Imagining,* chap. 4.

48. Dominick, *Environmental Movement,* 112–13. On pressure to conform to official ideology and express goals in Nazi language see Hans Klose to Richard Lohrmann, 21 September 1946, Bundesarchiv, Koblenz (BAK), Bundesamt für Naturschutz (B 245/253) (hereafter BAK B 245/253); Klose to Hermann Helfer, n.d. [1947?], BAK B 245/105.

49. See Hans Klose, "Naturschutz als Selbstverständlichkeit," *Naturschutz* 20, no. 1 (1939): 1–4.

50. Dominick, *Environmental Movement*, 85–95; Lekan, *Imagining*, 148–50; Uekötter, *Green and the Brown*, 30–42. On preservationists' hopes for spatial planning see Thomas Lekan, "'It Shall be the Whole Landscape!' The Reich Nature Protection Law and Regional Planning in the Third Reich," in Brüggemeier, Cioc, and Zeller, *How Green*, 73–74.

51. Uekötter, *Green and the Brown*, 16. See also his "Green Nazis? Reassessing the Environmental History of Nazi Germany," *German Studies Review* 30, no. 2 (May 2007): 267–87.

52. For recent critical assessments of the law see the essays by Charles E. Closmann, "Legalizing a Volksgemeinschaft. Nazi Germany's Reich Nature Protection Law of 1935" (pp. 18–42), and Lekan, "Regional Planning" (pp. 73–100), in Brüggemeier, Cioc, and Zeller, *How Green*; Uekötter, *Green and the Brown*, 62–75; Karl Ditt, "Die Anfänge der Naturschutzgesetzgebung in Deutschland und England 1935/49, in Radkau and Uekötter, *Naturschutz und Nationalsozialismus*, 116–25; Frohn, "Natur macht Staat," in Frohn and Schmoll, *Natur und Staat*, 164–76. See also Michael Wettengel, "Staat und Naturschutz 1906–1945: Zur Geschichte der Staatlichen Stelle für Naturdenkmalpflege in Preußen und der Reichsstelle für Naturschutz," *Historische Zeitschrift* 257, no. 2 (October 1993): 382–84; Dominick, *Environmental Movement*, 107–8.

53. On animal protection (1933) and hunting legislation (1934) see Dominick, *Environmental Movement*, 106–7; Heinrich Rubner, "Naturschutz, Forstwirtschaft und Umwelt in ihren Wechselbeziehungen, besonders im NS-Staat," in *Wirtschaftsentwicklung und Umweltbeeinflussung*, ed. Hermann Kellenbenz (Wiesbaden: Steiner, 1982), 118–19; Wettengel, "Staat und Naturschutz," 383; Edeltraud Klueting, "Die gesetzlichen Regelungen der nationalsozialistischen Reichsregierung für den Tierschutz, den Naturschutz und den Umweltschutz," in Radkau and Uekötter, *Naturschutz und Nationalsozialismus*, 77–106; Uekötter, *Green and the Brown*, 55–57. On forestry practices in Nazi Germany see Michael Imort, "'Eternal Forest—Eternal Volk': The Rhetoric and Reality of National Socialist Forest Policy," in Brüggemeier, Cioc, and Zeller, *How Green*, 43–72; Rubner, "Naturschutz, Forstwirtschaft und Umwelt," 112–15; Uekötter, *Green and the Brown*, 70–73; Wettengel, "Staat und Naturschutz," 382, 386–87.

54. Quotes on Klose's managerial style are found in Closmann, "Legalizing a Volksgemeinschaft," in Brüggemeier, Cioc, and Zeller, *How Green*, 34; and Uekötter, *Green and the Brown*, 74. The reasons for Schoenichen's fall remain unclear. Uekötter, *Green and the Brown*, 73–74, writes that Schoenichen was a dedicated Nazi and an able publisher but not a skilled manager, which the Reich Agency needed after passage of the RNG. Schoenichen also clashed with higher ranking Nazis, including Lutz Heck, the man who oversaw preservation in the Reich Forest Office and who had close ties to Göring. Oberkrome, "*Deutsche Heimat*," 182, also notes that Klose might have been transferred to the Reich Agency from the Reich Forest Office (where he had been since 1935) because he was viewed as a rival by Lutz Heck.

55. Closmann, "Legalizing a Volksgemeinschaft," in Brüggemeier, Cioc, and Zeller, *How Green*, 21–22.

56. Compare Klose, *Fünfzig Jahre*, 33; with Pflug, "200 Jahre Landespflege," 247; Mrass, *Organisation*, 10, 11–13; and Wolfgang Erz, "75 Jahre Bundesforschungsanstalt für Naturschutz und Landschaftsökologie im Spiegelbild deutscher Naturschutzgeschichte," *Jahrbuch für Naturschutz und Landschaftspflege* (hereafter *JfN&L*) (Greven: Kilda, 1983), 185.

57. *Reichsgesetzblatt* (1935) I. no. 68, 821–24. On earlier attitudes and laws that informed these portions of the RNG see Closmann, "Legalizing a Volksgemeinschaft," in Brüggemeier, Cioc, and Zeller, *How Green*, 20–26; and Jefferies, "Heimatschutz in Wilhelmine Germany," in Riordan, *Green Thought in German Culture*, 49.

58. Uekötter, *Green and the Brown*, chapters 4–5.

59. Zeller, *Strasse*, 132–37; Lekan, "Regional Planning," in Brüggemeier, Cioc, and Zeller, *How Green*, 90–93; and chapters 3 and 7 in this book.

60. Compare Walter Mrass, "Zu einem fast dreißig Jahre alten Änderungsentwurf des RNG," *N & L* 46, no. 1 (1971): 15–16, which is uncritical of the change, with the critique by Gröning and Wolschke-Bulmahn, *Natur in Bewegung*, 199.

61. Mrass, *Organisation*, 31, 40; Lekan, "Regional Planning," in Brüggemeier, Cioc, and Zeller, *How Green*, 91; Uekötter, *Green and the Brown*, 149. On commissioners' limited financial support see Klose, "Der unbekannte Naturschützer," *Naturschutz* 20, no. 2 (1939): 25–29; Klose, "Fünf Jahre Reichsnaturschutzgesetz," *Naturschutz* 21, no. 8 (1940): 85. Klose's complaints are ironic because in helping draft the RNG he had emphasized commissioners' honorary status to prevent the Reich Ministry of Finance from blocking the law.

62. Closmann, "Legalizing a Volksgemeinschaft," in Brüggemeier, Cioc, and Zeller, *How Green*, 26–35; Dominick, *Environmental Movement*, 107–8. On use of paragraph 24 see Uekötter, *Green and the Brown*, 142–45. On Göring's abuse of the category of "Reich nature reserve" see Heinrich Eberts [formerly in the Reich Ministry of Agriculture] to Egon Selchow, 16 July 1958, Verband Deutscher Naturparkträger Archive, Niederhaverbeck, Lüneburg Heath, binder labeled "Schriftwechsel 1958/59 A-G" (hereafter VDN Archive, "Schriftwechsel 1958/59 A-G").

63. See Schoenichen's "Appell der deutschen Landschaft an den Arbeitsdienst," *Naturschutz* 14, no. 8 (1933): 145–49; "Ödlandaufforstung?—Jawohl! Aber mit Bedacht," *Naturschutz* 15, no. 4 (1934): 78–82; and "Landschaftsgestalter an die Front!" *Naturschutz* 15, no. 5 (1934): 93–95.

64. On successes and shortcomings of constructing the Autobahn from an ecological standpoint see Zeller, *Straße*, 142–98, 203–9; Lekan, *Imagining*, 225, 234–43; Rollins, "Whose Landscape?" 508–9; Alwin Seifert, *Ein Leben für die Landschaft* (Düsseldorf and Cologne: Eugen Diederichs, 1962), 89.

65. Seifert's career has been examined by several historians with differing interpretations of his loyalty to the regime and his support for racial ideology. Compare Rollins, "Whose Landscape," passim; and Dominick, *Environmental Movement*, 109–111, 113, who view Seifert as only outwardly conformist, with Lekan, *Imagining*, chap. 5; and Gröning and Wolschke-Bulmahn, *Der Drang nach Osten*, 135–36, 138, 148–50, who maintain that Seifert embraced Nazi racial ideology. Thomas Zeller, "'Ganz Deutschland sein Garten': Alwin Seifert und die Landschaft des Nationalsozialismus," in Radkau and Uekötter, *Naturschutz und Nationalsozialismus*, 273–307, comes down in the middle, stressing Seifert's complex character and opportunism.

66. Alwin Seifert, "Die Versteppung Deutschlands," *Deutsche Technik* (September 1936): 423–27; (October 1936): 490–92; Seifert, *Ein Leben*, 100–112; Thomas Kluge and Engelbert Schramm, *Wassernöte: Sozial- und Umweltgeschichte des Trinkwassers* (Aachen: Alano, 1986), 191–96; Dominick, *Environmental Movement*, 109–10; Lekan, *Imagining*, 231–33; Blackbourn, *Conquest*, 285–87. On Seifert's political ties see Zeller, "Molding the Landscape," in Brüggemeier, Cioc, and Zeller, *How Green*, esp. 152–62; more extensive, Zeller, *Straße*, part 3.

67. Lekan, *Imagining*, 244; Rollins, "Whose Landscape?" 506, 510.

68. Zeller, *Straße*, 168–98; Lekan, *Imagining*, 228–29, 244–46, quote on p. 246; Thomas Potthast, "Naturschutz und Naturwissenschaft—Symbiose oder Antagonismus? Zur Beharrung und zum Wandel prägender Wissensformen vom ausgehenden 19. Jahrhundert bis in die Gegenwart," in Frohn and Schmoll, *Natur und Staat*, 364–75, 388–94, 404–9.

69. On reducing the impact of hydroprojects and river regulation see Zeller, "Molding the Landscape," in Brüggemeier, Cioc, and Zeller, *How Green*, 157; and chap. 3 below. On attitudes toward preservationists see Zeller, *Straße*, 198–202; Lekan, *Imagining*, 234–50.

70. On postwar competition see Gert Kragh to Hans Klose, 1 October 1946, BAK B 245/153; Klose to Kragh, 9 October 1946, BAK B 245/153; Potthast, "Naturschutz und Naturwissenschaft," in Frohn and Schmoll, *Natur und Staat*, 407–12.

71. Zeller, "Molding the Landscape," in Brüggemeier, Cioc, and Zeller, *How Green*, 158.

72. Gröning and Wolschke-Bulmahn, *Natur in Bewegung*, 197–204; Wettengel, "Staat und Natur- schutz," 395–96; Closmann, "Legalizing a Volksgemeinschaft," in Brüggemeier, Cioc, and Zeller, *How Green*, 34; Blackbourn, *Conquest*, 290; Uekötter, *Green and the Brown*, 154–55.

73. Klose, *Fünfzig Jahre*, 35; Klose, "Hermann Göring dem Schirmherrn des deutschen Natur- schutzes zum Geburtstage," *Naturschutz* 24, no. 1 (1943): 3; Ditt, "Naturschutzgesetzge- bung," in Radkau and Uekötter, *Naturschutz und Nationalsozialismus*, 124–25; Mrass, *Organisation*, 31; Wettengel, "Staat und Naturschutz," 389–91; Uekötter, *Green and the Brown*, 152–54; Blackbourn, *Conquest*, 280; Frohn, "Natur macht Staat," in Frohn and Schmoll, *Natur und Staat*, 176–87.

74. Zeller, "Seifert," in Radkau and Uekötter, *Naturschutz und Nationalsozialismus*, 279, 292–304.

75. Gröning and Wolschke-Bulmahn, *Drang nach Osten*, 26–35; Blackbourn, *Conquest*, 261– 78; Uekötter, *Green and the Brown*, 156–60.

76. Mechtild Rössler, "Die Institutionalisierung einer neuen Wissenschaft: Raumforschung und Raumordnung 1935–1945," *Geographische Zeitschrift* 75 (1987): 177–94; Mrass, *Organisa- tion*, 30–31. On spatial planning in the incorporated territories and the "greater" East see the essays in Rössler and Sabine Schleiermacher, eds., *Der 'Generalplan Ost': Hauptlinien der nationalsozialistischen Planungs- und Vernichtungspolitik* (Berlin: Akademie Verlag, 1993); Rolf-Dieter Müller, *Hitlers Ostkrieg und die deutsche Siedlungspolitik* (Frankfurt am Main: Fischer, 1991), 85–89, 94–97; Elke Pahl-Weber, "Die Reichsstelle für Raumordnung und die Ostplanung," in Rössler and Schleiermacher, *Der 'Generalplan Ost,'* 148–53.

77. On landscape architects' role in spatial planning in the East see Gröning and Wolschke-Bulmahn, *Drang nach Osten*, 26–61; Wolschke-Bulmahn, "Gewalt als Grundlage nationalsozialistischer Stadt- und Landschaftsplanung in den 'eingegliederten Ostgebieten,'" in Rössler and Schleier- macher, *Der 'Generalplan Ost,'* 328–38, and the translated version in Brüggemeier, Cioc, and Zeller, *How Green*, 242–56; Klaus Fehn, "'Lebensgemeinschaft von Volk und Raum': Zur na- tionalsozialistischen Raum- und Landschaftsplanung in den eroberten Ostgebieten," in Radkau and Uekötter, *Naturschutz und Nationalsozialismus*, 207–24; with more historical context, Black- bourn, *Conquest*, 251–78. See also Kiran Klaus Patel, "Neuerfindung des Westens—Aufbruch nach Osten. Naturschutz und Landschaftsgestaltung in den Vereinigten Staaten von Amerika und in Deutschland, 1900–1945," *Archiv für Sozialgeschichte* 43 (2003): 191–223, which dis- cusses how Nazi elites likened their expansion eastward to the US's conquest of the "wild" West.

78. Fehn, "Lebensgemeinschaft," in Radkau and Uekötter, *Naturschutz und Nationalsozialis- mus*, 213–21; Lekan, *Imagining*, 246; Blackbourn, *Conquest*, 287–90; Joachim Wolschke- Bulmahn, "All of Germany a Garden? Changing Ideas of Wilderness in German Garden Design and Landscape Architecture," in Mauch, *Nature in German History*, 86–90.

79. Mäding quoted in Blackbourn, *Conquest*, 290.

80. Gert Gröning, "Die 'Allgemeine Anordnung Nr. 20/VI/42'—Über die Gestaltung der Land- schaft in den eingegliederten Ostgebieten," in Rössler and Schleiermacher, *Der 'Generalplan Ost,'* 136–47; more extensive, Gröning and Wolschke-Bulmahn, *Drang nach Osten*, 82–143.

81. Robert N. Proctor, *The Nazi War on Cancer* (Princeton: Princeton University Press, 1999).

82. Lekan, *Imagining*, 247, 251; Joachim Wolschke-Bulmahn, "Violence as the Basis of National Socialist Landscape Planning," in Brüggemeier, Cioc, and Zeller, *How Green*, 245–46.

83. Erhard Mäding, *Landespflege. Die Gestaltung der Landschaft als Hoheitsrecht und Hoheits- pflicht*, 2d ed. (Berlin: Deutsche Landesbuchhandlung, 1943); Gröning and Wolschke-Bul- mahn, *Drang nach Osten*, 25; Wolschke-Bulmahn, "All of Germany a Garden?" in Mauch, *Nature in German History*, 87–88; Körner, *Theorie*, 43–56, 66–76.

84. Gröning and Wolschke-Bulmahn, *Drang nach Osten*, 58–59; Gröning and Wolschke, "Die Landespflege als Instrument Nationalsozialistischer Eroberungspolitik," *Arch + 81* (August 1985): 56–57; Blackbourn, *Conquest*, 290–93.

85. Tony Judt, *Postwar. A History of Europe since 1945* (New York: Penguin, 2005), 25–27.

Chapter 2

DEFENDING NATURE UNDER THE
ALLIED OCCUPATION, 1945–1955

With Germany's unconditional surrender on 8 May 1945, World War II in Europe ended. Central government in Germany collapsed and the country was divided into four zones of occupation under American, British, French, and Soviet military control. During the first years of the Allied occupation, many Germans suffered to a degree that they had not known during the war when the Nazi regime had had access to abundant natural resources and the spoils of conquest. In the wake of total defeat, Germany lost 25 percent of its prewar territory, surrendering the former provinces of Pomerania, Silesia, and East Prussia, which today form part of Poland and Russia. This transfer of land meant giving up well-stocked forests and productive large farms. In the western zones of occupation under US, British, and French administration, small farms prevailed. But thousands of these land holdings lay in ruins, making it difficult to feed the population adequately. Prolonging the scarcity of food were shortages of fertilizer and horses that hindered planting in the autumn of 1945 and below average harvests over the next few years.

Securing adequate housing posed additional challenges for occupation authorities. An estimated 20 percent of all dwellings in the four zones had been destroyed in the war. In the more industrialized Ruhr and Rhineland, an even larger percentage was lost, in some cases more than 50 percent. To rebuild homes, industry, and railway lines required vast amounts of timber and other raw materials that were in short supply because of territorial losses, reparations obligations, and tensions among the Allies. At the Potsdam Conference in the

---

Notes for this chapter begin on page 75.

summer of 1945, the Allies agreed that the more densely populated, industrial western zones of Germany would receive shipments of food and timber from the smaller, more agricultural eastern sector under Soviet control. In exchange, the Soviets would take some reparations from industries in the west that had escaped destruction. But mounting tensions between the western Allies and the Soviets over the latter's excessive reparations disrupted shipments of food and timber to the west. The global scarcity of food and natural resources brought on by years of fighting and by a temporary drop in international trade made it all the more difficult to secure imports needed to provide Germans with a minimum standard of living.

Compounding hardships in the western zones was the steady arrival of thousands upon thousands of refugees. Between 1944 and 1948 thirteen million people—refugees fleeing the Red Army, ethnic Germans brutally expelled from Eastern Europe (some of them only recently resettled in what had been Nazi-occupied territory), and other displaced persons—moved west, ending up in what became the British and American sectors. After taking into account the death toll from the war, the population in the western zones increased from 42 million in 1939 to 47.3 million in 1948, and to 49.3 million by 1950.[1] To feed and house an increased population in shrunken space required the exploitation of limited resources in what some conservationists referred to as "the remains of Germany," a phrase that conveyed the humiliation and regret they felt over the loss of East Prussia in particular, territory once settled by Germans but now under Polish and Soviet control and famous for its bison, birds, lakes, forests, and estates.[2]

But Germans were not alone in having to exploit natural resources that were inaccessible or in short supply in the aftermath of war. The United Nations Food and Agriculture Organization (FAO) was established in October 1945 to alleviate the global food crisis and to cope with the distribution of natural resources. Around the world, famine, drought, erosion, and population growth in developing countries compelled conservationists in industrialized nations to issue moralizing, neo-Malthusian warnings about societies' need to respect nature's limits.[3] For conservationists in the western zones of occupied Germany, the importance of heeding this counsel seemed especially urgent.

This chapter examines how conservationists grappled with what they perceived to be the most pressing problem of the occupation and early years of the Federal Republic, namely, the accelerated increase in demand for natural resources, first to restore stability and then to fuel economic prosperity. In a time of upheaval, conservationists looked to the mixed legacy they had inherited from the past to navigate their way into an uncertain future. With limited interruption, those involved in state-sponsored preservation continued on in their posts, reflecting little on their support for the Nazi regime. They used the RNG and the administrative apparatus it provided to pick up where they had left off, only slowly altering their views of nature and how and why it needed protection.

Initially, preservation groups struggled to resume their activities, but they, too, soon carried on much as before, pledging to protect "nature of the homeland . . . one of [our] most valuable possessions."[4]

At a time when overt nationalism was taboo, conservationists advocated protecting nature-as-*Heimat*—one of Germany's "most valuable possessions"—hoping thereby to aid in reconstructing a positive national identity. Protecting nature, they believed, would anchor the displaced and the disillusioned to a homeland that had remained untainted by the Nazi past and that provided fertile ground for cultivating patriotic citizens. Although the changing language of *Heimat* remained an important part of conservationists' discourse through the 1950s, they relied more and more on utilitarian arguments that stressed the role of *Naturschutz* in guiding the use of land and natural resources, a reform in the works since the late 1920s and made more pressing in the 1930s when Göring introduced the Four Year Plan to mobilize the economy for war.

Again under the occupation, reasons of state and the economy, as determined in important ways by the Allied powers, forced conservationists to emphasize the economic significance of their work. Convinced that Germany's economic revival was essential to the recovery of the rest of Europe, and eager to reduce the financial burden on American and British taxpayers funding the occupation, the US introduced aid to the western sectors through the Marshall Plan in 1947. As the future economic and political orientation of postwar Germany increased tensions between the western Allies and the Soviets, western Germany witnessed its rapid transformation from defeated enemy to Cold War ally. In 1948, the US, British, and French permitted Germans in their zones to write a constitution and instituted currency reform that contributed to economic stability eventually. In June 1949, one month after Stalin ended his eleven month blockade of West Berlin in protest of economic and political unity in the western zones, the Federal Republic of Germany was established as a democracy oriented toward the capitalist West. The country's first chancellor (1949–1963), Konrad Adenauer, the Catholic Rhinelander and former Cologne mayor, and his party, the newly formed anti-Marxist, non-denominational Christian Democratic Union (CDU), sought to recover from the Nazi past less by confronting it than by pursuing policies designed to secure the Federal Republic's place in the western block of nations. In 1951, West Germany joined France, Italy, and the Benelux countries in founding the European Coal and Steel Community, an organization that marked the first step toward the economic integration of Western Europe. By the early 1950s, West Germany's economy showed signs of recovery, growing 8 percent annually for the rest of the decade, due to many factors, among them increased international trade, limited permanent wartime damage to the infrastructure of businesses, policies encouraging investment in industry, and a large supply of skilled workers, including former refugees. In 1955, when the occupation officially ended, West Germany gained full sovereignty and joined NATO, a democratic ally in the fight against communism.[5]

But what did West Germany's rapid economic recovery and rehabilitation of its international reputation mean for conservation? In the simplest of terms, these significant changes contributed to an accelerated increase in land, water, and energy use, which threatened nature and underscored conservationists' inability to respond adequately. The same was true, of course, in communist East Germany. Yet in West Germany, closer cooperation with the US, Britain, and France also contributed to what scholars cautiously refer to as "Westernization," a complicated process involving cultural transfers, which included respect for democratic institutions and the protection of basic rights.[6] The development of democratic institutions opened up several avenues for reforming conservation. Forced by necessity to change, commissioners began to professionalize their work. New national and regional alliances emerged to protect threatened forests, water, landscapes, and wildlife, broadening the base of support for *Naturschutz* somewhat and contributing to the revival of civic life in the conservative political climate of Adenauer's Germany.[7]

Re-forming the "Green Front": Reconstructing Official Conservation

At the end of the war, the future looked bleak for the institution that had occupied a prominent place in the administration of preservation in Nazi Germany, the Reich Agency for Nature Protection. After fleeing west in February 1945 to escape the advancing Red Army, the agency's small staff settled in the Lüneburg Heath, converting a barrack into a make-shift office and resuming operations in what became the British zone of occupation.[8] Just weeks after the end of the war, Hans Klose, the agency's director, gloomily predicted that "[n]o matter how the borders of the future Germany will be drawn, one thing remains certain: as never before the German people will be 'a people without space.'" Reflecting lingering anxieties about implementation of the punitive Morgenthau Plan, which would have deindustrialized the country, but left it with more agricultural land in the East, Klose feared a "Chinaization of the land" as Germans were forced to cultivate what arable areas remained to feed an expanding population in shrunken space. Small plots of intensively used farmland stripped of hedges, trees, and wildlife—empty of features that gave landscapes their unique charm—would deprive his countrymen of a homeland, "which the German just simply needs."[9] For Klose, still in the grip of the state he had served for a decade if not wholly embraced, this *völkisch* language captured the reversal of fortunes caused by the defeat of Nazism and the collapse of its vision for a thousand year Reich. In the wreckage of National Socialism, Germans were living with less space, not more, on land that might no longer look "German," but barren, degraded, and "Asiatic."

Although Klose had been prominent in conservation during the Third Reich, he had little difficulty with denazification because he never joined the Nazi party and avoided ideological extremism in his administrative post. He also ended up in the British zone where the process was more lenient. Though he passed muster, he did not escape accusations that he was a Nazi sympathizer. According to Klose's own description, he was "a good democrat," just as the monarchists in England. Perhaps more revealing of his nationalist, conservative political views was the bronze bust of Kaiser William II that adorned his office in the heath.[10] A secondary school master by training, Klose had worked alongside Hugo Conwentz in the 1910s. In 1922, he was passed over as director of the Prussian Agency for the Care of Natural Monuments in favor of Walther Schoenichen, a decision Klose resented as he considered himself Conwentz's rightful heir. But when Schoenichen fell out of favor with higher-ups in the Reich Forest Office in 1938 and was forced into early retirement at 62, Klose replaced him as head of the agency. To Klose's immense irritation, after the war Schoenichen used his dismissal to claim he was a victim of National Socialism, rather than the supporter he was widely known to have been. In another example of what some West Germans referred to as the "restoration" of former Nazis, Schoenichen received a professorship at Braunschweig Technical University in 1950. Six years later, just prior to his death, he received the Federal Distinguished Service Medal for his scientific contributions.[11]

Scholars have examined the continued influence in the Federal Republic of landscape architects who had been prominent in the Third Reich, such as Konrad Meyer and Heinrich Wiepking-Jürgensmann, both of whom went on to occupy posts at the Technical University of Hanover. They have also noted the continued involvement in conservation activities of people like Alwin Seifert and Hans Schwenkel (whose commitment to Nazism had been "practically fanatical" according to Klose, but whose postwar influence was limited).[12] But what about the fate of rank-and-file volunteer commissioners (*Beauftragter*)? Initially the future prospects for commissioners looked grim. Unknown numbers had died during the war or remained in POW camps, while others were detained by occupation officials during denazification. Writing in 1946, Klose remarked that weeding out commissioners with a compromised past made the situation for preservation in most districts "so critical that one can view the future only with considerable mistrust."[13] Despite the upheaval associated with denazification, those involved with official conservation eventually resumed their work with a high degree of continuity that was typical among German civil servants.[14]

While writing references for colleagues undergoing denazification, Klose worked tirelessly with the cranky zoologist, Herbert Ecke, to preserve the Reich Agency, his mentor's legacy and the institution he viewed as central to preserving uniformity in conservation. The many statements Klose composed between 1945 and 1952 to convince British occupation authorities and German political leaders at the federal and state levels that the institute was essential left a paper trail of evidence of official conservation's shift from cultural and pedagogical emphases to economic and planning priorities associated with landscape care.[15] This change, in the works since the 1920s and 1930s, was made more expedient after 1946 and 1947 when the western Allies adopted a more lenient policy toward Germany, one that prioritized economic recovery.[16] In response, Klose stressed the importance of conservation in guiding the use of land and resources to prevent their exploitation. He especially hoped this line of reasoning would ensure the continued existence at the federal level of the Reich Agency—a measure opposed by several state governments (Bavaria in particular). Klose's efforts eventually paid off. Effective as of January 1953, the former Reich Agency became the Federal Institute for Nature Protection and Landscape Care (*Bundesanstalt für Naturschutz und Landschaftspflege*, or BANL), lodged in the Ministry of Agriculture (BML). The association with agriculture and forestry continued the administrative change forced through by Hermann Göring in 1935, which ended up marginalizing preservation. The continuation of this arrangement in the Federal Republic revealed an awareness of the economic aspects of conservation, yet it paradoxically encouraged a reductionist reading of "*Naturschutz*" as narrow preservation, an activity that seemed less significant than maximizing production in the rural economy.[17]

To pursue conservation in its expanded dimensions required strengthening its legal foundations. At the very least, it meant preserving gains made with the Reich Nature Protection Law of 1935. The RNG was never lifted officially in any of the four zones. British authorities recognized (and praised) it in 1946 after deleting authoritarian sections like those permitting the confiscation of property. This part of the RNG was invalidated through Article 14 of West Germany's constitution, the Basic Law, which required compensation for expropriating property.[18] Under the Federal Republic, the RNG remained in place as national legislation until 1958 when the Constitutional Court ruled that its comprehensive provisions in effect at the federal level violated the Basic Law, which gave the states primary authority for *Naturschutz*. Although the RNG had been progressive when introduced, several states amended it to better protect and renature landscapes that were being more intensively exploited to support the country's economic rebound.[19]

A significant change in the administration of conservation occurred when the Basic Law gave the states primary responsibility for *Naturschutz*. Conservation was just one of many areas affected by West Germany's federal structure, which was designed to serve as a corrective to the concentration of power at the center under National Socialism. The delicate balance of authority between the federal and state governments provided for in the constitution contributed to the Federal Republic's long term political stability. Klose, however, opposed refederalizing conservation, insisting that central control was necessary for administrative uniformity. He railed against the "contagion" of federalism that had "infected" West German political leaders intent on giving the states control over the protection of nature—a responsibility that had been theirs historically because of the view that *Naturschutz* was a cultural and scientific enterprise.[20] In a compromise, the Basic Law listed nature protection, landscape care, hunting, water management, and regional planning under Article 75, which specified areas of concurrent jurisdiction. Under this arrangement, the states had primary responsibility to legislate these matters, but the federal government could pass general guideline laws. It did so for conservation only in 1976.

Confronted with states' rights advocates who wanted to refederalize *Naturschutz*, Klose nostalgically recalled the latter half of the 1930s as the "high point" for conservation when central control seemed secure.[21] But his recollections were misleading for they implied that progress in preserving nature between 1935 and 1939 had resulted from greater centralization. More often gains had been made through informal liaisons with influential Nazis and by applying, or using the threat of, paragraph 24 of the RNG, which permitted officials to confiscate property without compensation. Klose also overestimated the benefits of central government oversight. In doing so, he overlooked the advantages that groups have when decisions about resources are made closer to the site of use, a point illustrated in the chapter case studies.[22]

Contrary to Klose's fears, state-sponsored conservation in West Germany was not weakened by refederalization. Rather, one of the greatest institutional hindrances to effective *Naturschutz* prior to the 1970s was that most officials adhered to the narrow view of conservation as a cultural and scientific matter. Rarely did they associate it also with planning the use of land and resources. Consequently, state governments separated *Naturschutz* from *Landschaftspflege* administratively, pigeonholing offices for *Naturschutz* either in ministries of culture or agriculture—or, less common but more promising, in interior ministries—where conservation officials lacked influence and an overarching perspective on resource use that was essential in guiding economic development.[23]

In 1954, after nearly a decade of lobbying to preserve the legal and administrative foundations of conservation, a weary Klose retired at 74. His replacement, Gert Kragh (1911–1986), came to the director's post determined to make landscape care more scientific and central to official conservation, to the chagrin of some preservationists.[24] This pastor's son and former member of the back-to-nature youth movement studied landscape and garden design at the University of Berlin between 1933 and 1937, working with Professor Reinhold Tüxen, the prominent plant sociologist, and Professor Heinrich Wiepking-Jürgensmann, the landscape architect who served under Himmler in the occupied Eastern territories. In the late 1930s, Kragh prepared vegetation maps for the Autobahn and managed Hanover Province's *Naturschutz* agency, where he opposed

Seifert's maneuvers to undermine local preservationists. Enlisted in the war, he served with an anti-aircraft artillery unit developing camouflage for fortifications on the western front and then on all fronts after being transferred to the navy. Kragh was exonerated for his wartime activities during denazification.[25]

As state conservation commissioner for Lower Saxony in the early 1950s and BANL director from 1954 until 1962, Kragh was instrumental in reviving landscape care, emphasizing that its planning competencies would help guide the economic recovery that everyone wanted. By pairing *"Naturschutz"* and *"Landschaftspflege"* more intentionally than in the past, Kragh signaled his desire to end the unconstructive competition between preservationists and landscape architects in hopes of strengthening the work of both. He was silent about the wartime fortunes of landscape architects who tested a racialized version of their craft in the East. But Kragh was not very different from other Germans at the time in remembering the Third Reich as a "normal" dictatorship, not a genocidal one.[26] After 1945, he and other conservationists rededicated themselves to the task of protecting and designing landscapes, ultimately to fulfill their vision for a Germany that would be strong again economically, yet still scenic and worthy of being called a homeland. But during reconstruction they struggled just to cope with classical preservation.

West Germany's approximately 560 honorary commissioners functioned as the "eyes and ears" of the conservation bureaucracy. Their abundant written records reveal a lot about the self-image of those involved in state-sponsored conservation and document how they tried to institutionalize and professionalize their efforts.[27] Since the 1920s, commissioners worked to broaden *Naturschutz* beyond "passive" preservation to include comprehensive land use planning, but coping with this added responsibility required more than they could deliver with their limited numbers, volunteer status, and chronic lack of funds.[28] Commissioners fretted about recruiting younger replacements, and indeed, well into the 1960s they tended to name men from the generation of 1900 to the honorary posts, often through an informal system of personal patronage that prized idealism and selfless devotion to the "green cause" more than expertise.[29]

They also lacked adequate financial support, particularly during the early years of the occupation. Otto Kraus, state commissioner for Bavaria until 1967, recalled the barrack that served as his temporary office and the financial support that came in small amounts from a Munich businessman. Gert Kragh operated Lower Saxony's conservation agency out of his home between 1949 and the early 1950s, and his replacement, Ernst Preising, did the same.[30] Conditions improved slightly as the economy recovered. Local commissioners in the district of Lüneburg, for example, reported in 1956 that their annual allowance to defray the cost of travel, telephone, postage and other expenses increased from the DM 100 that had been standard for years to between DM 600 and DM 1,000.[31] To some extent, limited funding reflected budgetary constraints of the lean postwar years. But it also stemmed from a misperception among officials that conservation was a cultural affair which could be carried out as an avocation by volunteers.

Although the RNG gave commissioners the responsibility for managing independent agencies advising conservation offices at the state, district, and county levels, and assured them a voice in public hearings over development projects, the law gave them little authority, a complaint voiced since the RNG's passage. Because some state commissioners, and most at district and local levels, served as volunteers well into the 1960s, they struggled to handle what amounted to a full-time job in addition to their occupation, typically as a teacher, forester, landscape architect, or engineer. Commissioners belonged to the professional middle class, but their occupational backgrounds rarely equipped them to address the range of problems they faced at an accelerated pace in the boom years.[32] No wonder, then, that throughout the 1950s, they claimed it was time to shed their image as "well-intentioned members of a beautification club" and transform themselves into uniformly trained professionals employed fulltime by the state.[33]

A modest beginning in the professionalization of conservation occurred in October 1947 when Klose convened twenty-four commissioners and other individuals from the western zones in a castle on the Wupper River to establish the Working Association of German Commissioners for Nature Protection and Landscape Care (*Arbeitsgemeinschaft Deutscher Beauftragter für Naturschutz und Landschaftspflege*, or ABN).[34] In 1957, the ABN's yearly gathering was designated German Conservation Day, which recalled annual meetings from previous decades that brought together commissioners, officials, and representatives of preservation groups. By meeting regularly, publishing congress proceedings, and sponsoring workshops on legislation and scientific research, the ABN helped commissioners forge a collective identity as professionals with a shared agenda. The reemergence in 1951 of the BANL-edited journal, *Naturschutz und Landschaftspflege,* a publication that served as the voice of official conservation, further united "the green front" of "comrades" in "fighting" for what many considered to be a selfless moral cause. In the 1950s, the publication resembled a voluntary association newspaper with its poems and honor roll, but by the 1960s its professional layout and technical articles on topics ranging from species preservation to renaturing mining pits reflected the development of conservation into a highly diversified scientific field.[35] Only in the 1970s did states replace agencies with government positions staffed by experts, a transition that did not pass without conflict. These new professionals prided themselves in their scientific, "objective," and rational approach to problems, and overlooked the cultural aspects of conservation, which they felt their predecessors had stressed to a fault.[36]

Despite legal and institutional obstacles, commissioners scored modest successes. Under the occupation, they urged state governments to include conservation in their constitutions and rebuilt archives of laws, ordinances, and maps lost during the war. They inventoried reserves and species under protection and took stock of what had survived the recent conflict. Although numbers do not convey how effectively areas were preserved, at the end of the 1950s when reliable figures were available, West Germany recorded an estimated 750 nature reserves, 3,800 larger, less stringently protected landscape reserves (*Landschaftsschutzgebiete*), and 38,000 natural monuments. Yet many of these had been under protection before 1945. Nonetheless, commissioners prevented a decline in their numbers. By the mid 1960s, the country reported 868 reserves, 5,930 protected landscapes, and around 40,000 natural monuments. Together these areas covered approximately 32,000 square kilometers, or 13 percent of the territory of the Federal Republic, an impressive accomplishment when one considers that by the early 1960s, 8.3 percent of the territory was used for industry, the military, housing, highways, railways, and airports. Yet preservation was like the proverbial finger-in-the-dike, wholly inadequate to stop the flood of economic growth that in the 1950s swallowed up over 60 hectares each day for settlement.[37]

Against the backdrop of accelerated land and resource use, commissioners' efforts to protect the beauty of regional landscapes appeared to be little more than quaint reminders of turn of the century preservation. They teamed up with private groups to oppose the careless placement of billboards along highways and in the countryside. In southern Germany, they fought against the "contagious spread" of cable cars on mountains, justifying their opposition by contrasting unfit urbanites, pocket radios in hand, with their ideal visitor, the introspective, solitary climber.[38] But often their cautious protests ended in compromise. In the mid 1950s, for example, Bavarian conservationists failed to block the installation of a cable car on Jenner Mountain in the middle of the Königsee nature reserve because they caved in to local authorities that pledged to leave other peaks in the area alone. It was apparent that this promise contained hollow words when local officials targeted the nearby Watzmann in the 1960s.[39] Eventually this peak was spared, accessible only on foot to visitors in Berchtesgaden National Park, which conservationists helped establish in 1978.

In publications, exhibits, public lectures, and radio programs, commissioners insisted on the need to protect the entire "household of the landscape." Yet they faced tremendous obstacles in conserving its "principle components," especially soil and water, which were being exploited at an increased tempo to support reconstruction, economic recovery, and the integration of thirteen million people forced to migrate west. As the commissioner in Hanover Province during the occupation, Gert Kragh had been right in 1945 in predicting that the "loss of living space" would require "inner colonization" to accommodate refugees who ended up in the western zones.[40] In the first postwar decade, Silesians and Pomeranians found a new *Heimat* in the remnant high moors of northwestern Germany that were being plowed into settlements.[41] In Bavaria, Hesse, Lower Saxony, and Schleswig-Holstein, where extensive land reclamation was underway to accommodate refugees, commissioners urged restraint in cultivating moors and draining bogs—the "regeneration cells" of landscapes, they explained—and helped to educate farmers about the role of wetlands in controlling erosion and protecting the groundwater supply.[42]

They also took part in drafting the land consolidation law of 1953 (*Flurbereinigungsgesetz*), the first piece of legislation to require landscape plans in conjunction with agricultural reforms merging small holdings to create larger, more productive farms that could be worked by heavy machinery. As these changes began in earnest in the late 1950s and 1960s, commissioners like Wolfgang Haber (1925–), later an internationally respected ecologist, cooperated with state ministries of agriculture to successfully convince farmers to plant shelterbelts for erosion control and to preserve hedges as a natural means of pest control. But measures like these did little to lessen the environmental harm that accompanied the mechanization of agriculture in West Germany and elsewhere in Europe as these nations strived to be competitive against major producers such as Argentina, Canada, and the US. As Ernst Rudorff had warned decades earlier, hedge removal caused species decline and soil erosion, and more irrigation added yet another stress on water supplies. Moreover, increased use of pesticides and artificial fertilizer containing nitrates and other chemicals ended up in the groundwater.[43]

Although commissioners did not ignore the obvious problem of water pollution from farming and industry (it had been visible for years), their primary concern was to reduce the threat that land reclamation, river regulation, and dam construction posed to regional supplies. In southern Germany, commissioners were unprepared for the spate of new dam projects promising to provide energy and drinking water to meet the country's rapidly rising demand for both. In 1949, state conservation commissioner Otto Kraus reported that more than seventy dams were in the planning stages in Bavaria alone. In a dozen instances in the 1950s and 1960s, he and other conservationists blocked or altered construction plans in the state. More often than not, however, commissioners and private groups caused only delays in, or modifications to, the dam projects of their more powerful opponents, the utility companies and the diverse groups who supported them. One dam they failed to block was among the country's largest, the Rosshaupten Dam on Bavaria's Upper Lech, completed in 1954. When opposing these hydroprojects, commissioners lost credibility by pointing to nuclear energy as a less invasive alternative. Yet their proposal reflected having witnessed over several decades the adverse consequences of hydrodams, as well as the search by each generation for a clean source of fuel.[44]

In confronting the variety of threats to nature during the hard times of the occupation and the more hopeful years of economic recovery, commissioners continued to view their activities as a form of moral instruction that would inoculate people, the youth in particular, against the ills of modern civilization, be it totalitarianism, materialism, apathy, or alienation. "Either we regard the green cause as a source of strength for clearing away the rubble in cities and souls of men," longtime district commissioner in the Catholic Rhineland and former Nazi Party member, Wilhelm Lienenkämper said, "or we give the spiritual confusion of our times free rein."[45] Embracing a conservative idealism in the tradition of Schiller, Kragh insisted in 1947 that the youth of the occupation, who grew up experiencing nature's abundance, would develop into citizens with a "deeply felt love of the homeland" and with the "primordial [*ursprünglich*] creative strength" necessary to "dutifully serve their countrymen and fatherland in their chosen profession." This new generation, he asserted, would be able to "master the future." Implicit in Kragh's commentary was a belief that immersion in nature and love of *Heimat* would give youth the inner strength they needed to overcome the resignation of the times and contribute to Germany's (organic) renewal.[46]

In the early years of the Federal Republic, when the economy recovered, commissioners did not lack this idealism and moral certitude, but they complained more frequently about the "step-mother treatment" they received from "utility fanatics" who regarded conservation as "a foolish matter for visionaries alienated from reality and the present."[47] Yet contrary to conservationists' complaint about being ignored, they had the support of several national and state leaders irrespective of political party, among them Federal President Theodor Heuss (FDP), Interior Minister Robert Lehr (CDU), *Bundestag* President Eugen Gerstenmaier (CDU), and minister-presidents Karl Arnold (North Rhine-Westphalia, CDU), Hinrich Wilhelm Kopf (Lower Saxony, SPD) and Wilhelm Hoegner (Bavaria, SPD). True, support from these high profile men was often more generalized and verbal than specific and activist. But their promotion of conservation suggests that it was viewed as a noble cause that transcended party politics. This also was the case elsewhere in western Europe where royalty often led conservation initiatives, most notably Prince Bernhard of the Netherlands and Prince Philip, Duke of Edinburgh.[48]

Complaints about being unheard and experiencing repeated setbacks were voiced by preservationists in earlier times and continue to be expressed by environmentalists today.[49] They communicate the desire to attract public attention to problems that seem pressing and sometimes immense, as well as frustration about the means available for addressing those problems. Konrad Buchwald, state conservation commissioner for Baden-Württemberg from 1955 until 1960, likened commissioners to fire fighters racing in vain to put out fires that already had burned. Working through the conservation bureaucracy, rushing from one local licensing hearing to another, commissioners were helpless to prevent "an area the size of a medium farm" from being "lost" each day to new industries, homes, and roads.[50]

Confronted with accelerated land use, commissioners made exaggerated claims and moral judgments to lend a sense of urgency to their cause. In doing so, they acquired a reputation for being uncompromising, elitist, old fashioned, and overly sentimental. Much as their predecessors had done, commissioners—and conservationists, in general—described the scenic landscapes they were trying to protect by using adjectives that suggested moral purity, such as "pristine" or "primeval." By contrast, they ascribed corrupting influences to nature's adversaries—technology, industry, and excessive materialism—to name the most frequently mentioned abstract threats. As a group more acutely aware of the human influences on nature than most of their fellow Germans, conservationists knew that the areas they defended were not untouched. As in earlier times, they used these terms in reference to landscapes that seemed to exhibit a harmonious blending of nature and human use, such as farming or small scale wine growing. In doing so, they expressed fear of even more intrusive changes to these intensively used landscapes if seemingly ubiquitous foes were not reined in.[51] In addition, however, their choice of words was a rhetorical ploy designed to give their argument moral weight in what one conservationist described as a David against Goliath battle against more powerful opponents.[52]

Yet along with these shrill sounding assertions, conservationists increasingly relied on economic and scientific arguments which carried more weight in postwar political decision making. Scholars investigating the fortunes of landscape architects after 1945 also note this scientification, and maintain that it was motivated at least partly by a desire to distance the profession from its ideological excesses during the Nazi period. By adopting a more rational, scientific approach, these scholars conclude, some landscape architects successfully modernized and reformed their field without having to confront wrongs of the past.[53] But this interpretation does not readily apply to conservationists outside of the profession of landscape architecture because it implies feelings of guilt, which a majority of conservationists did not openly harbor, and it suggests a degree of influence during the Third Reich that conservationists rarely had, despite their best efforts. It seems most likely that postwar conservationists used scientific and economic arguments more frequently to stay in step with international trends and to have greater leverage in decisions affecting the use of land and natural resources. By expressing their views in quantifiable terms, commissioners hoped to present themselves more convincingly as "neutral" experts in conservation affairs.[54]

With some effect, commissioners emphasized the economic benefits of scientifically based conservation. Relying on ecological insights associated with plant geography since the 1920s, Gert Kragh noted that "[e]very landscape has a certain reserve of energy," or "biotic potential," which is determined by water supply, soil condition, and local climate, and measurable by an inventory of plant and animal communities. According to Kragh, landscape care involved preserving, and where possible, increasing the land's "biotic potential" to support long term economic uses. Bavaria's state commissioner Otto Kraus arrived at a similar conclusion when he defined a biologically healthy landscape as one capable of supporting appropriate economic uses over the long term, while renewing itself and remaining a beautiful *Heimat*. Such explanations were similar to those expressed by their American contemporary, Aldo Leopold, whose land ethic asserted that "[a] thing is right when it tends to preserve the integrity, stability, and beauty of the biotic community. It is wrong when it tends otherwise."[55]

A common theme in the writings of conservationists in North America and parts of Europe since the 1920s was that of land health, a concept that referred to a landscape's capacity for regeneration. Diagnosing the health of landscapes meant relying on ecological assumptions of plant geographers who viewed land as an organism that exhibited signs either of wellness and balance or sickness and imbalance (often depending upon human economic practices). This view of nature was static and based on aesthetic judgments that were inherently subjective: if an area looked attractive, it was assumed to be in ecologically good health as well. Although the notion of land health had been distorted under National Socialism by some who equated it with the primordial native soil of the racially pure *Volksgemeinschaft*, in the 1950s commissioners relied even more on the idea of wellness to improve scientific methods of evaluation. Increasingly they understood their primary objective to be preserving and revitalizing the health of landscapes, more so than protecting nature-as-*Heimat*. But like all scientific approaches, this one reflected ideological assumptions, in this case a social conservatism that continued to associate cities with disease and imbalance and countryside with health and wholeness.[56]

Yet conservationists' emphasis on wellness encouraged more interaction with professionals in other fields who shared an interest in health, be it of people or the economy. Over time, the emphasis on health weakened the perceptual divide between humans and nature, and between urban and rural, enabling conservation to seem more central in addressing social problems. This was apparent in 1955 when commissioners gathered in the industrial city of Düsseldorf for the annual ABN conference that was organized around the theme of "Nature and Economy." At the meeting conservationists claimed a role for themselves in guiding economic recovery by pledging to protect and restore the health of landscapes where West Germans "worked, lived, and relaxed." Reflecting the importance assigned to economic arguments, they defined land health in terms of a landscape's productive capacity, but also in terms of its ability to provide physical and emotional healing for industrious people experiencing stress in the workplace. Accordingly, they declared their intention to set aside recreation areas in rural settings where the country's rising urban population might be restored to health and full productivity, a subject examined in chapter 4. With the adoption of the metaphor of health, commissioners claimed the right to participate in restoring health not only to landscapes, but also to people and the economy—all without abandoning their conservative critique of modern civilization.[57]

The Revival of Private Conservation Groups

In the difficult years of the occupation, Germany's impressive array of preservation groups established around the turn of the century struggled to resume their work, fighting against apathy, financial limitations, and in many cases, a tainted reputation from the recent past. After experiencing a drop in membership at war's end, many witnessed modest increases by the mid 1950s, though not until the 1970s did they achieve prewar numbers. As they had in the past, these organizations worked closely with commissioners and officials, often blurring the distinction between public and private. They relied on a reserved style of protest and a hierarchical structure in pursuit of traditional goals, turned to the state for financial aid, and depended upon publicly prominent individuals and independently wealthy people to serve as patrons or in leadership positions.[58] However top heavy their structure and conservative their rhetoric, existing groups and several new "working associations" contributed to the return of civil society in West Germany.

After the war Germany's largest conservation organization, the German League for Bird Protection (DBV), found its offices in Munich, Stuttgart, and Berlin in ruins and its membership down by 50 percent. The DBV had enthusiastically supported the Nazi regime at least outwardly, changed its bylaws in 1934 to exclude non-Germans, and watched its membership climb to 55,000 by 1943, an increase aided by Göring's directive in 1938 to consolidate bird protection societies under the league. After receiving official sanction by occupation authorities in 1946, the DBV unanimously elected Hermann Hähnle, son of Lina Hähnle, to serve as president. The organization continued to rely on low membership dues, the wealth of its leadership, and government subsidies (DM 20,000 per year from the federal government in the 1950s) to protect more than 200 bird sanctuaries it had established over the years through land purchases and leases. In the late 1940s, when its local chapters in the Soviet zone were subsumed under a mass organization for cultural affairs, the DBV lost several reserves to the GDR regime. In West Germany the DBV recruited new members gradually, surpassing the wartime high only in 1965 when membership reached 57,000, an increase attributed to its endorsement of Rachel Carson's controversial best-seller, *Silent Spring* (1962).[59]

It is not surprising that long-standing organizations avoided making significant reforms in their structure and agenda in the 1950s when most people preferred a return to stability and familiar activities. This was the case also for the Bavarian League for Nature Protection. In the 1920s, the league claimed 10,000 members, climbing to 28,000 just before World War II. Less conformist than the DBV, the league nonetheless had named a local Nazi as its "protector" and tailored its message to fit official ideology. Into the 1960s, the league still struggled to attract members to add to the 15,000 it had retained. It continued to be led by civil servants and relied on state government subsidies (DM 10,000 annually in the 1950s) to buy land for reserves.[60]

These few examples illustrate continuities in the postwar era with earlier activities of preservation groups. A closer examination of two organizations—the Nature Park Society (*Verein Naturschutzpark*, or VNP), founded in 1909, and the Association for the Protection of the German Forest (*Schutzgemeinschaft Deutscher Wald*, or SDW), established in 1947—underscores constancy in conservation groups' conservative rhetoric and their reliance on social and political elites for patronage. In protecting the Lüneburg Heath, one of Germany's prized nature reserves, and "the German forest" against foreign occupiers in the late 1940s and early 1950s, the VNP and the new SDW nationalized nature, cultivating a green patriotism that might aid in the country's organic revival. It would be misleading, however, to imply that nature was nationalized to the same degree in every case when protecting nature intersected with protesting foreign occupiers. In the mid 1950s, for example, when locals, scientists, preservationists, and youth protested the British Royal Air Force's use of Knechtsand in the Wattenmeer as a bombing range, they emphasized that the schelducks, which congregated on the large sandbank during the summer to moult, belonged not to Germans, but to all of humanity. The area, they argued, ought to become a symbol of freedom and peace, not military defense.[61] It is difficult to imagine such an argument during the early years of the occupation when many Germans felt victimized, ashamed, and defensive. Yet a closer look at the activities of the VNP and the SDW uncovers a gradual process of reform as these groups, too, sought to define their place in a new polity.

Liberating the Lüneburg Heath, a "Besieged" Homeland Landscape

In the autumn of 1945, British and Canadian occupation forces seized over 3,000 hectares of land in the Lüneburg Heath nature reserve to use as a military training area, and began detonating mines and explosives planted there by Germans during the war. The following spring they started conducting maneuvers in the southern part of the reserve, moving as far north as the quaint village of Wilsede, Wilsede Mountain, and Hannibal's Grave—some of the most scenic spots owned by the VNP.[62] The conversion of one of Germany's largest reserves into a training ground for an army of occupation angered conservationists, but no doubt also reminded them of how the area had been treated by the Nazis. The protected parts of the Lüneburg Heath became the first Reich nature reserve in 1935, and were to be elevated to the status of a national park after the war. In 1942, however, the regime began building a hospital in the middle of the nature park owned by the VNP, and planted mines and explosives in the central and southern sections of the reserve. Plans to lay down a small airfield, drill for oil, and transform Wilsede Mountain into a fortress with anti-aircraft towers did not materialize.[63]

A century earlier, few would have considered the Lüneburg Heath worthy of preservation. Until the 1800s, this low lying plain between Hamburg and Hanover seemed little more than a desolate wasteland. Once the Lüneburg Heath was rediscovered as scenic countryside exhibiting a harmonious blend of nature and traditional farming, local homeland preservationists collected donations to purchase land and protect it from private developers. Their efforts merged with those of the VNP whose members wanted to establish three large reserves representative of Germany's lowland, upland, and alpine landscapes as an alternative to the larger national parks in the United States.[64] By 1918, the VNP had purchased 3,400 hectares in the heath. After these encouraging beginnings, VNP members who supported National Socialism prevailed in the 1930s, dissolving the volunteer heath watch initiated by socialist youth and changing the charter in 1939 to exclude Jews from membership.[65]

The man who led the VNP from 1942 until 1953, Hans Domizlaff, was a cantankerous artist who made his money in industrial design. According to the *Gauleiter* of East Hanover who recommended him for the chairmanship, Domizlaff's "relations with the Führer" made him appear "to be the right man."[66] But Domizlaff experienced more failure than success in trying to protect VNP property from the misuses noted earlier. Arrested by the British in August 1945, he spent the next several months in detention. After Domizlaff's two year struggle through denazification, VNP members tried to oust him, faulting him for being "an autocrat—exactly in a Nazi sense" and of treating VNP land as his private domain.[67] His racial views and authoritarian style contributed to a drop in the organization's membership from 5,000 in 1945 to 2,000 in the early 1950s. Using the organization's journal, he spouted off *völkisch* claims, insisting, for example, that protecting nature of the homeland was the only way to "save the nation from otherwise unavoidable biological degeneration."[68] Working largely alone, he tackled the VNP's main challenge: protecting the heath from British forces conducting maneuvers in what a sympathetic reporter described as the "only jewel of untouched nature in the North German lowland."[69]

The natural beauty of the heath mattered little to the western powers as Cold War tensions mounted. In 1945, the British and Canadians had moved into the heath as an army of occupation, but after the establishment of the Federal Republic and the formation of NATO in 1949, they remained in the country as the alliance's forward troops, poised to stop the spread of communism. The sparsely populated Lüneburg Heath came into question for military training because theorists considered this vast plain in north central Germany a likely site for a Soviet launched attack. When the Korean War broke out in 1950, heightening fears about a growing communist menace, the area assumed even more strategic significance. Especially before the controversial reestablishment of a national army in 1955, few West Germans doubted the need for foreign forces on their soil to protect them from communist neighbors. But area residents wondered why Britain's Rhine Army could not make due with designated training spaces near, but not in, the Lüneburg Heath nature reserve, such as Fallingbostel, Munster, and Bergen. Indeed, by the early 1950s, the British Rhine Army had an estimated 60,000 hectares in the area at its disposal for training, but not all of it was suitable for use. Only in 1953, for example, was Munster cleared of mines planted by the *Wehrmacht,* and in some other designated areas, West Germans had planted trees for timber harvesting, limiting the amount of land for tank exercises.[70]

When the size of British and other NATO forces in the heath increased in 1952, Domizlaff appealed to Interior Minister Robert Lehr (CDU) to use his influence with the chancellery to prevent further damage in the reserve. But officials were intent on avoiding the embarrassment of West Germans protesting NATO forces at a time when diplomatic discussions were going on (in vain as it turned out) to create a European Defense Community, which was to include West German troops.[71] Weary of Domizlaff's one-man show, VNP members finally replaced him in December 1953, electing the multi-millionaire Hamburg entrepreneur, Alfred Toepfer, to the top office and pacifying Domizlaff with the title of honorary president.

In Toepfer (1894–1993), a VNP member for twenty-six years, the organization found an able leader with a murky past. Toepfer was a former *Wandervogel,* World War I veteran, and member of the Märker Free Corps, one of many paramilitary groups the weak coalition government of the early Weimar Republic had used to quell leftist revolutionary activities. Toepfer started his import/export firm in 1919 and saw it grow to be the largest business of its kind in the Federal Republic. He leaned toward the far right politically, yet avoided party politics (including the NSDAP), preferring to be "an eclectic pragmatist." Arrested in 1937 on suspicion of tax evasion, Toepfer spent a year in confinement. After his release, he served in France as a captain in the army. When the war ended, the British arrested him, suspecting that his wealth concealed Nazi assets. Those suspicions were proved wrong and he was released in 1947.[72]

The election of this well-connected businessman and philanthropist enabled the VNP to pursue its traditional goals with a more up-to-date, though still conservative, message. Toepfer increased VNP membership and secured the return of its park in Austria, Hohe Tauern, property the Allies had considered an "enemy asset." On VNP property, Toepfer used his wealth to create an open air *Heimat* museum of sorts that reflected his vision of an ideal landscape, one without cars or visible power lines (he had them buried), but with open spaces and scenic vistas, horse-drawn wagons, grazing sheep, and architecture that imitated regional styles.[73]

By the time Toepfer took over as chairman, British forces had withdrawn from the most scenic spots owned by the VNP, but half of its property continued to be torn up by daily military exercises.[74] To defend the heath against the defenders of Western Europe, Toepfer worked methodically and persistently through official channels to garner support of district and state officials, legislators, and federal security officer, Theodor Blank. In June 1954, he hosted fifty journalists from the region on a tour in horse-drawn wagons through the well-preserved eastern part of the park and the desert-like sections of the western area. With reporters in tow, he ventured through the Munster training area to dispel British fears that the danger of mines remained. His strategy to garner media coverage worked to some extent, as newspaper headlines declared that "Europe's largest nature monument" was becoming "scorched earth" because British tanks "continued their fatal work of destruction."[75] But neither sympathetic press coverage, resolutions by conservationists, major questions in the *Bundestag,* nor pressure on British officials by the International Union for the Conservation of Nature (IUCN) had much effect.[76]

What produced results were student protests and a change in West Germany's sovereignty. In July 1955, just after the Federal Republic gained full sovereignty and joined NATO, Blank, now Federal Defense Minister, assured the *Bundestag* that the British would not use the heath for training to the extent allowed previously. With West Germany negotiating as an equal partner now, a compromise would be reached.[77] Nearly a year later, the British withdrew from 600 hectares of the prized flat land in the reserve and most of the Canadian troops pulled out entirely. This retreat was triggered by fears that protests by German youth might end in sabotage. During the night of 23 June 1956, SPD *Bundestag* Deputy Herbert Wehner told over one thousand students that their torches burned as a sign of peace and understanding among peoples. The Federal Republic, he declared, was not a colony, but a sovereign entity.[78] Students' use of fire in this and other protests like Knechtsand recalled its historical use in the youth movement, including at its famous gathering at the Hoher Meißner in Hesse in 1913. Yet fire had also burned as a symbol of freedom and autonomy in Germany's national unity movement of the previous century. Area newspapers glorified the demand by German youth to "liberate the homeland" and their appeal to end "the humiliation and destruction inflicted on us by foreign troops."[79]

Another three years passed, however, before West German and British governments set the boundary of the Rhine Army's training area. The 1959 Soltau-Lüneburg Agreement gave the British access to a 345 square kilometer area from Soltau to Lüneburg. Within this training space, several "red zones" were created for intensive tank use, two of them within the Lüneburg Heath reserve. Together these two areas encompassed 1,800 hectares, 1,600 of which were VNP owned. In 1994, with the Cold War over, the two red zones were returned to the VNP and the process of renaturing the desert-like land began.[80]

In protesting the presence of foreign troops in the Lüneburg Heath in the mid 1950s, conservationists, students, politicians, and reporters referred to the nature reserve as a "national park," making it a symbol of national autonomy. As they sought to liberate this "colonial possession"—this homeland besieged by foreign forces—activists found a legitimate avenue for expressing feelings of national pride and asserting West Germany's new status as a fully sovereign nation. Yet protecting nature in this instance also provided a way to demonstrate the Federal Republic's commitment to international cooperation. As Blank and Wehner made clear in their public statements, opposing Britain's use of a nature reserve for military training was a legitimate expression of sovereignty, and did not lessen West Germany's desire to find a place among the community of nations.

It is not entirely clear if those who expressed national pride in this case did so because they felt an attachment to the Federal Republic as a nation-state or to the idea of an autonomous German nation. Scholars who have examined the process of constructing national identity after 1945 explain that in the 1950s and 1960s, few West Germans developed strong emotional ties to the Federal Republic, a political entity they viewed as a temporary arrangement until reunification. It was more common for them to convey a muted sense of pride in their country by focusing on its economic success.[81] Indeed, in a very tangible way the Lüneburg Heath became a space in which West Germans could express pride in their prosperity. "The five-day week will come," Toepfer predicted in the mid 1950s, and "industrious people" wanting relaxation but not a long drive would need access to "peaceful oases" in nature.[82] In 1956, the VNP chairman went public with his plan to address rising demand for recreation areas, using the preindustrial landscape he designed in the Lüneburg Heath as a model for new nature parks that he hoped to establish across the country, a subject explored in chapter 4.

Defending the "German Forest"

The adverse effects of the country's rapid economic recovery contributed to the formation of several new alliances to defend nature and curb pollution. In the 1950s and 1960s, building coalitions at the local, regional, and increasingly national levels was a widespread, common strategy, one that continued the reserved style of protest employed by preservationists in the first decades of the century. In the 1950s alone, there were local and regional campaigns against air and water pollution in the Ruhr and the Saar; against hydroprojects in southern Germany; against canalizing the Mosel and Neckar Rivers; against expanding airports in Frankfurt, Munich, and Stuttgart; and against confiscating nature reserves for military purposes, among other protests. (Only in the late 1960s did road construction spark opposition.) In general, the citizens who formed ad hoc local and regional alliances exhibited greater flexibility in their actions than members of conservation organizations, who shied away from public protest. Both groups of people, however, used a range of tactics in hopes of achieving narrow goals. They drafted resolutions, circulated petitions, staged rallies, lobbied parliamentarians, commissioned reports by experts, filed suits in administrative courts, and lobbied officials and politicians. But because their ultimate goal involved reaching a consensus among the parties involved, they viewed public protest as a last resort—an attitude illustrated in chapter 3.[83]

Among the oldest nationwide postwar alliances was the Association for the Protection of the German Forest (SDW), formed in 1947 as an act of protest against the Allied occupation for overcutting timber. As a result of postwar territorial adjustments, Germany surrendered 25 percent of its forested land, which dropped from 12,675,000 hectares in 1937 to 9,585,000 hectares in 1946, when the Allies began an extensive forest inventory of the four zones.[84] Even though Germany had imported timber since the mid 1800s, the Allies adopted a policy of "full exploitation" in the first two years of the occupation, felling 200 percent of annual growth to destroy the "war potential of German forests" and to meet the unprecedented demand for timber.[85] Wood was needed for reconstruction in Germany and in countries ravaged by the war, and was essential for repairing pit-props, truck beds, and miners' houses so that the mining of coal could resume. Timber also was needed for export to help Germans meet reparations obligations and to generate revenue to pay for badly needed imports.[86]

The forests that Germans rallied to protect during the occupation were the product of scientific management over two centuries. In the early 1800s, German foresters had responded to a shift in demand from hardwood for fuel to soft woods for timber and pulpwood by planting fast-growing evergreen species. Scientific management resulted in higher yields of commercial timber over the short run, but eventually created forests that were 70 percent evergreen (spruce and pine with some larch and fir) and 30 percent deciduous (largely beech and oak). These industrial forests gradually declined in productivity because of an increase in the acidity of the soil, which made trees susceptible to damage by windfall and insects and discouraged growth of vegetation on the forest floor. In response, foresters in the 1910s began planting some oak, beech and other hardwoods with different root systems and heights, increasing productivity and allowing foresters to cut no more timber than that which reached maturity each year. The Nazi regime deviated from this practice, ordering foresters to cut 150 percent of annual growth beginning in 1935. Though overcutting occurred each year, this goal was never reached.[87] By 1945, Germany's forests were overused, but to a degree disputed because reliable forest statistics had not been kept since 1938 and the most detailed inventory dated from the 1920s. In general, the country's forests survived the war in better shape than initially feared; around 6 percent of forested land in all four zones existed as clear-cuts, an amount not unusual after a major war.[88]

Nonetheless, Germans in the western zones complained bitterly about excessive over-cutting, casting themselves in the role of the victim of National Socialism and an exploitative occupation. Resentment over timber cutting was limited in the American sector, because it had the most forested land of all four zones (3,516,000 hectares) and US authorities gave Germans some control over harvesting and distribution. The French, in charge of 1,480,000 hectares of forest, caused uproar with their methods of extracting timber. After singling out stands near roadsides to be clear-cut (where transport would be easiest but more visible and shocking to passersby), they auctioned off lots to foreign firms who allegedly resold the wood at a higher price on the world market. Foreign companies came with their own laborers, sequestered homes, offices, and schools, and clear-cut the stands they had purchased, charging expenses to Germans in the zone. But the Soviets were the most rapacious, clear-cutting the best-stocked imperial forests as reparations, failing to replant, and forcing foresters to cut trees with crude tools and near-starvation rations. Between 1945 and 1949, the Soviets hauled away thirteen years of forest growth.[89]

Germans and foreign observers assumed that in the western zones the French were the most exploitive, but between 1946 and 1948 overcutting in the British zone was more severe. To oversee timber harvesting the British created the North German Timber Control (NGTC), one of many control boards the British established to manage industries in their zone. Typically NGTC set up camp in the center of a forested area, then hired displaced persons, occupation soldiers, and workers from German firms to clear-cut the surrounding woods. German forest service officials could recommend procedures, but British officers often ignored them.[90] Germans in the British zone had formed ad hoc groups in 1945 to prevent deforestation by Germans scrambling for wood. But the first organized protest developed in the spring of 1946 when the newly formed Zonal Advisory Council (*Zonenbeirat*), a body representing state and local governments, political parties, and unions, appointed a committee to study deforestation. Several members later played a leading role in SDW.[91] The committee conceded that overcutting in the current crisis was unavoidable, but faulted the British for excessive harvests and the NGTC for indiscriminate clear-cutting and trampling edible vegetation so critical in a time of food shortages.[92] The British Control Commission's standard reply to these kinds of complaints was that overcutting in its zone did not match the heavy losses inflicted on Britain's stock of trees in fighting two world wars. After exploiting the natural resources of other countries during WWII, Germans should expect that their forests would be overused temporarily.[93] In November 1946, the British began "Operation Woodpecker," dispatching three thousand soldiers armed with axes to fell trees in the Harz Mountains and Lüneburg Heath. By January 1947, 26,545 tons of wood had been exported to England for reconstruction.[94]

In this chilling winter, German conservationists and foresters heightened their criticism of the "purely businessman focus" of the British Military Government, warning in exhibits, lectures, and letters to officials about the long term dangers of clear-cutting.[95] Kurt Borchers, forester and district conservation commissioner for Braunschweig, conceded that Germany "must make sacrifices for the events of the past." But there was no justification for Allied exploitation of Germany's forests, a shortsighted policy, he argued, that exacerbated erosion, disrupted microclimates, and contributed to the kind of extreme flooding that northern Germany had recently witnessed.[96] Expressing exaggerated alarm, Gert Kragh, Hanover Province's conservation commissioner, stated in a program over Radio Bremen that Allied policies limiting coal supplies and requiring the use of good wood for fuel seemed driven by the desire "to destroy the German landscape, the German economy, and the German people." Delivering these comments in January 1947, during one of Europe's most brutally cold winters in half a century, Kragh conveyed the sentiments of other Germans who objected to the "dismantling" of forests and took up the protest out of sense of victimhood and patriotism.[97]

Similar responses were expressed by minister-presidents of state governments in all four zones when they gathered in June 1947 in Munich to discuss pressing economic issues. According to Bavaria's Minister of Agriculture, Dr. Josef Baumgartner (Bavaria Party) "the slaughter of German forests . . . and the exploitation of timber reserves that have been tended for decades" was a "catastrophe." The National Socialist regime had begun an "irresponsible exploitation" of Germany's forests, and Allied powers were continuing it at a rate that would hinder the economic recovery of Germany and Europe. The extent of overcutting in the western zones, he and other political leaders alleged, struggling for moral ground, violated the 1907 Hague Convention, which limited the amount of raw materials victors could extract from another country.[98] In explaining why such complaints fell on deaf ears, Borchers concluded that the Allied powers lacked the attachment to forests that Germans had cultivated over generations through sound forestry and through sagas, poetry, and music inspired by the woods.[99]

Though resentful of overcutting, Germans could not ignore that in August 1947, timber exports had produced an estimated $10 million in credit—second only to coal. A new level of industry plan from August 1947 called for increased production in the merged British and American zones, enabling more coal to be extracted from the Ruhr. Even though less timber was being cut and Germans gained more control over felling and distribution, in the British zone harvests for 1948 were to remain high, at 250 percent of annual growth.[100] Frustrated by the slow response of the occupying powers, prominent members of the British Zonal Advisory Council initiated a "people's movement" from above, establishing the Society for the Protection of the German Forest (SDW) in December 1947. In his opening remarks to 800 Germans representing state governments, forestry, and conservation, the pre-selected SDW president Robert Lehr (CDU) appealed to the "sense of justice of the English people."[101] "The Nuremberg Trials," he stated, "have revealed that the victors consider it to be a grave offense if an occupying power exhausts the economic potential of an occupied country for its own ends without regard for international law," namely the 1907 Hague Convention.[102] But moralizing by the SDW had little effect on British timber harvesting practices.

The United States' more lenient economic policy toward Germany evident in the Marshall Plan announced in 1947 was more decisive. US Military Governor General Lucius Clay criticized British harvest projections for 1947–1948, citing US forestry experts who considered it "more akin to reparations than to a sound economic proposal." Reflecting State Department policy, the US Military Government insisted that "All future felling in the bi-zonal area should be carried out in accordance with sound practices bearing in mind Germany's export responsibilities as a country receiving United States aid."[103] In 1948, the British dissolved the NGTC and replaced it with a body controlled jointly with the US. Direct timber harvesting by the occupying powers ceased in 1949 and rapid reforestation began.

Though Germans had limited influence on the Allies' plans for felling timber, the SDW seized the opportunity to shape how its own people viewed the forests and the occupation policies that called for exploiting them. In general, the SDW functioned as an educational arm of the forest service. It relied on public figures to lead state chapters that emerged between 1948 and 1949, first in the British and American zones and later in the French.[104] In exhibits, lectures, publications, and films, chapters emphasized the economic and ecological significance of well-tended forests, but also reminded people of what SDW literature described as an enduring cultural bond between the forest and *Volk*.[105] In September 1948, North Rhine-Westphalia's chapter opened an exhibit in Essen, "The Forest—Our Fate," informing 115,000 visitors—50,000 of them youth—about the forest as a living community, as lungs that purified the air of industrial cities, and as the "the true homeland landscape" of the German soul.[106] The SDW journal *Grünes Blatt* (later *Unser Wald*) first published by North Rhine-Westphalia after currency reform, declared the organization's intention to become a "people's movement" that would "rebuild our forest . . . in the interest of our economy, culture, and the continued existence of our people." But SDW's "main task," the article stated, was to strengthen Germans' "intuitive and spiritual bond to the forest."[107] Typical of SDW publications at the time, one book claimed that "life without the forest is unthinkable for us [Germans] not only for economic reasons . . . But above all, because our . . . spiritual existence swings in rhythm with it."[108]

Some SDW members were constantly on the road and over the radio generating awareness about the ecological functions of forests and the urgent need for reforestation. In over 400 lectures and articles, Erich Hornsmann urged his audiences to plant trees and shrubs, warning that powerful cultures in ancient times had declined in status after devastating the land, forests, and water supply that sustained them.[109] To foster idealism among the youth after the horrors of the Nazi past, SDW chapters enlisted girls and boys to help reforest the homeland—initially with fast-growing evergreen species (pine and spruce).[110] This organic rebuilding was symbolically linked to the country's economic revival when West Germany minted its new currency: the 50 pfennig coin bore the imprint of a barefoot woman planting an oak seedling, a tree considered to be authentically German, despite being an importation.[111]

With government funds, SDW chapters sponsored an annual "Day of the Tree," a nationwide event modeled after Arbor Day in the US and instituted in countries worldwide upon the recommendation of the FAO. In cities and towns throughout West Germany, public officials kicked off a day of celebration that featured planting trees, singing and dancing to folk songs, and viewing exhibits about the economic, ecological, and recreational value of forests.[112] On the first Day of the Tree in 1952, the new "protector" of SDW, Federal President Theodor Heuss (1949-1959, FDP), planted a tree in the garden of the university in the West German capital, Bonn. Other officials used the event to foster a positive national identity, one supposedly rooted in nature and sustained by the cultural heritage that grew out of it. In his speech, Lehr claimed that "Germans have always been connected to the forest in a . . . heartfelt way . . . Customs, ways of thinking, character—yes, our soul is deeply anchored in the forest, in the homeland of fairy tales and sagas." When Chancellor Adenauer addressed the West Berlin chapter of SDW in 1953, he, too, invoked the forest as a symbol of national identity and political stability, declaring that the German forest "is . . . deeply tied to the German essence . . . Whoever loves the German forest also loves an orderly political system. But he loves something more—he also loves the German homeland out of the depths of [his] soul."[113]

In their organized protest and public awareness campaign, prominent officials who led SDW chapters referred to the many distinct regional forests as one unified "German forest," expressing a desire for national unity that presumably was rooted in nature and linked to a better, distant past, immortalized and idealized in the country's cultural traditions. But they also believed that conserving the forest was essential in securing Germany's identity as an economically stable country in the future. Contrary to the conservative rhetoric about a mystical link between forest and *Volk*, however, it seems that Germans' tie to the forest was not so deeply anchored. According to a 1955 poll of approximately 2,000 people conducted by the Allensbach Institute, 55 percent responded they did not visit the forests often and another 11 percent indicated they had not been to the forests in years.[114] Not presumed mystical ties to the forests, but visible harm to them by worsening pollution generated more support for protecting the nation's woodlands after the mid 1950s, in particular by advocating clean air laws and challenging the free reign of industry.[115]

Democratizing Conservation and Building New National Alliances

Few conservation organizations were as explicit in nationalizing nature and naturalizing nationalism as the VNP and the SDW, because they did not directly confront the Allied occupation. More typical of several new national alliances was the aim to educate the public about *Naturschutz* in its many dimensions and to improve conservation legislation through the democratic process. Measuring the public impact of alliances' pedagogical initiatives, in particular, is difficult. So, too, is determining the size of their following. Frequently alliances uniting several organizations claimed to represent thousands of people who shared a moral concern to protect helpless nature and the common good from the ills of modern civilization. But their supporters probably were not as numerous as they maintained. Yet as recent scholarship emphasizes, precisely because these new national alliances lacked a natural clientele like traditional lobby organizations, they could claim to represent the common good.[116]

The largest new umbrella organization, the German Conservation Ring (*Deutscher Naturschutzring,* or DNR) was established in 1950 at the annual ABN congress by Klose and others who wanted to prevent the state from monopolizing preservation as it had during the Third Reich. The coalition was built on a tradition from the 1920s when the Nature Preservation Ring Berlin-Brandenburg had been created, an organization that Klose had chaired. He acknowledged that the DNR's member groups, which included "nature preservers" and "nature users," would sometimes disagree on issues. This did not prevent him from hoping that the new alliance would function as an "emergency association," responding to controversial matters on short notice and wielding political influence like the country's larger, more powerful lobby organizations representing labor and industry. But this ambitious goal was unrealistic because conservation still lacked strong institutional and financial support.[117]

At the founding meeting of the DNR, Dr. Hans Krieg (1888–1970), Munich zoology professor and director of Bavaria's Natural Sciences Collection, was elected president (to Klose's chagrin because Krieg had shown lukewarm support for the BANL, an institute with Prussian roots). The DNR proved to be a loyal supporter of the agency and adopted much of the agenda of official conservation as its own. By 1952 the alliance claimed sixty-one member organizations representing 760,000 people, an inflated estimate that overlooked individuals' membership in more than one DNR-affiliated group. In the organization's early years limited funds from membership dues restricted its influence primarily to Bavaria. (Only in 1973 was the main office moved from Munich to the capital, Bonn).[118]

Continuing *Naturschutz* organizations' traditional emphasis on pedagogy, the DNR was most active in educating the public about the importance of conservation. In publications and lectures, Krieg admonished contemporaries who seemed "enslaved" by the idea of progress for failing to see that conservation was about preserving a source of inspiration and moral truth. But, he emphasized, conservationists' concern to ensure "harmony in the landscape" had become a "vital" economic issue as erosion, large scale fish kills, and major disruptions in the water supply indicated.[119] The energetic DNR business manager and student of Krieg, Wolfgang Engelhardt (1922–2006), called for disciplinary action against officials who failed to enforce conservation measures, and drafted guidelines (adopted by West German ministers of culture in 1952) for improving biology instruction at all education levels.[120] A key player in postwar conservation and one of West Germany's representatives to the IUCN, Engelhardt tried to distance "modern *Naturschutz*" from the "sentimental and useless complaints about lost natural beauty" and associate it more clearly with ecology and "rigorous scientific form."[121]

Conservative, moralizing rhetoric remained a part of *Naturschutz* discourse into the 1970s, but was already muted in the 1950s as the base of support for conservation broadened somewhat, and economic and scientific arguments became expected in public debate. The Alliance for the Protection of Germany's Waters (*Vereinigung Deutscher Gewässerschutz*), formed in 1951 by Dr. Karl Imhoff, a pioneer in scientific water management, captured the modern sounding voice of postwar conservation with its emphasis on economic efficiency and health. Uniting groups representing fishermen, hunters, industry, and tourism, the alliance claimed to speak for one million people concerned about the water supply. As Erich Hornsmann warned in the first of the alliance's many publications, water had become a "scarce commodity" as greater demand outpaced an increasingly polluted and falling supply. Indeed, consumption had risen dramatically in the late 1940s with the influx of refugees and the revival of industry. Yet during reconstruction, governments emphasized urban and industrial renewal, leaving little money for installing treatment facilities in numbers needed to handle the rapid rise in use. And the groundwater supply was down because extensive land reclamation and river rectification drained water from the soil that should have absorbed it like a sponge. To meet the demand for water required drawing from surface waters that were growing more polluted with industrial, agricultural, and household effluents, oil, and radiation. Water pollution was becoming a costly, well-publicized problem, threatening the profitability of tourism and some industries and compromising the livelihood of commercial fishermen.

(Between 1949 and 1952, over one hundred major fish kills occurred each year.) Using ties to political leaders, the alliance helped draft federal laws to manage the water supply (1957), to require manufacturers to produce biodegradable detergents (1961), and to control oil pollution, a problem that worsened as West Germany's petroleum use increased. In the early 1960s, coal still supplied 75 percent of the country's total energy needs, but oil covered 21 percent, bringing more spills, leaking fuel tanks, and poisoned groundwater.[122]

The organization that deserves the most credit for passing conservation and environmental legislation is the non-partisan Interparliamentary Working Association for a Sustainable Economy (*Interparlamentarische Arbeitsgemeinschaft für eine naturgemäße Wirtschaft*, or IPA). Formed in 1952 by fifty federal and state parliamentarians who were involved in or abreast of international developments in conservation, the IPA attracted an additional 250 members by 1964 with its goal of promoting stewardship of natural resources in tandem with economic development. Expressing an environmental consciousness ahead of its time, the IPA warned that disruptions in the balance of the "household of nature" potentially threatened public health and the quality of life of future generations. Assigning a new, universal significance to conservation that contrasted sharply with older, yet still common, nationalistic and morally conservative arguments, IPA literature cautioned that careless exploitation of natural resources put freedom, justice, and peace at risk. In fulfilling what the IPA described as a "political duty" to "secure the natural foundations of life," members took the lead in drafting the Land Consolidation Law (1953), the Water Management Law (1957), the Clean Air Maintenance Law (1959), and the law requiring biodegradable detergents (1961).[123]

These examples suffice to illustrate the range of organizations that claimed responsibility for conservation in postwar West Germany. While some remained nationalistic in their aims (such as the VNP and SDW), others were more pragmatic (like the Conservation Ring and the Alliance for the Protection of Germany's Waters). A lesser number was like the IPA, guided by a universal concern to protect peace and freedom in pursuing pragmatic legal reform. The revival of old groups and the emergence of several new alliances in the late 1940s and early 1950s refutes the claim that *Naturschutz* was too tarnished by National Socialism to find support in the Federal Republic and it ensured that no group would monopolize conservation.

Yet the conservation leadership was dominated by a small circle of well connected social and political elites until the late 1960s.[124] The bank executive Georg Fahrbach (FDP) presided over several hiking organizations, founded a giant merger of six mass organizations for hiking and preservation, and served for years on the DNR executive committee.[125] The multi-millionaire Alfred Toepfer chaired the VNP, assumed a position on the DNR executive committee, and sat on the German Council for Land Cultivation, a body discussed in chapter 4.

The younger Wolfgang Burhenne (1924-) was cofounder of the progressive alliance for wildlife protection (*Schutzgemeinschaft Deutsches Wild*), served for years as the Secretary General of the IPA, went on to play a key role in the IUCN in legal affairs, helped establish the World Wildlife Fund in 1961, and later served on the DNR executive committee (as a rather disgruntled member).[126] This tendency of old and new groups to rely on a few well connected people to make most of the decisions and work behind the scenes to secure officials' support is not surprising for the generation of 1900, which received much of its political education under authoritarian systems and associated democracy with the unstable Weimar Republic. Nor was it out of place in the conservative political climate of the times. In the absence of a mass following, leading conservationists pursued a practical strategy by cultivating close ties to the state. In the process, they strengthened support for *Naturschutz*. In the case of individuals such as Burhenne and Engelhardt, they also assured West Germany's participation in international conservation.[127] Despite a lack of broad participation by members, the freedom of organizational leaders to participate in the public sphere of West Germany's restored democracy ensured the continuation of conservation after 1945 and contributed in some measure to the revival of civic life.

After World War II, the generation of 1900 that stayed on to shape postwar conservation clung to the belief that the condition of Germany's landscapes directly affected the spiritual and physical health of their countrymen. A few, like former VNP chairman Hans Domizlaff and former conservation commissioner Hans Schwenkel, still linked preservation to racial hygiene, but they found themselves marginalized. More common was the continued use of biologisms, as in the arguments of SDW leaders who claimed that Germans' spiritual essence and respected intellectual heritage were intricately connected to the forest. It therefore followed that protecting "the German forest" would preserve the nation's cultural roots and secure its economic future.

Conservationists also continued to advocate the protection of nature-as-an-idealized-*Heimat*. Yet the image of homeland they sought to protect underwent subtle change. Initially, they fought to protect a *Heimat* that presumably had remained "pure" and that provided fertile ground for cultivating patriotic citizens for a nation-in-waiting. As material conditions improved somewhat and environmental problems worsened in the 1950s, the *Heimat* they wanted to defend was not only prosperous and modern but scenic, healthy, and reminiscent of cherished traditions. However flexible the *Heimat* idea had shown itself to be, postwar conservationists resisted the subordination of *Naturschutz* to *Heimatschutz,* fearing that the broad cultural agenda of the latter would dilute efforts to limit the exploitation of land and natural resources, their greatest worry.[128]

The emphasis that the western Allies and German political leaders placed on economic recovery forced conservationists to adjust their goals and rhetoric to reflect this overriding concern. Those associated with state-sponsored conservation led the way in developing a more flexible response to the challenge of managing the country's resources and landscapes, conveying their goals by pairing *"Naturschutz"* with *"Landschaftspflege"* more intentionally than in the past. Accordingly, conservationists came to view themselves less as protectors and designers of homeland landscapes and more as stewards of land health, charged with protecting healthy landscapes and doctoring biologically sick ones—all in the interest of public wellness and economic prosperity. Yet even this presumably more rational approach to conservation was undergirded by a familiar cultural conservatism.

Without ignoring the ecological insights of preservationists of previous decades, one can view the 1950s as an important stage in the ecologization of *Naturschutz,* not only in West Germany, but internationally as well.[129] This change is not surprising after a global conflict that caused critical shortages of natural resources around the world, prolonging human misery, and slowing economic recovery. WWII made the interconnectedness of humans and nature, and nature and economies obvious. In West Germany, ecologization also was evident in the emergence of new alliances whose diverse member groups understood that harm to one part of nature affected the larger "household," as well as their economic and recreational interests. But one should not assume that ecological arguments carried more weight in public debate in the 1950s, especially when ecology was still not a widely respected science in West Germany. Unlike their North American cohorts who thought ecology provided an objective means of understanding and managing nature, West German ecologists contended that nature could not be understood in purely scientific terms. Partly for this reason, the scientific community regarded ecology as methodologically suspect. Reinforcing the point, the prominent German ecologist Wolfgang Haber recalled that his professor discouraged him from studying ecology because it had little prestige; he pursued biology, chemistry, and geography instead.[130] Furthermore, the compartmentalization of conservation in state ministries of culture, agriculture, or the interior meant that officials responsible for *Naturschutz* had difficulty appreciating the holistic perspective of ecological arguments. In general, West German officials and the public viewed *Naturschutz* as a cultural activity, a notion reinforced by conservationists' pedagogical activities that, ironically, tried to educate people about the expanded scope of caring for nature.

It is tempting to conclude that conservation was not overly successful in West Germany in the 1940s and 1950s. Although it acquired support from several new alliances and prominent public figures, it still lacked strong institutional and financial support and remained a minority cause with a rather narrow base and with influence primarily at the local and regional levels. And the social conservatives who dominated the leadership won few new converts with their elitist sounding message that preached against excessive materialism, the arrogance of technology, and contemporaries' alienation from nature. Although these familiar lamentations were right at home in the paternalistic climate of Adenauer's Germany, they failed to resonate with most people who only had begun to sample the fruits of prosperity. Yet as recent studies have shown, examining developments on the regional level where preservation had its traditional base of support reveals a more promising picture of early postwar conservation.[131] In the following case study from the Black Forest, social conservatives united thousands of supporters in an alliance to protect nature-as-*Heimat,* forcing a utility company to beat a small retreat and reach a partially green compromise.

Notes

1. Lucius D. Clay, *Decision in Germany* (New York: Doubleday, 1950), 263–80; Ulrich Kluge, "West German Agriculture and the European Recovery Program, 1948–1952," 157, and Jeffry M. Diefendorf, "America and the Rebuilding of Urban Germany," 348, both in *American Policy and the Reconstruction of West Germany, 1945–1955,* ed. Diefendorf, Axel Frohn, and Hermann-Josef Rupieper (New York: Cambridge University Press, 1993); Alan Bullock, *Ernest Bevin,* vol. 3, *Foreign Secretary, 1945–1951* (New York: Norton, 1983), 20, 232, 389; Christoph Kleßmann, *Die doppelte Staatsgründung: Deutsche Geschichte 1945–1955,* 5th ed. (Göttingen: Vandenhoeck & Ruprecht, 1982; Bonn: Bundeszentrale für politische Bildung, 1991), 48–53, 357; David Childs, *Germany in the Twentieth Century* (New York: Harper Collins, 1991), 122.
2. "Holzversorgungslage Restdeutschlands," *Grünes Blatt* (March 1949): 8. On postwar myths about lost lands see Blackbourn, *Conquest,* 311–22.
3. On the FAO see John McCormick, *Reclaiming Paradise: the Global Environmental Movement* (Bloomington: Indiana University Press, 1989), 27–28. Postwar neo–Malthusian texts include Henry Fairfield Osborn, Jr., *Our Plundered Planet* (New York: Little, Brown and Company, 1948); William Vogt, *The Road to Survival* (New York: William Sloane, 1948); and Adolph Metternich, *Die Wüste droht. Die gefährdete Nahrungsgrundlage menschlichen Gesellschaft* (Bremen: Friedrich Trüjen, 1947).
4. Hermann Hähnle, German League for Bird Protection, Activities Report, 2 November 1946, available at <http://www.nabu.de/nabu/history/bericht1946.htm> (accessed 10 August 2000).
5. Mary Fulbrook, *The Divided Nation. A History of Germany, 1918–1990* (New York: Oxford University Press, 1992), chapters 6–7, pp. 181–85 on economic growth; Childs, *Germany,* chapters 7–8; Jeffrey Herf, *Divided Memory. The Nazi Past in the Two Germanys* (Cambridge: Harvard University Press, 1997), 220.
6. Konrad Jarausch, *After Hitler: Recivilizing Germans, 1945–1995,* trans. Brandon Hunziker (New York: Oxford University Press, 2006), 104–5, 111–20, 127–29.
7. On modernizing social changes in the conservative climate of the "long 1950s" see Axel Schildt and Arnold Sywottek, eds. *Modernisierung im Wiederaufbau: Die westdeutsche Gesellschaft der 50er Jahre* (Bonn: Dietz, 1998). Refer also to Robert G. Moeller, ed. *West Germany under Construction. Politics, Society, and Culture in the Adenauer Era* (Ann Arbor: University of Michigan Press, 1997); Hanna Schissler, ed. *The Miracle Years: A Cultural History of West Germany, 1945–1968* (Princeton: Princeton University Press, 2001).

8. Hans Klose, "Zusammenbruch und Wiederaufbau: Die Reichsstelle für Naturschutz seit 1943," *N & L* 26, no. 5/6 (1951): 56–58; no. 7/8 (1951): 86–87; no. 11/12 (1951): 130; Klose, *Fünfzig Jahre*, 42–44.

9. Hans Klose, "Über die Dringlichkeit stärksten Naturschutzeinsatzes," printed in *N & L* 56, no. 9 (1981): 314. "Volk ohne Raum" was the title of Hans Grimm's 1926 novel, a bestseller among rightwing politicians, which advocated expanding Germany's borders in the east. On Germans' fears about the Morgenthau Plan see James F. Byrnes, *Speaking Frankly* (New York and London: Harper, 1947), 181.

10. Hans Klose to Richard Lohrmann, 2 May 1947, BAK B 245/253; Klose to Ilse Waldenburg, 17 November [n.y. 1947?], BAK B 245/255; Klose to Hermann Helfer, 1947, BAK B 245/105; Friedrich Goethe to Klose, 31 March 1949, BAK B 245/237; Klose to Goethe, 6 April 1949, BAK B 245/237.

11. On Klose's career see Hans Schwenkel, "Lebensbild von Dr. Hans Klose," *Nachrichtenblatt für Naturschutz und Landschaftspflege* 25, no. 6 (1954): 21–23; Wettengel, "Staat und Naturschutz," 382–84; Gröning and Wolschke-Bulmahn, *Natur in Bewegung*, 189–90. On Schoenichen's career see Gröning and Wolschke-Bulmahn, *Natur in Bewegung*, 142–44; Hans Schwenkel, "Professor Dr. W. Schoenichen zum Gedächtnis," *N & L* 32, no. 4 (1957): 58–59; "Prof. Dr. Schoenichen beigesetzt," *Goppinger Kreisnachrichten*, 27 November 1956, clipping in BAK B 245/254. On the Klose–Schoenichen rivalry see Klose to Friedrich Goethe, 6 April 1949, BAK B 245/237; and Klose to Walter Effenberger, 3 February 1946, BAK B 245/250.

12. On the continued influence of landscape architects and conservationists after 1945 see esp. Gröning and Wolschke-Bulmahn, *Natur in Bewegung;* Oberkrome, *"Deutsche Heimat";* Körner, *Theorie.* On Hans Schwenkel see Hans Klose to Richard Lohrmann, 21 September 1946, BAK B 245/253; Dominick, *Environmental Movement*, 119; Uekötter, *Green and the Brown,* 186–87. For evidence of his waning influence see Gert Kragh to Schwenkel, 21 January 1955, BAK B 245/254.

13. Hans Klose to Richard Lohrmann, 4 July 1946, BAK B 245/253. See also Max Bromme, "Natur– und Landschaftsschutz im Regierungsbezirk Wiesbaden," *Verhandlungen* (1948): 70.

14. Oberkrome, *"Deutsche Heimat,"* 396–404; Uekötter, *Green and the Brown,* 164–65, 187–88, 192.

15. Compare Klose's early statements that stress protecting nature–as–*Heimat*, such as "Grundsätzliches zur Frage der obersten Naturschutzbehörde," 20 June 1945 and "Dringlichkeit," both published in *N & L* 56, no. 9 (1981): 313–15; with later ones stressing economic contributions: "Zweite Denkschrift zur Frage der Angliederung der bisherigen Reichsstelle für Naturschutz an die Verwaltung für Ernährung, Landwirtschaft und Forsten," 20 June 1948, BAK B 245/238.

16. On the Allies' policy toward Germany see Carolyn Eisenberg, *Drawing the Line. The American Decision to Divide Germany, 1944–1949* (New York: Cambridge University Press, 1996), chap. 1; Alec Cairncross, *The Price of War: British Policy on German Reparations* (New York: Blackwell, 1986), 86–99, 230–31; James Byrnes, "Restatement of U.S. Policy on Germany," 6 September 1946, in *Germany 1947–1949. The Story in Documents*, ed. United States Department of State (Washington, DC: U.S. Government Printing Office, 1950), 5.

17. On Hans Klose's struggle to preserve the former Reich Agency despite budgetary constraints and states' rights advocates see Klose, *Fünfzig Jahre*, 44–46; Klose's correspondences in BAK B 245/238; Klose to *Ministerialrat* Gustav Mitzschke (Hesse), 11 October 1950, BAK B 245/253; Klose to Carl Kraemer, 8 February 1951, BAK B 245/252. On competition between the Federal Ministry of Agriculture and the Federal Ministry of the Interior for authority over conservation in the early 1950s see BAK B 245/247, especially Klose to Federal Ministry of Agriculture, 27 June 1950, BAK B 245/247 and Federal Minister of the

Interior to Federal Ministry of Agriculture, 7 May 1950, copy in BAK B 245/247. Instructive secondary accounts of these developments include Dominick, *Environmental Movement*, 120–21; Uekötter, *Green and the Brown*, 189–91; more extensively, Frohn, "Naturschutz macht Staat," in Frohn and Schmoll, *Natur und Staat*, 194–212.

18. Headquarters of the Military Government, North Rhine Region to *Oberpräsident*, North Rhine Region, 15 March 1946, BAK B 245/237; Hans Klose to Carl Duve, 27 May 1947, BAK B 245/137. On British officials' praise of the RNG see Duve, "Niederschrift über die Besprächung mit Forstmeister Behm, Sacharbeiter für Lt. Col. Brooke, Chef–Offizier für Jagd–Angelegenheiten d. Britischen Zone," 12 February 1947, BAK B 245/237; Uekötter, *Green and the Brown*, 142–43, 188, 191.

19. Klose, *Fünfzig Jahre*, 33–41; Dominick, *Environmental Movement*, 120; Erwin Stein, "Recht des Natur– und Umweltschutzes," in *Natur– und Umweltschutz in der BRD*, ed. Gerhard Olschowy (Hamburg: Paul Parey, 1978), 878–82.

20. Hans Klose to Carl Kraemer, 8 February 1951, BAK B 245/252; Klose, *Fünfzig Jahre*, 42–50.

21. Klose, *Fünfzig Jahre*, 33.

22. Radkau, "Germany as a Focus of European 'Particularities,'" in Lekan and Zeller, *Germany's Nature*, 18–21.

23. Mrass, *Organization*, 64. In five of the eleven states, conservation was housed in the ministry of culture. In Bavaria and Bremen, it was under the ministry of the interior. In Schleswig–Holstein and Hesse, the ministry of agriculture had oversight, and in North Rhine-Westphalia and West Berlin, the ministry for public works was responsible.

24. Gert Kragh to Hans Klose, 1 October 1946; Klose to Kragh, 9 October 1946, both in BAK B 245/153.

25. Gert Kragh, "Lebenslauf," 28 February 1953; Kragh, "Bericht über meine bisherige berufliche Tätigkeit," 28 February 1953, both in BAK B 245/153. See also Herbert Ecke, "Gert Kragh," *Nachrichtenblatt für Naturschutz und Landschaftspflege* 25, no. 5 (1954): 17–19. On Kragh's criticisms of Seifert see Zeller, *Straße*, 199.

26. Gert Kragh to Minister of Culture, Lower Saxony, 3 September 1953, BAK B 245/153; Engels, *Naturpolitik*, 53. More extensive on West Germans' memories of the Nazi past is Herf, *Divided Memory*, chapters 7–8.

27. Wey, *Umweltpolitik*, 196–98; Dominick, *Environmental Movement*, 117–18, 148; Brüggemeier, *Tschernobyl*, 201–2. The number of commissioners stated is from 1956. See *Verhandlungen* (1957): 39.

28. Gert Kragh, "Der Beitrag der Naturschutzstellen bei Planungsarbeiten im Städtebau," 24 October 1950, BAK B 245/153; Carl Duve, "Landschaftspflege in der Stadtlandschaft," *Verhandlungen* (1948): 18–22; Johannes Sigmond, "Landschaftspflege am Niederrhein," *Verhandlungen* (1948): 22–26; Richard Lohrmann, "Von den Wirkungsmöglichkeiten der Naturschutzbeauftragten in der praktischen Landschaftsgestaltung," *N & L* 27, no. 5/6 (1952): 55.

29. Mrass, *Organisation*, 41–42, table 26; Oberkrome, *"Deutsche Heimat,"* 396–404; Engels, *Naturpolitik*, 66.

30. Hans Klose, "Über die Lage der Landes– und Bezirksstellen," *Verhandlungen* (1948): 5; Bromme, "Natur– und Landschaftsschutz im Regierungsbezirk Wiesbaden," *Verhandlungen* (1948): 70–71; Otto Kraus, *Über den bayerischen Naturschutz* (Munich: Öko–Markt, 1979), 16–18; Kragh, "Lebenslauf," 28 February 1953, BAK B 245/153; Ernst Preising, interview by author, 12 May 1992, Oberhaverbeck, Lüneburg Heath.

31. "Haushaltmittel für Naturschutz und Landschaftspflege," *Verhandlungen* (1956): 120–21, 126–28; Rudolf Schaper, "Kreis– und Bezirksnaturschutzstellen," *N & L* 34, no. 11 (1959): 167–72.

32. Lekan, "Regional Planning," in Brüggemeier, Cioc, and Zeller, *How Green*, 91; Bergmeier, *Umweltgeschichte*, chap. 3.

33. Quote from Wilhelm Lienenkämper, "Gedanken zur Tätigkeit der Naturschutzbeauftragten," *Verhandlungen* (1949): 33–34. On efforts to make commissioners fulltime government employees see Kragh, "Der Beitrag der Naturschutzstellen," 24 October 1950, BAK B 245/153; Johannes Sigmond, "Zur Hauptamtlichkeit der Bezirksbeauftragten," *Verhandlungen* (1949): 36–37, among many examples. On commissioners' profile see Mrass, *Organisation*, 40–41, and tables 10–17, 23, 24, and 25.

34. Klose, *Fünfzig Jahre*, 47–48.

35. The BANL journal, first published as *Naturschutz* in 1922, ceased publication in 1944. In 1953 the title was changed to *Natur und Landschaft*. See Engels, *Naturpolitik*, 47, 63–64.

36. Mrass, *Organisation*, 41; Engels, *Naturpolitik*, 46; Stefan Körner, "Die Entwicklung des Naturschutzes und der Landschaftsplanung nach dem Zweiten Weltkrieg," in Brüggemeier and Engels, *Natur– und Umweltschutz*, 92–100.

37. Klose, *Fünfzig Jahre*, 35; Heinrich Lohmeyer, "Unser Lebensraum ist in Gefahr!" *N & L* 36, no. 3 (1961): 34, 36; Herbert Offner, "Bewahren, Pflegen und Neu Gestalten," *N & L* 40, no. 6 (1965): 101; Andersen, *Traum*, 127ff.

38. Erich Kühn, "Natur und Wirtschaft," *Verhandlungen* (1955): 33–34; Heller, "Reklame in freier Landschaft," *Verhandlungen* (1948): 89–91; Uekötter, *Naturschutz im Aufbruch*, chap. 2; Rommelspacher, "Zwischen Heimatschutz und Umweltprotest," 79.

39. Fritz Lense, "Neue Bergbahnprojekte in den Deutschen Alpen," *N & L* 27, no. 7/8 (1952): 70–71; Heinrich Menke, "Die Seilbahnseuche geht durch die deutschen Lande," *N & L* 28, no. 3 (1953): 44–45; Dominick, *Environmental Movement*, 133; Andersen, *Traum*, chap. 4.

40. Gert Kragh, "Gesunde Landschaft bedingt die Zukunft des Volkes," 13 December 1945, BAK B 245/153. See also Erich Hornsmann, *Innere Kolonisation oder man made desert* (Stuttgart: Verlag der Pflanzenwerke im Verlag Oscar Angerer, 1948).

41. Blackbourn, *Conquest*, 325.

42. Karl Koch, "Hemmungen und Mißerfolge unserer Arbeit," *Verhandlungen* (1948): 11; Otto Kraus, "Über die Bedeutung des engeren Naturschutz," *Verhandlungen* (1950): 81–88; Kraus, "Vom Primat der Landschaft (1949)," in *Zerstörung der Natur. Unser Schicksal von morgen? Der Naturschutz in dem Streit der Interessen* (Nuremberg: Glock und Lutz, 1966), 10–14; Ernst Preising, interview by author, 12 May 1992; Dominick, *Environmental Movement*, 106, 120.

43. Hans Schwenkel, "Die Wünsche des deutschen Naturschutzes für die Flurbereinigung," *Verhandlungen* (1949): 95–104; Wilhelm Lienenkämper, *Grüne Welt zu treuen Händen. Naturschutz und Landschaftspflege im Industriezeitalter* (Stuttgart: Franckh'sche, 1963), 88–96; Oberkrome, *"Deutsche Heimat,"* 407–11, 496–97; Wolfgang Haber, interview by author, 20 June 1992, Freising. On parallel reforms in France see Bess, *Light–Green Society*, 40–41.

44. ABN, "Entschließung über Verschmutzung der Gewässer," *Verhandlungen* (1949): 50; ABN, "Entschließung über Kraftwerke," *Verhandlungen* (1949): 28–29; Hermann Schurhammer, "Wasserkraftwerke und Naturschutz," *Verhandlungen* (1949): 21–26; Otto Kraus, "Kraftplanung in Bayern," *Verhandlungen* (1949): 26–28; Kraus, *Über den Bayerischen Naturschutz*, 35–38; Blackbourn, *Conquest*, 327–28; Dominick, *Environmental Movement*, 125–34; Bergmeier, *Umweltgeschichte*, 154–69. See also Kraus, *Bis zum letzten Wildwasser? Gedanken über Wasserkraftnutzung und Naturschutz im Atomzeitalter* (Aachen: Georgi, 1960).

45. Lienenkämper, "Gedanken," *Verhandlungen* (1949): 35. See also ABN Resolution, *Verhandlungen* (1949): 37; Otto Kraus, "Vom Naturschutz unserer Zeit," *N & L* 26, no. 1/2 (1951): 4; Engels, *Naturpolitik*, 63–71.

46. Gert Kragh, "Naturschutz und Landschaftspflege––oder Katastrophe!" transcript of radio broadcast, 13 January 1947, BAK B 245/153.

47. Lienenkämper, "Gedanken," *Verhandlungen* (1949): 33; Koch, "Hemmungen," *Verhandlungen* (1948): 13.

48. Engels, *Naturpolitik,* 51–52; Bergmeier, *Umweltgeschichte,* 154–59; Dominick, *Environmental Movement,* 123, 129–30.

49. For a critical appraisal of these complaints see Frank Uekötter, "Erfolglosigkeit als Dogma? Revisionistische Bemerkungen zum Umweltschutz zwischen dem Ende des Zweiten Weltkriegs und der 'ökologischen Wende,'" in Brüggemeier and Engels, *Natur– und Umweltschutz,* 105–23.

50. Konrad Buchwald, "Unsere Zukunftsaufgaben im Naturschutz und in der Landschaftspflege," *Verhandlungen* (1957): 33.

51. Stefan Körner, "Kontinuum und Bruch: Die Transformation des naturschützerischen Aufgabenverständnisses nach dem Zweiten Weltkrieg," in Radkau and Uekötter, *Naturschutz und Nationalsozialismus,* 418.

52. See Otto Kraus, "Primat der Landschaft," in Kraus, *Zerstörung der Natur,* 10–13; Lienenkämper, "Gedanken," *Verhandlungen* (1949): 33; Koch, "Hemmungen," *Verhandlungen* (1948): 13. The David against Goliath metaphor is mentioned in Kühn, "Natur und Wirtschaft," *Verhandlungen* (1955): 40. On its use in attracting sympathetic media coverage see Engels, *Naturpolitik,* 198–99, 412.

53. Zeller, *Straße,* 228ff.; Körner, *Theorie,* 86–87.

54. See comments by Otto Kraus in *Verhandlungen* (1949): 45. On the scientification of conservation and environmentalism in the US see Samuel Hays, *A History of Environmental Politics Since 1945* (Pittsburgh: Pittsburgh University Press, 2000), chap. 11. On the relationship between scientific expertise and environmental politics see Bocking, *Nature's Experts.*

55. Kragh, "Der Beitrag der Naturschutzstellen," 24 October 1950, BAK B 245/153; Otto Kraus, "Vom Naturschutz unserer Zeit," *N & L* 26, no. 1/2 (1951): 4; Aldo Leopold, "The Land Ethic," in *A Sand County Almanac* (New York: Oxford University Press, 1949; Ballantine, 1966), 237–64.

56. Körner, "Entwicklung des Naturschutzes," in Brüggemeier and Engels, *Natur– und Umweltschutz,* 90–92; and more extensive, Körner, *Theorie,* 99ff.

57. Mitman, "In Search of Health," 184–89; Herbert Offner, opening remarks, *Verhandlungen* (1955): 22–24; Mrass, *Organisation,* 8; Wey, *Umweltpolitik,* 198; Körner, *Theorie,* 99ff. Engels, *Naturpolitik,* 86–93, is skeptical of the view that landscape care was modernized by these economic and scientific emphases.

58. Engels, *Naturpolitik,* chap. 1.

59. Helge May, "Hundert Jahre für Mensch und Natur. Ein Streifzug durch die Geschichte des NABU," <http://www.nabu.de/nh/199/history100.htm> (accessed 10 August 2000); Anna-Katharina Wöbse, "Lina Hähnle und der Reichsbund für Vogelschutz: Soziale Bewegung im Gleichschritt," in Radkau and Uekötter, *Naturschutz und Nationalsozialismus,* 309–28; Erich Ficker (Soviet Zone) to Hermann Hähnle, 10 December 1946, <http://www.nabu.de/nabu/history/sbz1946.htm> (accessed 10 August 2000); Dominick, *Environmental Movement,* 83, 102–4, 122–24, 249, n. 8.

60. Ernst Hoplitschek, "Der Bund Naturschutz in Bayern. Traditioneller Naturschutzverband oder Teil der neuen sozialen Bewegungen? (PhD diss., Free University of Berlin, 1984), 93–95, 117, 140–43; Dominick, *Environmental Movement,* 49–51, 55–56, 104, 123–24.

61. Engels, *Naturpolitik,* 162–64, 177–80; Anna-Katharina Wöbse, "Zur Visuellen Geschichte der Naturschutz– und Umweltbewegung," in Brüggemeier and Engels, *Natur– und Umweltschutz,* 237–38.

62. Jens Tönnießen and Gottfried Vauk, "Heide statt Kanonendonner," *Nationalpark,* no. 74 (January 1992): 21; Hans Klose to Friedrich Kantak, 17 December 1946; Klose to

Erich Künstler, 1 February 1947, both in BAK B 245/252. See also Herbert Ecke, "Truppenübungen in Naturschutzgebieten," *Verhandlungen* (1949): 46–48; and clippings in BAK B 245/83.

63. On plans for a national park see Lutz Heck (Reich Forest Office) to Carl Duve, 31 March 1942, Verein Naturschutzpark Archive, Niederhaverbeck, Lüneburg Heath, binder labeled "VNP Landschaftspflege/Einzelverfahren, Bereisungen" (hereafter VNP Archive, "VNP Landschaftspflege/Einzelverfahren, Bereisungen"). On plans to drill for oil see Reich Forest Master (Göring) to President, District of Lüneburg, 6 January 1940; Hans Klose to Reich Forest Master, 10 February 1940, both in BAK B 245/82. Wartime developments are discussed in Hans Domizlaff, "Die volkspsychologische Dringlichkeit des Naturschutzproblems," *Naturschutz* 25, no. 3 (1944): 39; Domizlaff, editorial, *Naturschutzparke* (December 1947): 2.

64. Wilhelm Carl-Mardorf, "Die Lüneburger Heide," *Naturschutzparke*, no. 3 (1955): 59; Henning Eichberg, "Stimmung über der Heide," in Großklaus and Oldemeyer, *Natur als Gegenwelt*, 197–208; Lütkepohl and Tönnießen, *Naturschutzpark Lüneburger Heide*, 28–33.

65. Dominick, *Environmental Movement*, 54–55, 98, 104–5; Lütkepohl and Tönnießen, *Naturschutzpark Lüneburger Heide*, 30–37; Knaut, *Zurück zur Natur!*, 378–82.

66. *Gauleiter* Telschow to Walther Keller [honorary VNP president, publisher of *Kosmos*], 3 January 1942, BAK B 245/82.

67. On denazification see Domizlaff, editorial, *Naturschutzpark* (December 1947): 3–4; Dominick, *Environmental Movement*, 120; Goerke to Heinz Appel, 1 November 1947, BAK B 245/83. On efforts to remove Domizlaff and adopt a more democratic charter see BAK B 245/83.

68. Hans Domizlaff, editorial, *Naturschutzpark* (May 1952): 1.

69. "Naturschutzpark in Gefahr. Wieder Truppenmanöver am Wilseder Berg," *Hamburger Echo*, 7 December 1948, clipping in BAK B 245/83.

70. "Dem Herz der Heide droht Verwüstung," *Hamburger Freie Presse*, 1 July 1950; Claus Lafrenz, "Dringender Hilferuf aus der Lüneburger Heide," *Die Welt*, 3 July 1954, clippings in BAK B 245/83; Alfred Toepfer, "Der Tätigkeitsbericht des Vorsitzenden," *Naturschutzparke* (Winter 1954/1955): 17–18; Lütkepohl and Tönnießen, *Naturschutzpark Lüneburger Heide*, 138.

71. Max Kochskämper to Hans Domizlaff, 4 June 1952, BAK B 245/83.

72. Hans Mommsen and Winfried Marx, "Alfred Toepfer in der deutschen Politik von 1913 bis 1945," in *Alfred Toepfer: Stifter und Kaufman; Bausteine einer Biographie—Kritische Bestandsaufnahme*, ed. Georg Kreis, Gerd Krumeich, Henri Ménudier, Hans Mommsen, and Arnold Sywottek (Hamburg: Christians, 2000), 29–84, quote on p. 37.

73. Kurt Conrad, "60 Jahre Alpenpark," *Naturschutz– und Naturparke* (Second Quarter, 1974): 74–80; Lütkepohl and Tönnießen, *Naturschutzpark Lüneburger Heide*, 42; Engels, *Naturpolitik*, 102–3.

74. "Der Heidepark im Spiegel der Presse," *Naturschutzparke* (Autumn 1954): 8–9; Toepfer, "Tätigkeitsbericht," *Naturschutzparke* (Winter 1954/1955): 17.

75. "Der Heidepark im Spiegel der Presse," *Naturschutzparke* (Autumn 1954): 8–9; Lafrenz, "Dringender Hilferuf," *Die Welt*, 3 July 1954, clipping in BAK B 245/83.

76. Toepfer, "Tätigkeitsbericht," *Naturschutzparke* (Winter 1954/1955): 17–18.

77. Deutscher Bundestag. 94 Sitzung, Bonn, 6 July 1955, pp. 5311–12; "Aussicht auf Panzer–Ruhe in der Heide," *Hamburger Abendblatt*, 7 July 1955, clipping in BAK B 245/83.

78. An enthusiastic communist in the 1920s, Wehner later settled on the conservative side of the West German SPD, leading the party in supporting the Godesberg Program of 1959, which abandoned revolutionary rhetoric for a more moderate stance.

79. *Harburger Anzeiger und Nachrichten,* 25 June 1956, typed copy in BAK B 245/83. On the symbolism of fire see Engels, *Naturpolitik,* 188.

80. Tönnießen and Vauk, "Heide statt Kanonendonner," *Nationalpark,* no. 74 (January 1992): 19–23; Lütkepohl and Tönnießen, *Naturschutzpark Lüneburger Heide,* 137–40; Tönnießen to the author, June 20, 1994.

81. Konrad H. Jarausch, Hinrich C. Seeba, and David Conradt, "The Presence of the Past. Culture, Opinion, and Identity in Germany," in *After Unity: Reconfiguring German Identities* (Providence: Berghahn, 1997), 40–41; ed. Jarausch, *Recivilizing Germans,* chap. 5.

82. Toepfer quoted in Lafrenz, "Dringender Hilferuf," *Die Welt,* 3 July 1954, clipping in BAK B 245/83.

83. Dominick, *Environmental Movement,* 134–35, 144, 169–79; Brüggemeier, *Tschernobyl,* 194; Bergmeier, *Umweltgeschichte,* chap. 3; Rommelspacher, "Zwischen Heimatschutz und Umweltprotest," 75–84; Ueköter, *Rauchplage,* 410; Zeller, *Straße,* 286. On styles of activism see Engels, *Naturpolitik,* chap. 4.

84. United States Office of Military Government for Germany (hereafter OMGUS), Special Report of the Military Governor, *The German Forest Resources Survey* (1 October 1948): 5.

85. Kurt Borchers, *Der Wald als deutsches Volksgut* (Lüneburg: Im Kinau, 1948), 53; OMGUS, *A Year of Potsdam: The German Economy Since the Surrender* (Washington, DC: U.S. Government Printing Office, 1946), 69–70.

86. SDW, "Niederschrift über die Sitzung des Hauptvorstandes und der Vertreter der Landesverbände am 30. Mai 1949 in Frankfurt a./M," p. 6, BAK B 245/230.

87. OMGUS, *German Forest Resources Survey* (1 October 1948), 6–8; Borchers, *Wald,* 25–39; Rubner, "Naturschutz, Forstwirtschaft und Umwelt," 110–16; Curt Meine, *Aldo Leopold: His Life and Work* (Madison: University of Wisconsin Press, 1988), 353–54; Arvid Nelson, *Cold War Ecology. Forests, Farms, and People in the East German Landscape, 1945–1989* (New Haven: Yale University Press, 2005), 16–22, 34–37; Küster, *Geschichte des Waldes,* 185–95; Scott, *Seeing Like a State,* 11–22.

88. OMGUS, *German Forest Resources Survey* (1 October 1948): 2, 6–7; Nelson, *Cold War Ecology,* 43.

89. Institut für Besatzungsfragen, *Einwirkung der Besatzungsmächte auf die Westdeutsche Wirtschaft* (Tübingen: Institut für Besatzungsfragen, 1949), 99–109. The British cut 348.4 percent of annual growth over this three year period compared with 285 percent in the French zone and 188.9 percent in the American zone. But the British scaled back overcutting each year, dropping from 419 percent in 1946 to 250 percent in 1948. The French, by contrast, increased harvests, felling 380 percent of annual growth in 1948. On the French compare Freda Utley, *The High Cost of Vengeance* (Chicago: Henry Regnery, 1949), 278–79 and *Einwirkung,* with the more sympathetic view in Frank Roy Willis, *The French in Germany, 1945–1949* (Stanford: Stanford University Press, 1962), 138–39. On the Soviet Zone see Nelson, *Cold War Ecology,* chap. 3.

90. Institut für Besatzungsfragen, *Einwirkung,* 105.

91. Document 16, "2. Sitzung des Zonenbeirats der britischen besetzten Zone," 26–27 March 1946, item 19, "Erhaltung des Waldes," in *Akten zur Vorgeschichte der Bundesrepublik Deutschland 1945–1949,* ed. Bundesarchiv and Institut für Zeitgeschichte, vol. 1, *September 1945–Dezember 1946,* ed. Walter Vogel and Christoph Weisz (Munich: Oldenbourg, 1976), 372–74. Among the ten committee members were Hinrich Wilhelm Kopf, *Oberpräsident* of Hanover; Dr. Schlange–Schöningen, Director of the Central Office for Food and Agriculture; and Robert Lehr, *Oberpräsident* of North Rhine Province.

92. Hinrich Wilhelm Kopf's report, "Erhaltung des deutschen Waldes," 26 April 1946, BAK B 245/230; Document 19, "3. Sitzung des Zonenbeirats der britischen besetzten Zone,"

2–3 March 1946, item 43, "Bericht des Forstausschusses," in Bundesarchiv and Institut für Zeitgeschichte, *Vorgeschichte der Bundesrepublik Deutschland*, vol. 1, 465–67, and notes 58–63.

93. Document 27, "6. Sitzung des Zonenbeirats der britischen besetzten Zone," 14–15 August 1946, item 135, "Bericht des Forstausschusses," in Bundesarchiv and Institut für Zeitgeschichte, *Vorgeschichte der Bundesrepublik Deutschland*, vol. 1, 694, n. 118.

94. "Holzhacker in Uniform," *Spiegel*, 22 February 1947, 15.

95. Kurt Borchers to Heinz Appel, 29 September 1947, BAK B245/230. See also [Borchers?], "Aus einem Schreiben des braunschweigischen Landesbeauftragter für Naturschutz," 7 March 1947, BAK B 245/230; Karl Oberkirch to several city managers, 10 December 1946, BAK B 245/230; Gert Kragh, circular letter to commissioners, Lower Saxony, 15 December 1946, BAK B 245/153.

96. Kurt Borchers, "Das Schicksal des deutschen Waldes," 18 October 1946, BAK B 245/230.

97. Kragh, "Naturschutz und Landschaftspflege––oder Katastrophe!" 13 January 1947, BAK B 245/153.

98. Document 32A, "Ministerpräsidentenkonferenz München," 6–7 June 1947, item 10b, "Diskussion über die Referate zur deutschen Wirtschaftsnot, Wald–und Holzfrage," in *Akten zur Vorgeschichte der Bundesrepublik Deutschland 1945–1949*, ed. Bundesarchiv and Institut für Zeitgeschichte, vol. 2, *Januar 1947–Juni 1947*, ed. Wolfram Werner (Munich: Oldenbourg, 1982), 545–47.

99. Borchers, *Wald*, 67–73. See also SDW, *Uns ruft der Wald. Ein Buch deutscher Dichter und Waldfreunde* (Rheinhausen: Verlagsanstalt Rheinhausen, 1949). On German attitudes toward the occupation see Barbara Marshall, "German Attitudes to British Military Government 1945–1947," *Journal of Contemporary History* 15 (1980): 655–84; Josef Fochepoth, "German Reaction to Defeat and Occupation," in Moeller, *West Germany under Construction*, 73–89.

100. "British Defend Use of German Timber," *New York Times*, 25 August 1947, 4; Jack Raymond, "Ruhr Coal Output faces New Hitch," *New York Times*, 12 December 1947, 11; Clay, *Decision in Germany*, 193–95; OMGUS, *Statistical Annex to the Report of the Military Governor*, no. 29 (July 1949): 204; Institut für Besatzungsfragen, *Einwirkung*, 99.

101. On the choice of Robert Lehr as president see "Hornsmann erinnert sich: Die Gründerjahre der SDW," *Unser Wald* 39, no. 5 (1987): 173. Over his long public service career, Lehr was mayor of Düsseldorf (1924–1933), a founding member of the CDU, *Oberpräsident* of North Rhine Province, a member of the state parliament of North Rhine-Westphalia (1947–1950), and Federal Minister of the Interior (1950–1953).

102. "Protokoll der Gründungs–Versammlung und ersten Arbeitstagung der 'Schutzgemeinschaft Deutscher Wald,' Bad Honnef," 5 December 1947, BAK B 245/230.

103. Lucius Clay to NOCE, 24 May 1947, CC 9296 "Secret," in *The Papers of General Lucius D. Clay, Germany 1945–1949*, vol. 1, ed. Jean Edward Smith (Bloomington: Indiana University Press, 1974): 366–67; Jack Raymond, "U.S. Britain Clash on German Timber," *New York Times*, 18 April 1948, 15.

104. SDW, "Niederschrift über die Mitgliederversammlung des Hauptverbandes am 31. Mai 1949 in Frankfurt am Main," BAK B 245/230; "Hornsmann erinnert sich," *Unser Wald* 39, no. 5 (1987): 173–74.

105. SDW, "Protokoll der Gründungs–Versammlung," 5 December 1947; pamphlet entitled, "Der deutsche Wald ist in Gefahr!" n.d. [December 1947?], both in BAK B 245/230. On chapter activities see descriptions in BAK B 245/231. Among SDW films is "Der Wald braucht junge Freunde," [late 1950s?], directed by Vera Meyendriesch, film #249, Film Archiv, Auswertungs– und Informationsdienst für Ernährung, Landwirtschaft und Forsten, Bonn–Bad Godesberg (hereafter AID Film Archiv).

106. "Der Wald unser Schicksal," *Grünes Blatt* (November 1948): 5–6. See guides to other exhibits in BAK B 245/230.

107. Statement about goals, *Grünes Blatt* (November 1948): 7.

108. SDW, *Uns ruft der Wald*, 10. See also "Der Wald im Märchen," *Grünes Blatt* (December 1948): 7–9.

109. Erich Hornsmann, "Radio Stuttgart Sendung 'Die Landvernichtung in der Welt,'" *Grünes Blatt* (September 1949): 2–4, among several of his articles in *Grünes Blatt*.

110. SDW, "Protokoll der Gründungs–Versammlung," 5 December 1947; SDW, "Der deutsche Wald ist in Gefahr!" pamphlet, n.d. [December 1947?], both in BAK B 245/230. On efforts to engage the youth see Karl Korfsmeier, "Der Wald im Schulunterricht," *Grünes Blatt* (March 1949): 2; Johannes Sigmond, "Jugend und Walderneuerung," *Grünes Blatt* (November 1948): 9.

111. On how the oak acquired significance in Germany as a symbol of freedom during the French Revolution and of national unity later in the nineteenth century see Annemarie Hürlimann, "Die Eiche, heiliger Baum deutscher Nation," in *Waldungen. Die Deutschen und Ihr Wald*, ed. Bernd Weyergraf (Berlin: Nicolaische Verlagsbuchhandlung, 1987), 62–9; and Küster, *Geschichte des Waldes*, 176–84.

112. SDW, "Merkblatt zur Durchführung des 'Tag des Baumes,'" 10 March 1952; "Jahresbericht 1954 des Landesverbandes Rheinland–Pfalz der SDW," 21 March 1955, both in BAK B 245/231.

113. Lehr's speech is excerpted in "Westdeutschland feiert den 'Tag des Baumes,'" *Nachrichtenblatt für Naturschutz* 23, no. 5/6 (May/June 1952): 13. Adenauer is quoted in "Treubekenntnis zum deutschen Wald," *Unser Wald*, no. 3 (1953), in BAK B 245/231.

114. The poll is referenced in "Zur Erhaltung des Wildbestandes. Ergebnisse einer Bevölkerungs–Umfrage," May 1955, BAK B 245/242.

115. Oberkrome, *"Deutsche Heimat,"* 429–30.

116. Engels, *Naturpolitik*, 23, 418.

117. Hans Klose, file notes for DNR founding meeting, 26 August 1950; Klose, "Aufruf zur Bildung des Deutschen Naturschutzrings," 20 May 1950, both in BAK B 245/236; "Zur Begründung des Deutschen Naturschutzrings," *Verhandlungen* (1950): 125–26. See also Martin Leonhard, *Umweltverbände: zur Organisation von Umweltschutzinteressen in der Bundesrepublik Deutschland* (Opladen: Westdeutscher Verlag, 1986), 63, 133–36; Oberkrome, *"Deutsche Heimat,"* 417–20; Engels, *Naturpolitik*, 23.

118. Hans Klose to Erich Griebel, 22 September 1950, BAK B 245/251; Klose to Professor Dr. Eberhard Stechow, 3 January 1951, BAK B 245/255; Wey, *Umweltpolitik*, 168–69; Deutscher Naturschutzring, *25 Jahre Deutscher Naturschutzring* (Siegburg: Buch- und Offsetdruckerei Daemisch-Mohr, 1976), 9. On finances see DNR *Rundschreiben*, no. 18 (6 December 1954): 2, in BAK B 245/236.

119. Hans Krieg, "Vom Sinn des Naturschutzes," *Verhandlungen* (1950): 103–6; Krieg, "Naturschutz––eine Schicksalsfrage," *Kosmos* 50, no. 10 (1954): 486.

120. Wolfgang Engelhardt, "Fünf 'Offene Worte' zur Lage," *N & L* 31, no. 1 (1956): 17–20; DNR *Rundschreiben*, no. 10 (18 March 1953): 1, in BAK B 245/236.

121. Wolfgang Engelhardt, *Naturschutz: seine wichtigsten Grundlagen und Forderungen* (Munich: Bayerischer Schulbuch Verlag, 1954), 4. See also Potthast, "Naturschutz und Naturwissenschaft," in Frohn and Schmoll, *Natur und Staat*, 401–2.

122. Dominick *Environmental Movement*, 140–43; Lienenkämper, *Grüne Welt*, 96–104; Wey, *Umweltpolitik*, 66, 173, 180; Brüggemeier, *Tschernobyl*, 187–88; Knud Ahlborn, "Feststellungen zur 'Ölpest,'" *N & L* 28, no. 7 (1953): 106–7; Wolfgang Engelhardt, "Gefährdung des Grundwassers durch Mineralölprodukte," *Kosmos* 57, no. 4 (1961): *132–*34.

123. Küppers, Lundgreen, and Weingart, *Umweltforschung*, 102–3; Wey, *Umweltpolitik*, 156–57, 178–79; Dominick, *Environmental Movement*, 141; Lienenkämper, *Grüne Welt*, 72–73, 103.

124. On collaboration between the leaders of private conservation groups and public officials see Oberkrome, *"Deutsche Heimat,"* 437–511. See also Engels, *Naturpolitik*, 51–53.

125. Georg Fahrbach, a former member of the back-to-nature youth movement, presided over the Swabian Alb Society, the German Youth Hostel Enterprise, and the League of German Mountaineering and Hiking Societies. In 1952, he and Karl Arnold (CDU), Minister–President of North Rhine-Westphalia (1949–1956) and head of the German *Heimat* League, formed the Working Association of German *Heimat*, Hiking, and Conservation Organizations (including the DNR). On Hans Klose and Hans Krieg's criticisms of the merger see BAK B 245/235.

126. Schutzgemeinschaft Deutsches Wild, *Leitsätze, Geschäftsordnung, Satzung der Schutzgemeinschaft Deutsches Wild* (Munich: Selbstverlag Schutzgemeinschaft Deutsches Wild, 1952), 4-7; DNR *Rundschreiben Neue Folge*, no. 18 (20 September 1968). On Burhenne's rise to prominence in international conservation in the 1950s see Anna-Katharina Wöbse, "Naturschutz global—oder: Hilfe von außen. Internationale Beziehungen des amtlichen Naturschutzes im 20. Jahrhundert," in Frohn and Schmoll, *Natur und Staat*, 681, 704.

127. On West Germany's involvement in international conservation organizations in the 1950s see Wöbse, "Naturschutz global," in Frohn and Schmoll, *Natur und Staat*, 672–90.

128. See Hans Klose to Hans Krieg, 15 December 1952; Krieg to Klose, 23 December 1952, both in BAK B 245/235.

129. Körner, "Entwicklung des Naturschutzes," in Brüggemeier und Engels, *Natur– und Umweltschutz*, 87–102; Blackbourn, *Conquest*, 330; Küppers, Lundgreen, and Weingart, *Umweltforschung*, 25–26, 80ff.

130. Potthast, "Wissenschaftliche Ökologie," in Radkau and Uekötter, *Naturschutz und Nationalsozialismus*, 240–41, 246–48; Wolfgang Haber, interview by author, 20 June 1992. On developments in ecology in the US during the 1950s see Worster, "Ecology of Order and Chaos," in *Wealth of Nature*, 156–70; Michael Barbour, "Ecological Fragmentation in the Fifties," in Cronon, *Uncommon Ground*, 233–55, 510–18; Bocking, *Ecologists and Environmental Politics*, 68–76.

131. Uekötter, *Natur im Aufbruch*, illustrates measured successes in North Rhine-Westphalia. Bergmeier, *Umweltgeschichte*, is less optimistic about developments in Bavaria.

Chapter 3

PRESERVING THE
WUTACH GORGE IN THE 1950s*

After twelve years of Nazi dictatorship and four years of Allied occupation, West Germans were reluctant to enter the public sphere of their restored democracy. They registered their political apathy in "no opinion" or "don't know" answers to public opinion polls and adopted an *ohne mich* (without me) attitude, retreating to the sanctuary of home, family, and the local community.[1] And yet scholars have shown that the conservative, paternalistic 1950s were a critical incubation period in the re-emergence of a civil society, a view reinforced by the following case study of activism to protect nature-as-*Heimat* in the southwestern state of Baden-Württemberg (pop. 1950: 6.4 million). In the early 1950s, conservation officials and a broad coalition of 80,000 citizens launched a successful protest to rescue the Wutach River and Gorge—"a natural wonder" of the Black Forest homeland—from being developed by the powerful utility company, *Schluchseewerk Aktiengesellschaft* (SSW). As supporters of nature and homeland protection squared off against SSW in a debate that lasted throughout the 1950s, both sides relied on recently reinstated democratic institutions to advance their views of how nature should be used to achieve the greatest public good. At the end of the decade, Baden's "homeland-loving loyal citizens" expressed relief that their involvement in the democratic process paid off: the Wutach River was spared and the scenic gorge remained preserved. Moreover, through their activism, they contributed to the rebuilding of a civic culture that expected and respected the protection of citizens' rights.

The Wutach conflict illustrates the possibilities and limitations of traditional preservation in the face of unprecedented economic growth. In terms of goals, rhetoric, and strategy, the campaign to save the Wutach had far more in common with early twentieth century homeland preservation than with the urban based grass roots initiatives of the 1970s. Those leading the movement appealed to the ideals traditionally associated with *Heimat,* uniting thousands of individuals in their attachment to the nature that gave the region its charm and supported the livelihood of local farmers and entrepreneurs. Defenders of the Wutach embraced *Heimat* preservation as a familiar way to express alarm over the transformation of their region by industrial development and population growth over the last half century, and by rapid postwar rebuilding that brought more industry and housing, dams and reservoirs, power lines and pollution. By framing their fight as a moral battle to protect "pristine" nature from being defiled by the materialism and greed of modern civilization, conservationists hoped to give their local conflict universal dimensions.[2]

In their strategies, too, leaders of the campaign mimicked preservationists of previous decades. Individuals prominent in their local communities built a broad coalition of middle and upper middle class civic organizations, cooperated closely with officials to work through layers of bureaucracy, and turned to the state government in Stuttgart—in their view a party that ought to be neutral—to settle their case judiciously.[3] Largely because the conflict was played out at the state and local levels, not at the national level where regional preservationists had limited means to influence decision making, they experienced some success. Yet as the Wutach controversy captures so well, not only during the Miracle Years but for most of the twentieth century, conservationists tended to settle for small victories that did little to slow the advance of industry. Indeed, although SSW failed in its bid to tap into the Wutach, one of many tributaries of the Rhine, it was a small price to pay in pursuit of more lucrative projects in the region.

The Wutach Between Weimar Democracy and Nazi Dictatorship

At the heart of the Wutach controversy was a scenic gorge, a geological marvel created some 70,000 years ago, when glacial water from Feldberg Mountain diverged from its original eastward path as part of the Danube and gradually forced its way to the southwest to become a tributary of another river system, the Rhine. On its new route to the Rhine, the Wutach dropped 400 meters in little more than thirty-eight kilometers. With tremendous force at the point of its sharp diversion southwest, the river eroded away layers of rock that lay behind it. Over centuries the water and debris it carried carved out the deep gorge that extends thirty kilometers between the towns of Achdorf and Neustadt.

When warmer spring weather melts the snow that has covered the peaks and slopes of the sub-alpine mountains of the Black Forest, the streams that feed the

Wutach swell into floodwaters that rush through the narrow gorge, crashing against the steep stone walls, loosening rock and clearing away sand and gravel. Where high water has washed up sediment and deposited it on the shores, wild grasses thrive, but gradually these spaces will make room for alder and willow trees and eventually, for deciduous forests of ash, alder, sycamore, and mountain elm. Because of the humid climate and varied terrain, flora and fauna typically not found together are concentrated in the gorge. Over 100 species of birds inhabit the area, as well as a multitude of insects, reptiles, rare amphibians, and small mammals. Until the latter nineteenth century, the Wutach was one of central Europe's finest fishing streams. But in the late 1800s the paper factory of Neustadt began dumping its effluents into the Wutach, endangering its population of trout and other fish. Annual spring floods aided the river's natural purification process, but improvement in the quality of the water came only in the mid 1950s when Neustadt installed treatment facilities. Even then, the problem persisted well into the late 1970s when the city installed a wastewater treatment plant that provided full biological purification.[4]

The early postwar conflict over the Wutach Gorge was actually the continuation of a debate begun nearly two decades earlier when *Schluchseewerk* was established by the state-owned *Badenwerk* and one of Germany's utility giants, the Ruhr-based *Rheinisch-Westfälisches Elektrizitätswerk* (RWE). In fact, SSW's creation in 1928 was a small part of the much larger story of organizing electricity production more efficiently in Germany to respond to the rising demand after World War I. Between 1913 and 1927, electricity consumption in Germany increased fourfold. South Germany's "white coal," or hydropower, seemed essential in helping to meet this growing demand, all the more so because the country had surrendered 40 percent of its coalfields in the Versailles treaty. Thus, the 1920s witnessed the coming together of private and publicly owned local and regional electricity suppliers to form mighty combines, among them RWE. RWE competed with other powerful combines in linking its coal-fired plants in the north with hydroplants in the south, creating a vast north-south network. But in 1927, RWE conceded Bavaria to its Prussian-based competitors, concentrating on Baden in the southwest. The following year RWE and *Badenwerk* established SSW to exploit the 620 meter drop between Lake Schluchsee and the Rhine to generate electricity at times of peak demand. Peak-load facilities like SSW perform a vital role in any large electric power grid, in this case the network linking coal-fired plants in the Ruhr with hydroplants on the Upper Rhine.[5]

When SSW's parent company, *Badenwerk*, presented the Baden parliament with its proposal to create SSW, it offered an unwritten "gentleman's agreement" to leave the Wutach alone in exchange for developing Lake Schluchsee—a minor concession to local preservationists who were then campaigning to protect the river and gorge. Parliamentarians approved the creation of SSW, but they also responded to pressure from preservationists by unanimously approving a resolution to establish a nature reserve in the Wutach-Gauchach Valley.[6] Yet it was a token gesture in light of the trend in Germany and other industrialized nations in the 1920s to build more and bigger dams to help meet the rising demand for electricity and water.

Ten years passed before the Wutach was protected, partly because of opposition from forestry officials and property owners who feared restrictions on land use, and from local leaders like the mayor of Neustadt, who anticipated the imposition of costly cleanup measures on the town's polluting paper mill that provided a living for 400 people.[7] Although the Reich Nature Protection Law of 1935 gave preservationists greater leverage to confiscate property, in the Wutach case they relied on agreements with land owners, avoiding the legal disputes that might have accompanied outright dispossession. Finally in 1939, Baden's Ministry of Culture and Education (as the state office responsible for conservation), with the approval of the Reich's highest conservation office under Göring, issued an ordinance establishing a 579 hectare nature reserve around the Wutach Gorge. The protected area extended from the lower Gutach River to just below the confluence of the Wutach and Gauchach Rivers. In the early 1940s, however, the same supreme conservation office that made possible the gorge's protection did an about-face, approving SSW's plans, which threatened to compromise the reserve.[8]

SSW proposed to increase its production of electricity by drawing water from several small feeder streams of the Rhine, among them the Alb, Murg, and Ibach to the west of Schluchsee, and the Wutach to the east. The most controversial part of SSW's plan, finalized in early 1942, was its intention to install a dam in the nature reserve where the Haslach and Gutach rivers converged and flowed into the Wutach. The two arms of the V-shaped reservoir would have extended approximately four kilometers up the Haslach and Gutach, leaving the upper end of the nature reserve along the Gutach under water. Most troubling to conservationists was SSW's proposal to drain water from the reservoir and direct it through an underground tunnel to the power station at Witznau, a move, they rightly feared, that would critically reduce the amount of water that fed into the Wutach River and drain the "living element" from the gorge.[9] Standing behind paragraph 20 of the RNG, which required authorities to consult preservation authorities before approving measures that might significantly alter the landscape, Baden conservation officials stalled SSW's project for a year and forced the utility company to modify its plan: rather than drain 83 percent of the water from the Wutach, SSW would tap "only" around 65 percent.[10]

But SSW's project was enthusiastically endorsed by the General Inspector for Water and Energy, Albert Speer and the Reich governor and *Gauleiter* of Baden, Robert Wagner. Late in 1942, Wagner suspended normal bureaucratic procedures and deprived lower-level preservation officials of their decision-making power, appealing to the supreme preservation office in Berlin to intervene directly in support of SSW's project, which was, he insisted, of decisive military importance. Under pressure from Speer's office, the Reich Conservation Office under Göring overruled Baden officials, declaring in March 1943 that it would "put aside the concerns of nature preservation in this particular instance" and permit SSW to go ahead with its expansion. The timing of the decision was no coincidence; it came just weeks after the Sixth Army's crushing defeat at Stalingrad and in the wake of Nazi Propaganda Minister Joseph Goebbels's famous speech calling for "total war."[11] The March 1943 decision placed some restrictions on SSW's use of the Wutach based on recommendations by Alwin Seifert, the landscape architect dispatched to the Wutach to conduct what local preservationists considered to be a superficial investigation of the area.[12] Even after the supreme preservation office handed down its decision, preservationists like Klose worked behind the scenes to recruit influential Nazis to their cause. In 1943, they enlisted the ardent National Socialist and poet Ludwig Finckh to win over Heinrich Himmler, but the SS leader was too preoccupied with implementing the "Final Solution" to intervene.[13] Ultimately, the war brought SSW's expansion to a temporary halt.

Building a "People's Movement" to Save the Wutach, 1949–1954

SSW did not proceed with plans for the Wutach until 1949. In the meantime, however, the company invested substantial sums of money expanding the Witznau power station and beginning construction of the Waldshut facility to accommodate the eventual addition of water from the Wutach. By the late 1940s, the core of SSW's pumped-storage installations consisted of three power stations and reservoirs at different elevations: Häusern, in use since the early 1930s; Witznau, operational in 1943; and Waldshut, completed in 1953. Each of these stations included turbines capable of pumping water from the Rhine and the reservoirs at Witznau and Häusern through underground tunnels back up to Schluchsee and other storage areas where the water would be held until demand required that it be released to generate electricity.[14]

When SSW began underground drilling in the Wutach nature reserve as a preliminary step in completing its plans, it claimed to have permission to do so with the decision Göring's office delivered in 1943. Throughout the 1950s, however, officials disagreed on whether or not the approval granted in 1943, in a time of total war, remained valid. As will be seen, the uncertainty that surrounded this issue benefited conservationists. By confusing district officials and causing disagreement among state ministries, the questionable validity of the 1943 decision meant repeated delays for SSW in securing the license it needed to pursue its project.

The bureaucratic wrangling so characteristic of this and other conflicts over resource use was evident from the start. In February 1950, South Baden's (formerly Baden)[15] superior conservation office moved to block SSW from proceeding any further by declaring the 1943 ruling invalid and reminding the company that the 1939 ordinance protecting the area remained in effect. SSW responded by filing suit in administrative court in Freiburg and lodging a complaint with South Baden's president, Leo Wohleb (CDU). Although SSW would not be easily deterred in completing its expansion plans, conservation officials used the administrative options available to reopen the debate.[16] In a lengthy statement justifying the measures taken by the superior conservation office, Karl Asal, the able jurist who oversaw preservation in Baden's ministry of culture since 1936, argued that SSW never properly secured legal approval to use the river. Indeed, only after a public hearing in which the company's clearly laid out plans for the Wutach were approved by the district government in Neustadt would SSW be able to claim it had the right to use the river. In the "atmosphere created by total war," Asal contended, the Reich Conservation Office in Berlin had decided the fate of the Wutach without adequately assessing the impact SSW's plans would have on the water supply or the nature reserve. But times had changed since 1943. "Everywhere in Germany, particularly in Baden," he wrote, conveying the worries of conservationists at the time, "technology's intrusions in nature . . . have increased in number and severity," making places such as the Wutach that have remained in "relatively untouched condition" all the more precious. In choosing between protecting the Wutach with its "primeval character," "impressive beauty," unique geology, and species diversity, or supporting a company with an unfavorable record in developing other rivers of the Black Forest, the decision seemed obvious. "Technology [SSW]," Asal moralized, "must learn to recognize its limits" and abandon its plan to tamper with this "unique natural treasure."[17]

Conservation officials were not alone in using the available administrative options to obstruct SSW's expansion. The Society of Those Affected by the Construction and Operation of *Schluchseewerk*, an organization formed in 1928 by communities, businessmen, and farmers seeking financial redress for material losses caused by the company's expansion, doubted the government's ability to make objective decisions where SSW was concerned. The alliance's spokesman, retired building official Theodor Röttges, bluntly informed President Wohleb in October 1950 that the government could hardly claim to be a disinterested party because the state-owned *Badenwerk* possessed 30 percent (37 percent after 1952) of its daughter company, *Schluchseewerk*. Particularly disconcerting was the potential conflict of interest for South Baden's Minister of Finance, Dr. Wilhelm Eckert (CDU), who also served as chairman of the board of directors of *Badenwerk*. This arrangement, however, was not unusual for the utilities industry where public, private, and hybrid firms coexisted. In Bavaria, too, *Bayernwerk* was state owned until 1994, a reflection of a utopian view in the early twentieth century that public utilities were preferable to companies privately owned by "profit-seeking" monopolists.[18]

In December 1950, SSW began the process of securing official approval to draw water from the Murg and the Ibach. It appeared that the company would do the same with the Wutach, especially after the state government overruled conservation officials and allowed the decision of 1943 to remain in effect. The government's decision reflected postwar shortages of energy, not only in Germany but throughout Europe. Continued underproduction of coal required expanding other sources of energy, and in mountainous regions that meant more hydroprojects. For this reason, *Bayernwerk* pushed through its controversial plan (despite sabotage by locals) to divert the Rißbach into Walchensee, an Alpine lake that had been converted into a reservoir in the 1920s and that already had drawn significant amounts of water from the Isar River. For this reason, France's government owned *Electricité de France* installed an arch dam on the Isère River at Tignes in Savoy (1952), despite sabotage by peasants who were relocated. Similar hydroprojects, protested by locals, were completed in Tirol in Austria (1952) and in Rheinau, near Zurich, Switzerland (1952–1954).[19] Capturing the prevailing mindset in Europe and West Germany at the time, the conservative newspaper *Die Welt* declared that "too many advantages" and energy demands were at stake for the state to block SSW.[20]

Just when it seemed that the utility company had cleared the major hurdles in its way, the state administrative court in Freiburg ruled in 1951 in an unrelated case that granting an exception to standard bureaucratic procedure in no way gave a party the right "to undertake decisive action" on construction. This decision reinforced conservationists' position that the 1943 decision did not give SSW approval to begin its probes in the nature reserve or draw water from the Wutach. Only after being granted permission to use the river in a public hearing at the district level could SSW claim to be following proper procedures. But the company had not yet requested such a hearing. For conservation officials, the hearing was decisively important, because by law they would be permitted to voice their objections to the company's plans. Until SSW requested such a hearing, they could do little. Even if district officials rejected the proposal, the state government could overturn their decision. Traditionally, and according to state laws regulating water use, district officials approved or rejected applications for water rights and construction plans, but final authority rested with the state government, which had primary jurisdiction over water management.[21]

The controversy might have died down until the company requested a licensing hearing were it not for some determined individuals who refused to give bureaucrats sole decision-making power. Hermann Schurhammer, a retired hydrologist, public official, and chairman of the local Black Forest Society, was unwilling to stand on the sidelines, waiting passively for officials to determine the fate of the gorge he had worked so hard to protect. In the 1930s, Schurhammer had been instrumental in negotiating agreements with 124 private property owners and a dozen communities to recognize the protected status of the nature reserve. As state conservation commissioner for Baden since 1939, Schurhammer almost got his agency shut down by the Nazi *Gauleiter,* Robert Wagner, for defending the Wutach. After the war, he continued to use his public and private leadership positions to denounce SSW's plans, insisting that they would drain the gorge of "the living element" that created and sustained it.[22] In 1952, one of Schurhammer's newest recruits in protecting the Wutach, the chief forester for the area, Fritz Hockenjos, proposed forming a broad-based coalition of organizations to save the gorge and take action in ways that official conservation could not. Preservationists had successfully used this strategy in the late 1920s when they won the Baden parliament's approval to establish the Wutach nature reserve.[23] When Schurhammer died unexpectedly late in 1952 at the age of 71, the Black Forest Society resolved to preserve his legacy.

In early 1953, just three weeks after Schurhammer's death, members of the Black Forest Society established the Working Association "Homeland Protection in the Black Forest." Under the banner of *"Heimatschutz"* the coalition united fifteen organizations behind the common cause of protecting the region's waters as well as the many uses these rivers supported. In another context, the 80,000 individuals representing potentially conflicting interests might have found themselves at odds with one another. In this case, the participants of a largely middle class background emphasized what united them—an attachment to the streams and rivers that gave their Black Forest homeland its unique character and supported the local economy. The idea of homeland preservation was broad and fluid enough to accommodate the varied interests of its member organizations, which included hiking and ski clubs, the youth hostel enterprise, and socialist Friends of Nature, hunters, foresters, farmers, and natural science enthusiasts, as well as proponents of tourism, commerce, and industry. Sympathetic nonmember organizations such as the DNR and the Swabian Alb Society stepped in at critical times to aid the coalition in garnering support outside of the region.[24]

The largest group in the Wutach conflict—the Black Forest Society with 20,200 members—assumed the leading role in the initiative. Established in 1864 in Freiburg by entrepreneurs and innkeepers who wanted to make the Black Forest more accessible, the organization seemed to be an unlikely leader of a protest action. A largely non-political club with a tradition of maintaining hiking rails and protecting nature and regional folklore, the society preferred compromise with industry rather than confrontation, in part because businessmen were among its members. Yet because some of the people who belonged to this civic organization had spent the last two decades trying to protect the gorge, they were not about to concede defeat or agree to a compromise. The society's leaders also felt betrayed by SSW for its "dishonorable" behavior in breaking what they viewed to be the gentlemen's agreement made in 1928, namely that the company would leave the Wutach alone in exchange for freedom to develop other rivers in the area. In addition, the society regretted that postwar reconstruction seemed to emphasize economic development without a corresponding concern for protecting the region's natural beauty. Only recently in 1950, for example, conservation and tourist organizations had failed to prevent the installation of high tension power lines on scenic Feldberg Mountain.[25] Such setbacks spurred the Black Forest Society to collaborate with other organizations to ensure that at least some areas of their homeland remained protected.

The need to do so seemed especially urgent in this sub-alpine region that had witnessed significant industrial and population growth over the last half century with the development of hydroelectricity on the High and Upper Rhine. Lacking rich deposits of coal found in the north, Baden turned to hydropower to supplement increasing energy needs around the turn of the century, not long after the technology became available. Initially, hydroelectricity was romanticized as a clean, renewable, and conflict-free source of power (tapping into the water supply would not involve strikes which disrupted coal mining). Lured by the promise of inexpensive electricity (it turned out not to be so cheap) and an abundance of water, new industries emerged in the region, bringing more settlements and hydroprojects on the Rhine and its tributaries.[26]

Attempts to block water engineering projects in the region had come to naught because protesters were no match for the powerful coalition of officials, companies, and engineers that backed the plans. In 1904, for example, the German League for Homeland Preservation was established partly to prevent the construction of a hydrodam at Laufenburg on the High Rhine, the site of a series of impressive rapids and salmon runs. Despite a nationwide public awareness campaign (which stressed aesthetic concern about the loss of a scenic homeland landscape to "materialism" and "mammon") and lobbying (including a resolution with 150 signatures of prominent individuals from across Germany), the Baden government approved the project because it promised the usual: new industries and more jobs. After the dam was completed in 1914, the rapids disappeared and salmon stocks died out.[27]

An even more invasive water engineering project was the Rhine Lateral Canal (Grand Canal d'Alsace), but protests against it had even less chance of succeeding. France had begun construction of the canal in 1921, after winning the right to control the left bank of the Upper Rhine in the Treaty of Versailles. The plan called for diverting large amounts of water from the Rhine between Basel and Strasbourg into a parallel canal outfitted with hydrodams and locks, to generate electricity, improve transport, and stimulate regional commerce. Completion of the first hydroelectric plant at Kembs in 1932 jeopardized the water table, causing hardships for Baden farmers, and accelerated the establishment of highly polluting aluminum, chemical, and textile industries on the Upper

Rhine. France resumed construction of the side canal in the 1950s, installing three more hydrodams and locks that further threatened Baden's water supply. Only when pressed to return the Saar to West Germany in the mid 1950s, did France agree to correct problems caused by the canal.[28]

As these examples illustrate, river development had generated controversy in the region for decades, preconditioning popular skepticism. Yet the 1950s marked the beginning of a quarter-century of dam building at an unprecedented pace—not only in West Germany, but also around the globe. Construction reached a high in the 1960s when 400 new dams were installed each year worldwide. But in contrast to the world's largest multi-purpose dam projects of the era—one thinks, for example, of the Hoover Dam on the Colorado River built in the 1930s (the largest at the time), the dams the Soviets installed on the Volga and other rivers beginning in the late 1930s, and the Aswan High Dam constructed on the Nile in the 1960s—West Germany's dam projects were smaller in scale and less invasive. Their primary purpose was to supply electricity and drinking water.[29] Even among dams being built in Europe at the time, the Wutach project would have been on the small side, with a projected 60 meter tall dam and an 18 million cubic meter reservoir. By contrast, one of West Germany's largest dams, the Rosshaupten Dam in Bavaria, is 41 meters high, with a reservoir of 165 million cubic meters. The Tignes Dam in Savoy, France, is even larger, with a 180 meter tall dam and a 230 million cubic meter reservoir.[30] Set in this context the Wutach protest appears to be a relatively insignificant effort to rescue one small tributary of the Rhine from the grasp of the utilities industry. But locals did not view their activism as unimportant, hopeless, or quaint. Sounding little different from preservationists in the Laufenburg protest half a century earlier, those most intensely involved in the Wutach conflict believed that theirs was a struggle to defend intangible moral values against the all pervasive power of technology and business, which prized electricity and profit over beauty and restraint.

In addition to moral conviction and historical experience, recent political events probably generated support for defending the Wutach. In the campaign leading up to the December 1951 plebiscite on creating Baden-Württemberg out of South Baden, Württemberg-Baden and Württemberg-Hohenzollern, citizens formed coalitions such as the "Working Association Baden" and "Alliance Baden-Württemberg" to sway popular opinion for and against the merger. Of the 59 percent of registered voters who participated in the plebiscite, 70 percent approved the new state. In South Baden, however, nearly two-thirds of voters opposed it, disinterested in joining a state without historical roots and worried about undue influence from rival Württemberg.[31] The alliance "Homeland Protection in the Black Forest" no doubt built on this recent political experience in democracy. But its formation also must be understood as an expression of regional pride against the outcome of the plebiscite. With the state government now located farther north in Stuttgart, coalition members resented that decisions affecting the Black Forest would be made by officials who lacked local knowledge of the issues at stake.[32]

Immediately after forming the alliance, participating groups elected a five member executive committee to develop a strategy and coordinate activities. Three of the five men chosen to serve on the executive body were associated with official conservation in some capacity, illustrating the overlap of state-sponsored and private conservation so common in Germany. The newly elected chairman of the working association, Fritz Hockenjos, was an active Black Forest Society member, the young chief forester in the area, and conservation commissioner for the county that included the Wutach Gorge. Walter Fries, an engineer, was district commissioner for conservation in Freiburg. The jurist Karl Asal had years of experience in conservation offices and during the conflict was elected president of the Black Forest Society (1956–1965). The remaining two members of the coordinating committee were civil servants who chaired the Friends of Nature and led the Society of Those Affected by the Construction and Operation of *Schluchseewerk*. By taking advantage of restored democratic institutions, these respected local elites ensured that the coalition's voice was heard in the public sphere. They wrote pamphlets and press releases, organized lectures and tours through the gorge, staged rallies locally and in Stuttgart, and lobbied parliament.[33]

Concerned about public perception, alliance publications declared that protecting the Wutach was "a reasonable demand." The coalition did not oppose economic development of the region's rivers, leaders explained, "if vital public interests made it unavoidable." At stake in this case, however, "was not just any river or landscape," but "our last bit of primeval landscape, our last wild river in the sub-alpine mountains." In an increasingly "mechanized" world, they insisted, people needed to be able to relax in "rugged" nature.[34] Although the Wutach was not a pristine landscape, to its defenders it seemed more "original" and "natural" than it would be if it were dammed and drained. Ascribing moral correctness to the coalition's objectives, Schurhammer's son insisted the Wutach Valley "without water would be a shocking indictment against the spiritual deprivation that unfortunately rules over an increasing part of our world—a world in which nothing is sacred but facts and figures."[35] With these familiar arguments, conservationists claimed the moral high ground, depicting themselves as idealistic defenders of the common good and of vulnerable natural landscapes against the corrupting influences of modern civilization.[36]

Convinced of the rightness of their cause, the alliance launched a twopronged assault against SSW in the spring of 1954. In April, "Save the Wutach Gorge" was published as the first of several pamphlets put out by the coalition in the developing propaganda war with SSW. The cover featured an idyllic sketch of the gorge, drawn as if the viewer were standing on the banks of the Wutach River looking up at cliffs whose many layers of rock recorded thousands of years of geological change. Inside the pamphlet were highly technical arguments challenging SSW's claims that it had official approval to pursue its plans, that developing the Wutach was essential, and that the project would not harm nature in the gorge.

Based on a cost-benefit analysis in this and subsequent publications, the alliance concluded that "draining the Wutach" was too high a price to pay for a project of limited economic benefit. After spending hours studying the company's technical plans, the engineer Fries concluded that the peak power generated through the project would be inconsequential in terms of the country's production of electricity, supplying a mere 0.33 percent of the total (based on figures from 1952). But this argument was misleading, for peak power will always be low in quantity, but high in cost and value. Nonetheless, Fries asserted that developing the Wutach had less to do with serving the "interests of the political economy" than with "the egotistical operational interests of *Schluchseewerk*."[37] The coalition did not dispute the need for peak power, but insisted that the 30,000 kilowatts that could be available with the additional water from the Wutach was not worth what would be destroyed in the process.[38] The same amount of energy, the alliance proposed, could be generated by hydroelectric plants under construction in less settled regions of the Austrian Alps or, even more controversially, from nuclear power plants. Though neither suggestion offered much in the way of alternatives, the executive committee defended the former proposal more easily than the latter. According to one outside observer writing in 1954 in *Der Volkswirt*, a Frankfurt-based financial newspaper favoring liberal economic policies, the "twisted local patriotism [of the coalition]" had gained new momentum with its nuclear proposal. The public, the author warned, ought to be wary of such "preservationist . . . hullabaloo."[39] But in the 1950s it was not uncommon for conservationists, particularly those in southern Germany who had witnessed the harm caused by hydropower, to consider nuclear fission to be a less destructive if not wholly understood alternative. (At the turn of the century, hydropower had been greeted with even greater enthusiasm.) Two decades after the Wutach protest, Hockenjos was among those who opposed the state government's nuclear program.[40]

More irksome to SSW than the battle of words was the association's effort to demonstrate that it had broad support for preserving the Wutach. Drawing inspiration from their Swiss neighbors engaged in an unsuccessful struggle between 1952 and 1954 to stop the construction of a power station at Rheinau, the working association, together with the Swabian Alb Society, made a bold political move in starting a petition drive to "save the Wutach Gorge." Although the coalition emphasized that several rivers of the Black Forest were at risk of being "drained" to generate electricity, its primary concern was the Wutach—the "most beautiful, unique and most precious nature reserve of the area."[41] Between April 1954 and the end of the year, members demonstrated impressive organization skills in collecting an estimated 178,900 signatures of voters primarily from Baden-Württemberg and an additional 15,000 from people living outside the state and a few from abroad. Support also came from the neighboring Swiss canton of Schaffhausen where citizens gathered signatures for their own petition against the project.[42] Though they could add no signatures to the long list, East German conservationists on the other side of the Iron Curtain showed solidarity with their western comrades who were battling powerful "capitalists" to save "a national possession of the entire German people."[43]

Viewed from today's perspective, signing a petition does not appear to be a radical move. And certainly earlier preservationists had circulated petitions. But in the most well-known cases, they either collected fewer signatures (only 150 people from around the country in the early twentieth century Laufenburg protest) or collected signatures in a limited area (in just one community in the Rißbach conflict in Bavaria in the late 1940s, though with public demonstrations, including a sensational funeral rally, which several thousand citizens attended and which culminated in a resolution that went to the *Landtag*). More comparable with the Wutach case was the protest organized by the Swiss in Rheinau. In this action, too, a non-partisan coalition circulated a petition that 156,000 people signed. Admittedly, this regional activity was limited when compared with the nation-wide petition drive carried out between 1957 and 1958 by peace activists who opposed arming the *Bundeswehr* with nuclear weapons; their petition found the support of over 1.5 million citizens.[44]

What made the Wutach petition drive more daring was the historical and political context. As Hockenjos commented two decades after the protest, it was unusual in the early 1950s for West Germans to support an issue so publicly because denazification had made many wary of associating their name with a cause. To be sure, Germans had staged protests against the Allies' dismantling of factories and forests, the treatment of veterans and expellees from Eastern Europe, the conditions for workers, and the decision by the *Bundestag* to rearm the *Bundeswehr* and join NATO.[45] Compared with these issues, defending the Wutach seemed less politically charged. But by getting behind the seemingly non-political cause of protecting nature and *Heimat*, people became politicized, identifying themselves as citizens who had rights that ought to be protected and respected. The most plausible explanation for the long list of supporters is that the majority of those who signed the petition belonged to groups in the coalition and they were better informed about the debate than most. Others, however, were won over after taking an educational hike through the gorge organized by the alliance. There also were some who had never laid eyes on the Wutach, but signed the petition out of a conviction that "money should not destroy everything."[46] Whatever their motive, those who affixed their signature to the petition, and especially those who led the drive, remained uncertain about what their protest would accomplish. They were pleasantly surprised when sympathetic media coverage of their "David-against-Goliath" campaign attracted a record number of visitors to the gorge. In the first seven months of 1954, when trails were often muddy, over 10,000 people trekked through the area, compared with the 3,000 recorded annually in the three previous years.[47]

The petition drive fanned the conflict, prompting SSW to launch an expensive counterattack to discredit its opponents. In 1954 alone, the company spent DM 100,000, compared with DM 9,000 put forward by the coalition.[48] In a direct response to the petition drive, SSW paid for a half page insert in large daily newspapers, accusing the executive committee of using "dictatorial" measures reminiscent of the Nazi era to coerce unwilling individuals to support the coalition's cause (a charge alliance leaders dismissed as evidence of the company's disregard of the rights of citizens). SSW also alleged that the working association's "propaganda lectures" exaggerated the effects of tapping water from the Wutach and failed to inform the public adequately of the restrictions on the company's use of water. Conservationists' slide presentations of remarkable cliffs and vegetation, SSW warned, left the "clueless public" to assume that the Wutach Gorge and its vegetation would disappear.[49]

Claiming to have the public good foremost in mind, the company clarified that water from the Wutach was to be used to generate highly prized, costly peak power. Not having sufficient electricity available at those times of the day and year when demand was highest would result in power outages and limits on use. SSW's pumped-storage installations would prevent these kinds of problems for they could generate peak power in a mere 100 seconds, far more quickly and less expensively than the steam powered plants the working association identified as an alternative. The company emphasized that "[e]lectricity is the most important fundamental element for trade and industry, and creates jobs for millions of . . . citizens." With local communities standing to benefit from new tax revenue from SSW and so many people "fighting for work and bread," no "productive person" could comprehend the extremist position of private conservationists and their "absolute rejection of a compromise solution." The company pointed out that South Baden had fifty-three nature reserves covering over 10,000 hectares, and fifty protected landscapes encompassing an even larger area. Ordinances protecting the beauties of nature had a certain importance, SSW conceded, but they should not infringe upon the "freedom of movement necessary" for economic development. In describing its project as an "unavoidable intrusion in the water supply of the upper Wutach," however, SSW revealed its own inflexibility.

Presenting itself as the agent of compromise that had the common good foremost in mind, the company insisted that nature conservation *and* technology were the solution to the conflict.[50] Developing imagery to reinforce this view, one SSW flyer featured a panoramic view of the entire valley with the reader's eyes drawn to the center where the planned dam merged harmoniously with forested hills and held back the placid waters of a reservoir. Sailboats appeared to glide atop the man-made lake, while below the dam, the cliffs of the gorge towered above the river unchanged. What the coalition considered the center of focus, the gorge, was for SSW one part of a much larger picture, implying that the company's broader vision ought to prevail over conservationists' supposedly narrow and inflexible goal.[51]

Although protecting the Wutach remained the coalition's central focus, its concerns went beyond preservation. To give their position objective spin, alliance leaders assembled an impressive array of scientific and economic opinions. They were keenly aware, however, that experts had their own biases and that their conclusions could be used to the advantage of the other side. Such was the case when local foresters (excluding Hockenjos) concluded that reducing the flow of water in the Wutach would probably not adversely affect area forests.[52] SSW, too, found that its own facts and figures could be used to support the opposition. Citing experts, the company assured the public that the Wutach Gorge and its vegetation would not be noticeably altered, because its project would not affect the rivers and streams that fed into the river below the dam. Yet it was obvious that drawing an annual average of 68 percent the water from tributaries *above* the dam would seriously disrupt the ongoing evolution of the gorge.[53]

In general, the specialists and professionals alliance leaders called upon to reinforce their position raised legitimate, and by the 1950s, familiar concerns about the adverse effects of hydroprojects. Dams flood river valleys and block the routes of migratory fish. By trapping silt and sediment behind the dam (along with chemicals and heavy metals from industry), they reduce the sediment load carried downstream, depriving aquatic life and fields of vital nutrients and increasing riverbed erosion. Some hydroprojects require the diversion underground of water from one or several rivers to a reservoir (as with the Wutach project), but the tunnels can absorb groundwater, causing a lowering of the water table.[54] The biggest worry in the Wutach conflict was that drawing water from the rivers and streams that feed the Wutach above the dam would disrupt the hydrology of the area. Mineralogists in particular balked at SSW's plan to control the spring floodwaters that were essential for washing away rock and gravel that otherwise would build up in the gorge.[55] Although promoters of dams historically have touted their usefulness in flood control, area farmers were less concerned about seasonal inundations than about a reduction in the groundwater supply, which they depended on to maintain their meadows and fruit groves.[56] Commercial fishermen rightly pointed out that fish would struggle to survive if the water level below the dam dropped too low and the temperature of the water increased, or if effluents from manufacturing in Neustadt collected in the bottom of the reservoir behind the dam wall.[57]

Representatives of local industries had a number of concerns as well. They predicted that with far less water in the Wutach and other rivers, the fifteen sawmills, ten textile factories, three paper factories, and other industries in the area would struggle in their daily operations and might face limitations on how they expanded in the future. This was an understandable concern, but one that illustrates the public's reluctance to prioritize water conservation in the 1950s. Area industries also worried that draining water from the Wutach, Murg or Ibach would reduce the self-cleaning capacity of these rivers and force communities to install expensive treatment facilities—a reminder that many still did not have them. Throughout the 1950s, only 40 percent of West Germans was hooked up to wastewater treatment plants, and just 10 percent had access to water that had been treated not only mechanically, but also biologically. This situation stemmed partly from a lack of funds during reconstruction for the installation of water purification systems in numbers needed to handle the surge in demand. Even in the mid 1970s, just over half of the population had access to fully treated water.[58]

Tourist associations predicted the gloomiest of outcomes. Their argument that SSW would drain enough water from the Black Forest to disrupt the local climate so crucial for area health resorts was exaggerated because the reservoir would help stabilize temperatures. But they were right to express skepticism of the company's slick brochures that promised a beautiful reservoir for recreation. Although SSW would be required to keep the reservoir full in summer during peak tourist season, that only applied in years with normal rainfall; in years with less than normal precipitation, the water level in the reservoir would be lower. Few people, tourism representatives asserted, would want to boat on a body of water that was lined with slime and rarely filled to capacity. Although this image was as misleading as SSW's, it pointed to some of the features of reservoirs that make them visibly distinct from lakes: their frequent fluctuations in water level and their near-naked shores—the latter a consequence of the former. Because of constant changes in the water level of reservoirs, vegetation and animal life have difficulty settling on the shoreline, though new species of flora and fauna find a niche in the new environment. And over time, reservoirs can become eutrophic, especially as they accumulate effluents, a significant concern at a time when water treatment remained inadequate.[59]

The working association's activism on behalf of the Wutach peaked in 1954 and 1955. In leading the coalition, Hockenjos and Fries found that their work as private citizens frequently overlapped with their duties as volunteer conservation commissioners. In several instances, the distinction between activist and commissioner conveniently blurred. In his capacity as a commissioner, for example, Fries wrote two of the most detailed and technical publications that appeared in the coalition's series and made use of official channels to distribute the literature to individuals in federal government posts and the *Bundestag*.[60] Little could be done at the federal level to resolve the Wutach conflict, however, because the states had primary responsibility for water management and conservation, a fact that meant coalition leaders had more options to shape the final outcome than would have been the case had the matter been decided in Bonn. This did not prevent the office of Ludwig Erhard, federal economics minister, from appealing to the BANL director, Gert Kragh, to mediate between SSW and the coalition so that "highly valuable peak power" could be produced "without further public disturbance," a clear indication that paternalistic federal officials found the coalition's activism to be meddlesome. (Federal officials had registered their support for the Rißbach diversion, too.)[61]

In their capacity as commissioners, Fries and Hockenjos also turned to the national network of conservation officials and commissioners, the ABN. In a show of support for the regional cause, the ABN held its annual meeting in Freiburg in 1954 and put Hockenjos on the agenda to talk about the coalition's "fight against the hollow materialism of our time," as he described it.[62] State conservation commissioner Otto Kraus was particularly sympathetic because he was embroiled in a conflict with Bavaria's state utility company over the height of a dam (one of several) on the Lech River. "What we are experiencing here," Kraus commented, "is an exemplary . . . offensive by conservation, not against technology . . . but against the hubris of technology."[63] In language that blended the rhetoric of traditional preservation with a growing appreciation for participatory democracy, the 250 attendees from across the country passed a resolution (a political activity conservationists frequently used, but one involving limited risk) supporting a "true movement of the people" to save the Wutach and "raising sharp protest against the sacrifice of irreplaceable values of the homeland for the benefit of economic efficiency."[64]

However routine the ABN meeting sounds to our contemporary ears, SSW interpreted the events in Freiburg as unfair. Otto Henninger, a member of the board of directors of SSW, complained to BANL Director Kragh that the company had been "attacked" without getting the chance to provide another point of view, an indication that SSW, like officials in the Federal Ministry of Economics, had little tolerance for outspoken opponents who chose to exercise their rights as citizens.[65] Just after the Freiburg conference, Henninger invited Kragh to tour the proposed construction site, entreating him to make certain "that our work is not constantly disturbed by private interests, especially because our efforts to provide additional peak power serve the public interest."[66] Responding to pressures from SSW and Ludwig Erhard's office, the ever-diplomatic Kragh accepted SSW's invitation to tour the site of the proposed dam in the spring of 1955. His intervention, reminiscent of Seifert's in the early 1940s, left Hockenjos and Fries feeling betrayed and the even-tempered Asal furious.[67] Fries flatly told the BANL chief that the federal institute's intervention in the Wutach conflict, which "consumed one-fifth of [his] job and is [his] greatest worry," was an "overtly unfriendly" act against those who had been battling SSW with limited funds and countless volunteer hours.[68] When Kragh suggested that they meet with SSW representatives, Fries refused. "A discussion with *Schluchseewerk* is completely useless," he wrote, because "two world views stand at odds with one another."[69]

Fries and Hockenjos reached this conclusion after colliding with the company on two occasions in particular. In October 1954, SSW led state legislators serving on the committees on water and energy, and economics and transportation through their facilities and took them on a tour of the Wutach Valley, but ignored deputies' request to include conservationists to present another point of view. In February 1955, when Hockenjos delivered a public slide lecture at the University of Freiburg, SSW unloaded two large buses of employees to circulate through the audience and disrupt the talk with boisterous remarks, a public display of bad manners that conservationists associated with Nazi bullies (but a tactic that would be used frequently by students in revolt in the 1960s and by environmental activists in the 1970s).[70] Kragh postponed his meeting with SSW, convinced that relations between the company and commissioners had deteriorated to such an extent that gentlemanly negotiations, which conservationists preferred, were not possible.[71]

The Final Round in the Wutach Conflict, 1955–1960

The conflict dragged on for another five years before being resolved in 1960 at the highest level of the state government. A combination of developments contributed to the final outcome in favor of conservationists. First, parliamentarians in Stuttgart took up the Wutach cause as part of a larger challenge to improve management of the state's water supply. In 1956, representatives led by Deputy Friedrich Vortisch (FDP/German Peoples' Party), an attorney well informed about water management issues, including the vexing Rhine Lateral Canal, pressured the state government to provide a non-partisan study of SSW's plans for the Wutach, and more importantly, to develop a comprehensive water management plan for the entire state. Vortisch effectively capitalized on the fact that badly needed federal guideline legislation for water management, at the time under deliberation in the *Bundestag,* would require the states to develop substantive plans to manage their water resources. Vortisch was one of the political leaders who insisted that SSW's Wutach project needed to be considered not in isolation, but in relation to other proposals for using the region's lakes, rivers, and streams.[72] Hoping to prevent plans for the Wutach from getting hung up in parliamentary debates on this complex issue, in December 1956 the Ministry of the Interior, as the office responsible for water management, instructed district officials in Neustadt to open the local licensing hearing for SSW's use of the Wutach. Clearly the ministry hoped that the company would secure a license for the project without a water management plan for the state. Such tactics, by no means unique to the Wutach conflict, only made the public less trusting of government officials.[73]

A second factor that shaped the outcome of the controversy was SSW's over-reach. When the local licensing hearing opened in January 1957, it was apparent to those who had a voice in the proceedings, including conservation officials, that the company had revised its wartime proposal substantially, going well beyond what had been approved in 1943. According to the new plan, 74,000 kilowatts of electric power (not the 30,000 kilowatts promised earlier) would be produced, because SSW now intended to drain an annual average of 75 percent (not the 68 percent estimated previously) of the water from the Wutach's tributaries above the dam. The new estimate reflected SSW's revised request to remove 20 cubic meters of water per second from the Wutach above the dam—far more than the maximum of 7.5 cubic meters stipulated in 1943. The company also intended to hold back nearly all of the floodwaters in the reservoir (compared with 80 per-cent earlier) to control flooding below the dam and guarantee farmers a steady supply of water, even in times of drought. But these potential advantages for agriculture would be purchased at a high price, namely the spring floods that shaped and sustained the gorge.[74]

The company's strategy for addressing water pollution inspired little confi-dence. To prevent effluents from Neustadt from building up in the reservoir, SSW proposed diverting the tainted water around the reservoir, running it through a treatment system to remove an estimated 75 percent of the impurities, and then feeding it into the Wutach below the dam.[75] With little water expected to flow in the river, however, its self-cleaning capacity would be limited. Beyond these weaknesses, SSW's plans for the Wutach were compromised further by the fact that at the end of the decade, it had grander projects underway which made this one seem insignificant—and clearly unnecessary. Ironically then, SSW's successful expansion elsewhere helped conservationists achieve their narrow ob-jective of protecting the Wutach.

The persistent, organized opposition of conservationists also determined the end result of the Wutach conflict. As a private organization, the working associa-tion had no legal right to voice objections in the local licensing hearing when it opened in early 1957, so it used other channels to keep its protest alive. Through the media, alliance leaders accused SSW of forging ahead with its plans without an objective impact statement on the Wutach project or a comprehensive water management plan for the region. Citing similar reasons, they lodged a formal complaint against the Ministry of the Interior for failure of duty (*Dienstauf-sichtsbeschwerde*), a move that proved to be a dead end. At the same time, coali-tion leaders publicly announced their intentions to present the *Landtag* with the 180,000 signatures its members had collected to remind parliamentarians that thousands of citizens opposed developing the Wutach. But they did not follow through with this move, perhaps concerned about the political fallout for them-selves and others for staging a protest against SSW, and thus indirectly against the state as part-owner of SSW's parent company, *Badenwerk*.[76]

In their capacity as commissioners, Hockenjos and Fries also recruited the nationally respected state conservation commissioner, Konrad Buchwald, to attract sympathetic press coverage beyond the region. In a half page article in the *Stuttgarter Zeitung* published a month into SSW's hearing, Buchwald took the state government of Baden-Württemberg to task (as the owner of SSW's parent company) for its apparent willingness to use citizens' taxes to "destroy" an "irreplaceable" nature reserve for a project of questionable economic merit. "[E]ven in these times of materialistic thinking," he stated, using a local conflict to preach a familiar sounding moral lesson, political leaders ought to "preserve the far-sighted values of the homeland, which cannot be quantified monetarily."[77] In response to the article, SSW filed a complaint with the Ministry of Culture (as the supreme conservation office), accusing Buchwald of spreading misleading information and misusing his post by intervening in a proceeding in which he had a part. Nothing came of the charge, but it illustrates how both sides used the legal and institutional options open to them to advance their cause.[78]

In the final stage of the controversy (1958–1959), the coalition, renamed "Homeland Protection in South Baden" to reflect its expanded area of activity, finally presented the state government with the list of 180,000 signatures from the petition drive.[79] Claiming to express the will of "tens of thousands of homeland-loving loyal citizens," Hockenjos and Asal asserted that approving plans for the Wutach "would be a sin against the common good." This was especially the case because SSW was involved in licensing hearings for two other expansion projects (one promising 449,000 kilowatts, the other 514,000 kilowatts), which would supply far more electricity than the Wutach (74,000 kilowatts).[80] At a carefully organized rally in the gorge in 1959, alliance leaders, dressed in suits and traditional attire to emphasize the seriousness and orderliness of their public protest, presented a resolution that made a final appeal to the state government to stop the Wutach project.[81] Referencing events of the past for political effect, the working association instructed the state government of Minister-President Kurt Georg Kiesinger (1958–1966, CDU) to feel "more obliged" to support the unanimous, democratic decision of the Baden parliament in 1928 to preserve the Wutach, rather than the "questionable exception" granted by Göring in 1943.[82] The implication here was that only Nazis and self-serving capitalists supported the project.

Another year passed before Kiesinger stepped in to resolve the conflict, which was bogged down in government bureaucracy—another critical factor that determined the outcome of the controversy. Throughout the decade, one of the main obstacles preventing a timely decision on the Wutach was disagreement over the validity of the 1943 decision. SSW's licensing hearing in Neustadt had stalled because officials there wanted assurances that the decision was indeed legitimate before proceeding. But neither the Ministry of the Interior (as the office responsible for water management) nor the Ministry of Culture (as the supreme conservation office) could provide clarity because they remained at loggerheads over the question until the end of the decade. Inter-ministerial conflicts such as this one were typical of the competency struggles that stalled decision making in many controversial development projects in the Federal Republic.[83] Sometimes they indirectly benefited conservationists, as appears to have been the case here. But this was only apparent once the struggle was over.

Not even studies by experts on the impact of the Wutach project could overcome the government gridlock. With controversial development projects it was standard practice for ministries and other parties involved to rely on specialists for presumably objective assessments that might serve as the basis for compromise. But opinions by experts are not value neutral, and this case was no exception. By the summer of 1958, several studies of the Wutach project had been completed, giving SSW hope that the stalled licensing proceedings might move forward. Experts concluded that SSW's proposed reservoir would help stabilize the microclimate and introduce only minimal changes in local vegetation in the gorge (findings that ignored the flooding of vast areas behind the dam). Studies challenged conservationists' idealized description of the area around the Wutach Gorge as untouched, pointing to scars from human use, such as forest monocultures and logging roads. They also noted the unpleasant odor, brown color, and foam buildup on parts of the river caused by industrial effluents that long ago had endangered trout and other fish populations. Experts conceded, however, that reducing the flow of water would lower the groundwater and adversely affect the gorge by allowing rock and gravel to accumulate in the riverbed. Whether or not the Wutach project was carried out, there was consensus that more needed to be done to reduce water pollution.[84] Rather than engage the findings of studies they repeatedly demanded the state to commission, the coalition and parliamentarians like Vortisch rejected them as biased, complaining that some conclusions were based on research conducted for an earlier report prepared at SSW's request.[85]

Despite the completion of reports that supported SSW yet also demanded improvements in water management, the two ministries remained at an impasse. With several other ministries interested in an end to the controversy, the Wutach affair was referred to the cabinet council in 1959. Here, however, the interests of conservation appeared to be at a distinct disadvantage for three reasons: the Minister of Finance was representative chairman of the board of directors of *Badenwerk,* the current Minister of Economics, Dr. Hermann Veit, was chairman of the board of directors of SSW, and the Minister of Culture had comparatively limited power by virtue of the state constitution.[86] Elsewhere in West Germany as well, state ministries responsible for conservation typically had less clout than those responsible for economic development or finance; in times of conflict the former frequently lost out to the latter.[87] In the Wutach controversy, however, Minister-President Kiesinger intervened. With the 180,000 signatures of concerned citizens before him and clear evidence that SSW's revised plans exceeded what had been approved in 1943, he suspended the water rights hearing.[88] But SSW also conceded defeat. Confronted by an organized coalition of citizens, the company retreated in the battle over the Wutach, freeing itself to pursue more profitable projects in the region.

Although SSW lost in the Wutach conflict, it did not suffer a serious setback. At the end of the decade, the company had projects in the works that made the Wutach expansion seem insignificant. In the early 1960s, SSW was touted as the most important pumped-storage facility in Baden-Württemberg and the largest peak-load facility of its kind in Europe.[89] But the controversy indicated that SSW faced some limits on how it expanded in the future, and those restrictions would reflect not only decisions made by its board of directors and powerful parent companies, but to a limited extent, the convictions and pragmatic concerns of citizens. Similar to other emergency coalitions, but by no means typical, "Homeland Protection in South Baden" continued to exist after the conflict. Although few participants were radicalized by their involvement in the protest, their activism ensured that the Wutach Gorge remained protected for future generations. Members kept alive the memory of having foiled the company's plans and launched other campaigns in the region under Hockenjos's experienced leadership. When SSW revived the Wutach project in 1975, the company had no success.[90] Although still active in the 1970s, the alliance lost influence to more confrontational environmental initiatives.[91]

When Hockenjos recalled the Wutach conflict after the social and political upheaval of the late 1960s and 1970s, he concluded that he had been involved in one of West Germany's first citizens' initiatives. Some studies of political activism argue that the initiatives of the 1950s and early 1960s were formed not as an alternative to political parties or in opposition to the state as was the case in the 1970s, but as an act of civic virtue carried out on behalf of others.[92] Indeed, the coalition believed that it conveyed the sentiments of thousands of patriotic citizens in wanting to protect an irreplaceable natural wonder for present and future generations. Expressing the idealism that long had been associated with preservationist campaigns (as distinct from the more urban-based, pragmatic, and professionalized public health movement to fight pollution), leaders of the coalition encouraged followers to see themselves as "homeland-loving loyal citizens" (despite their dissent), fighting for a noble goal that served the common good. When protesters in the Wutach case, like West German conservationists more generally, referred to their activities as apolitical, they meant that their goals were not a reflection of partisan struggles, but a desire to serve the common good. Yet in this instance and so many others, local self-interest also was involved in seeking to limit outside interference from disrupting the economic and political status quo.[93] Whether or not the coalition's campaign should be called a citizen initiative is debatable because of the overlap with official conservation. But it clearly is an example of democracy in action in the politically conservative 1950s.

The blending of private and official conservation in the Wutach conflict—a pragmatic strategy carried over from earlier preservationist campaigns in Germany—expanded the options of conservationists and gave them greater flexibility. Whereas commissioners and officials had greater leverage when the conflict was being addressed in public licensing hearings, the coalition wielded more influence outside of these administrative channels. Aided by their social standing and official positions, coalition leaders used the press and orderly public rallies to publicize their views, and turned to sympathetic officials and deputies in the legislature to represent their cause and cast it in broader terms of managing the state's water supply. Less typical and most daring of all in the early postwar context was the coalition's organized petition drive, a measure that appeared to challenge the state as part owner of SSW's parent company. Yet even in the Wutach controversy where officials' conflict of interest was apparent, conservationists ultimately looked to the state to resolve the matter fairly. But in this and other protests in West Germany at the time, protesters' tone had a sharper edge than in early preservation campaigns.[94]

In forming a broad coalition to protect the *Heimat,* conservationists cooperated closely with representatives of business, agriculture, and tourism. Their goal, however, remained narrowly focused on protecting the Wutach. They succeeded partly because of leaders' limited aims, but also because it meant that they did not obstruct SSW's expansion elsewhere. The company's bigger projects at the end of the decade dwarfed plans for the Wutach. In this conflict and so many others during the Miracle Years, conservationists settled for a limited victory that, however significant, did not slow the advance of industry. But as an exasperated Fries had explained in the middle of the campaign, just fighting to protect the Wutach required money and volunteer time that were hard to come by. Bureaucratic delays prolonged the fight, making it even more costly. Had the project been subject to the approval of federal officials in Bonn, however, it most likely would have gone through without much of a fight, as communications from Erhard's office implied. As it was, the states had primary jurisdiction over water management. When the interior ministry in Stuttgart tried to push through SSW's plans in 1957, conservation officials, *Landtag* deputies, and the coalition used networking, lobbying, the media, and bureaucratic maneuvering to obstruct the move.

But neither side claimed a decisive victory. For each side there were partial gains and losses, and a "partial greening" of society. Although alliance leaders framed their fight as a David against Goliath battle to defend "pristine" nature against the "egotistical" ambitions of SSW, they also stressed that they did not oppose "progress," only a one-sided interpretation of what it meant. The progress they envisioned could be achieved best through compromise: through using natural resources carefully but insisting on the preservation of unique places such as the Wutach. By the end of the decade, more West Germans had reached a level of material comfort that made them more receptive to conservationists' qualified definition of progress, which included not only prosperity but also natural beauty and respect for citizens' rights. But to pursue these potentially conflicting goals required better planning of the use of space and resources, a competency that seemed best left to governments and experts. As chapter 4 illustrates, renewed emphasis on spatial planning in the late 1950s and 1960s benefited conservation to some degree, yet it also potentially reduced the role that citizens might play in decisions that affected their local communities.

Notes

*   This chapter is a revised version of Sandra Chaney, "Protecting Nature and Practicing Democracy in West Germany," in Mauch, et. al., eds., *Shades of Green. Environmental Activism Around the Globe*. Rowman & Littlefield, 2006.

 1. Jarausch, Seeba, and Conradt, "Presence of the Past," in Jarausch, *After Unity*, 38–39.
 2. Engels, *Naturpolitik*, 196–99.
 3. Engels, *Naturpolitik*, 205–7.
 4. Fritz Hockenjos, *Wanderführer durch die Wutach- und Gauchachschlucht*, 5th ed. (Freiburg, 1989), 11–74; Hermann Schurhammer, "Das Naturschutzgebiet Wutach-Gauchach und seine Bedrohung," *N & L* 26, no. 9/10 (1951): 97–99; Walter Fries, *Rettet die Wutachschlucht! Eine Antwort auf die Pläne der Schluchseewerk AG* (Freiburg: Karl Schillinger, 1954), 8–10, in Bundesamt für Naturschutz (BAN), Naturschutzarchiv, Wutach (0831513) (hereafter BAN Naturschutzarchiv 0831513). On paper and pulp manufacturing see Cioc, *The Rhine*, 124–25.
 5. Blackbourn, *Conquest*, 217–28, p. 227 for figures on increased energy consumption; Herbert Gätschenberger, "Energieversorgung," in *Baden-Württemberg. Staat, Wirtschaft, Kultur*, ed. Theodor Pfizer (Stuttgart: Deutsche Verlags-Anstalt, 1963), 275; Schluchseewerk AG (hereafter SSW) homepage, <http://www.schluchseewerk.de> (accessed 24 July 2004).
 6. Fries, *Rettet*, 3–4; Fries, *Muss die Wutach abgeleitet werden? Wirtschaftliche Betrachtungen zum Plan der Wutachableitung durch die Schluchseewerk AG* (Freiburg: Karl Schillinger, 1955), 3, 5, in BAN Naturschutzarchiv 0831513; Engels, *Naturpolitik*, 175; Uekötter, *Green and the Brown*, 126–27.
 7. Uekötter, *Green and the Brown*, 127–28.
 8. Karl Asal, "Stellungnahme der Höheren Naturschutzbehörde zur Frage der Wutachbeileitung," 23 May 1950, BAK B 245/6.
 9. SSW, *Ist die Wutach-Schlucht wirklich gefährdet?* (Freiburg: [privately published?], 1953), 1–5, in BAN Naturschutzarchiv 0831513; SSW, *Schluchseewerk Aktiengesellschaft*, 2d ed. (Freiburg: [privately published?], 1952), in BAN Naturschutzarchiv 0831513; Hockenjos, report on the working association, in *Verhandlungen* (1954): 75; Fries, *Rettet*, 4.
10. Hockenjos, report in *Verhandlungen* (1954): 75; SSW, *Ist die Wutach-Schlucht wirklich gefährdet?*, 1–4; SSW, *Schluchseewerk Aktiengesellschaft;* Fries, *Rettet*, 4; Uekötter, *Green and the Brown*, 129–33.
11. Reich Forest Master [Göring] to General Inspector for Water and Energy [Speer], 9 March 1943, BAK B 245/6. See also Hans Klose to Dr. Ludwig Finckh, 18 June 1943, "Vertraulich," BAK B 245/6. On the wartime context see Uekötter, *Green and the Brown*, 129–30.
12. Reich Forest Master to General Inspector for Water and Energy, 9 March 1943; Klose to Finckh, 18 June 1943, both in BAK B 245/6; Asal, "Stellungnahme," 4–5, 23 May 1950, BAK B 245/6. Fries, *Rettet*, 5–6, explains that Seifert recommended that the reservoir remain filled

from July through October, but this was not included among the requirements handed down to SSW. Neither was Seifert's insistence that the Neustadt paper factory above the dam cease its production of pulp to prevent effluents from accumulating behind the dam. Ludwig Finckh to Klose, 16 June 1943, BAK B 245/6, suggests that Seifert thought the strict conditions he set would discourage SSW from pursuing the Wutach project. Nonetheless, local conservationists resented his intervention, a reaction not unique to them. See Lekan, "Regionalism and the Politics of Landscape Preservation," 396.

13. Finckh to Klose, 16 June 1943; Klose to Finckh, 18 June 1943, both in BAK B 245/6; Uekötter, *Green and the Brown*, 133–34.

14. SSW, *Ist die Wutach-Schlucht wirklich gefährdet?*, 2–3; SSW, "Wozu Unterschriften zur Rettung der Wutachschlucht?" April 1954, BAN Naturschutzarchiv 0831513; SSW, *Schluchseewerk Aktiengesellschaft.*

15. After 1945, the Allies redrew the boundaries of Baden and Württemberg to form three states: in the French zone were South Baden with its capital in Freiburg and Württemberg-Hohenzollern with its capital in Tübingen; in the US zone was Württemberg-Baden with its capital in Stuttgart. After a plebiscite, the three states merged to form Baden-Württemberg in 1952.

16. Karl Asal to Hans Klose, 23 May 1950, BAK B 245/6.

17. Asal, "Stellungnahme," 5–9, 23 May 1950, BAK B 245/6.

18. Theodor Röttges to Leo Wohleb, 23 October 1950, archive of the Schwarzwaldverein, Bonndorf Chapter, in possession of the current first chairman, Friedbert Zapf, Wutach Gorge, binder # 6.5, pp. 52–53 (hereafter SWV-B, Wutachschlucht, #6.5, 52–53). On ownership of utility companies see Ulrich Linse, "'Der Raub des Rheingoldes': Das Wasserkraftwerk Laufenburg," in Linse, Falter, Rucht, and Kretschmer, *Bittschrift*, 60–62; Gätschenberger, "Energieversorgung," in Pfizer, *Baden-Württemberg*, 276; Blackbourn, *Conquest*, 219–20, 228.

19. On the Rißbach project see Falter, "Walchenseekraftwerk," in Linse, Falter, Rucht, and Kretschmer, *Bittschrift*, 106–15; Dominick, *Environmental Movement*, 45–46, 125–26. On Tignes see Robert L. Frost, "The Flood of 'Progress': Technocrats and Peasants at Tignes (Savoy), 1946–1952," *French Historical Studies* 14, no. 1 (Spring 1985): 117–40. On these projects in general see Rommelspacher, "Zwischen Heimatschutz und Umweltprotest," 78.

20. Jürgen Buschkiel, "Technik besiegt Naturschutz. Die Wutachschlucht im Schwarzwald wird zum Stausee ausgebaut," *Die Welt*, 19 February 1951; "Industrie siegt über Naturschutz. Großkraftwerk entsteht in der romantischen Wutachschlucht," unidentified newspaper, 30 December 1950, clippings in BAK B 245/6.

21. Fritz Hockenjos, "Urlandschaft oder elektrischer Strom?" in *Wutach-Brevier*, ed. Arbeitsgemeinschaft "Heimatschutz Schwarzwald" (Freiburg: [Karl Schillinger?], 1955), 50, in BAN Naturschutzarchiv 0831513; Fries, *Rettet*, 6.

22. Asal, "Stellungnahme," 1, 23 May 1950; Klose to Finckh, 18 June 1943, both in BAK B 245/6; Schurhammer, "Das Naturschutzgebiet Wutach-Gauchach," *N & L* 26, no. 9/10 (1951): 99. A Nazi Party member only in 1937 and thus presumably a reluctant one, Schurhammer also worked as the only engineer on Seifert's elite team of landscape architects in the 1930s. See Uekötter, *Green and the Brown*, 126; and Zeller, "Alwin Seifert," in Radkau and Uekötter, *Naturschutz und Nationalsozialismus*, 293.

23. Fritz Hockenjos, "Wutachschlucht Erinnerungen," *Der Schwarzwald*, no. 2 (1979): 62.

24. Hockenjos, "Erinnerungen," 62; Georg Wagner, "Die Wutachablenkung—100 Jahre Flußgeschichte," *Blätter des Schwäbischen Albverein* 59, no. 6 (1953): 93–94, in BAN Naturschutzarchiv 0831513. Hockenjos, report in *Verhandlungen* (1954): 76, states that the coalition represented 140,000 people.

25. Asal, "Stellungnahme," 7, 23 May 1950, BAK B 245/6; "Industrie siegt über Naturschutz," [unidentified newspaper], 30 December 1950, clipping in BAK B 245/6.

26. Blackbourn, *Conquest*, 217–20.

27. Linse, "Laufenburg," in Linse, Falter, Rucht, and Kretschmer, *Bittschrift,* 11–62; Rollins, *Greener Vision,* 141–43.

28. Cioc, *The Rhine,* 66–67, 130–33, 142. See below chap. 5.

29. Geoff Petts, "Water, Engineering and Landscape: Development, Protection and Restoration," in *Water, Engineering and Landscape. Water Control and Landscape Transformation in the Modern Period,* ed. Denis Cosgrove and Petts (London: Belhaven, 1990), 189–97; McNeill, *Something New,* 157–82; Blackbourn, *Conquest,* 228–32, 327.

30. "Neue Runde im Kampf um die Wutach," *Badische Volkszeitung* [Karlsruhe] 5 January 1957, clipping in BAK B 245/6; Frost, "Flood of 'Progress,'" 127. Technical information about the Rosshaupten and Tignes dams is available at <http//www.structurae.de> (accessed 24 July 2007).

31. Landeszentrale für politische Bildung Baden-Württemberg, "Baden-Württemberg. Kleine politische Landeskunde," <http://www.lpb.bwue.de/publikat/politischelandeskunde/suedweststaat.htm> (accessed 24 July 2003).

32. Arbeitsgemeinschaft "Heimatschutz Schwarzwald," *Trockenlegung des südlichen Schwarzwaldes* (Freiburg: privately published, n.d. [1953?]), 10, in BAN Archiv C 63710.

33. Fritz Hockenjos, interview by author, 19 May 1992, St. Märgen; Hockenjos, "Erinnerungen," 62.

34. Working Association "Heimatschutz Schwarzwald," flier entitled, "Eine vernünftige Forderung," n.d., in BAN Naturschutzarchiv 0831513; Fritz Hockenjos to coalition members and participants in the action "Save the Wutach Gorge!" 21 April 1954, BAN Naturschutzarchiv 0831513.

35. Hermann Schurhammer, Jr., "Naturschutzgebiet Wutachschlucht in Gefahr," *Kosmos* 50, no. 6 (1954): 277.

36. Engels, *Naturpolitik,* 196–99.

37. Fries, *Muß die Wutach abgeleitet werden?,* 3, 16. Frost, "Flood of 'Progress,'" 128, notes similar arguments in the Tignes project.

38. Fries, *Rettet,* 16–18.

39. "Naturschutz kontra Hydroenergie," *Volkswirt,* 10 July 1954, clipping in BAK B 245/6.

40. For references to the Austrian Alps as an alternative see Fries, *Muß die Wutach abgeleitet werden?,* 13; Hockenjos, "Urlandschaft oder elektrischer Strom?" in Arbeitsgemeinschaft "Heimatschutz Schwarzwald," *Wutach-Brevier,* 59; "Ein Gesamtplan der Wasserwirtschaft gefordert," *Badische Zeitung* [Freiburg], 4 November 1954; "185,000 Unterschriften für die Wutachschlucht," *Stuttgarter Nachrichten,* 27 October 1954, clippings in BAK B 245/6. Nuclear power is mentioned as an alternative in Fries, *"Rettet,"* 19; Konrad Buchwald, "Muß die Wutachschlucht wirklich geopfert werden?," *Stuttgarter Zeitung,* 6 February 1957, 12, clipping in BAK B 245/6; DNR *Rundschreiben,* no. 19 (10 February 1955): 2. On enthusiasm for hydropower in the early 1900s see Blackbourn, *Conquest,* 219. On Hockenjos's opposition to nuclear power see Günther Reichelt, *Wach sein für Morgen. 40 Jahre Bürger für Natur-und Umweltschutz in Baden-Württemberg* (Stuttgart: Theiss, 1992), 18.

41. Signature sheet and accompanying instructions, "Unterschriftsammlung, 'Rettet die Wutachschlucht,'" n.d. [April 1954?], BAN Naturschutzarchiv 0831513.

42. Hockenjos, report in *Verhandlungen* (1954): 79.

43. Kurt Kretschmann, "Rettet die Wutachschlucht!" *Natur und Heimat,* no. 11 (Nov. 1954): 326.

44. Linse, "Laufenburg," 28; and Falter, "Walchenseekraftwerk," 107–8, both in Linse, Falter, Rucht, and Kretschmer, *Bittschrift;* Rommelspacher, "Zwischen Heimatschutz und Umweltprotest," 77–78; Jarausch, *Recivilizing Germans,* 160.

45. Jarausch, *Recivilizing Germans,* 158–60.

46. Hockenjos, "Erinnerungen," 62. On the radical implications of the petition drive see Reichelt, *Wach sein*, 19–20; Engels, *Naturpolitik*, 183.

47. Hockenjos, report in *Verhandlungen* (1954): 78–79; "Kampf um die Wutachschlucht geht weiter," *Badische Neueste Nachrichten* [Karlsruhe], 4 November 1954; "Interessen des Naturschutzes bleiben gewahrt," *Südwest Rundschau* [Freiburg], 26 October 1954, clippings in BAK B 245/6.

48. Hockenjos, report in *Verhandlungen* (1954): 78–79.

49. SSW, "Wozu Unterschriften?" April 1954, BAN Naturschutzarchiv 0831513. For the coalition's reply to SSW's accusations see Hockenjos to coalition members, 21 April 1954, BAN Naturschutzarchiv 0831513.

50. SSW, "Wozu Unterschriften?" April 1954, BAN Naturschutzarchiv 0831513.

51. The graphic is reprinted in Reichelt, *Wach sein*, 16.

52. Compare Prof. Dr. Eduard Kirwald to Forestry Division, South Baden, "Über die Beeinträchtigung der Belange der Forstwirtschaft durch die Beileitung von Wutach, Ibach und Murg," 5 April 1954, BAK B 245/6 with Hockenjos's report to the Forestry Division, South Baden, 13 April 1954, excerpted in Arbeitsgemeinschaft "Heimatschutz Schwarzwald," *Wutach-Brevier*, 22–27.

53. SSW, *Ist die Wutach-Schlucht wirklich gefährdet?*, 12–13.

54. Cioc, *The Rhine*, 130–33; Blackbourn, *Conquest*, 228–36; McNeill, *Something New*, 157–82.

55. Excerpt by Schneiderhöhn in Arbeitsgemeinschaft "Heimatschutz Schwarzwald," *Wutach-Brevier*, 10–11.

56. Stifel, Baden Agricultural Association, statement of 10 March 1955, in Arbeitsgemeinschaft "Heimatschutz Schwarzwald," *Wutach-Brevier*, 19–21.

57. Dr. W. Koch [South Baden State Fisheries Association], statement of 1 March 1955, 28–32; Dr. Elster [hydrologist], public lecture of 4 December 1954, 17–18, both excerpted in Arbeitsgemeinschaft "Heimatschutz Schwarzwald," *Wutach-Brevier*.

58. Verein der durch Bau und Betrieb des Schluchseewerkes Betroffenen, "und was sagt die Industrie?" 4 July 1955, in Arbeitsgemeinschaft "Heimatschutz Schwarzwald," *Wutach-Brevier*, 35–39. On the country's water management challenges see Wey, *Umweltpolitik*, 173–80; William Russell Mangun, *The Public Administration of Environmental Policy: A Comparative Analysis of the United States and West Germany* (Bloomington: Institute of German Studies, 1977), 66.

59. Arbeitsgemeinschaft "*Heimatschutz* Schwarzwald," *Trockenlegung*, 2–4, 6–7, in BAN Archiv C 63710; statement by Arbeitsgemeinschaft "*Heimatschutz* Schwarzwald," 15 April 1955, in *Wutach-Brevier*, 33–34. See also Fries, *Muß die Wutach abgeleitet werden?*, 14. On SSW's requirements see SSW, *Ist die Wutach-Schlucht wirklich gefährdet?*, 12–13; SSW, "Wozu Unterschriften?" April 1954, BAN Naturschutzarchiv 0831513. On the environmental impact of dams and reservoirs see Blackbourn, *Conquest*, 228–36; McNeill, *Something New*, 157–82.

60. Walter Fries to BANL [Gert Kragh], 26 May 1954, BAK B 245/6.

61. Federal Ministry of Economics to Gert Kragh, 24 September 1954, BAK B 245/6; Falter, "Walchenseekraftwerk," in Linse, Falter, Rucht, and Kretschmer, *Bittschrift*, 110.

62. Hockenjos, report in *Verhandlungen* (1954): 79.

63. Otto Kraus in *Verhandlungen* (1954): 79. Parallels between the Wutach and Lech conflicts are striking, though with the Lech the height of the dam was at issue. *Bayernwerk* agreed to lower the height to not flood the Litzauer Loop, one of the state's few stretches of unregulated river. See Dominick, *Environmental Movement*, 128–30; Bergmeier, *Umweltgeschichte*, 154–69.

64. The resolution is printed in *Verhandlungen* (1954): 91–92.

65. Otto Henninger, SSW to Gert Kragh, 27 August 1954, BAK B 245/6.

66. SSW to BANL [Kragh], 7 September 1954, BAK B 245/6.

67. Gert Kragh to Konrad Buchwald, 17 December 1954; Walter Fries to Kragh, 24 May 1955, both in BAK B 245/6.

68. Walter Fries to Gert Kragh, 24 May 1955, BAK B 245/6.

69. Walter Fries to Gert Kragh, 26 May 1955, BAK B 245/6.

70. Fritz Hockenjos to Gert Kragh, 23 May 1955, BAK B 245/6; Fries, *Muss die Wutach abgeleitet werden?*, 14; "Interessen des Naturschutzes bleiben gewährt. Landtagsausschüsse informierten sich über Wutachableitung, *Südwest Rundschau* [Freiburg], 26 October 1954, clipping in BAK B 245/6. For a comparison of forms of environmental activism that includes an analysis of the Wutach protest see Engels, *Naturpolitik*, 183–92, 369–76, 378–88.

71. Konrad Buchwald to Gert Kragh, 8 June 1955, BAK B 245/6.

72. Resolution by Friedrich Vortisch and others for a comprehensive water management plan, "Antrag," 26 June 1956, in Landesarchiv Baden-Württemberg, Hauptstaatsarchiv Stuttgart (HStA S), Innenministerium (EA 2/006)/Büschel 311 (hereafter HStA S EA 2/006/Bü 311). On the federal law see Wey, *Umweltpolitik*, 173–80; Dominick, *Environmental Movement*, 139–43.

73. Fritz Hockenjos, "Wutach-Ableitung (Erläuterungen zur Presse-Besprechung am 24.I.1957)," (hereafter "Erläuterungen 1957"), SWV-B, Wutachschlucht, #6.4. On officials' intervention in favor of utility companies see Falter, "Walchenseekraftwerk," in Linse, Falter, Rucht, and Kretschmer, *Bittschrift*, 114; more generally, Bergmeier, *Umweltgeschichte*, chap. 3.

74. "Neue Runde im Kampf um die Wutach," *Badische Volkszeitung*, 5 January 1957, clipping in BAK B 245/6; Hockenjos, "Erläuterungen 1957," 4–5, SWV-B, Wutachschlucht, #6.4; Fritz Hockenjos and Karl Asal (for Arbeitsgemeinschaft "*Heimatschutz* Südbaden"), "Darlegung der für die Beurteilung der . . . geplanten Wutach-Ableitung," 1 March 1959 (hereafter "Darlegung," 1959), SWV-B, Wutachschlucht, #6.4.

75. Hockenjos, "Erläuterungen 1957," SWV-B, Wutachschlucht, #6.4; Otto Henninger and Bassler to District Government Office (*Landratsamt*), Neustadt, 16 October 1956, HStA S, Kultusministerium (EA 3/102)/Bü 28 (hereafter HStA S EA 3/102/Bü 28).

76. "Vermutungen des 'Heimatschutzes.' Will das Schluchseewerk seinen Antrag 'durchpeitschen'?" *Badische Volkszeitung* [Karlsruhe], 5 January 1957, 17a, clipping in BAK B 245/6; Hockenjos, "Erläuterungen 1957," SWV-B, Wutachschlucht, #6.4; Gebhard Müller, Minister-President, Baden-Württemberg to Arbeitsgemeinschaft "Heimatschutz Schwarzwald," 12 February 1957, HStA S EA 3/102/Bü 29; "Der Ministerpräsident sagt eingehende Prüfung des Wutachprojektes zu," *Stuttgarter Zeitung*, 6 February 1957, p. 12, clipping in BAK B 245/6.

77. Buchwald, "Muß die Wutachschlucht wirklich geopfert werden?" On vertical alliances in this and other cases see Engels, *Naturpolitik*, 167–72.

78. Dr. Eugen Melchinger, SSW to Ministry of Culture, Baden-Württemberg, 27 February 1957, HStA S EA 3/102/Bü 29/doc.# 63; Buchwald to Ministry of Culture, Baden-Württemberg, 8 April 1957, HStA S EA 3/102/Bü 29, doc.# 72.

79. State Conservation Agency, Baden-Württemberg to Ministry of Culture, Baden-Württemberg, 6 February 1958, HStA S EA 3/102/Bü 29/doc.#109.

80. Fritz Hockenjos and Karl Asal, "Stellungnahme der Arbeitsgemeinschaft 'Heimatschutz Südbaden' zur gegenwärtigen Lage im Konzessionsverfahren bezüglich der Wutach-Ableitung," 31 May 1958 (hereafter "Stellungnahme," 1958), SWV-B, Wutachschlucht, #6.4.

81. Engels, *Naturpolitik*, 189.

82. Hockenjos and Asal, "Darlegung," 1959, SWV-B, Wutachschlucht, #6.4.

83. On the inter-ministerial disagreement over the 1943 decision see esp. Ministry of Culture, Baden-Württemberg to Ministry of the Interior, Baden-Württemberg, 31 October 1957, HStA S EA 3/102/Bü 29/doc.# 98; Ministry of the Interior, Baden-Württemberg

to Ministry of Culture, Baden-Württemberg, 17 April 1958, HStA S EA 3/102/Bü 29/ doc.#113. On similar struggles in other cases see Bergmeier, *Umweltgeschichte*, 261–63; Engels, *Naturpolitik*, 181–82, 205.

84. Ministry of the Interior, Baden-Württemberg, "Allgemeine Erläuterung zum wasserwirtschaftlichen Gesamtplan für das Wutachgebiet," n.d. [July 1958?], HStA S EA 2/006/ Bü 311.

85. Dr. Kübler, Ministry of the Interior, Baden-Württemberg, file note, 9 July 1958, HStA S EA 2/006/Bü 311/p. 97; Reichelt, *Wach sein*, 17.

86. Minister of Culture, Baden-Württemberg [Wilhelm Simpfendörfer] to Minister-President Gebhard Müller, draft, 30 June 1958, HStA S EA 3/102/Bü 29/doc. #120; Ministry of Culture, file note, 19 January 1959, HStA S EA 3/102/Bü 29/doc. #131.

87. Bergmeier, *Umweltgeschichte*, passim.

88. Hockenjos, "Erinnerungen," 64.

89. Gätschenberger, "Energieversorgung," in Pfizer, *Baden-Württemberg*, 275.

90. The Wutach-Gauchach Nature Reserve was expanded in 1989 beyond the original 579 hectares to encompass 950 hectares and was redesignated the "Wutachschlucht Nature Reserve." See "Naturschutzgebiete im Hochschwarzwald, Hotzenwald und Kaiserstuhl," available at <http://www.frsw.de/nsg.htm> (accessed 2 October 2006).

91. Untitled clipping from *Südwestpresse*, 21 March 1975 in HStA S EA 2/006/Bü 311; Engels, *Naturpolitik*, 343–44.

92. Karl-Werner Brand, Detlef Büsser, and Dieter Rucht, eds., *Aufbruch in eine andere Gesellschaft. Neue soziale Bewegungen in der Bundesrepublik* (Frankfurt am Main: Campus, 1983), 85.

93. On preservationists' "non-political" goals see Engels, *Naturpolitik*, 192–96, 205–6. On local self-interest see Bergmeier, *Umweltgeschichte*, chap. 3; Engels, *Naturpolitik*, 172–80.

94. Uekötter, "Erfolglosigkeit," in Brüggemeier and Engels, *Natur- und Umweltschutz*, 122; Falter, "Walchenseekraftwerk," in Linse, Falter, Rucht, and Kretschmer, *Bittschrift*, 110.

Chapter 4

ORDERING LANDSCAPES AND "LIVING SPACE" IN THE MIRACLE YEARS, 1956–1966

In the 1957 federal elections, Chancellor Konrad Adenauer's CDU party and its sister party of Bavaria, the Christian Social Union (CSU), promised "Prosperity for All." Their campaign slogan came from the title of a book ghostwritten that year for Ludwig Erhard, Federal Minister of Economics and architect of West Germany's "economic miracle." The publication called for economic growth to continue unimpeded to produce national wealth that would benefit all citizens. The country's remarkable recovery was already evident in industrial production, which had more than doubled since 1945.[1] Into the 1970s, with the exception of the recession in 1966–1967, West Germany's annual rate of economic growth surpassed that of other industrialized nations, leaving its economy in third place behind the US and Japan. Yet the liberal economic policies that contributed to postwar prosperity favored industry and commerce. By the mid 1960s, a minority of the population controlled much of the country's wealth. But few people protested because unemployment was low at 0.5 percent in 1965, and average disposable household incomes rose steadily, quadrupling between 1950 and 1970.[2]

"Prosperity for All" was a nice campaign promise. But it was a hard one to keep. In general, the country's expanding urban areas experienced prosperity more than the rural regions. By 1961, roughly one-third of the country's 56.5 million people lived in cities having more than 100,000 inhabitants; another 46 percent lived in smaller urban areas. At the end of the decade, 45 percent

---

Notes for this chapter begin on page 140.

of West Germans lived in twenty-four densely populated metropolitan areas, with at least 1,250 people per square kilometer. These conurbations covered 7 percent of the country's total area. For many urbanites, city life meant the chance to enjoy new levels of prosperity. Average household monthly incomes of blue and white collar workers and the self-employed doubled between 1955 and 1965, and more West Germans owned an automobile—a symbol of affluence. The 500,000 vehicles recorded in 1955 climbed to four million by 1960, an increase that accompanied the spread of low density cities which required people to commute from homes in the suburbs to jobs in the city. By 1961, over 30 percent of all employees commuted to work, compared with 18 percent from a decade earlier.[3]

These general trends apply less readily to rural regions where the agricultural sector was rapidly shrinking. Between 1949 and 1965, 488,000 small farms of ten hectares or less ceased operation. Over this same period, those employed in agriculture dropped from 23 percent of the working population to 13 percent, or from five million to three million people. In these rural communities, governments struggled to attract modern industries to strengthen their tax base and modernize infrastructure. The story was much the same for the eastern border zone, a forty-kilometer wide area that extended from the Baltic Sea, along the East German and Czechoslovak borders, and then south to Passau. This zone covered 19 percent of West Germany's total area and was home to 12 percent of the population.[4]

During the Miracle Years, the Federal Republic was like other nations of Western Europe in strengthening spatial planning (*Raumordnung*) at all administrative levels in order to address the disparities in infrastructure and economic opportunity. Since the 1930s, industrialized nations from the Soviet Union to the United States placed greater emphasis on centralized planning. In Nazi Germany, the regime had established the Reich Agency for Spatial Planning in 1935 to oversee regional offices throughout Germany and made area research (*Raumforschung*) a scientific discipline in several universities. In the Old Reich, planners pursued their work pragmatically, but many of their colleagues in the eastern occupied territories used their expertise in developing plans that supported ethnic cleansing. Because the institutional apparatus for spatial planning in the Old Reich remained in place under the Federal Republic, some officials concluded that *Raumordnung* was little more than a relic of Nazism; others associated it with communist dictatorships. In either case, spatial planning seemed incompatible with a democratic society and free market economy.[5]

But postwar realities convinced most officials that some degree of centralized planning was needed to restore order to society and the economy. The influx of millions of refugees, the disruption of trade between east and west with the division of the country, and the rapid pace of reconstruction created a number of challenges that officials hoped to address with effective territorial planning.[6] With the return to economic stability in the 1950s, *Raumordnung* also promised to lessen the gap between prosperous and poor regions. West Germany's constitution already mandated a "unity of living standards" across the states (Article 107), a goal that was partly achieved "through federal re- distribution" of specific tax revenues to poorer states and through payments from financially wealthier *Länder* (Baden-Württemberg, Hamburg, and Hesse) to poorer, often more rural ones (Bavaria, Lower Saxony, Rhineland- Palatinate, and Schleswig-Holstein). Guided by the Basic Law's guarantees of liberty, social equality, and security, postwar planners came to view *Raum- ordnung* as a vital policy tool that would enable them to guide the country's economic development in more rational directions, ultimately preventing the social inequality (and chaos) they feared would result from *too much* freedom in the economic sphere.[7]

Paradoxically, the constitutional guarantees of liberty, equality, and secu- rity were being compromised by the affluence that made more West Germans supportive of their democracy. Beginning in the 1950s, West Germany and other industrialized nations witnessed an accelerated increase in land use, the burning of cheaper fossil fuels, and the pollution of water, soil, and air. The democratization of consumer technology, especially during the 1960s, en- abled more people to afford household appliances that saved labor and time, but used more energy and created new environmental problems. Washing machines created mounds of suds on lakes and rivers, the result of new deter- gents containing phosphates that stimulated plant growth, which in turned fueled a population explosion of oxygen-consuming zooplankton, with nega- tive consequences for aquatic ecosystems. Mass motorization, the increased use of oil for home heating, and the expansion of the petroleum products industry heightened demand for oil. This in turn contributed to more spills and leaking fuel tanks—problems collectively dubbed the "oil plague," a term newly minted during the 1950s.[8]

As West Germans concentrated less on bread and butter issues and focused more on quality of life concerns, conservationists joined cautionary voices across the political spectrum in linking prosperity to worsening pollution and haphazard development. Engineers responded to these threats to health and well-being by developing new technologies to reduce air pollution, and by cooperating with medical researchers to draft guidelines for air quality and acceptable noise levels in cities and the workplace. For their part, conservation- ists renewed longstanding hopes to play a partnership role in managing land use. During the Miracle Years, conservationists were forced to modernize their practices by adopting more professional and objective scientific standards. In- fluenced by the prevailing enthusiasm for rational planning during the 1960s, some cooperated more closely with planners, embracing their progressive, technocratic ambition to design the places where people lived, worked, and relaxed into ordered spaces where each individual enjoyed health, prosperity, and dignity.[9]

The most tangible result of this uneasy and unequal alliance between conservationists and planners was the nature park program, a topic that forms an important part of this chapter. When launched in 1956 by VNP chairman, Alfred Toepfer, the nature park program appeared to be an example of "conservation as usual": a private group teamed up with commissioners to combat the perceived ills of modernity, establishing recreational "oases of calm" in idyllic rural settings to offset the "mechanization" of daily life in "denatured" cities. But as federal and state governments devoted more resources to spatial planning at the end of the 1950s, the nature park program became a planning project overseen by experts who could settle competing claims on space made by multiple parties. Regional planners' involvement forced conservationists to view nature parks not merely as scenic landscapes for rejuvenation (*Erholungslandschaften*), but as "model landscapes" (*Vorbildslandschaften*) that might illustrate how to use the country's territory more efficiently and equitably.

The nature park program illustrates in a microcosm what influential conservationists wanted to do on a grander scale through inclusion in territorial planning. Influenced by spatial planners' goals, and concerned about deteriorating environmental conditions, conservationists warned in the late 1950s and early 1960s that West Germany's entire "living space" (*Lebensraum*) was at risk. Although tainted, this term conveyed ecological awareness that problems ranging from erosion to pollution to sprawl had cumulative effects that directly threatened public health and the quality of life. Two decades after the Nazi regime waged a genocidal war for living space, prominent conservationists rehabilitated the concept, divorcing "*Lebensraum*" from its geopolitical association and using it to give tangibility and definition to a domestic problem. In naming the problem—a living space endangered by West Germany's economic success—conservationists asserted their professional expertise in restoring the country's urban and rural landscapes to ecologically healthier conditions. They believed that by helping design a "more natural" and "orderly" living space, they would assist planners in addressing a larger social challenge, namely protecting the dignity and well-being of each individual.

To increase their leverage in decisions about land use, leading conservationists strengthened university degree programs for landscape planning experts and participated in the creation of the German Council for Land Cultivation (*Deutscher Rat für Landespflege,* or DRL), an elite advisory body that turned landscape planners into political actors. The cultivation of landscape planning professionals contributed to the modernization of state-sponsored *Naturschutz*, yet frequently these new experts were disappointed by their inability to influence planning decisions to the same degree as their counterparts representing more powerful interests, such as industry, transportation, and agriculture. In addition, by the late 1960s and early 1970s, professional landscape planners lost touch with "ordinary" lay activists who found new leadership in public figures with a more confrontational message and style.

Protecting Prosperity and Health: The Nature Park Program

The modernization of West German conservation was not all that evident in the mid 1950s. As the economy rebounded, conservationists more frequently billed their work as a social amenity, with a familiar rationale. Their worry that fast-paced urban living threatened physical and emotional health echoed early twentieth century critiques of industrial society, which reflected an ambivalence toward modernity and fears about "uprooted," unruly laboring classes and youths. Such arguments also sounded like a modified version of claims advanced in some circles since the early twentieth century that the health of racial groups was organically linked to the health of their surroundings. But heightened concern about unhealthy conditions in the country's expanding cities also revealed an understanding of health beyond the absence of disease. Higher expectations for general well-being were indicative of an improved standard of living in West Germany and other advanced industrial countries.[10] In addition, a growing body of medical research linked physical illnesses to unhealthy conditions in cities, most visibly air pollution. In the 1950s, doctors viewed worsening air pollution as the number one threat to public health.[11]

But some physicians identified a much larger problem. "[N]ot a day goes by," one doctor reported in 1955, "without a number of patients complaining about the two cardinal ailments of our time: nervousness and chronic fatigue." Higher instances of stress-related illness (*Managerkrankheit*) and so-called diseases of civilization (*Zivilizationskrankheiten*)—high blood pressure, heart disease, and cancer—reported in North American research and observed in their own patients, convinced some West German physicians that people were "no longer at home" in the hectic, automated urban environment they had created. According to Joachim Bodamer, the conservative Catholic neurologist and psychologist whom conservationists often cited, the modern world that humans made "threatens to be our enemy because our body, mind, and sensory organs originally were made for another world and can no longer adapt." Bureaucratization, mechanization, and the frantic pace of urban life, he argued, caused an emptiness of the spirit, a loss of individual identity, and an inability to cope with solitude. To combat this perceived cultural malaise, he prescribed relaxation in natural surroundings, advice that benefited conservationists by giving their cause a clear social orientation and by offering medical research that might reinforce their conservative critique of modern society.[12]

The idea to establish public parks for recreation developed in conjunction with the urban public health movement, which emerged in the mid nineteenth century. By the twentieth century, laws and constitutions recognized the importance of protecting nature for public well-being, including the RNG, which declared in its preamble that the state had the responsibility to provide "even the poorest citizen his share of the beauties of nature." Several constitutions of West Germany's new *Länder* also obliged the state to establish public parks for recreation.[13] The idea found concrete expression in the early 1910s when the VNP purchased land for three public parks, and later in the 1930s when conservationists set aside large landscape reserves in the Rhine and Mosel valleys.[14] In the early 1950s, the Swabian Alb Society cooperated with conservation commissioners and officials to establish "peaceful oases" closed to automobiles in three counties in the region. At the same time, the German Working Group for Fighting Noise (*Deutscher Arbeitsring für Lärmbekämpfung*), another broad alliance formed in the early 1950s by doctors, engineers, industrialists, and representatives of tourism, promoted "noise-free areas for relaxation."[15]

Organizations viewed these measures as a partial antidote for a mounting problem. According to a 1955 poll conducted by the Bielefeld-based Emnid Institute, 41 percent of the people interviewed said that noise disturbed them daily. Nearly a quarter claimed that they suffered physical or emotional harm as a consequence of noise from traffic, industry, airplanes, radios, and youth.[16] Conservationists tended to view noise pollution as a matter of maintaining public order, related only indirectly to their work, but they agreed that fighting the problem was "urgently necessary" in the interest of public health. Thus, they encouraged the creation of "oases of calm" closed to automobiles.[17] Not until the early 1960s was research available to establish a clear link between noise pollution and health. According to the Max Planck Institute for Occupational Physiology, low levels of noise caused psychological reactions, but middle range levels could disrupt normal circulation and contribute to anxiety in some people; higher levels of noise could impair hearing permanently. In response to such findings, the Working Group for Fighting Noise and the Society of German Engineers developed guidelines for acceptable levels of noise, which were used to update the civil code and support new ordinances and laws, including federal legislation in 1965 protecting people from construction noise.[18]

In the 1950s, before guidelines and supporting scientific research were available, conservationists responded to noise and air pollution by setting aside "oases of calm" in the countryside. In June 1956, the VNP captured public attention and government endorsement when Toepfer unveiled a plan to establish "spacious, noise-free nature reserve parks" for "the welfare of those seeking rest and recovery, for the satisfaction of youths who love to hike, and for the best of research and science." Before an audience that included Federal President Heuss and other dignitaries, Toepfer argued that DM 10 million in support from the federal government—a mere fraction of the DM 10 billion spent on defense—was a small price to pay to "promote public health" and to "strengthen love of the homeland."[19] West Germany, he emphasized, lagged behind other densely populated nations such as the Netherlands, Japan, and Great Britain in providing its hard working urban population with "quiet oases."[20] A media blitz packaged the parks as "nature's treasure trove," and as "sources of strength" for people and the economy. In these "landscapes for rejuvenation," office and factory workers would stretch their limbs (quietly and orderly), temporarily escape the pollution that plagued the cities, and return to their jobs fully restored and ready to work.[21]

Originally Toepfer intended for the VNP and other organizations to purchase land for approximately six parks and administer them privately (as was the case with VNP property in the Lüneburg Heath). This modest plan quickly expanded to include twenty, and then thirty-six potential parks, ruling out land purchases, but calming farmers' and foresters' fears of dispossession. Yet the core of Toepfer's socially oriented, conservative vision remained in tact for the time being. A number of popular scenic areas from the North Sea to the Alps would be preserved (in a static state) and accessible to the public free of charge.[22] By spending time in rural landscapes that recalled the country's preindustrial past and represented its regional homelands, Toepfer reasoned, urbanites would strengthen their bonds of loyalty to the new democratic German homeland.[23] For Toepfer and Herbert Offner, the officer for conservation in the Federal Ministry of Agriculture (BML), oases of calm would cultivate industrious, dependable citizens who derived moral and physical strength through quiet, solitary activities in nature. According to Offner, "[w]hoever in this time of automation has not forgotten to listen to their inner voice will confirm . . . that immersing one's self in God's creation contributes to a renewal of mental and spiritual powers, strengthens and steels the body, and heals what is not well. Whoever lives in nature, whoever . . . acts in accordance with nature . . . will be a well-balanced, peace-loving, more communicative—in short, better—human being."[24] Worried that city folk were "wasting" their free time watching Hollywood films, playing sports, listening to the radio, dancing to rock and roll, and later, viewing television—preferences confirmed by scholarship on West Germany's emerging mass consumer culture—Toepfer hoped that nature parks would facilitate a presumably more constructive use of leisure time. Setting aside nature parks, he explained in the conservative daily *Die Welt,* "involves not only preserving the scenery of landscapes and the nature of our homeland, but also cultivating the labor of inhabitants of our major cities, and sensibly shaping leisure time, more of which will be available to us with increasing prosperity."[25]

Conservationists were not alone in their paternalistic concern to promote constructive use of leisure time. As more West Germans enjoyed their Saturdays off, and as the average workweek shortened from a high of 49 hours in 1955 to approximately 46 hours at the end of the decade, politicians, clergymen, professionals, and intellectuals fretted that "the masses" would squander their free time on cheap (American influenced) entertainment, or engaged in immoral activities. Despite their worries, however, most West Germans stayed close to home reading, gardening, listening to the radio, and visiting with family and friends. Some also opted to spend a portion of their leisure time outdoors, as was evidenced by the two million visitors to the Lüneburg Heath in 1955 and the 20,000 cars parked near Titisee in the Black Forest on Pentecost in 1957. But as Toepfer pointed out, West Germany had a limited number of large parks—too few to satisfy the growing demand for outdoor recreation areas near urban centers. And until the 1960s, few people had the money and time for long distance weekend getaways. Thus, Toepfer's plan to establish several nature parks engaged a pressing social issue by providing factory and office workers with affordable options for using their leisure time in ways deemed appropriate.[26]

Yet the renewed popularity of recreation in nature had its drawbacks. As in previous decades, conservationists complained about people who trampled vegetation, pitched tents and fished in unauthorized locations, left trash along trails, in woods and streams, and disrupted nature's calm with rowdy activities, and now transistor radios.[27] Some conservationists feared that nature parks would only encourage such behavior. To assuage these concerns (which they sympathized with), Toepfer, Offner, and supportive conservationists informed critics that parks would be carefully mapped out to improve the management of tourists, whose numbers only would increase.[28]

Toepfer's attempt to lay down rules for "orderly conduct" in the nature parks revealed a paternalistic desire to guide the uninitiated in experiencing nature properly, i.e., according to the preferences of a veteran *Wandervogel* who nostalgically recalled solitary nature walks that encouraged introspection and cultivated self-discipline and self-reliance. But his old fashioned concern for order also expressed a need to balance preservation with public recreation more effectively, a challenge that accompanied democratized access to the outdoors. Nature park supporters were confident, however, that disruptive visitors could be controlled in landscapes that would be transformed into well-ordered "natural" spaces that inspired disciplined conduct and served as a model for social harmony.[29] Yet the specter of unruly urbanites flocking to areas designated as nature parks, and invading tranquil forests and quiet villages, compelled some communities and forestry officials to resist the program, especially in Baden-Württemberg where the first nature park was erected only in the early 1970s.[30]

In general, however, the nature park program found widespread support among federal, state, and local leaders, irrespective of political party. To ensure the program's success, Toepfer turned to government agencies that could balance competing claims on land by agriculture, industry, the military, recreation, and communities seeking to expand their economic base. Thus, he worked closely with Offner and Theodor Sonnemann, state secretary (1949–1961) to Federal

Minister of Agriculture, Heinrich Lübke (CDU). Three federal institutes helped determine the location of parks and prepared general guidelines for the states to use in erecting them: the Federal Agency for Nature Protection and Landscape Care (BANL) under the BML; and the Federal Agency for Regional Geography and the Institute for Regional Planning, both under the Ministry of the Interior (BMI).[31] Between 1957 and 1963, twenty-six parks encompassing over 15,000 square kilometers were established across the country, primarily in the heavily industrialized northern states of North Rhine-Westphalia, Hamburg, and Hesse. By the mid 1970s, Bavaria had the most parks with a total of fifteen. Two decades after the program began, over fifty nature parks had been erected on 15.6 percent (38,828 square kilometers) of the total area of the Federal Republic. By the time of unification in 1990, the former West Germany had sixty-four nature parks covering 22 percent of its territory, a much greater percentage than neighboring France, which in the 1990s had thirty-three similar parks covering 11 percent of its (larger) territory.[32]

Behind this picture of cooperation and success were disagreements over the parks' primary purpose. In keeping with the VNP's traditional emphasis on preservation, publicity initially stated that the parks would give equal attention to recreation and stringent preservation. But Toepfer quickly retreated from this position because of protests from farmers and foresters who feared restrictions on the use of their property, and under pressure from Offner, a forester by training.[33] Indicative of the mindset that delayed West Germany's establishment of national parks and large, stringently protected reserves like other European countries (including heavily populated ones), Offner maintained that "[i]n our densely populated fatherland every square meter of ground serves an economic purpose. A synthesis between nature protection and economics must be found that—with good will on both sides—will not cause any difficulties."[34] Thus, park advocates struck a compromise: they placed few restrictions on traditional economic uses in the nature parks. When property owners continued to raise objections, park promoters reminded them of their responsibilities to the public weal, including making their property accessible. In turn, Toepfer assured them, visitors would respect the rights of landowners by being "considerate, quiet, and tidy."[35]

In the first two years of the program, those involved in the research, design, and implementation of the parks remained uncertain about what to call them. BANL Director Gert Kragh, and Toepfer on occasion, referred to them as "national parks" to justify public funding and to convey that these scenic landscapes formed the core of the country's natural heritage.[36] But Kragh also hoped that conservation commissioners might oversee the administration of the new "national" parks, and thus qualify to receive government salaries and increase their leverage in decisions about land use.[37] Interest in calling the areas "national parks" also reflected considerable activity in the 1950s and 1960s to erect national parks in Europe and elsewhere, and eagerness on the part of West

Germans to conform to western models in protecting nature as a tourist attraction.[38] But the national park designation would have been inappropriate for what West Germans were planning. The areas to be set aside were large relative to the size of the country, but most would be administered by private bodies, not the state, as was expected in national parks. In addition, all of the areas had been influenced by farming or forestry, traditional uses that continued with few restrictions in nature parks. Moreover, the parks did very little to protect nature, one of the core objectives of national parks. It was Offner who found a solution, recommending that West Germany follow the example of Sweden where large recreation areas that permitted some economic use were called "nature parks."[39]

This designation, too, caught fire from critics who argued that it conjured images of "amusement parks," not "peaceful oases," or who justifiably noted that "protection" (*Schutz*) was absent from the term (and would be from the parks as well).[40] Because of limited attention to preservation, conservation commissioners grew critical of the program.[41] They were especially annoyed when officials not responsible for conservation drafted ordinances for the new nature parks that weakened the protection of existing reserves now included in the parks. They also worried that with so much publicity devoted to nature parks, other responsibilities associated with conservation would receive less government funding.[42]

Because of conservation commissioners' misgivings, Toepfer and Offner preferred working with regional planners and thus turned to them in 1959 for an appraisal of the VNP's evolving proposal. When Toepfer first went public with the nature park idea, he was responding to the so-called diseases of civilization—a more up to date version of criticisms of modernity. But planners challenged Toepfer's understanding of nature parks as the antithesis of "denatured" cities, viewing them instead as extensions of urban areas.[43] "We have a form of existence [today]," the planner Gerhard Isbary argued, "in which work and recreation . . . are inseparable parts of a whole . . . we need rejuvenation outdoors for total rehabilitation of our personality."[44] Regional planners especially took issue with Toepfer's backward looking vision to preserve idyllic landscapes from the inevitability of social and economic change. Although there was a decisive social orientation to his plan to make the country's most popular landscapes accessible to the public free of charge, it overlooked the plight of rural inhabitants whose agrarian way of life was becoming a thing of the past. From the institute's point of view, nature parks were not natural landscapes needing protection in a static state, but spaces requiring reorganization and design. "In a time of intense structural transformation of society and the economy," planners asserted, "the idea of *preservation* is no longer adequate . . . For people of the present, landscapes of the present must be designed, so that the inhabitants of the city find beauty, satisfaction, peace and relaxation, and the country dweller makes a good living."[45]

Toward this end, planners proposed establishing nature parks in less economically developed areas of the Federal Republic, which were experiencing population loss as people left struggling small farms behind and migrated to cities in search of better paying jobs. The guiding hand of experts would transform poor rural areas into attractive "model landscapes" (*Vorbildslandschaften*) that would demonstrate how to use the country's territory more equitably and efficiently.[46] The institute referred to nature parks as "model landscapes," not because they fulfilled an ideal of a scenic area with little sign of development, but because they would serve as the building blocks of spatial planning. In theory, "model landscapes" would reduce sprawl, provide recreation areas for the well-being of an industrious urban labor force, and improve economic conditions in the rural areas designated as nature parks.[47] Literally speaking, planners sought to "order the space" (*Ordnung des Raumes*) in which people conducted their daily lives, ultimately to improve the quality of life for all of the country's inhabitants.

But shaping nature parks into model landscapes was a difficult goal to achieve because of inadequate funding for planning and long term maintenance and because of the economic priorities of local governments.[48] Until 1962, the federal government provided the bulk of funding to establish nature parks, after which the states, communities, and legal sponsors assumed a greater share of the burden of financing new parks and paying for the upkeep of existing ones. And it was a burden because most communities and sponsors lacked the means to adequately fund comprehensive planning for and constant oversight over the parks.[49] State conservation and planning offices laid the groundwork for the parks, but sponsor organizations at the local level assumed the work of establishing and maintaining them.[50] The majority of sponsors were registered private associations, with members including local communities, private organizations, firms, and individuals. Other sponsors took the form of public associations, wherein several communities united for the purpose of running a park (*Zweckverband*).[51] In 1963, nature park sponsors formed the Association of German Nature Parks (*Verband Deutscher Naturparkträger*, VDN) with Toepfer as president.

Ideally, local officials were to draft detailed plans for nature parks within the context of state level territorial plans. In the first decade of the program, however, parks came into being as a result of initiatives at the local level before sufficient planning had been done to manage the parks in conjunction with surrounding areas. In fact, during the 1960s, 80 percent of the funding for nature parks was spent not on long-range planning, but on trails, parking lots, restrooms, campgrounds, and other structures.[52] Nature parks themselves were organized in three zones to manage the flow of visitors and to serve up an ideal of nature that was clean, ordered, well-furnished, and ready for mass consumption. The outermost area, designed to handle the heaviest impact from tourists, included parking lots, campgrounds, picnic areas, hostels, hotels, gas stations, concessions, and public restrooms, and in some cases, entire vacation villages. Within the core of the parks were benches, lookout towers, hiking, biking, and horseback riding trails, and paths where visitors could learn about flora and fauna. To ensure that people could relax and move about freely, the parks were to be at least 200 square kilometers. But the size varied, from 38 square kilometers (Harburger Berge, Hamburg) to 2,908 square kilometers (Altmühltal, Bavaria).[53]

The first new nature park, Hoher Vogelsberg in central Hesse, was established in 1958 to serve as a recreation area for the Rhine-Main region. Though situated in an area experiencing a decline in agriculture, little was done to ensure that the park might ease locals' transition to a service-oriented economy. The park's legal sponsor lacked funds to hire experts who might have drafted plans to help attract appropriate businesses and services. Instead, the limited money available was spent primarily on recreational facilities. By 1971, Hoher Vogelsberg recorded forty pensions, three hostels, four ski lifts, one stable, a small wildlife reserve, three campgrounds, over 90 kilometers of hiking trails, and nearly thirty parking lots for 1,500 automobiles. Just over 1 percent of this 385 square kilometer park was stringently protected.[54]

Because of the lack of planning prior to establishing Hoher Vogelsberg, most states later required sponsors to provide evidence that they had a concrete landscape plan to follow before they were eligible to receive funding.[55] A park better planned in relation to the surrounding area was Rothaargebirge, established in North Rhine-Westphalia in 1963. Extensive planning prior to and after the opening of the park took into account that the area was making the transition from a farming economy to one based on tourism. But this park, too, was first and foremost a recreation area, with sixty-two ski lifts, over 100 small parking lots to accommodate 2,500 automobiles, nine playgrounds, over 1,400 kilometers of hiking trails, seven youth hostels, and forty pensions. Less than one percent of the 1,130 square kilometer park was stringently protected.[56]

The nature park program epitomizes the partially green compromises reached during the Miracle Years. Nature parks responded to consumer demand for recreation areas and helped local economies by stimulating tourism. But the program led the public to believe that steps were being taken to protect nature without restricting economic growth. As conservationists had predicted, preservation was rarely effective in nature parks because their ordinances prioritized recreation and placed few restrictions on forestry and farming or on the settlement of new industry. Some found their sentiments aptly expressed by a conservation commissioner in Aachen who concluded in the late 1960s that many of the parks were threatening nature in their attempt to provide an assortment of recreational activities to satisfy ever diversifying expectations, from "fairytale forests" to mini-golf courses. Partly because of inadequate concern for protecting nature, a vocal minority of conservationists forged ahead with plans to establish West Germany's first national park where stringent preservation would be a priority, the subject of chapter 7.[57]

Despite disappointments with the program, commissioners' participation in setting up nature parks contributed to reforms in the states' outdated approach to conservation. By conceptualizing nature parks as a planning challenge, some commissioners joined a growing body of experts shaping decisions about land use and regional development. Viewing nature parks as an aspect of territorial planning elevated the importance of conservation, yet simultaneously subordinated it to broader, more abstract planning decisions. To the frustration of conservationists, planners seemed to consider nature to be little more than "green space" that could be arranged on a map, as part of a larger process of rationally ordering economic development to distribute the fruits of prosperity more evenly among the population. Indicative of the excessive rationalism that pervaded expert planning, by the late 1960s those involved in establishing recreation areas devised a system that allowed them to quantify "objectively" the recreational value of an area, for example, by measuring the distance between meadows and forests or the length of shores. That the parks had more to do with spatial planning than with conservation is indicated by the fact that "nature park" first became a legal category in federal and state laws for territorial planning passed in the 1960s.[58]

Modernizing and Professionalizing Conservation

During the Miracle Years, conservationists were most concerned about the steady replacement of fertile landscapes with industrialized farms and urban sprawl. Those involved with official conservation hoped to correct this undesirable development by drafting legally binding landscape plans (for areas with few inhabitants) and land use plans (for areas that included settlements) in cooperation with regional planners. As their work overlapped more frequently with planners—most clearly through the nature park program—they joined these experts in linking urban and rural landscapes, conceptualizing them as unified space needing better planning, order, and design.[59]

Enthused about the possibilities for strengthening conservation by assuming a partnership role in spatial planning, BANL Director Gert Kragh organized the 1959 German Conservation Day around the theme "order in the landscape, order of space." His move was an attempt to improve communication between commissioners and planners who were at odds over the goals of the nature park program. Another reason for the conference focus was a cost cutting proposal to unite the BANL with the Institute for Spatial Planning in the BMI. The merger did not take place, though as Kragh noted, it might have strengthened the agency by giving it the overarching perspective needed not only to plan nature parks, but also to advise ministries in water management, pollution abatement, and nuclear waste removal.[60]

In many ways the 1959 annual conference showed state-sponsored conservation at a crossroads. The keynote speaker, Erich Dittrich, Director of the Institute for Spatial Planning, challenged commissioners to abandon cherished assumptions about their work and adopt a more modern, technocratic perspective. For starters, the concept "landscape," defined as "countryside" in the RNG, needed to be expanded to reflect the spread of industry, housing, and transportation into what had been countryside. Conservation must not halt where the country meets the city, Dittrich insisted, because that boundary was less clear. Just as urban planners viewed the city in its relationship to the surrounding area and the entire region, conservationists likewise needed to consider their work in connection with urban centers and with people's needs foremost in mind. Like planners in other industrialized nations at the time, Dittrich believed that regional planning could impose a rational, more harmonious order upon society. Through spatial planning, the state would create the agreed upon conditions for order in the spaces where people conducted their daily lives, ultimately guaranteeing social equality, freedom, and security.[61]

Kragh accepted the challenge of participating in this ambitious undertaking, explaining to skeptical colleagues that while regional planners refereed competing social, political, economic uses of space, conservationists would be there with plans that defended the landscape, ensuring that it remained healthy for citizens' well-being. A "healthy landscape," he clarified, underscoring the economic and recreational value of nature, was one with its "household" in balance and capable of maximum productivity over the long term. But it also was one free of pollution harmful to human health and with the potential to heal people physically, emotionally, and spiritually. For Kragh and other reformers, an ecologically "healthy landscape" looked little different from the landscape ideal that preservationists of previous decades had embraced. It was a patchwork of fertile fields and open meadows, of orchards and parcels of forest with diverse green hues, all stitched together by rows of hedges on a backing with rolling hills. But unlike their predecessors who had envisioned a harmonious blending of nature and technology—of rural tradition and modern engineering—Kragh and other reformers viewed vanishing rural areas as cultural landscapes needing protection from additional intrusions by technology. Disagreeing with the planners, they viewed countryside as space that needed to be preserved in a static state, much like smaller scale nature reserves, to offset the country's highly engineered landscapes that were rapidly increasing in number. Yet Kragh did not omit conurbations from his reform agenda, for even mechanized cityscapes could be made "more natural" and healthier with parks, gardens, forests, and cleaner air and water.[62]

According to Kragh, the science of ecology offered the most accurate means of assessing the health of rural and urban landscapes. After inventorying soil, vegetation, bodies of water, and terrain of a specific area, plans would indicate where legally protected reserves existed or ought to be established, where new development projects could be tolerated, and what kind of measures would be needed to restore an ecologically healthy order to places harmed by exploitative use. These plans would be presented at licensing hearings for construction projects or would aid officials in developing strategies for balancing conservation and economic growth.[63]

A vocal minority of commissioners resisted Kragh's timely reform initiative that aimed to professionalize and securely institutionalize conservation. By August 1959, around thirty commissioners had formed the "Bayreuth Circle" opposing the agenda. Led by 70-year-old Carl Duve, long-time commissioner for Hamburg, the group insisted in outdated fashion that their primary duty involved "fulfilling and securing Germans' longing for primeval nature." Those who felt inspired to protect nature, Duve argued, were individuals who understood that the "dynamism of the natural creative force" could not be grasped using statistics, scientific facts, or abstract plans. "[A] one-sided specialized education" in landscape planning, they maintained, did not automatically qualify people to serve as fulltime commissioners. It was no substitute for idealism, they implied.[64] The Bayreuth Circle dissolved in a matter of months, but deserves mentioning because it captured the faint echo of a dying voice in landscape care.

Arguments of the Bayreuth Circle also offer evidence of the friction that Kragh and other reformers caused when they tried to modernize conservation by taking on additional planning responsibilities, a move that made nature's care more reliant on ecology, yet also more abstract and technocratic. Kragh's colleague and second chairman of the ABN, Otto Kraus, a proponent of scientifically based preservation, concluded that Kragh should step down as chair because his recommendations seemed overly reliant on abstract planning. (Kragh himself was not fond of planners' tendency to refer to nature and landscapes as "green space.")[65] In 1962, Kragh left the BANL for a position with the Landscape Association Rhineland (*Landschaftsverband Rheinland*) in Cologne-Deutz, one of a growing number of planning organizations to emerge outside of the conservation bureaucracy.[66] The BANL remained under the Federal Ministry of Agriculture where it merged with the Institute for Vegetation Science (*Vegetationskunde*) in 1962, forming the Federal Institute for Vegetation Science, Nature Conservation, and Landscape Care (hereafter BAVNL). Beginning in the mid 1960s, the institute became more research oriented, a telltale sign of the scientification of state-sponsored conservation, which increasingly set it apart from private organizations. The BAVNL went on to complete several studies for federal ministries, among the most important an ecological assessment of "Strains on the Landscape," published in 1969 as an early state of the environment report.[67]

But state-sponsored conservation was slow to change because there still were too few qualified people to take on responsibilities associated with land use planning, a weakness highlighted in chapter 5, a case study on canalizing the Mosel River. Most state-level conservation commissioners were employed fulltime by the 1960s, but those at the district and local levels continued to hold honorary posts into the 1970s when their agencies were replaced with bureaucratic positions occupied by experts.[68] At the local level, where important decisions about economic development were made, few commissioners had professional training qualifying them to assist with land use planning. In the 1960s, of West Germany's 575 local commissioners, forty-one percent (235) had a background in pedagogy. Foresters represented the next highest group at 18 percent (104), followed by civil servants at 13 percent (77), and garden architects at 12 percent (69). Moreover, in 1967 roughly one-third of local commissioners were over sixty-five; a few were over eighty.[69]

Cultivating a younger generation of professionals to take on expanded planning responsibilities required updating training programs at technical schools and universities.[70] And here the Miracle Years witnessed noteworthy achievements, thanks to the efforts of individuals like Konrad Buchwald (1914–2003), another veteran of the back-to-nature youth movement, a former state conservation commissioner, and a self-described proponent of ecology from the right. As Director of the Institute for Landscape Care and Conservation at the Technical University of Hanover (1960–1979), Buchwald was instrumental in strengthening existing programs in the mid 1960s to better reflect the range of competencies a new generation of professional landscape planners would need to fill the growing number of jobs with government planning, construction, and transportation offices, and in the private sector. In addition to general courses in chemistry, biology, botany, and physics, there were specialized ones in fields ranging from soils, hydrology, and meteorology, to animal ecology and synecology. Because human beings were at the center of all efforts to develop and conserve the landscape, Buchwald argued, students needed exposure to human ecology, sociology, public health, urban planning, and architecture, as well as the legal foundations of regional and land use planning. After completing exams and a thesis, the candidate earned a masters degree in horticulture and entered a two year probationary period.[71] To be sure, "horticulture" was an inadequate designation for a program with such breadth. But the label serves as a reminder of the influence that garden and landscape architecture traditionally had on conservation in Germany and elsewhere in Europe, where hybrid landscapes sculpted by human use were the object of protection and design. This degree program was but one of many that were eventually instituted in technical schools and universities to cultivate experts who could approach decisions about conservation and land use from a holistic perspective, one grounded in the social and natural sciences.

In search of a label that would express the broad range of competencies associated with the new class of professional landscape planners, Buchwald dusted off the concept "*Landespflege*," which literally means "land cultivation," and gave it a more precise definition. "Land cultivation," he explained, had three dimensions: the preservation of species, biotopes, and rural landscapes (in his view, the embodiment of ecologically healthy land); the greening of urban areas; and the ecological restoration of land adversely affected by economic uses. A term with roots in the Enlightenment, "land cultivation" came to be associated with state planning on a grand scale during the Third Reich when landscape architects used it to express their ambitious racial plan for total planning authority in transforming land in the East into a living space that would sustain the Aryan race. In the Federal Republic, "land cultivation" remained a technical term used in diverse ways by professionals with training in landscape architecture. During the 1960s, however, the practice of *Landespflege* as outlined more precisely by Buchwald served as the primary vehicle for modernizing state-sponsored conservation by linking it to spatial planning and giving it clear ecological underpinnings. According to Buchwald, insights from ecology—the science concerned with the reciprocal relationship between animals, plants, and their surroundings—were needed to come to terms with the threatened "environment" (*Umwelt*) of human beings. But no science, including ecology with all of its branches, is value neutral.

In theory and in practice, ecologized *Landespflege* expressed the social conservatism of its principle proponent. A conservative at heart, Buchwald still fretted in the early 1960s that too many people took early retirement because of health problems stemming from lost spiritual ties to nature and from living in the "denatured urban environment."[72] Never before, he argued, had humans made such demands on "their living space, the landscape." In less than a generation, the human created world of managed forests, mechanized farms, high rises, suburbs, industrial complexes, airports, highways, and rail networks had been layered more thickly over the natural world, rapidly replacing it, creating out of a "near-natural environment" an "artificial Ersatz world" which threatened physical and emotional health. And there was ample evidence to support these views in new research by the Max Planck Institute for Occupational Physiology, which linked illnesses to pollution and hectic work environments and in official reports, such as one by the US Outdoor Recreation Commission, which emphasized nature's therapeutic value.[73] But if humans had built these unhealthy surroundings, Buchwald asserted, expressing tempered optimism about technocratic solutions, professional landscape planners could restore them to a "more natural" order and ensure that a "life of dignity remained possible."[74] Such views indicate that Buchwald's vision for modernizing conservation contained not only conservative elements, but progressive ones as well. His agenda was progressive in its concern to protect individual dignity, but paternalistic in its conviction that only expert planners could impose a presumably more rational, natural, and healthy order on the environment for the benefit of the masses.

Toward the Protection of "Living Space"

Whether socially conservative or politically liberal, a number of influential West Germans reached a consensus in the late 1950s and early 1960s that the country's agglomerations where a near majority of the population lived had become "disordered," unhealthy, and a threat to individual dignity. Efforts to control urban pollution in the Federal Republic have been examined in numerous articles and books, and thus do not need a detailed discussion here.[75] Suffice it to say that the boom years were a time of unprecedented media coverage and legislative activity aimed at mitigating worsening pollution. The Federal Republic was not alone in focusing on pollution control in the late 1950s and early 1960s, passing laws to manage the water supply (1957), to maintain clean air (1959), and belatedly to ban DDT (1972), eight years after Rachel Carson's *Silent Spring* appeared in translation and quickly became a top ten best seller in West Germany.[76] Increased concern throughout the industrialized world about pollution and the quality of life in cities reflected a tendency in these countries to shift attention to the negative aspects of prosperity after a period of steady economic growth. This had been the case also in the 1890s and the 1920s.[77] In addition, however, a more affluent population with higher expectations for the good life had grown less tolerant of pollution.

Moreover, threats to the water supply and air pollution had increased to the extent that they could not be ignored without compromising public health. To note some of the more glaring examples, the country's largest lake, Lake Constance, was dying from industrial effluents and untreated sewage that had tipped its ecosystem out of balance, compromising its recreational value and its ability to supply communities with drinking water. Plans in the 1960s to lay an oil pipeline along the Austrian side of the lake and to build a shipping canal connecting Lake Constance to the Rhine at Basel were abandoned in the face of determined opposition from conservationists and city governments, such as Stuttgart which tapped into the lake for their water supplies.[78] The Rhine registered the impact of an even longer period of exploitative use by riparian states. Over several decades, chemical industries and the hydroelectric, petroleum, and nuclear companies they relied on, had reduced the river to "one long 'sacrificed stretch'" that was declared "near-dead" in the mid 1970s.[79] Despite water management laws, West Germany's rivers, lakes, and coasts grew more polluted until the trend began to be reversed in the 1970s.

Slightly more hopeful were efforts to reduce air pollution, a problem that had grown intolerable in the 1950s in the Ruhr, prompting organized protests from city governments and educated middle class citizens who formed local emergency alliances in cities like Duisburg, Essen, and Bochum. At the end of the decade, some citizens ratcheted up the pressure on polluters and lawmakers by bringing charges against industrial firms. In addition, in 1961, West Berlin mayor Willy Brandt (SPD) made air quality and public health central issues in his unsuccessful campaign against Adenauer for the chancellor's post. Seeking support from the eight million voters in the Ruhr, Brandt called for "blue skies" over the industrial region, justifying the novel focus of his political campaign with research linking air pollution to higher instances of cancer. The winning CDU/CSU parties trivialized the "blue skies" slogan, even though that year 1.5 million tons of particulate matter rained on the Ruhr and four million tons of sulfur dioxide put over 400 square kilometers of forest in the region at risk.[80] By the mid 1960s, air quality actually improved somewhat because of new laws, federal emissions guidelines (issued in 1964), and better technologies. The installation of electric filters in industry in the Ruhr reduced particulate matter (dust decreased from 310,000 tons in 1963 to 245,000 tons in 1968) and higher smokestacks distributed sulfur dioxide in lower concentrations, though without reducing the amount of gas emitted. But these measures did not address the growing threat from motor vehicles emitting lead and carbon monoxide.[81]

The challenge facing advanced industrial societies such as West Germany involved more than fighting pollution in the urban environment. According to the liberal *Süddeutsche Zeitung,* 10 percent of the country was built over with homes, industry, highways, rail networks, and airports, or saturated with "the waste of civilization" in the form of pollution, toxins, and garbage. And it seemed as if the hunger for space would not subside because every year an area the size of Munich was converted into a city or road.[82] By the mid 1960s, West Germany had over three thousand kilometers of highway, more than nearly all other western European nations combined, and second behind the US.[83] The face of the countryside, too, was changing radically as land consolidation accelerated under pressure to compete within the European Economic Community (EEC) and in the global marketplace. Researchers with the BANL reported in 1961 that each day in West Germany, 60 hectares of farmland (primarily holdings of 10 hectares or less) went out of production, replaced by new homes, industries, or roads, or by large scale farming operations run by fewer people. Rationalized agriculture meant that more food could be produced on less land. Yet it also meant more monocultures and fewer plant and animal species, more heavy machinery that compacted the soil, and heavier applications of pesticides and fertilizers that poisoned drinking water with excess nitrogen and phosphorus.[84]

But some of the statistics bandied about at the time were misleading. If 10 percent of West German territory was covered by settlement (an area that corresponded to the country's two dozen urban concentrations), then around 90 percent was not. According to regional planners writing in the late 1970s, 84 percent of the country's "economic space" existed in the form of forests or farmland, in their estimation "a remarkably high proportion for a densely populated industrial state."[85] Furthermore, not all of the farms that fell out of production became a factory, road, or housing settlement. Without underestimating the dramatic changes effected by the crisis in agriculture (like that in mining occurring simultaneously as West Germans and other Europeans shifted to oil as a cheaper source of fuel), it is important to point out that some farmland was "recycled" back into use as forests or recreation areas. Similarly, abandoned gravel pits, mines, and harbors became the focus of renaturing projects in and near metropolitan areas.[86] But in the face of rapid, exploitative land use, these efforts seemed insignificant. As the crisis in agriculture transformed the countryside at a dizzying pace and polluted cities spread outward, conservationists viewed urban and rural areas as unified "living space" needing better planning, order, and design.[87]

The most promising and democratic vision for addressing the cumulative problems that seemed to threaten West Germans' "living space" was expressed in the Green Charter of Mainau, an often cited document made public in 1961 by the Swedish-born nobleman, Graf Lennart Bernadotte, President of the German Horticulture Society.[88] In the latter 1950s, Bernadotte convened a series of roundtable discussions, or "Green Parliaments," on the Island of Mainau on Lake Constance attended by prominent individuals in government, science, and culture to examine threats to nature and public health.[89] Eager to convert roundtable talks into a concrete reform program, Bernadotte organized a commission that included some of the country's most influential conservationists from the field of landscape architecture, including Buchwald and Kragh, to draw up a charter of principles that would serve as the "green" conscience of the nation.[90]

Unveiled in June, the Green Charter declared that "[t]he basic foundations of our life have fallen into danger because vital elements of nature are being dirtied, poisoned and destroyed." The document asserted that the "the dignity of human beings is threatened where his natural environment (*Umwelt*) is damaged." Grounded in Articles 1, 2, and 14 of the Basic Law, which guaranteed the protection of human dignity, liberty, and the right of inheritance respectively, the charter insisted that a "healthy living space" in city and country was a basic inviolable human right. "For the sake of human beings," the twelve demands of the charter called for regional planning at all levels of government to consider the natural conditions of an area, and for landscape plans to guide the construction of housing, industries, and transportation in all communities. It demanded public access to mountains, lakes, rivers, forests, and scenic landscapes, and adequate space for recreation in and near cities. Because the "living space" was already damaged, however, the charter called for more effective soil and water conservation to restore "a healthy household in nature" and insisted that measures should be taken to repair unavoidable intrusions from mining and construction. Realizing these goals, the charter emphasized, required more research, better laws, heightened public awareness through improvements in education, and "a readjustment in thinking by the entire population."[91]

The Green Charter did not mark a bold departure from current practices, but the consolidation of years of work by many. Since the mid 1950s, for example, federal and state governments had worked together to improve spatial planning. The year the charter was published, the federal government issued a comprehensive spatial planning report, which pledged to make the Basic Law's guarantees of liberty, equality, and security the basis for territorial planning. In conjunction with the nature park program, the BANL worked to make legally binding land use plans an integral part of regional planning, and private organizations and state and federal officials had begun to set aside "green spaces" for public recreation. The charter's reference to sustainable agriculture reflected the federal government's "Green Plan," which appropriated funds to encourage farmers to plant shelterbelts to control erosion. For nearly a decade, organizations like the DNR and the ABN had demanded better instruction in the biological sciences. Finally, since its founding in the early 1950s, the IPA had taken the lead in passing laws to control pollution and practice conservation in tandem with development.

To transform the charter's ambitious principles into deeds, in 1962 Bernadotte convinced Federal President Lübke (1959–1969, CDU) to serve as the official patron of the German Council for Land Cultivation (*Deutscher Rat für Landespflege*, or DRL). The DRL was a body of publicly prominent individuals who weighed in on controversial proposals such as the Upper Rhine canal and the establishment of the country's first national park in the Bavarian Forest, two projects it opposed. The council's membership, which fluctuated between eleven and fourteen members in its early years, initially included men who overwhelmingly came from the generation born in the late Wilhelmine Empire. Several also had helped draft the charter (leaving some private conservation groups to grumble about the preponderance of landscape architects).[92] In addition to Bernadotte, the council included Buchwald, IPA chairman Otto Schmidt, Professor Erich Kühn, a specialist in urban and land use planning at the Technical University in Aachen, federal constitutional court justice Erwin Stein, and Theodor Sonnemann, former state secretary in the federal agriculture ministry and the new president of the *Raiffeisenverband*, a league representing farmers' interests. In 1963, Alfred Toepfer came on board as did Gerhard Olschowy, later director of the BAVNL (1964–1976). The country's leading ecologist, Wolfgang Haber, joined the elite group in 1980, serving as the council's speaker from 1991 until 2003. Like so many other conservation initiatives in Germany, the DRL united private and public efforts, an arrangement that gave it semi-official status and increased its influence, primarily in the 1960s while Lübke remained in office. (Lübke resigned in 1969 after it was proven that he had drafted plans for concentration camps.) The DRL's relations with subsequent federal presidents would never be so close, nor would it acquire the political clout its founder desired.[93]

Some historians question the significance of the DRL, arguing that it did little to alter public consciousness or political institutions.[94] Yet the council deserves attention because it is an example of professional landscape planners functioning as political experts to address societal concerns. Contrary to the DRL's claim to be an independent body offering objective assessments of issues for the common good, however, it was a self-selected group of men that tended to view problems from the narrow perspective of landscape planning and was not immune to trumping the views of locals with the opinions of nationally known specialists who reflected the council's preferences. The DRL espoused a conservatism that was evident in its political strategy. In the words of one recent study, it was "conservative, harmonizing, [and] elitist" in presuming to know what was best for the public good, yet also "progressive [and] technocratic" in relying on the authority of specialists to sway public opinion on issues that ranged from managing solid waste to balancing tourism and preservation in the Bavarian Alps.[95]

Partly because of the Green Charter's association with a nobleman and an exclusive circle of government officials and experts, its democratic vision did not produce public outcry or inspire protests.[96] And yet the document left an important legacy in maintaining that "individual and . . . political freedom can unfold only in a living space with healthy conditions for existence," an assertion that made healthy surroundings an inviolable human right. It affirmed that having a space in which one could live with dignity and realize one's potential was fundamental to an improved quality of life. Moreover, the emphasis on protecting humanity's living space expressed recognition of the need to confront vast new problems threatening West Germans in whatever space they lived—in the countryside or the city.[97] In contrast to some old guard conservationists who continued to presume that urbanites needed to flee the city for the countryside on occasion to restore their sense of well-being, the charter (if not all DRL members) viewed the city as an environment in which the individual could find fulfillment. In addition, it expressed a vision for placing conservation on the same level as, not subordinate to, economic development.[98] Finally, the charter brought together problems that heretofore had been considered independently, prompting conservationists to demand administrative reforms.

Not long after the charter was publicized, DNR President Hans Krieg complained to a *Bundestag* deputy that the present organization of official conservation, with its lack of funding and qualified personnel would amount to "pitiful piecework" when confronted with the daunting challenge ahead: the "protection of living space." To ensure a holistic approach in tackling this problem, Krieg proposed the establishment of a new ministry for living space (*Lebensraum*) with departments for species preservation, pesticide control, water and air purity, and landscapes (which, he explained, included parks and reserves, social hygiene, and climate).[99] Adenauer did not establish a ministry for protecting living space or for spatial planning (as Kragh had suggested), but he did create a new Ministry for Health Affairs in 1961, which was responsible for air, noise, and water pollution, along with public health.[100]

To contemporary readers, it appears that Krieg was appealing for an environment ministry, but his and other conservationists' choice of terminology was odd, for "*Lebensraum*" was a concept with a troubled past. In the early twentieth century, plant geographers had used "living space" to refer to a niche that supported a community of plants (*Lebensgemeinschaft*). Some preservationists applied these scientific insights in commentaries on homeland landscapes, suggesting that the natural geography of a particular place played a key role in shaping its human occupants, in some cases approaching geographic determinism. During the 1930s and 1940s, *Lebensraum* had come to be associated with the primordial soil from which a racially pure *Volk* would be sustained and uplifted.[101] In the latter 1950s, conservationists rehabilitated the concept, suppressing its association with the expansionist, genocidal policies of the Nazi regime and using it to capture their sense of alarm about the rapid loss of space that remained fertile, scenic, and pollution free. How, they implied, could people living in such unhealthy surroundings continue to prosper economically, culturally, and physically? Such concerns sounded uncomfortably similar to those expressed by some landscape architects during the Nazi era, who had claimed that the German *Volk*, with its "biological origins in nature," needed "healthy" scenic landscapes to remain racially pure and physically robust.[102] Yet such racialized understandings of the relationship between humans and nature do not appear in conservationists' statements from the 1950s and 1960s. Nor is there evidence that conservationists even considered using their appeal to safeguard *Lebensraum* as a mask for discriminating against the growing number of non-Germans living within their borders. (Between 1960 and the early 1970s, the Federal Republic's population of foreign guest workers from southern Europe and Turkey increased from 279,000 to around two million.[103])

In its most basic scientific definition, *Lebensraum* means "habit," but it also implies an understanding of the reciprocal relationship between a species and its surroundings—in this case the human species. Unlike familiar terms such as *"Naturschutz"* and *"Landschaftspflege,"* the concept of a threatened "living space" gave tangibility to conservationists' fear that people had constructed an environment which had become so engineered—so denatured—that it threatened their health and compromised their quality of life. Reflecting these changes in human surroundings, "nature" was displaced somewhat in conservationists' discourse by the more abstract and versatile concept "space" (*Raum*). This discursive shift was significant, for it expressed a weakening of the mental association of "nature" with scenic rural landscapes, and opened up the possibility for seeing urban areas as "natural" to their human occupants.

Conservationists' concern to protect *Lebensraum* was reinforced by federal and state government efforts to implement spatial planning (*Raumordnung*). It also appears to have reached a crescendo in 1961, the year the Berlin Wall went up, making reunification with East Germany seem more remote. The increased use of "living space" was perhaps, on some level, if not a conscious one, an expression of some conservationists' attempts to come to terms with the Federal Republic's eastern political boundary. Their near obsession with a loss of space after WWII had, by the Miracle Years, shifted to a concern about the lack of order in the increasingly urban, industrial space that remained theirs to shape. A film produced by the Federal Ministry of Agriculture in the mid 1960s captures this change in perception. Entitled "Landscape, our Living Space," footage documented how an increase in population, wealth, and wants consumed more and more land for housing, industry, and transportation. To compete in the EEC and global market, less land was farmed more intensively, exhausting the soil while leaving other tracts fallow. The consequences of disorderly development were evident in stinking lakes, dead rivers, poisoned soil, smog and constant noise, and gravel pits that became garbage dumps filled with the waste of consumer society. But, the film emphasized, "[w]e suffer less from a lack of space than from a lack of 'order in this space.'"[104]

Before the term "environment" (*Umwelt*) was popularized around 1970 and environment ministries were established, West German officials attempted to address interrelated threats to human surroundings as a whole by establishing public health ministries and strengthening spatial planning at all administrative levels. In 1965, after a decade of work, the Federal Spatial Planning Act was passed, establishing general guidelines for imposing order on the future development of the entire country. The law stipulated that land use plans were to include measures to protect nature, maintain clean air and water, protect the public against noise, and set aside spaces for recreation. The *Länder*, which had primary jurisdiction over spatial planning as they did for conservation and water management, were responsible for drafting statewide territorial plans, working closely with lower level officials to meet local needs. Communities had the final say in planning decisions that affected them directly—in general a desirable arrangement. But too often during the economic boom years local leaders were more concerned to attract revenue-generating industries for the short term than to conserve resources and protect public health over the long term.[105] But the basic premise of postwar *Raumordnung*—to promote constitutional guarantees of liberty, social equality, and security—had taken root in public consciousness, arguably as part of a larger process in West Germany of "internalizing democratic values."[106] These democratic ideals served as a rallying point for early advocates of environmental protection (*Umweltschutz*).

During the Miracle Years noise, air, and water pollution, sprawl and exploitative land use rapidly changed the face of cityscapes and countryside, capturing unprecedented attention in the media, political campaigns, opinion polls, and stirring concern among more diverse groups of society. As historian Raymond Dominick maintained some years ago, the environmental movement of the 1970s did not emerge suddenly, but "grew gradually out of strong antecedents," including those of the 1950s and 1960s. During these years, the West German government enacted federal guideline laws to manage the water supply, reduce air pollution, and consider conservation in the context of spatial planning. The states, which had primary jurisdiction over these areas, passed more substantive legislation, though implementation varied in effectiveness. The Federal Ministry of Health Affairs, established in 1961, assumed responsibility for air, noise, and water pollution, but no specific office or ministry existed at the federal or state level to administer threats to human surroundings as a whole. After several months of close attention to pollution, sprawl, and related environmental problems, media coverage temporarily leveled off in the mid 1960s. Public interest waned and new crises erupted over the outdated education system and the mining industry. In addition, some grew frustrated over the cost of reducing pollution, while others concluded that threats to "living space" were being managed through diverse measures, from establishing nature parks to investing in new technologies for controlling pollution.[107]

In the late 1950s and early 1960s, when environmental conditions deteriorated perceptibly, conservationists found themselves at a crossroads. To prevent marginalization, individuals such as Kragh, Buchwald, and Bernadotte modernized *Naturschutz* by strengthening its institutional foundations and by engaging some of the most pressing social issues of the Miracle Years. Through participation in the nature park program, for example, conservationists helped address public health concerns and spatial planning challenges, though rarely to the extent they desired. By improving university degree programs for professional landscape planners, Buchwald and others ensured that experts employed full-time in the bureaucracy eventually replaced honorary conservation commissioners. Armed with specialized scientific knowledge, these new professionals hoped to have greater leverage than their idealistic predecessors in political decisions about the use of resources and space. There is some truth to the charge that landscape planners like Buchwald hoped to transform their field into a discipline with significant planning authority. Privileged by their scientific expertise, they expected to play a leading role in spatial planning, not merely a supporting one. As professional landscape planners, they would set the ground rules for using resources and space, determining whether or not those uses conformed to their conservative ideal of healthy landscapes and of healthy living. But this "claim to power" was ultimately incompatible with democracy.[108]

While this argument rings true to a degree, it is overstated. When viewed in the context of the 1960s—a decade marked by euphoria over rational planning across the industrialized world—landscape planners' bid for greater influence is understandable. Their ambitions also reflected the desire to set ecological considerations on equal footing with economic ones, a goal that required increasing landscape planners' political leverage vis-à-vis other powerful interests, most notably industry, the military, and agriculture. Spatial planning laws of the 1960s marked only the first step in this direction. But what of conservationists' commitment to democratic ideals? Although conservationists were like other social conservatives in remaining skeptical of mass democracy, the Green Charter of

Mainau stands as a clear statement of their support for constitutional guarantees of liberty, security, and individual dignity.[109]

Influenced by policy makers' attention to spatial planning, leading conservationists came to view urban and rural landscapes as a unified living space, one increasingly at risk and—critical for a more democratic outlook—a threat to individual dignity. Yet they, like government officials, remained unclear about the role that citizens should play in planning the development of their communities. The institutionalization and scientification of landscape planning widened the gap between experts and "ordinary" citizens, the former relying on presumably objective knowledge to make decisions for the public good and the latter often prioritizing personal experience. The new German Council for Land Cultivation, for example, assumed that an alliance of professional landscape planners and social and political elites could wield influence at the highest levels of government, remaining above partisan politics while implementing an ambitious vision expressed in the Green Charter—without the participation of citizens who were its central concern. This is not an entirely unusual development in contemporary politics where technocratic expertise exists in tension with democratic decision making.[110] But as Vilma Sturm, an editor for the conservative *Frankfurter Allgemeine Zeitung*, wrote in 1966, citizens needed to take more responsibility for a "green environment" by holding political leaders accountable for development decisions, demanding fewer kilometers of highway, and reducing the amount of trash they generated.[111] In the latter 1960s, a minority of West Germans were increasingly angry over their exclusion from planning decisions adversely affecting the quality of life in their communities.[112] By then, they were more willing to respond to appeals like Sturm's and the one made in 1966 by Bernhard Grzimek, the DNR president (1963–1968) and popular television personality making his debut as a charismatic and confrontational leader in West German conservation: "We all live in a democracy [where] public opinion matters." Rather than look to him to take action on their behalf, Grzimek urged supporters, "do something yourself. Have civil courage."[113]

Grzimek issued this challenge in increasingly turbulent times. In 1966, economic recession, growing dissent from an emerging New Left, and increased support in state parliamentary elections for a right-wing neo-Nazi party convinced political leaders that a strong, stable government was essential. As support for Chancellor Ludwig Erhard (1963–1966) collapsed, the CDU/CSU formed a coalition government in November 1966 with the other major party, the Social Democrats. The former Nazi, Kurt Georg Kiesinger (CDU) became Chancellor and the anti-Nazi Willy Brandt (SPD) served as Foreign Minister. But the Grand Coalition (1966–1969) left some West Germans feeling as though they had no means to express dissent within the political system. This view was strongest among the younger generation who had come of age in an affluent society and had grown increasingly critical of the wartime generation which seemed to have become too comfortable, complacent, and conservative. Encouraged by the emergence across the industrialized world of a counterculture opposed to consumerism, war, and conformity, and by expanded access to universities (which were overcrowded and had outdated curricula and authoritarian professors), West German students, supported by leftist intellectuals, insisted that only "extraparliamentary opposition" (*Außerparlamentarische Opposition*, or APO)—activism outside of traditional political institutions—would challenge the status quo. Students' sensational public protests, the sharp tone of their leftist anti-establishment rhetoric, and their fundamental questioning of modern industrialism left an indelible mark on the political culture in which environmental reforms of the 1970s were debated and implemented, a topic picked up again in chapter 6.[114]

Notes

1. Klaudia Prevezanos, "Propaganda für den Markt. Ludwig Erhard: Wohlstand für Alle," *Zeit* (1999), available at <http://www.zeit.de/zrchiv/1999> (accessed 17 July 2006).
2. Berghahn, *Modern Germany*, 226–28; Fulbrook, *Divided Nation*, 183–84.
3. Christoph Kleßmann, *Zwei Staaten, eine Nation. Deutsche Geschichte 1955–1970* (Göttingen: Vandenhoeck & Ruprecht, 1988; Bonn: Bundeszentrale für politische Bildung, 1988), 30, 32, 36–37; Georg Kluczka, "'Raumordnung'—Regional Planning and Spatial Planning and Spatial Development," in *Federal Republic of Germany: Spatial Development and Problems*, ed. Peter Schöller, Willi Walter Puls, and Hanns J. Buchholz (Paderborn: Schöningh, 1980), 14; Andersen, *Traum*, 127–35; Axel Schildt, "Urban Reconstruction and Urban Development in Germany after 1945," in *Towards an Urban Nation. Germany since 1780*, ed. Friedrich Lenger (Oxford and New York: Berg, 2000), 141–61, commuter statistics from p. 153. For automobile statistics see Schildt, "Freizeit, Konsum und Häuslichkeit in der 'Wiederaufbau'-Gesellschaft. Zur Modernisierung von Lebensstilen in der Bundesrepublik Deutschland in den 1950er Jahren," in *Europäische Konsumgeschichte: zur Gesellschafts- und Kulturgeschichte des Konsums (18. bis 20. Jahrhundert)*, ed. Hannes Siegrist, Hartmut Kaelble, and Jürgen Kocka (Frankfurt am Main: Campus, 1997), 333.
4. Childs, *Germany*, 187; Kluczka, "Raumordnung," in Schöller, Puls, and Buchholz, *Spatial Development*, 14–15.
5. Rössler, "'Area Research,'" 135–37; Rössler, "Institutionalisierung," 177–94; Winifred Süß, "'Wer aber denkt für das Ganze?' Aufstieg und Fall der ressortübergreifenden Planung im Bundeskanzleramt," in *Demokratisierung und gesellschaftlicher Aufbruch. Die sechziger Jahre als Wendezeit der Bundesrepublik*, ed. Matthias Frese, Julia Paulus, and Karl Teppe (Paderborn: Schöningh, 2003), 349.
6. Kluczka, "Raumordnung," in Schöller, Puls, and Buchholz, *Spatial Development*, 11; Norman Wengert, "Land Use Planning and Control in the German Federal Republic," *Natural Resources Journal* 15 (July 1975): 511–28.
7. Kluczka, "Raumordnung," in Schöller, Puls, and Buchholz, *Spatial Development*, 11–16; David Conradt, *The German Polity*, 4 ed. (New York: Longman, 1989), 22; Fulbrook,

Divided Nation, 181–85. On planning in centralized France see Bess, *Light-Green Society*, 49–52.

8. Pfister, ed. *Das 1950er Syndrom;* Arne Andersen, "Das 50er-Jahre-Syndrom—Umweltfragen in der Demokratisierung des Technikkonsums," *Technikgeschichte* 65, no. 4 (1998): 329–44; Rommelspacher, "Zwischen Heimatschutz und Umweltprotest," 76. See also the following essays in Siegrist, Kaelble, and Kocka, *Europäische Konsumgeschichte:* Michael Wildt, "Die Kunst der Wahl. Zur Entwicklung des Konsums in Westdeutschland in den 1950er Jahren," 307–25; Schildt, "Freizeit, Konsum und Häuslichkeit," 327–48.

9. Michael Ruck, "Ein kurzer Sommer der konkreten Utopie—Zur westdeutschen Planungsgeschichte der langen 60er Jahre," in *Dynamische Zeiten. Die 60er Jahre in den beiden deutschen Gesellschaften,* ed. Axel Schildt, Detlef Siegfried, and Karl Christian Lammers (Hamburg: Christians, 2000), 362–401. See also Scott, *Seeing Like a State,* and the following essays in Frese, Paulus, and Teppe, *Demokratisierung:* Karl Lauschke, "Von der Krisenbewältigung zur Planungseuphorie. Regionale Strukturpolitik und Landesplanung in Nordrhein-Westfalen," 451–72; and Gabriele Metzler, "'Geborgenheit im gesicherten Fortschritt.' Das Jahrzehnt von Planbarkeit und Machbarkeit," 777–97.

10. On parallel developments in the United States see Samuel Hays, *Beauty, Health and Permanence. Environmental Politics in the United States, 1955–1985* (Cambridge: Cambridge University Press, 1987).

11. Gerd Spelsberg, *Rauchplage: Hundert Jahre Sauerer Regen* (Aachen: Alano-Verlag, 1984), 82.

12. Gerhard Venzmer, "Wir haben es zu eilig," *Kosmos* 51, no. 4 (1955): 175; Joachim Bodamer, *Gesundheit und technische Welt,* 2d ed. (Stuttgart: Ernst Klett, 1960 [1955]), 21. For conservationists' references to Bodamer see Konrad Buchwald, "Gesundes Land—Gesundes Volk. Eine Besinnung zum Gesundheits- und Erholungsproblem," *N & L* 32, no. 6 (1957): 94–98; Otto Kraus, "Millionen gegen Almosen," *Verhandlungen* (1956), 37–39. On the larger context for Bodamer's critique see Hermann Glaser, *Kleine Kulturgeschichte der Bundesrepublik Deutschland 1945–1989* (Munich: Carl Hanser, 1991; Bonn: Bundeszentrale für politische Bildung, 1991), 178, 241–42.

13. Hans-Dietmar Koeppel and Walter Mrass, "Natur- und Nationalparke," in *Natur- und Umweltschutz in der Bundesrepublik Deutschland,* ed. Gerhard Olschowy (Hamburg: Paul Parey, 1978), 803.

14. Udo Hanstein, *Entwicklung, Stand und Möglichkeiten des Naturparkprograms in der Bundesrepublik Deutschland,* Beiheft 7, *Landschaft + Stadt* (Stuttgart: Eugen Ulmer, 1972), 6–7.

15. Georg Fahrbach, "Oasen der Ruhe," *Kosmos* 54, no. 10 (1958): 410–13. See also Richard Lohrmann (Swabian Alb Society) to BANL, 28 November 1955; Konrad Buchwald to BANL, 1 December 1955; "Protokoll der Besprechung zwischen dem Deutschen Arbeitsring für Lärmbekämpfung und der BANL," 10 November 1955, all in BAK B 245/240.

16. F. v. Tischendorf, "Gesundheitsgefährdung durch Lärm," *N & L* 32, no. 6 (1957): 92.

17. "Protokoll der Besprechung zwischen dem Deutschen Arbeitsring für Lärmbekämpfung und der BANL," 10 November 1955; Otto Kraus to BANL, 1 December 1955; Richard Lohrmann to BANL, 28 November 1955; Konrad Buchwald to BANL, 1 December 1955, all in BAK B 245/240; DNR *Rundschreiben,* no. 22 (16 January 1956): 3; "Entschließung der SDW Landesverband NR-W, 11.7.56," [draft], BAK B 245/231.

18. Hans Wiethaupt, "Rechtsfragen der Lärmbekämpfung," *N & L* 38, no. 8 (1963): 125–27.

19. Alfred Toepfer, "Naturschutzparke—eine Forderung unserer Zeit," *Naturschutzparke* (Autumn 1957): 172–74.

20. At the time, West Germany had an average population density of about 200 people per square kilometer and no national parks. Great Britain had 208 people per square kilometer and ten national parks, all established in the 1950s. Japan, with 232 people per square kilometer, boasted seventeen national parks by the mid 1950s, two erected in 1955. The

Netherlands, with 308 people per square kilometer, had three national parks at the time. See the UN List of Protected Areas at <http://www.wcmc.org.uk/protected_areas/UN_list/index.htm.> (accessed 8 August 2001).

21. There are over fifty newspaper clippings covering Toepfer's public announcement in the VDN Archive, Niederhaverbeck, Lüneburg Heath, binder entitled "Neue Naturparke. Die einzelnen Gebiete und Presse, 1956." "Schatzkammer der Natur," and "Naturschutzparke— Kraftquellen unseres Volkes," two films produced in 1956 by Eugen Schuhmacher to promote the program, are available in the VNP Archive.

22. "Wann kommen die Oasen der Ruhe?" *Die Welt,* 5 June 1956, and other clipping in VDN Archive, "Neue Naturparke. Die einzelnen Gebiete u. Presse 1956." On Toepfer's concern to keep parks accessible see "Das Programm des Vereins hat allgemein Zustimmung und starkes Interesse gefunden," *Naturschutzparke,* no. 10 (Autumn 1957): 302–4.

23. Confino, "Nation as a Local Metaphor," 62–64.

24. Herbert Offner, "Naturparke. Ein Problem unserer Zeit," 4–5, published lecture, 9 November 1957, VDN Archive.

25. Alfred Toepfer, "Wie helfen wir dem Großstadtmenschen? Naturschutzparks—ein Gebot der Stunde," *Die Welt,* 11 May 1957. On trends in consumer culture and leisure time activities see Axel Schildt, "'Mach mal Pause!'" Freie Zeit, Freizeitverhalten und Freizeit-Diskurse in der westdeutschen Wiederaufbau-Gesellschaft der 1950er Jahre," *Archiv für Sozialgeschichte* 33 (1993): 357–406. On the influence of American popular culture in Germany see Ute Poiger, *Jazz, Rock, and Rebels: Cold War Politics and American Culture in a Divided Germany* (Berkeley: University of California Press, 2000); Fehrenbach, *Cinema in Democratizing Germany.*

26. Schildt, "'Mach mal Pause!,'" 358–65, 395–401; Engels, *Naturpolitik,* 97–101; Jarausch, *Recivilizing Germans,* 120–24; Toepfer, "Der Tätigkeitsbericht des Vorsitzenden für die Zeit von Dezember 1955 bis Anfang April 1956," *Naturschutzparke* (May 1956): 136; Walter Fries to VNP, 18 June 1957, VDN Archive, "Baden-Württemberg 1.1.57-1.8.61."

27. E. Blaser, "Die grüne Welle kommt," *N & L* 36, no. 8 (1961): 144–46.

28. Alfred Toepfer, "Naturparke—Idee und Verwirklichung," *Naturschutzparke* (January 1962): 3–6. See also Herbert Offner, "Erholung durch Naturparke," *Kosmos* 57, no. 1 (1961): 18, 20.

29. Engels, *Naturpolitik,* 103–8.

30. On opposition in Baden-Württemberg see VDN Archive, "Baden-Württemberg, 1.1.57-1.8.61"; Eberhard Bopp, "Warum man in Baden-Württemberg keine Naturparke schafft," *Naturschutzparke,* no. 30 (August 1963): 31–32.

31. Toepfer, "Naturparke—Idee und Verwirklichung," *Naturschutzparke* (January 1962): 4; Theodor Sonnemann, "Bereitstellung großräumiger, lärmgeschützter Naturparke—eine soziale Verpflichtung," *Naturschutzparke,* no. 13 (September 1958): 436–38; BANL, "Empfehlungen zur Planung und Einrichtung von National-Parken," n.d. [spring 1957], VDN Archive, "Schriftwechsel mit den Bundesanstalten und Gutachten 1957."

32. Koeppel and Mrass, "Natur- und Nationalparke," in Olschowy, *Natur- und Umweltschutz,* 803–4; *N & L* 50, no. 10 (1975): 266–73; "Naturparke in der Bundesrepublik Deutschland," *N & L* 66, no. 4 (1991): 205–9; Bess, *Light-Green Society,* 221–22.

33. Herbert Offner, "Naturparke—ein Anliegen der Menschheit, 2. Teil," *Naturschutzparke,* no. 11 (Winter 1957/1958): 346; Offner, "Naturparke. Ein Problem unserer Zeit," 9 November 1957, VDN Archive; Offner, "Planung und Einrichtung von Naturparken," in *Das Naturpark-Programm und seine Probleme,* Schriftenreihe des Vereins Naturschutzpark e.V., ed. Verein Naturschutzpark e.V. (Stuttgart and Hamburg: privately published, n.d. [1962?]): 43. See also Hanstein, *Entwicklung,* 7–9.

34. Herbert Offner, "Ansprach des Naturschutzreferenten im Bundesministerium für Ernährung, Landwirtschaft und Forsten," *Verhandlungen* (1959): 110.

35. Offner, "Naturparke—ein Anliegen der Menschheit, 2. Teil," *Naturschutzparke,* no. 11 (Winter 1957/1958): 345–46; Egon Selchow, "Wie steht es mit den neuen Naturschutzparken?" *Naturschutzparke,* no. 10 (Autumn 1957): 307; quote from Toepfer, "Ansprache Dr. h.c. Alfred Toepfer auf der 52. Hauptversammlung in Hannover," *Naturschutzparke,* no. 22 (July 1961): 48. See also Prof. Dr. Herbert Krüger, "Die öffentliche Verantwortung des Eigentümers," in Verein Naturschutzpark e.V., *Das Naturpark-Programm und seine Probleme,* 99–103.

36. Alfred Toepfer, "Wie helfen wir dem Großstadtmenschen?" *Die Welt,* 11 May 1957. Among many examples of using the terms interchangeably are Toepfer, "Das Programm des Vereins hat allgemein Zustimmung und starkes Interesse gefunden," *Naturschutzparke,* no. 10 (Autumn 1957): 302–5; Hans Krieg, "Wir brauchen Naturschutzparke!" *Kosmos* 52, no. 5 (1956): 202, 205.

37. "Protokoll der Landesbeauftragten-Konferenz vom 10./11.5.1957 in Wilsede; and Egon Selchow, file note, "Besprechung mit Oberregierungsrat Kragh am 9. Mai 1957," 10 May 1957, both in VDN Archive, "Schriftwechsel mit den Bundesanstalten 1957"; Gert Kragh, "Naturschutz und Landschaftspflege in Ballungsräumen," *N & L* 35, no. 11 (1960): 161–64.

38. Karl Ditt, "Naturschutz und Tourismus in England und in der Bundesrepublik Deutschland 1949–1980," *Archiv für Sozialgeschichte* 43 (2003): 29–49.

39. Offner, "Naturparke—ein Anliegen der Menschheit, 2. Teil," *Naturschutzparke,* no. 11 (Winter 1957/1958): 350; Hanstein, *Entwicklung,* 5, n. 2.

40. *Ministerialrat* Ziegler, Ministry of the Interior, Baden-Württemberg to Egon Selchow, 15 March 1960; *Landesforstpräsident* Hubert Rupf, Ministry of Agriculture, Baden-Württemberg to Selchow, 23 December 1959, both in VDN Archive, "Baden-Württemberg, 1.1.57-1.8.61."

41. Gert Kragh to Alfred Toepfer, 18 February 1957; Kragh to Toepfer, 1 March 1957, both in VDN Archive, "Schriftwechsel mit den Bundesanstalten 1957"; Egon Selchow to Kragh, 7 October 1958, VDN Archive, "Schriftwechsel mit Institut für Landeskunde und BANL, 1.1.58-1.9.61."

42. "Protokoll der Landesbeauftragten Konferenz 1957"; Hildmar Poenicke [state conservation commissioner, Hesse] to Gert Kragh, 5 August 1957, both in VDN Archive, "Schriftwechsel mit den Bundesanstalten 1957"; Kragh to Egon Selchow, 2 October 1958; Kragh to Toepfer, 17 March 1960, both in VDN Archive, "Schriftwechsel mit Institut für Landeskunde und Bundesanstalt für Naturschutz, 1.1.58-1.9.61."

43. Toepfer, "Ansprache Dr. h.c. Alfred Toepfer auf der 52. Hauptversammlung in Hannover," *Naturschutzparke,* no. 10 (July 1961): 47; Toepfer, "Warum Naturparke?" *Naturschutz und Naturparke,* no. 41 (Second Quarter 1966): 6. See also Hanstein, *Entwicklung,* 7–8.

44. Gerhard Isbary, "Aufgaben der Erholungslandschaften im Einzugsbereich von Ballungsräumen," 3 September 1961, special printing of public lecture, in VDN Archive.

45. Erich Dittrich, "Der Ordnungsgedanke der Landschaft und die Wirklichkeit," *Verhandlungen* (1959): 127. See also Dittrich to Alfred Toepfer, 10 September 1959; Toepfer to Institute for Regional Planning, 25 August 1959, both in VDN Archive, "Bundesbehörde und Anstalten."

46. Gerhard Isbary, "Naturparke als Vorbildslandschaften," in Verein Naturschutzpark e.V., *Das Naturpark-Program und seine Probleme,* 30–31; Dittrich, "Ordnungsgedanke," *Verhandlungen* (1959): 126–29; Hanstein, *Entwicklung,* 11–13.

47. Dittrich, "Ordnungsgedanke," *Verhandlungen* (1959): 127–29; Isbary, "Naturparke als Vorbildslandschaften," in Verein Naturschutzpark e.V., *Das Naturpark-Program und seine Probleme* 30.

48. Theodor Sonnemann, "Der Naturschutz- und Naturparkgedanke in der Sicht der Raumordnung," *Naturschutzparke,* no. 27 (October 1962): 1–6, esp. 5; Alfred Toepfer, "Naturschutz,

Naturparke und Landschaftspflege," *Naturschutzparke*, no. 33 (April 1964): 47; Herbert Offner, "Die ländliche Umwelt in ihrer Bedeutung für die verstädterte Bevölkerung," *Naturschutz und Naturparke* (Third Quarter 1966): 40–43; Hanstein, *Entwicklung*, 11–16, 28.

49. In 1957, the federal government provided DM 250,000, but increased this amount to DM 900,000 the following year. Between 1959 and 1966, federal funding for nature parks and other recreation areas fluctuated between DM 1,350,000 and DM 1,800,000. Federal support fell after the 1966–1967 recession. Between 1967 and 1970, appropriations ranged from DM 752,000 to DM 809,000. Between 1956 and 1959, the states spent DM 307,000 on nature parks, but their contributions increased steadily, reaching DM 7,132,000 in 1975 (roughly equal to the federal government's outlay for recreation areas that year.) Third party contributions grew from DM 350,000 in 1957 to DM 11,677,000 in 1975, or roughly 44 percent of the total expenditures for nature parks. See Koeppel and Mrass, "Natur- und Nationalparke," in Olschowy, *Natur- und Umweltschutz*, 807; Koeppel, "20 Jahre Naturparkprogramm—Finanzierung und aktueller Entwicklungsstand," *N & L* 51, no. 5 (1976): 130–36.

50. Gert Kragh, "Empfehlungen zur Planung und Einrichtung von National-Parken," n.d. [May 1957] to state conservation commissioners, VDN Archive, "Schriftwechsel mit den Bundesanstalten 1957"; Hanstein, *Entwicklung*, 23–28.

51. Hanstein, *Entwicklung*, 64–79. Koeppel and Mrass, "Natur- und Nationalparke," in Olschowy, *Natur- und Umweltschutz*, 806.

52. Udo Hanstein, "Landespflege in Naturparken—Voraussetzungen, Stand und Möglichkeiten," in *Wiedergabe von Vorträge, 3/4 Oktober 1969, Mitgliederversammlung des Verbandes Deutscher Naturparke*, Schriftenreihe des Vereins Naturschutzpark e.V., ed. Verein Naturschutzpark e.V. (Stuttgart and Hamburg: privately printed, 1969): 9–15, esp. 12. See also the January 1968 issue of *Garten und Landschaft*, especially articles by Udo Hanstein, "Sind die Naturparkträger ihren Aufgaben gewachsen?" 14–15; Wolfram Pflug, "Landschaftspflege und Grünordnung im Naturpark Nassau," 8–12; and Gottfried Heintze, "Landschaftsplanung—Grundlage für die Entwicklung der Naturparke zu Vorbildslandschaften," 4–7.

53. Friedrich Wilhelm Dahmen, "Planung und Einrichtung von Naturparken," in *Handbuch für Landschaftspflege und Naturschutz. Schutz, Pflege und Entwicklung unserer Wirtschafts- und Erholungslandschaften auf ökologischer Grundlage*, ed. Konrad Buchwald and Wolfgang Engelhardt (Munich: Bayerische Landwirtschafts-Verlag, 1969), 80–87; Ulrich Nickel and Walter Mrass, "Zum Entwicklungsstand der Naturparke in der BRD," *N & L* 48, no. 6 (1973): 165–67.

54. Hanstein, *Entwicklung*, 64–65; Nickel and Mrass, "Entwicklungsstand der Naturparke," *N & L* 48, no. 6 (1973): 168–69. The size of the park is based on figures from 1975. There is no indication of how much land in the park was protected in the form of nature reserves at that time, so figures from the early 1990s are used. See VDN, "Naturparkliste. Stand Januar 1992," in author's possession.

55. Heintze, "Landschaftsplanung," *Garten und Landschaft* (January 1968): 4.

56. Herbert Prott, "Planung des Naturparkes Rothaargebirge," in Buchwald and Engelhardt, *Handbuch für Landschaftspflege und Naturschutz*, 92–96; Nickel and Mrass, "Entwicklungsstand der Naturparke," *N & L* 48, no. 6 (1973): 168–69. On planning nature parks in North Rhine-Westphalia see Oberkrome, *"Deutsche Heimat,"* 420–45. The size of Rothaargebirge is based on figures available from 1975. The percentage given for the stringently protected area reflects figures from the early 1990s.

57. Hanstein, "Naturparkträger," *Garten und Landschaft* (January 1968): 14–15; H. J. Bauer [district conservation commissioner, Aachen], "Vorbildslandschaften oder Erholungsindustrie in Naturparken?" unpublished manuscript, n.d. [March 1969?], VDN Archive, "Institut für Landeskunde, Dt. Gartenbaugesellschaft, Inst. für Raumordnung, Nsch.beauftragte, ABN, ABL"; Bernhard Grzimek to Alfred Toepfer, 17 April 1967, DNR Archive, binder entitled "Nationalpark Bayerischer Wald, 1966–1967."

58. Körner, "Entwicklung des Naturschutzes," in Brüggemeier and Engels, *Natur- und Umweltschutz,* 92–96; Koeppel and Mrass, "Natur- und Nationalparke," in Olschowy, *Natur- und Umweltschutz,* 806.

59. See esp. Konrad Buchwald, "Unsere Zukunftsaufgaben im Naturschutz und in der Landschaftspflege," *Verhandlungen* (1957): 33; Buchwald, "Naturschutz, Landschaftspflege, Landesplanung," *N & L* 33, no. 7 (1958): 113–15; Gert Kragh, "Ordnung der Landschaft—Ordnung des Raumes," *N & L* 34, no. 8 (1959): 113–17.

60. Director of the Institute for Regional Planning (Erich Dittrich) to Dr. Keßler, Federal Ministry of the Interior, 17 April 1959, copy in BAK, Federal Ministry of Agriculture (B 116)/10831 (hereafter BAK B 116/10831).

61. Dittrich, "Ordnungsgedanke," *Verhandlungen* (1959): 111–34; Dittrich, "Vom Schutz der Natur zur Ordnung der Landschaft," *N & L* 34, no. 5 (1959): 65–66.

62. For the definition of "healthy" landscapes see Gert Kragh, "Vom Naturschutz zu Landschaftspflegeplan," *Verhandlungen* (1959): 138; Konrad Buchwald, *Die Zukunft des Menschen in der industriellen Gesellschaft und die Landschaft* (Braunschweig: Hans August-Stolle, 1965), 43. For images of healthy landscapes see Kragh's "Erhaltung der Natur und der natürlichen Hilfsquellen in Europa," *N & L* 37, no. 2 (1962): 19; and "Naturschutz und Landschaftspflege in Ballungsräumen," *N & L* 35, no. 11 (1960): 166. On opposition to merging technology and culture in rural areas see Körner, *Theorie,* 107.

63. Kragh, "Landschaftspflegeplan," *Verhandlungen* (1959): 134–40. See also Kragh's "Ordnung der Landschaft, eine ungelöste Aufgabe," *N & L* 35, no. 5 (1960): 65–67; and "Naturschutz für die Stadt," *N & L* 35, no. 4 (1960): 49–53.

64. Carl Duve (for the Bayreuth Circle) to conservation commissioners, August 1959, VDN Archive, "Schriftwechsel mit Institut für Landeskunde und BANL, 1.1.58-1.9.61."

65. Otto Kraus's views are implied in Carl Duve to Dr. Schmitz (with the VNP), 7 February 1960, VDN Archive, "Schriftwechsel mit Institut für Landeskunde und BANL, 1.1.58-1.9.61." On Kragh's dislike of planners' abstract terminology see Wolfram Pflug, "Er is uns näher denn je," *N & L* 61, no. 9 (Sept. 1986): 321.

66. Pflug, "200 Jahre Landespflege," 258.

67. Gerhard Olschowy, "Über die Aufgaben und Arbeitsgebiete der Bundesanstalt," *N & L* 40, no. 3 (1965): 43–46; Frohn, "Natur macht Staat," in Frohn and Schmoll, *Natur und Staat,* 232–41, 254–62.

68. Buchwald, "Zukunftsaufgaben," *Verhandlungen* (1957): 36; Mrass, *Organisation,* table 24; Engels, *Naturpolitik,* 46. State commissioners in Rheinland-Palatinate, Schleswig-Holstein, and Bremen still held honorary posts. District commissioners were employed fulltime in Baden-Württemberg (with four) and North Rhine-Westphalia (with six). In Bavaria, three of seven district commissioners had fulltime positions. Figures for district commissioners in Saarland, Schleswig-Holstein, Hamburg, Bremen, and West Berlin are unavailable.

69. Mrass, *Organisation,* 41, table 25. See also Wolfgang Engelhardt, "Naturschutz in Deutschland heute und morgen," DNR *Informationsbrief* (September 1965): 6–8.

70. Wolfgang Engelhardt to Gert Kragh, 2 September 1955, BAK B 245/235; Engelhardt, "Fünf 'Offene Worte zur Lage,'" *N & L* 31, no. 1 (1956): 17–20.

71. Konrad Buchwald, "Wie studiert man Naturschutz und Landschaftspflege?" *N & L* 40, no. 1 (1965): 2–7.

72. On Buchwald's conservative route toward modernizing landscape planning see esp. Körner, *Theorie,* 99–121.

73. Konrad Buchwald, "Der Mensch in der Industriegesellschaft und die Landschaft," *N & L* 36, no. 12 (1961): 212–17; Buchwald, *Zukunft des Menschen,* 7, 15–17, 24; Buchwald, "Landschaftspflege und Naturschutz in der industriellen Gesellschaft," in *Naturschutz—eine politische Aufgabe,* ed. Georg Fahrbach (Stuttgart: Fink, 1965), 61–105.

74. Buchwald, *Zukunft des Menschen*, 8, 15, 41.

75. See for example Brüggemeier, *Tschernobyl;* Brüggemeier and Rommelspacher, *Blauer Himmel;* Dominick, *Environmental Movement;* Wey, *Umweltpolitik;* Uekötter, *Rauchplage;* Kluge and Schramm, *Wassernöte;* Mangun, *Environmental Policy.*

76. "Schädlingsbekämpfung. Schweigen im Walde," *Spiegel,* 14 November 1962, 118–22.

77. Dominick, *Environmental Movement,* 183–87; McCormick, *Reclaiming Paradise,* 49.

78. Dominick, *Environmental Movement,* 172–73; Cioc, *The Rhine,* 62–64, 148, 184, 199; Richard Brunnengräber, *Deutschland—Deine Landschaften. Ein Geographiebuch zum Thema Umweltzerstörung,* 2d rev. ed. (Munich: Deutscher Taschenbuch Verlag, 1985), 185–95; DRL, ed., *Bodenseelandschaft und Hochrheinschiffahrt,* Schriftenreihe des Deutschen Rates für Landespflege, no. 3 (Bonn: Buch- und Verlagsdruckerei Ludwig Leopold, 1965).

79. Cioc, *The Rhine,* chap. 5, quotes from p. 143.

80. "Zu blauen Himmeln," *Spiegel,* 9 August 1961, 24, 25; Brüggemeier, *Tschernobyl,* 188; Dominick, *Environmental Movement,* 202–3; Wey, *Umweltpolitik,*187. Gerhard Olschowy, "Die Pest, die sich so grausam ausbreitet," *Unser Wald,* no. 8 (August 1960): 193–95. See also Spelsberg, *Rauchplage,* 205–8. On the political impact of Brandt's 1961 campaign, see Hünemörder, *Frühgeschichte,* 51–64.

81. Rommelspacher, "Zwischen Heimatschutz und Umweltprotest," 82–84; Uekötter, *Rauchplage,* 460–70; Mangun, *Environmental Policy,* 58–59; Wey, *Umweltpolitik,* 187–90; Brüggemeier and Rommelspacher, *Blauer Himmel,* 67–69; Dominick, *Environmental Movement,* 191–93; Spelsberg, *Rauchplage,* 208–14.

82. Wolf Schneider, "Das große Landsterben," *N & L* 36, no. 1 (1961): 1–2, reprinted from *Süddeutsche Zeitung,* 29 December 1960.

83. Vilma Sturm, "Verantwortung der Bürger für ihre grüne Umwelt," *Der grüne Kreis* (July 1966): 12. See also Zeller, *Straße,* 216; Dietmar Klenke, "Bundesdeutsche Verkehrspolitik und Umwelt. Von der Motorisierungseuphorie zur ökologischen Katerstimmung," in *Umweltgeschichte: Umweltverträgliches Wirtschaften in historischer Perspektive,* ed. Werner Abelshauser (Göttingen: Vandenhoeck & Ruprecht, 1994), 163–89.

84. Heinrich Lohmeyer, "Unser Lebensraum ist in Gefahr," *N & L* 36, no. 3 (1961): 35; Gerhard Olschowy, "Über Gliederung und Gestaltung der bäuerlichen Kulturlandschaften," *N & L* 37, no. 4 (1962): 49–54; Brüggemeier, *Tschernobyl,* 186. See also Norwich Rüße, "'Agrarrevolution' und agrarpolitische Weichenstellungen in Nordrhein-Westfalen nach dem Zweiten Weltkrieg," in Frese, Paulus, and Teppe, *Demokratisierung,* 473–91; Lienenkämper, *Grüne Welt,* 89–96; Lohmeyer, "Agrarischer Strukturwandel und Landschaft," *N & L* 38, no. 11 (1963): 169–71; *Verhandlungen* (1967); Scott, *Seeing Like a State,* 262–73.

85. Kluczka, "Raumordnung," in Schöller, Puls, and Buchholz, *Spatial Development,* 13.

86. Gerhard Olschowy, "Der Beitrag des Landschaftsplaners zur Erhaltung von Naturlandschaften und Entwicklung von Kulturlandschaften," *N & L* 41, no. 11 (1966): 246–51.

87. Lohmeyer, "Lebensraum ist in Gefahr!" *N & L* 36, no. 3 (1961): 36. See also Lohmeyer, "Die Bedrohung unseres Lebensraumes und Maßnahmen zu seiner Pflege und Erhaltung im Zahlenspiegel," *N & L* 30, no. 8 (1964): 124–33.

88. Several studies mention the charter, including Bergmeier, *Umweltgeschichte,* 15–16; Brüggemeier, *Tschernobyl,* 200–201; Dominick, *Environmental Movement,* 144–46; Hermand, *Grüne Utopien,* 129; Oberkrome, *"Deutsche Heimat,"* 430–35; Wey, *Umweltpolitik,* 169–70; most extensively, Engels, *Naturpolitik,* chap. 3.

89. Heinrich Lübke, "Gesunde Luft, gesundes Wasser, gesunder Boden," in *Grüner Lebensraum um des Menschen willen,* 4. *Mainauer Rundgespräche, April 24, 1960,* Schriftenreihe der Deutschen Gartenbau-Gesellschaft, ed. Deutsche Gartenbau-Gesellschaft, no. 8 (privately published, 1960), 2–7.

90. Graf Lennart Bernadotte to Gerhard Olschowy, 9 December 1960, BAK B 116/10842; Olschowy, in-house memorandum, 3 February 1961, BAK B 116/10842.
91. "Grüne Charta von der Mainau," *N & L* 36, no. 8 (1961): 151.
92. Wolfgang Engelhardt to Gert Kragh, 5 December 1961, BAK B 245/235; Georg Fahrbach to Hans Krieg, 8 August 1962, BAK B 245/235.
93. Engels, *Naturpolitik,* 139–43.
94. Wey, *Umweltpolitik,* 170.
95. Engels, *Naturpolitik,* 139–54, quote from p. 152.
96. Engels, *Naturpolitik,* 149.
97. Chaney, "For Nation and Prosperity," in Mauch, *Nature in German History,* 105–6.
98. Engels, *Naturpolitik,* 131–35; Bergmeier, *Umweltgeschichte,* 15–16.
99. Hans Krieg to an unidentified *Bundestag* deputy, 24 October 1961, BAK B 245/235.
100. Gert Kragh to Hans Krieg, 7 November 1961, BAK B 245/235. On the new health affairs ministry see Dominick, *Environmental Movement,* 200, 203.
101. Lekan, *Imagining,* 114–16, 244–47.
102. Lekan, *Imagining,* 244.
103. Berghahn, *Modern Germany,* 227.
104. "Landschaft unser Lebensraum," produced by the Land- und Hauswirtschaftlicher Auswertungs- und Informationsdienst, AID Film Archiv, film # 8164.
105. Rudolf Stich, "Naturschutz in Raumordnung und Landesplanung," *N & L* 40, no. 9 (1965): 161–64; Stich, "Bauplanungsrecht und Naturschutzrecht," *N & L* 41, no. 9 (1966): 207; Bergmeier, *Umweltgeschichte,* 26–46.
106. On West Germans' gradual acceptance of democracy see Jarausch, *Recivilizing Germans,* 139–47, quote from p. 139.
107. Dominick, *Environmental Movement,* 183–93, 257 n. 7, 207, quote from p. viii. See also the opinion poll from 1963 in Elisabeth Noelle and Erich Peter Neumann, *The Germans. Public Opinion Polls, 1947–1966,* trans. Gerard Finan (Allensbach and Bonn: Verlag für Demoskopie, 1967; reprint, Westport, CT: Greenwood Press, 1981), 158. More research is needed on the role of Catholic and Protestant Churches in conservation. For evidence of Protestants' concern see Gustav Dessin, "Naturschutz als Dienst am ganzen Menschen," *N & L* 34, no. 8 (1959): 117, reprinted from *Evangelische Welt;* Eberhard Amelung, "Unsere Verantwortung gegenüber der Natur," *N & L* 39, no. 2 (1964): 17–18, reprinted from *Evangelische Verantwortung. Politische Briefe des Evangelischen Arbeitskreises der CDU/CSU* 11, no. 6 (1963): 1–2; no. 8/9 (1968): 28.
108. Körner, *Theorie,* 121.
109. Compare Engels, *Naturpolitik,* 135, 142–43, 149. Engels concludes that drafters of the charter referenced the Basic Law primarily as a tactical move to associate their agenda with high politics.
110. Bocking, *Nature's Experts,* 4, 14, 21–22.
111. Sturm, "Verantwortung der Bürger," 12.112. Dieter Grunow and Hildegard Pamme, "Kommunale Verwaltung: Gestaltunsspielräume und Ausbau von Partizipationschancen?" in Frese, Paulus, and Teppe, *Demokratisierung,* 518–28.
113. Grzimek, "Die Zivilcourage," DNR *Informationsbrief* (March 1966): 5–6. For a critical analysis of Grzimek's appeal to have civil courage, see Engels, *Naturpolitik,* 250. See also Engels's, "Von der Sorge um die Tiere zur Sorge um die Umwelt. Tiersendungen als Umweltpolitik in Westdeutschland zwischen 1950 und 1980," *Archiv für Sozialgeschichte* 43 (2003): 297–323, for a compelling discussion of Grzimek's central role in using television to make conservation a legitimate issue on which to express dissent.
114. Bess, *Light-Green Society,* 79–81; Jarausch, *Recivilizing Germans,* chap. 6.

Chapter 5

LANDSCAPING THE MOSEL CANAL, 1956–1964*

The Miracle Years did not lack for people with the civil courage Bernhard Grzimek called for, nor were the boom years absent of groups and individuals willing to stage organized protests against the adverse effects of rapid economic recovery. The success or failure of their activism depended upon many factors, including whether decisions about resource use were made by distant authorities or by officials closer to home. This chapter examines the debate over canalization of the Mosel River as well as its transformation into a canal between 1956 and 1964. Unlike the regional conflict over the Wutach unfolding at the same time, the controversy surrounding the Mosel had international dimensions. Pursuing a pragmatic diplomatic course that would integrate the Federal Republic into Western Europe, and facing immense pressure from France, Chancellor Konrad Adenauer had little choice but to agree to build the canal. In terms of foreign policy, the Mosel was much more useful as a transportation route symbolically serving as a bridge between West Germany and France and linking two industrial regions in economic unity than it would have been had it remained a scenic river in a wine producing valley.

Before Adenauer asserted his authority in another example of chancellor democracy and agreed to transform the Mosel into an international shipping lane, he had to confront stiff opposition at home from members of his cabinet, Ruhr industrialists, the German Federal Railway, and nature and homeland preservationists. Closer study of the debate over canalization, particularly in the spring of 1956, confirms that ecological concerns played only a minor role in top level deliberations. Just when the decision was about to be made, however, conservation-minded men, women, and youth directed their written appeals to the highest levels of the federal government, hoping to convince officials that the Mosel was more than just another potential transportation artery. But unlike West Germans embroiled in the Wutach conflict, these activists had limited possibilities for democratic action because the decision about canalization was the chancellor's to make. Nonetheless, they flooded the foreign office and the chancellery with postcards and letters that demanded protection of a popular tourist destination, a protected landscape of immeasurable value to the German "homeland," a "living river" that supported diverse plant and animal life, and a critical source of drinking water that had to be kept clean. Although understandable, their uncompromising stance against canalization was unrealistic in light of Adenauer's foreign policy and West Germany's vulnerable position within the western bloc.[1] At a time when the Federal Republic sought a secure place among the nations of Western Europe, some conservationists' reliance on the nativist language of homeland preservation did little to strengthen their position. Nonetheless, citizens' concerns to protect the scenic beauty of the Mosel landscape and to maintain water quality were integrated into the canal treaty, albeit in general terms.

But the story does not end here. Once the government officially agreed to canalization in October 1956, the results of this engineering project rested in the hands of experts. A number of leading conservationists hoped to be involved at each stage of planning and construction between 1956 and 1964 to help ensure that the outcome would be a carefully engineered landscape that was in better ecological health than before. But for a canalized Mosel to be more attractive and biologically healthier than it previously was—and capable of supporting additional economic uses—more planning, money, personnel, and legal support were needed than were available at the time. For conservationists involved in the project, the Mosel canal highlighted the severe limitations of official conservation in guiding major development projects along ecologically sustainable paths. At the same time, their experiences left them all the more convinced that landscape and land use planning were the primary vehicles for professionalizing their field and increasing their leverage in decisions that affected the country's natural resources and space.

The Mosel Transformed since Roman Times

Since the early 1800s, Europeans engineered their rivers into "organic machines," fusing the mechanical and the natural to create waterways that served multiple human uses. The grandest river rectification project of the nineteenth century, begun after the Congress of Vienna (1815) which ended the Napoleonic Wars, transformed the romantic Rhine into a global transportation route that supported free trade and ensured a steady supply of water for farming, settlement, industrial production, and power generation. But more than a century of "correction" projects destroyed habitats, created a shorter, straighter, faster flowing Rhine, and increased flooding—not in the natural floodplain, but on the Middle and Lower Rhine where in recent years "hundred-year floods" have recurred.[2]

Rectification projects continued at a more rapid pace after World War II as the nations of Western Europe expanded international shipping networks to support economic unity. In the early postwar years, European ministers of transport identified several rivers they hoped to link to the Rhine, the continent's main transportation artery. The most massive long term project was the revived Rhine-Main-Danube canal, completed in 1992. Other rivers singled out for canalization included the Rhône, the Neckar, and the Mosel. All three of these projects sparked protests, but only in the case of the Rhône were plans for canalization eventually abandoned in 1997. The Neckar and the Mosel Rivers experienced a different fate; they were engineered into multi-purpose organic machines during the Miracle Years.[3]

The Mosel flows north from its source in the Vosges Mountains in Alsace through the French cities of Nancy, Metz, and Thionville in the industrial heartland of Lorraine. It curves along the Luxembourg-German border for 40 kilometers, and then makes an uneven and winding descent through steep wooded banks in the wine producing region of Rhineland Palatinate. Along its 545 kilometer course to the Rhine, the Mosel drops from an elevation of over 730 meters to about 60 meters, and drains 28,500 square kilometers in the Vosges, Ardennes, Hunsrück, and Eifel Mountains. The Mosel had been an important waterway since antiquity, serving as a strategic and commercial transportation route for Romans, medieval merchants, princes, and kings and supplying water for millers, vintners, and local industrialists. By virtue of its location between two regions with major river systems, the Rhine and the Saar-Lore-Lux regions, the Mosel assumed significance as a political boundary dividing these areas at times, and linking them economically at others. The success or failure of efforts to canalize the river over the centuries reflected the constantly shifting relations between these two regions.

In the first half of the nineteenth century, France and Prussia carried out projects to improve travel on the Mosel, but the river's uneven gradient caused delays in shipments, and extreme fluctuations in the water level from season to season made it less dependable than the more efficient railway system. In the latter half of the century, however, canalizing the Mosel increased in importance as technological developments in steel production made it desirable to connect the vast supply of coal in the Ruhr basin with the ore abundantly available in Lorraine. But when France lost Alsace and northern Lorraine to Germany after the Franco-Prussian War, it had little interest in exploiting the river's potential as a transportation route. France and Germany agreed in the Frankfurt Peace

Treaty of 1871 to continue canalizing the Mosel within their borders, but at the end of the decade it had been developed only to Metz.

In the late nineteenth and early twentieth centuries, efforts to improve the navigability of this route to the Rhine met with fierce opposition, primarily from Ruhr steel manufacturers and the Prussian railway. As steel producers in the Ruhr sought better access to Swedish ore with its high content of iron, they grew less interested in a waterway that would link them to Lorraine's deposits of ore, which had sulfur impurities. The Prussian railway considered the canal to be an unwanted source of competition that might force it to reduce freight rates. After regaining Alsace and Lorraine at the end of WWI, the French government hesitated to canalize the Mosel past Metz because of a lack of financial resources and an unwillingness to connect the industry in Lorraine with the Ruhr. In the late 1920s, however, Lorraine industrialists and area chambers of commerce successfully lobbied the French government to apply war reparations from Germany toward construction of a side canal between Metz and Königsmacher, which by 1932 accommodated 350 ton barges.[4]

The Nazi Regime sought to develop the Mosel's economic potential while also preserving its cultural heritage and natural beauty. Because of the scenic charm of the region with its vineyards, flora, fauna, unique geology, and cultural traditions dating back to the Roman Empire, regional preservationists succeeded in placing the Mosel valley between Trier and Koblenz under legal protection (*Landschaftsschutz*) in 1940. This less stringent category of preservation did not bar economic development, but did restrict uses that threatened to despoil the beauty of the river and valley, and harm plant and animal life. After the regime annexed Alsace and Lorraine in the early 1940s, it moved forward with plans to canalize the remaining stretch of the Mosel. The war, however, prevented doing little more than dredging some of the shallow sections of the riverbed to create a more even descent and beginning the construction of a dam, lock, and power generating facility at Koblenz. The project at Koblenz slowed to a standstill by 1944, but was resumed in 1947 and finally completed in 1951.[5]

The Diplomacy of Western Integration: Trading the Saar for the Mosel Canal

After World War II, canalization of the Mosel figured prominently in negotiations over Western European integration and Franco-German reconciliation. Initially, interest in the canal was confined to the region because of opposition from powerful representatives of Ruhr industry and the French and West German federal railroads, and because of uncertainty about how the project would be funded. But when French Foreign Minister Robert Schuman pressed for greater economic cooperation by establishing the European Coal and Steel

Community (ECSC), French steel producers, particularly those in Lorraine who worried about competition from Ruhr steel manufacturers, lobbied for compensation in the form of the Mosel canal. Thus, a regional concern assumed national and international dimensions.[6]

The French National Assembly ratified the Schuman plan in December 1951 on the condition that the French government would negotiate an agreement to canalize the Mosel before establishing a common market for coal and steel. An inexpensive waterway linking Lorraine's steel industry with the abundant supply of coke and coal in the Ruhr was one of the most important gains the French could make with European integration.[7] Pressure from the French National Assembly to canalize the Mosel came as no surprise to West German officials studying the issue in the early 1950s. But they cautioned Adenauer against approving the project that would improve Lorraine's access to Ruhr coke and coal and yet have unknown effects on West German railway revenues, Ruhr industry, and the water supply, and perhaps limit West Germany's jurisdiction over the Mosel.[8]

In 1956, the French government applied significant pressure on Adenauer to canalize the Mosel, after losing control of the Saar. In hopes of retaining some of the advantages it had reaped as a result of postwar economic occupation of this coal rich region, France had supported plans from the early 1950s to Europeanize the Saar while insisting on continued "economic unity" with the region. In 1954, Premier Pierre Mendès-France secured Adenauer's approval of this arrangement by forcing the chancellor into a difficult situation. Facing political opposition at home to West German rearmament, Mendés-France made ratification of the Paris Agreements of October 1954 (which ended the occupation and admitted the Federal Republic into NATO) contingent upon West Germany's acquiescence to the Europeanization of the Saar. The chancellor's challenge, one historian writes, was to "keep the Saar question subordinate to the restoration of Germany's sovereignty without openly sacrificing what his countrymen considered part of Germany."[9] In October 1955, however, over 65 percent of the voters in the Saar rejected Europeanization in a referendum. The newly elected Saar government declared itself a part of West Germany in January 1956.[10]

When these developments made it clear that France had lost the Saar, Adenauer had to perform a delicate balancing act in order to not jeopardize the formal return of the territory to West Germany and to ensure the continuation of European integration. During the final round of negotiations on the Saar between February and October 1956, France insisted on compensation that included construction of the Mosel canal. West Germany initially rejected this demand, calling for the return of the Saar without delay and proposing the electrification of the railway line along the Mosel as an alternative. But the French threatened to break off negotiations. By March, Adenauer agreed to canalization, but demanded in exchange that France correct problems caused by the Rhine lateral canal. France had resumed construction of the canal after WWII, applying Marshall Plan funds toward the installation of three more hydrodams and locks that further threatened Baden's water supply. In talks on the Saar, France assured West Germany that on the section of the canal yet to be built, such problems would be avoided. (In completing the project in the 1960s the French used a "Loop Solution" that returned water to the Rhine below each of four new hydrodams.)[11] In October 1956, the two countries signed a series of agreements on the Saar. One of the treaties, also signed by Luxembourg, provided for canalization of the Mosel between Thionville and Koblenz.[12]

The Mosel Canal in Domestic Power Politics, 1956

At the time of these high level talks, Adenauer told a Danish journalist that "a German-French agreement [on the Saar] must not fail because of the Mosel canal question."[13] He had arrived at this position with the support of Foreign Minister Heinrich von Brentano who told Adenauer that "we will only come to a satisfactory solution [on the Saar] when there is an agreement between France and Germany on the . . . Mosel Canal." After the loss of the Saar and recent humiliating defeats in its crumbling colonial empire, Brentano reasoned, the French government needed a face saving measure. The French public would not allow its government to return the Saar to West Germany without some compensation.[14] Dr. Hans Globke, the controversial former Nazi official who headed the Chancellery since 1953, informed Adenauer that if West Germany agreed to the canal, the French would scale back some of their demands for compensation for the loss of the Saar.[15] Officials in the Ministry of Defense also endorsed the canal, arguing that it would strengthen the Federal Republic's ties to the West and serve as a cheaper transport route, not only for Lorraine but also Rhineland-Palatinate, a border state that had played the role of "Cinderella in West Germany's economic ascent."[16]

Although foreign policy considerations proved decisive, Adenauer had to weigh them against domestic concerns. Economics Minister Ludwig Erhard feared that if France financed a significant portion of the construction costs, it might expect to exercise "a decisive influence" on administering the waterway, determining canal tolls, and distributing electricity generated by the hydrodams.[17] Federal Minister of Transportation Hans-Christoph Seebohm shared Erhard's concerns about a loss of sovereignty over the river, but also feared that the German Federal Railway, already running a large deficit, would struggle to compete with the canal.[18]

The most powerful opponents of canalization were not cabinet members in Bonn, but organizations representing industry and commerce in the Ruhr. The Federal Association of German Industry (*Bundesverband der Deutschen Industrie,* or BDI) in Cologne,[19] the German Association of Chambers of Commerce (*Deutscher Industrie und Handelstag,* or DIHT), the Economic Association of the

Iron and Steel Industries (*Wirtschaftsvereinigung der Eisen- und Stahlindustrien,* or WVESI),[20] and the German Federal Railway (*Deutsche Bundesbahn,* or DBB) emerged as formidable opponents in the early 1950s. These organizations lobbied to convince Adenauer that a canalized Mosel would do little to further Western European unity because it promised to benefit Lorraine's heavy industry almost exclusively. By opposing the canal, these groups intended to protect their own regional economic advantage while claiming it was in the national interest to do so.

Relaying exaggerated fears about unfair competition, the BDI and DIHT noted that after WWII West Germany's industries were being dismantled while Lorraine's were expanding. Lorraine steel manufacturers would reap yet another advantage over their West German competitors with the proposed canal. The waterway would lower the cost of ore deliveries to the Ruhr from Lorraine, but industrialists made clear their preference for higher quality ore from Sweden.[21] Issuing alarmist predictions, industrialists and the DBB warned that if France paid for more of the canal's construction costs, West Germany might lose control over the Mosel, or perhaps watch it become internationalized.[22] According to supporters of the canal in France, such arguments reflected Ruhr industrialists' attempts to stifle legitimate economic competition.

Ruhr industrialists and the DBB viewed the Mosel canal as a bad investment. If constructed, it would reduce the amount of freight carried on federal and local rail lines and thus devalue investments already made in the region's rail network. The federal railway currently transported goods between Lorraine and the Ruhr, but was still not operating to full capacity. The already strapped DBB, they warned, would turn to the state to cover its losses or raise the cost of freight within West Germany. As a more economical alternative to the canal, they proposed increasing the railway's capacity by electrifying the line along the Mosel.[23] In arguing that canalization was not economical these organizations failed to recognize that canals are constructed not because they are economical, but because they serve special purposes—in this case, opening up a cheaper transportation route to the Rhine for Lorraine and Rhineland-Palatinate, expanding economic development of the Mosel region, and promoting European unity.

When these organizations—representing industrial and railroad interests—had mounted formidable opposition to the canal by the early spring of 1956 when talks on the Saar entered a delicate stage, Adenauer held a two-hour meeting with them, hoping to diffuse a potentially volatile situation.[24] In the 5 March meeting, State Secretary Walter Hallstein stated that rejecting the Mosel canal would jeopardize talks on the Saar and delay the region's return to West Germany. If the Federal Republic hoped to have support from the US and Great Britain in securing the return of the Saar, West Germany needed to cooperate with the French government on canalization. Foreign Minister

Brentano explained that if the French government failed to secure West Germany's support for the Mosel canal, it would be viewed at home as another foreign policy defeat and would provide political capital for five and a half million communist voters. None of these arguments swayed most of the representatives of industry, who remained decidedly against the project.[25] Some threatened to withhold financial support from the governing political parties if they agreed to canalization.[26]

The *Bundestag* did not extensively debate canalization of the Mosel because most of the details were determined in diplomatic negotiations. Initially, however, the major political parties tended to be cautious out of the concern that the canal would negatively affect Ruhr industry. On 8 May 1956, however, the CDU's coalition partner, the FDP, forced the issue by calling a major question in parliament, which required a government response. When Brentano appeared before the *Bundestag,* he evasively reported that the Mosel canal was one of several issues being examined by the Foreign Office in conjunction with the Saar; another was the Rhine lateral canal. Although Adenauer expected the Saar to return to Germany, Brentano reported, the chancellor anticipated that France would demand a corresponding sacrifice from West Germany (i.e., the Mosel canal). By June, none of the parties opposed canalization if it helped secure the Saar's return.[27]

In the debate over canalization, the concerns of Rhineland-Palatinate, the state through which the Mosel flowed and which would be most directly affected by canalization, played a limited role because of the overriding foreign policy considerations.[28] Nonetheless, when the *Landtag* debated the issue, the FDP denounced the canal as a "transportation subsidy" for Lorraine's industry, while an SPD deputy declared that its construction was "entirely un-European" and warned that in the future it might become known as a "reparations canal." Minister-President Peter Altmeier (CDU) overcame such objections when he convinced deputies that it was ultimately a foreign policy matter the federal government had to decide.[29]

In contrast to the *Landtag*'s reluctant approval, the Industry and Chambers of Commerce of Trier and Koblenz emerged as enthused proponents early on. They conceded that the canal would benefit their own state more than others by attracting new industries and making limestone, timber, ore, and other natural resources more accessible. Widening the river would improve the microclimate and reduce the danger of frost, enhancing conditions for wine production and agriculture. Tourism, too, would profit because the river would be opened for passenger ship travel year round. Careful planning and engineering would ensure that power plants and other structures did not mar the scenery, which made the Mosel so appealing to vacationers. Beyond these advantages for the region, they insisted, the Mosel canal would promote economic cooperation within Western Europe by dismantling economic barriers.[30]

In general, local government and planning officials in communities along the Mosel shared these optimistic expectations. But they wanted assurances that widening and dredging the river would not adversely affect the supply of drinking water or the river's fish population. Although some raised concerns about an increase in flooding, particularly in the spring, they concluded that the canal would afford greater control of the river and thus provide more reliable protection against seasonal inundation. Most local officials expected an increase in tourism, but a minority shared the concerns of Rhenish homeland preservationists who predicted that canalization would despoil the beauty of this popular vacation spot and that increased traffic would disturb the tranquility of the valley. Local officials did not mention the issue, but it remained unclear how property owners would be compensated for damages that resulted from constructing the canal.[31]

It comes as no surprise that the majority of arguments for and against the canal by government officials, politicians, and industrialists registered little, if any, interest in the Mosel as part of nature. A few worried about the impact the engineering project would have on the water supply and some cautioned that canalization might despoil the scenery of the river landscape so vital to regional tourism. But for most people, the debate was about western European unity, the return of the Saar, and regional economic development. In this context, it seems all the more remarkable that an organized letter writing campaign in early 1956 by nature and homeland preservationists forced federal officials to consider a range of cultural, moral, and ecological concerns that had been overlooked in the high level negotiations.

Conservationists' Protest of Words

West German conservationists had conflicting opinions about canalization. Most shared the sentiments of Rhineland-Palatinate's state commissioner for conservation, the aged Heinrich Menke, who warned that binding "a living river in a landscape so rich in scenic and artistic value" in a "technical straitjacket" would permanently harm the river's flora and fauna and despoil one of the country's beloved historic areas.[32] Veteran landscape architect Alwin Seifert tried to dispel such anxieties, arguing that advances in engineering would preserve the attractiveness of the river valley and "create new beauty where none is to be found today [along parts of the Mosel]." Those who fretted that canalization would transform the Mosel into a "mechanized landscape," he editorialized, failed to recognize that the valley was less a "cultural landscape" than a "steppe of vineyards."[33]

Seifert was among a minority of conservationists who focused on the river's less than pristine condition. When plans were in place to expand the canal in the early 1940s, he had been asked to prepare a professional opinion on how the project would affect the valley. Reflecting Seifert's alarmist predictions about the steppification of Germany and his own racial prejudices, his study had bemoaned the "steppes" of vines on hillsides above long stretches of the Mosel and the "American weeds" that had "invaded" the shoreline.[34] But other conservationists also noted that by the early part of the twentieth century, shrubs and trees had been cleared from the hillsides along the Mosel to make way for growing grapes. The spread of vines along the hills, in meadows, and on farmland indicated a landscape with "an impoverished" diversity of plant and animal life. Revealing their continued reliance on aesthetic judgments, they noted that by the twentieth century, the valley's bright spring and autumn hues from diverse deciduous trees (poplar and willow along the shores, elm in the water meadows, and ash near the slopes) had been replaced by the darker tones of "monotonous evergreen forests," which were more vulnerable to "insect calamities" and, because of their shallow root system, less effective in controlling erosion.[35]

Conservationists also pointed out that the Mosel had not escaped the problem of pollution. Seifert's report from the Nazi era noted that residue from the thriving industries in Lorraine and the Saar had blackened the water and settled on the riverbed. In addition, research from the late 1950s indicated that effluents from Lorraine's salt mines flowed into the Mosel, fostering the growth of plants suited to saline conditions.[36] Such changes in vegetation were less visible than the billboards that cluttered the hillsides, the "uncontrolled trash dumps in vineyards on the slopes, in the woods, and on the Mosel's shores," and the numerous fish kills in recent years caused by effluents from the region's industry.[37] Given such undesirable conditions, these conservationists were among those who pragmatically argued that canalization in conjunction with land use planning and design could improve the ecological health and appearance of the river and valley.

The majority, however, opposed canalization for a variety of moral, cultural, and ecological reasons that transcended economic and diplomatic considerations. Beginning in late February 1956, their letters and postcards poured into the Chancellery, the Foreign Office, and government offices in Rhineland-Palatinate, urging officials to reject canalization. By raising their voices at a critical stage in negotiations on the Saar, they ensured that their concerns would not be ignored entirely. According to civil servants in the Foreign Office who reviewed the correspondence, some of the letters were indeed worrisome. Their "sharp attacks on the federal government" were overtly political and confrontational and their apparent origin from "all social classes of the population" raised the specter of public disorder.[38]

Between February and May, at least 500 cards and letters eventually reached the Foreign Office claiming to represent, by conservative estimates, at least 1.5

million West Germans, most of them of middle class standing. Because many of the letters appeared to be scripted, officials quickly concluded that they were not dealing with a spontaneous "protest action," but a letter writing campaign orchestrated by a few organizations like the DNR. Nonetheless, the correspondences are a rich source for studying the arguments West Germans used to justify preservation in the mid 1950s. Even as the Federal Republic became more firmly established in the Western Bloc, the ideas and rhetoric associated with traditional nature and homeland preservation shaped letter writers' understanding of what was at stake in the debate. Officials were less moved by these concerns, however, than by those outlining threats to the water supply.

Echoing turn of the century preservationists, DNR President Hans Krieg told officials in his letter claiming to represent 800,000 people that canalization would be "an extensive intrusion in the scenery (*Landschaftsbild*) of the Mosel Valley." Although this argument afforded a way to consider the river and valley as an integrated aesthetic whole, it overlooked less visible problems such as a loss of plant and animal species and changes in the supply of ground and surface water. Repeating arguments that were the staple of conservation rhetoric, Krieg explained that the DNR did not oppose economic growth in and of itself and understood "that the . . . preservation of cultural values would have to wait if technological and economic developments would allow for no other solution." But alternatives to the canal existed, such as electrification of the railway line along the Mosel, or construction of a canal, long in planning, between the Rhine and Meuse Rivers.[39] In their response to Krieg's letter and others of similar content, officials in the Foreign Office explained that France was demanding canalization as one of the conditions for the return of the Saar; the outcome of negotiations would "depend on how European unity and the vital interests of the German people, particularly the Saar population, could be served best."[40]

A Hamburg woman expressed the sentiments of many other letter writers, however, when she asserted that it was not in Germany's best interest to concede to canalization in exchange for the Saar. Why should the "destruction" of this "German landscape" be made a condition for the return of this territory? The loss of the "unique" Mosel River and valley that was rich in "beauty, history, tradition and nature" she concluded, "would make us substantially poorer."[41] She was not alone in emphasizing values that were less tangible, but no less real. Nor was she unique in describing the Mosel valley as landscape that was distinctly German.

Correspondence frequently referred to the Mosel as a "German landscape," a "unique landscape of national significance," or a "jewel [*Kleinod*] of the German homeland."[42] In claiming to defend the "uniquely German" Mosel River and valley from the "economic interests of a foreign nation,"[43] or the "material interests of a small group of French heavy industrialists,"[44] letter writers conveyed a sense of [wounded] national pride and moral superiority vis-à-vis their neighbors. For them, the Mosel River and valley was a source of national pride that merited protection from France's potentially damaging economic ambitions. By assigning national significance to the Mosel they also expressed resentment over France's continued influence on West Germany's foreign policy and outrage over its ability, so it seemed, to determine the fate of a treasured part of Germany's natural heritage. For many, the prospect of a canalized Mosel symbolized the Federal Republic's tenuous status as a sovereign nation.

Letters and postcards that ended up in the Foreign Office, however, offer evidence of a range of attitudes toward France and of views about West Germany's place within Europe. A Bremen architect urged Adenauer to let the "warning voices of responsible citizens" bolster the "government's resistance to the shameless . . . unreasonable requests [that stemmed from] French national egotism, which contradicts . . . the spirit of understanding among the people of Europe."[45] One man wondered why "we Germans always must humble ourselves and crawl before the French," and reproached the government for not having "more backbone" to demonstrate that West Germany was once again a sovereign nation.[46] On behalf of the 250,000 members of the League of German Mountaineering and Hiking Associations, Georg Fahrbach wrote with somewhat less rancor that if Germany demanded that France canalize one of its beloved rivers, France would refuse. It would be "irresponsible" for the government to sacrifice one of Germany's few remaining "unspoiled and original" valleys such as the Mosel "for France's sake."[47] Expressing a much more conciliatory tone, one similar to that adopted by youth involved in the Knechtsand conflict with the British RAF, the Young Eagles of Düsseldorf's Youth Movement identified themselves as "enthusiastic supporters" of the "European idea" and of "efforts to achieve German-French reconciliation." They believed, however, that conceding to canalization in exchange for the return of the Saar—a matter already decided by a "democratic referendum"—would be "too great a sacrifice" and only would "build walls between the two nations."[48]

More frequently, the letter writers viewed plans to canalize the Mosel as confirmation of their fears that West Germany was losing its scenic landscapes to urbanization and industrial development at an alarming pace. They understood their campaign as yet another struggle to defend noble cultural values and nature—the embodiment of timeless moral truths—against the corrupting influences of modern civilization in the form of excessive materialism and the hubris of technology.[49] A teacher in the Cologne area lamented that so many beautiful landscapes already had been lost to housing developments or to technology in general. One would get the impression, she wrote, that people in Germany now have concern only for "material values." Another woman worried that West Germans would leave a bad impression on "fellow Germans in Central Europe" if they conceded to a plan that amounted to nothing more than "crass materialism."[50]

Several people asserted that protecting the Mosel for present and future generations would foster idealism, strengthen morality, and nurture the spiritual essence of the German people. As Karl Arnold asserted in his letter on behalf of the 400,000 members of the German *Heimat* League, "canalization is not only a political and economic problem, but also a spiritual one. In a heavily materialistic world," he warned, "the German people must be circumspect about preserving the sources of its strength [in] undiminished [form]." One of these sources included experiencing nature in a landscape such as the Mosel—one of the "last untouched river valleys in West Germany."[51] A CDU district official in Hamburg expressed a similar belief that Germans had a unique bond with nature, arguing that "the spiritual substance of our people is closely tied to the landscape. One cannot destroy the one without damaging the other," she asserted.[52] The head of the Homemakers' League of Einbeck agreed, urging Adenauer "not to destroy our Germany through industry. You take from us a refuge where our hearts find nourishment, and we must preserve the heart or we will all go asunder."[53]

In a similar vein, Henry Koehn, the local conservation commissioner on the island of Sylt, insisted that a people's sagas and poetry, myths and music, had their roots "in the mysterious powers of living nature." Only if a landscape remained "primordial" (*ursprünglich*), or at least retained its "natural character," he clarified, was that landscape capable of positively influencing a people and its culture and serving as a source of spiritual regeneration. Like Koehn, many letters described the Mosel River and valley as "original," "pristine," and "relatively unspoiled." In doing so, they perpetuated the myth of an ideal picturesque landscape which conveniently left out evidence that the Mosel had been transformed by decades of development. Envisioning the Mosel as one of the last, largely untouched landscapes in the country only heightened the sense of loss that supposedly would come with canalization and led to an uncompromising, alarmist stance. Koehn exclaimed that a country as densely populated as West Germany could not afford the "loss" of a landscape as large as the Mosel Valley. If Germany were to fulfill its role as the geographic center of Europe and justify its claim to be "a people of rank in the world," then it had to counteract the destructive forces of modern society by not sacrificing the Mosel to "technology and the economy."[54] As in the Wutach conflict, descriptions of the Mosel as "pristine" or "original" were a partly rhetorical ploy that aimed to give protests moral weight against more powerful opposition. But this language also expressed opposition to more changes to already engineered landscapes such as the Mosel. The Mosel River in its current condition seemed more "original" than the Mosel would be after it was outfitted with locks, sluices, hydrodams, and barges.

Though heavily laden with emotional appeals and exaggerated fears, letters and postcards also contained numerous references to "diseases of civilization"

and related public health issues receiving renewed attention with the launch-
ing of the nature park program. A miner from Cologne queried, "[I]sn't our
homeland ruined and over-mechanized enough?" It made little sense to him
that as nature conservation organizations worked to save the "last oases in
nature," one of those areas was about to be lost because of "profit seeking
foreigners."[55] An engineer from Duisburg believed in the therapeutic value of
nature, explaining that for those who "spend the largest part of our lives in a
gray environment," the Mosel "brings us not only good wine" but also "peaceful idyllic nature in which the tensed-up nerves can relax and the soul can gain
new strength."[56] This interest in setting aside scenic areas for recreation and
rejuvenation reflected not only contemporary concerns about public health and
emotional well being, but also the need for affordable vacation areas at a time
when West Germany's currency was still was not that strong and its people
might not have been welcomed elsewhere.

In correspondence from scientific societies and professionals in the natural
sciences, it was not uncommon to find descriptions of the Mosel as one of the
last "natural" river valleys left in the country. But their letters also emphasized
that adding locks, dams, and concrete retaining walls would drastically alter the
appearance and ecological condition of the river and valley. Habitats would be
lost and sediment and pollutants would build up behind the dams.[57] A Hamburg area forestry biologist explained that the Mosel was as an organic whole
from its source to its mouth, including the tributaries. Changing the river at one
or several locations, he explained, would lead to unanticipated consequences for
the course of the river, its drainage area, the water supply, and vegetation.[58] Only
a few letters expressed worry that canalization would increase traffic on the Mosel and thus contribute to worsening air, noise, and water pollution.[59]

Among the most influential correspondence was a resolution passed by the
5,000 member State Fishery Association of Rhineland-Rhinehessen, which
called upon the Adenauer Government not to make the Mosel "a chain of
drainage basins for French industrial effluents." The Fishery Association maintained that the Mosel was one of the cleanest rivers of the Federal Republic,
except for the section above Trier where the accumulation of tailings from
coal mining in particular had caused fish kills. This material, which originated in the industrial regions of Lorraine, entered the Mosel by way of the
Saar. The association feared that with canalization, even more sediment and
pollutants would build up on the floors of the dams, destroying the habitat
of fish, threatening the livelihood of fishermen, and jeopardizing the drinking water of communities along the Mosel. France's inadequate laws against
water pollution, the resolution stated, would do little to prevent businesses
and industries from dumping their allotted waste into the river.[60] The resolution did not mention West Germany's tainted rivers, which lacked protection
because of inadequate water purity laws. Because the *Bundestag* was debating

guideline legislation for water management at the time, however, the Foreign Office acted upon the resolution, recommending that the October 1956 treaty for the canal contain provisions to prevent "excessive" pollution of the river, a vague term open to interpretation.[61]

Landscaping the Mosel Canal, 1957–1964

On 27 October 1956, West Germany signed a treaty with France and Luxembourg to canalize the Mosel between Thionville and Koblenz. Eight years and over DM 770 million (approximately $195 million) later, engineers had built thirteen new locks and dams, nine in West Germany, two along the Luxembourg-West German border, and two in France. They had transformed the Mosel River into a step-like series of ponds that made the waterway navigable by 1,500 ton ships throughout the year. The eleven new hydroelectric plants on the West German stretch of the river generated an estimated 750 million kilowatt-hours of electric power per year.[62]

Construction began in 1958 at dam sites on the upper and lower sections of the Mosel (Lehmen, Trier, and Detzem), though the most extensive work occurred between 1961 and 1963. The cost of installing the thirteen new dams and locks, five security harbors, and eleven hydroelectric plants exceeded original estimates by more than DM 200 million. By the time the canal was completed, it had rung up a bill of DM 770 million. France ultimately paid the International Mosel Corporation,[63] the organization specially created to finance the project, more than two-thirds of the cost, DM 518 million, while the Federal Republic contributed DM 250 million, and Luxembourg added DM 2 million.[64]

Adenauer's decision to build the canal signaled a defeat for those who hoped to preserve the Mosel in its present state, but it offered other conservationists the opportunity to use their technical expertise to try to improve upon the river's undesirable conditions and moreover, to naturalize the engineered channel. Before beginning construction of the dams, the district governments of Koblenz and Trier held hearings to approve the plans for each site and to finalize the expropriation of property. Engineers and other specialists in the water management offices of Koblenz and Trier tried to make certain that contractors' plans would not jeopardize the water supply, sewer systems, or the flow of the Mosel's tributary rivers and streams. Despite their efforts, an estimated 4,000 complaints surfaced in these hearings, primarily over water rights (2,600) and the dispossession of property (1,400). Officials boasted, however, that through an orderly process they resolved complaints to the satisfaction of most parties involved.[65]

Ideally the canal's design would reflect not only effective engineering, but also careful landscape and land use planning. Landscape plans would determine the placement of dams, power plants, water treatment facilities, and roads, and would ensure that appropriate vegetation was replanted or planted anew along the shores. More encompassing land use plans would ensure careful development of the shorelines of communities located on the river and of the entire valley, including the placement of new roads and rail lines. At the time of construction, conservationists were told that their fears about increased settlement by industry were unwarranted. The narrowness of the valley that charmed tourists made it less attractive to industries needing space for expansion. Such assurances were misleading and failed to anticipate local governments' desire to attract new enterprises to strengthen their tax base.[66]

Seifert had high hopes that the canal would "be a showpiece" of "technical construction in conformity with nature," just as the stretch of the Autobahn through the Ruhr had been.[67] But his optimism proved to be misplaced, in part because of the limited number of people working on the project at any one time who were qualified to address planning from an ecological perspective. During the critical phase of planning between 1957 and 1960, there were usually six people, at most eight, employed by the five offices and agencies participating in canalization to address land use and landscape planning, and few of these individuals could devote attention exclusively to the Mosel. Concerned about the lack of personnel, the state government of Rhineland-Palatinate hired Seifert in 1957 to serve as a consultant on the project. In 1963, a year before the canal opened, eleven landscape architects and horticulturists helped draft landscape plans, but by then their proposals functioned as addendums to the approved engineering plans, recommending chiefly what type of vegetation to plant along the shores and at dam sites.[68]

Furthermore, neither the Ministry of Culture of Rhineland-Palatinate (as the supreme conservation office), nor officials responsible for conservation at the district level had individuals with the training necessary to competently see that canalization did not compromise the Mosel's status as a legally protected landscape. Honorary commissioners also were limited in the extent to which they could assist. After the death of state commissioner Heinrich Menke in 1956, a very able forester took over the volunteer post, but readily admitted that he lacked the expertise to tackle problems which arose in conjunction with canalization. He made only two trips on the Mosel during the six years that it was under construction. At the district level, the two volunteer conservation commissioners in Trier and Koblenz could devote little time to the Mosel because they were fulltime secondary school teachers and had other preservation projects to address. This situation highlighted a major weakness in state-sponsored conservation—that of relying on honorary commissioners with some expertise, but little authority (and often too little time) to advise the non-specialist officials responsible for administering conservation.[69]

The effectiveness of land use planning was also limited because of weaknesses in the legal provisions for building the canal. The October 1956 treaty stipulated that the "needs of utilities, soil conservation and land reclamation, fisheries, water management and tourism shall be taken into consideration" during construction. The agreement also stated vaguely that the canal should be built "with special care" not to damage the scenery (*Landschaftsbild*) of the Mosel and surrounding area whenever it was "practicable." Emphasizing the importance of the scenery meant that little was done to improve the less visible but more important ecology of the landscape and left room to argue that it was not "practicable" to avoid damaging the beauty of the river and surroundings to a certain degree. Requiring the canal to be built "with special care" did not clarify contractors' legal obligations. Under the treaty, the contractor was required to repair what had been damaged or altered by canalization, but nothing more. If dredging or flooding destroyed the few remaining islands or the shoreline, the contractor had to restore the islands and replant reeds and willow bushes to reinforce the shore. But there was no incentive to improve upon the ecological condition of the shores, as some had hoped would be the case.

Existing laws also were of limited help. According to the RNG, navigation had priority over conservation. Nor did the state water maintenance law of 1960, which replaced the outdated Prussian law of 1913, help to clarify contractors' obligations in terms of caring for the landscape. The law stipulated that the contractor had to take measures to protect the public interest and safeguard private property, even at the expense of conservation. But the law also contained a section that required the contractor to consider preservation and landscape design "to the extent that this is economical and compatible with the purpose of the project." It was not legitimate to saddle the company with higher costs related to conservation if "the same or equivalent success can be reached through lesser means." This did not absolve contractors from protecting the landscape, but it repeatedly subordinated conservation to the overarching goal of cutting costs and converting the Mosel into a canal quickly.[70]

Although canalization was not complicated from a technical point of view, engineers and conservationists faced several challenges. Dredging the river so that it would be at least 2.9 meters deep and 40 meters wide amassed several hundred thousand cubic meters of stone and gravel which were deposited in unattractive heaps near Enkirch, Lehmen, and in the Monteneubel Valley. Near Lehmen in particular, landscape design successfully used the material to support a new forest of shrubs and trees that protected the area against flooding.[71] Dredging the river proved difficult and costly where the bed was unusually hard and difficult to penetrate with machinery. Adopting a technique used successfully by a Swedish company, the contractor bored and exploded the riverbed meter by meter. An air shield around the area of the explosion protected fish from the powerful waves. Despite these measures, dredging the river killed off enough fish to prompt fishermen to turn to the courts for compensation.[72]

One of the greatest challenges with canalization was protecting the water supply of the communities on the river, particularly those near the sites of dams. Because most of the cities and towns along the Mosel did not have central sewage plants or adequate water treatment facilities prior to development of the river, they had to be installed quickly before canalization. This expensive undertaking, which generated considerable debate among local, state, and federal officials over who ought to foot the bill, was essential and helped control pollution of the Mosel after canalization.[73] Most of the towns and cities on the Mosel obtained drinking water from wells dug in the gravel and sand of the river's foreshore. In the case of twenty-seven communities, widening the river hampered securing water from these sources. They either had to modify existing wells, dig new ones, or have new collective water supply systems built. Particularly serious was the situation for the city of Traben-Trarbach, which had obtained most of its drinking water from two wells located near the shore, just above the dam and lock being built at Enkirch. Dredging to create the navigation channel for the lock damaged the area that had functioned as a natural filter for the water supply. By law the contractor had to find an alternate source of water for the community, but did so only after the state government intervened.[74]

Communities near the new dams worried about an increase in the groundwater level and potential flooding. By installing drainage systems and pumps to return water to the Mosel, builders were able to control the potential problem of high water.[75] In the case of Mehring, a town located upstream from the dam planned at Detzem, more drastic measures were necessary. Because constructing the dam was expected to raise the groundwater level near Mehring by an estimated six meters, something needed to be done to protect the low lying part of the community. Eventually, the vulnerable section of town was torn down, the area elevated, and then rebuilt. Of the seventy-two property owners directly affected by this restoration project, twelve accepted a cash settlement and moved elsewhere, seven rebuilt in other designated locations, and the rest remained in the area.[76] To the disappointment of conservationists assessing the canal project, the architects in charge of designing the newly raised section of the town consulted a landscape architect only in 1964; by then he could do little more than make recommendations for planting vegetation.[77]

With damming the Mosel and reinforcing the new banks, at least 50 percent of the vegetation that previously lined the shores was lost, along with a variety of biotopes and rare aquatic plants. As the law required, the new shores eventually were restored by planting reeds and sedges, willows, poplars, ash, and elm trees, but even in the early 1970s some of the riverbanks looked bare. But replanting vegetation along the banks was not always possible. Widening and damming the river required some roads and railroad tracks to be raised, rebuilt, or newly constructed. Had landscape planners been involved in assisting the state highway administration in drawing up guidelines for building or reconstructing roads in the early stages of planning, they would have rerouted some of them further away from the shore. In general, however, the roads were closer to the Mosel than previously, and even the newly constructed sections had little space separating them from the river. Not only did this mean a loss of habitat and "green space" along the river, it necessitated sturdy walls of flagstone to protect the shore. The reinforcement required for some of the stretches of road, critics complained, did more to make the Mosel look like a canal than did canalization.

Before the channel was built, just under one-third of the shore of the Mosel within Germany needed to be supported by an embankment of flagstone to support railroad tracks and roads. After construction was completed, almost half (47 %) of the 450 kilometer long shore was outlined by a bank of either concrete or stone. This impoverished the area of plant and animal species and ruled out the option of protecting the riverbank from erosion by planting sedges and other plants suited to the local environment. In a few experimental cases, the Federal Institute for Hydrology successfully implemented a pioneering and cheaper method of securing the shores using gravel and sedges and rushes that thrive in marshy areas. In addition, some sections of the shore were protected by stones, which allowed vegetation to be planted and resulted in a biologically healthier shore than either flagstone or concrete retaining walls.[78]

With canalization, the river's water level remained higher throughout the year than previously and no longer receded to low levels in summer months. Damming and widening the Mosel made it resemble a lake in places and expanded the surface area of the water by about 25 percent, a change that slightly increased the humidity of the local climate. Vintners welcomed the higher humidity because it stabilized temperatures and reduced the threat of frost.[79]

Because the Mosel resembled a lake during most of the year, however, it took several years for flora and fauna to adapt to the new environment. Prior to canalization, eel, pike, white fish, and salmon (driven to the Mosel because of the pollution in the Rhine), were among fish that flourished in the river and provided a livelihood for commercial fisheries that leased the rights to fish there. During construction, fishing along some sections of the river proved to be temporarily impossible. As the canal was being built, engineers installed fish ladders on the dams and carved out calm pools along the shore so that young fish could mature and find protection from the swift current. Despite these measures, not all fish easily adapted to the newly created environment. Canalization destroyed the Mosel as a destination for salmon and other migratory fish; even eels struggled. According to one study, of 1,000 eels that attempted to swim upstream over four dams, all but 60 of them were killed or injured. To compensate for these engineering failures, the state of Rhineland-Palatinate restocked the river with eel, carp, pike, perch, and other species to help restore their populations. Only in the late 1990s, when Germany, France, and Luxembourg set plans in motion to outfit the Mosel's channel to handle two-way traffic did they also agree to restore the migration route of salmon by improving fish passages on the dams.[80]

There were some examples of successful cooperation between engineers, landscape architects, and conservationists, but they tended to achieve cosmetic results. The persistence of state conservation officials and commissioners ensured that dams, locks, and power plants were located at cities and towns rather than in more rural areas. Below each of the dams, reeds, sedges, willow, poplar, ash, and elm trees eventually were planted (in some cases long after the canal was opened in 1964) and successfully "greened" the sites of dams and locks. Less successful were the placement and design of sewer treatment plants.[81] Conservationists also were frustrated by the slow response of local governments in developing landscape plans for the shorelines. An exasperated Seifert expressed hope that some communities might "bring order" to the "completely neglected" areas along the riverbanks for the benefit of locals and tourists.[82] As of the mid 1960s when construction was completed, sixty-two of the 110 communities on the Mosel had developed plans for using the limited space along the shore, promising landing stages for ships, new roads, gardens, parks, and pathways. A number of cities and towns also envisioned new industrial settlement. A regional plan for Trier and its surroundings, for example, anticipated industry that eventually would spread beyond the outskirts of the city, up and down both sides of the Mosel, claiming farmland and catchment areas in the process.[83]

When the Mosel canal was completed, conservationists viewed the results with a critical eye. In its assessment of the project, the DRL regretted disruptions to the water supply, the significant loss of shoreline vegetation, the proximity of roads to the river, the extensive use of concrete and flagstone to reinforce the shores, and the unavoidable lake-like conditions created by the dams. The council also predicted that the increase in industrial settlement without adequate planning would add to water pollution.[84] Conservationists conceded that their vision for improving upon the appearance and health of the Mosel remained largely unfulfilled, frustrated by a lack of qualified personnel, pressure from France to complete the project by 1963, and weaknesses in the October 1956 treaty and existing laws. (Only in 1965 did the *Bundestag* pass the Federal Regional Planning Law which required ecological investigations and land use plans to accompany construction plans, rather than supplement them after a project was finished.) In his appraisal of the canalized Mosel, Professor Wolfram Pflug, an official responsible for landscape care in Rhineland-Palatinate's Ministry of Agriculture at the time of construction, concluded that "certainly [the river] has changed. Perhaps here and there [it is] more beautiful, but on most other places more empty, functional, cleaner, and thus less natural than previously."[85] For those like Pflug who hoped to strengthen conservation by linking it to landscape and land use planning, the Mosel project was a source of disappointment, a timely reminder of the inadequacies of official conservation and of the pressing need for reform.

The story of the Mosel's conversion from a somewhat developed river landscape to an "organic machine" is a cautionary one for proponents and opponents alike. Conservationists who warned that canalization would "destroy" the "largely untouched" Mosel overstated their case. Employing a familiar strategy, the DNR and other large umbrella organizations launched a letter writing campaign to warn officials that canalization would leave the country somewhat poorer morally, culturally, and ecologically. According to their socially conservative, moralizing stance, they were acting in the nation's best interest, defending the "pristine" Mosel from corruption by "crass materialism" or by "foreigners" allegedly acting out of narrow economic interests. Despite their old fashioned, provincial sounding arguments, they expressed an alternative understanding of prosperity, one less preoccupied with materialism and more mindful of less tangible values supposedly embodied in this "jewel of the German homeland," such as moderation, respect for tradition, and general well being. Although their guarded activism could have only a limited impact on a decision being made at the federal level by the chancellor, their protest was not without impact. Because the correspondence arrived when it did and in such impressive numbers, officials took note, ensuring that the October 1956 treaty at least acknowledged the concerns to protect the scenic beauty and ecological integrity of the river. With or without their letters, however, West German negotiators would still have demanded measures to protect the water supply that was so vital to the region's economy.

The people of Rhineland-Palatinate viewed the canal as a route toward regional prosperity and assumed that careful engineering would enable the river to support more diversified uses than before. When construction began, their hopes were frustrated temporarily because of worries about flooding and the expense of securing sewer and water treatment systems. Once the canal was opened, cities such as Trier and Koblenz attracted new industries relatively quickly, but their hinterlands, Hunsrück and Eifel, experienced limited economic growth. Communities along the Mosel recorded an increase in tourism, and even fishing had a rebound: between 1962 and 1966, the number of recreational fishermen doubled from 16,000 to 32,000 per year. But salmon and sea trout had disappeared from the river, unable to clear the dams that blocked their former migration route. New industries and the increase in commercial and recreational traffic on the river added to noise and water pollution, though the latter problem was mitigated somewhat by the recent improvements in water purification systems.[86]

When the waterway was opened to traffic in 1964, longstanding supporters praised it as a symbol of European economic unity. Indeed, the development of this route to the Rhine demonstrated the Federal Republic's efforts to reorient its transport routes away from the East and toward the West. But traffic on the

Mosel only gradually increased. Before the canal could support a heavier flow of commercial traffic and link a number of the industrial regions of Western Europe, other waterways in Lorraine and the Saar needed to be developed or expanded. Those who had opposed the canal also needed to adjust their claims. As expected, Lorraine obtained cheaper access to coke and coal, but this did not undermine the competitiveness of heavy industry in the Ruhr. The French contributed more of the construction costs, but they did not seek to control the Mosel. By 1964, each country assumed responsibility for maintaining and operating its section of the canal.[87]

And what of the predictions of conservationists who claimed that the Mosel Canal would "be a showpiece" of "technical construction in conformity with nature"? In some instances, landscape and land use planning helped to renature sections of the channel. More frequently, however, canalization exposed the inability of official conservation in its current organization to guide the development of the Mosel into an organic machine that could support multiple uses, yet retain its scenic beauty and ecological health. In his matter of fact assessment of the project, Pflug commented that,

> the Mosel Valley, like all cultural landscapes, must succumb to the constant striving of mankind to construct and design an environment that corresponds to his essence and needs, [an environment] in which he can live and make a living. That which is new will naturally blend in to the Mosel landscape and be scarcely noticeable—if it is good. That which has been changed but does not conform—not even the mantle of love will be able to conceal.[88]

The results of canalization were another reminder that the organization of state-sponsored conservation needed to be overhauled to give those responsible for it more influence in planning decisions. As the next chapter illustrates, however, ecological landscape planning could be only a partial response to the daunting challenge of managing the human environment.

Notes

* This chapter is a revised version of Sandra Chaney, "Water for Wine and Scenery, Coal, and European Unity: Canalization of the Mosel River, 1950–1964," in Anderson and Tabb, eds., *Water, Culure and Politics in Germany and the American West*. Peter Lang, 2001.
1. Ronald J. Granieri, *The Ambivalent Alliance. Konrad Adenauer, the CDU/CSU, and the West, 1949–1966* (New York: Berghahn, 2003).
2. Richard White, *The Organic Machine. The Remaking of the Columbia River* (New York: Hill and Wang, 1995); Blackbourn, *Conquest*, chap. 2; Cioc, *The Rhine*.
3. Bess, *Light-Green Society*, 207. On the Rhine-Main-Danube canal see Bill Bryson, "Main-Danube Canal," *National Geographic* 182, no. 2 (August 1992): 3–31; Cioc, *The Rhine*,

204; Keith Boucher, "Landscape and Technology: the Gabčikovo-Nagymaros Scheme," in Cosgrove and Petts, *Water, Engineering, and Landscape,* 174–87.

4. Jean Cermakian, *The Moselle: River and Canal from the Roman Empire to the European Economic Community* (Toronto: University of Toronto Press, 1975), 12–83, 116–17; Ludwig Vogel, "Der Ausbau der Mosel zur Gross-Schiffahrtsstraße 1945–1957," *Geschichte im Westen* 11 (1996): 73–74; Louis Lister, *Europe's Coal and Steel Community. An Experiment in Economic Union* (New York: Twentieth Century Fund, 1960), 379–82.

5. K. Fraaz, "Der Ausbau der Mosel," in *Landschaft und Moselausbau,* Schriftenreihe des Deutschen Rates für Landespflege, ed. Deutscher Rat für Landespflege, no. 7 (Bonn: Buch- und Verlagsdruckerei Ludwig Leopold, 1966), 15.

6. Vogel, "Ausbau der Mosel," 73–78.

7. Interministerial Committee on the Mosel to the Federal Government, "Zur Frage der Moselkanalisierung," 1 December 1953, Bundesarchiv-Zwischenarchiv, St. Augustin-Hangelar (BAStA), Bundeskanzleramt (B 136), Moselkanalisierung (1551), I Band 2, p. 24 (hereafter BAStA B 136/1551/I Bd. 2/24); Cermakian, *Moselle,* 97–98; Frank Roy Willis, *France, Germany, and the New Europe, 1945–1963* (Stanford: Stanford University Press, 1965), 94, 102, 223; William Diebold Jr., *The Schuman Plan* (New York: Praeger, 1959), 182.

8. Vogel, "Ausbau der Mosel," 78–81.

9. Willis, *France, Germany, and the New Europe,* 190, 197–209.

10. Winfried Schumacher, "Konrad Adenauer und die Saar," in *Die Saar 1945–1955: Ein Problem der europäischen Geschichte,* ed. Rainer Hudermann and Raymond Poidevin (Munich: Oldenbourg, 1992), 49–74; Willis, *France, Germany and the New Europe,* 190–91; Per Fischer, *Die Saar Zwischen Deutschland und Frankreich. Politische Entwicklung von 1945–1959* (Frankfurt am Main: Metzner, 1959), 186–90.

11. "Saar. Pariser Verhandlungen. Hallstein flüsterte," *Spiegel,* 29 February 1956, 18–19; Vogel, "Ausbau der Mosel," 82; Fischer, *Saar,* 232–34; Cioc, *The Rhine,* 67–68.

12. Fischer, *Saar,* 232–34; Willis, *France, Germany, and the New Europe,* 208–9, 224; Jacques Freymond, *The Saar Conflict, 1945–55* (New York: Praeger, 1960), 197–202. In exchange for political unity with the Saar by 1 January 1957 and economic unity by 1960, West Germany agreed to canalization along with other economic concessions. For example, France had the right to extract 66 million tons of coal from the Warndt mines until 1980 and was guaranteed annual shipments of 1.2 million tons of coal from the Saar. France also received reparations of Fr. 3 billion for the loss of the Völklingen steel mills to the Röchling family (who had collaborated with the National Socialist regime).

13. Konrad Adenauer, *Teegespräche 1955–1958,* ed. Rudolf Morsey and Hans-Peter Schwarz (Berlin: Siedler, 1986), 81–82.

14. Heinrich von Brentano to Adenauer, 25 February 1956, BAStA B 136/1552/I Bd. 3/87.

15. "Saar Problem," *Spiegel,* 14 March 1956, 11; Dr. Hans Globke, "Dem Herrn Bundeskanzler vorzulegen," to Adenauer, 20 March 1956, BAStA B 136/1552/I Bd. 3/137.

16. Dr. Eugen Schilken (Federal Ministry of Defense, Foreign Division, Koblenz), "Der Moselkanal—Auch ein deutsches Anliegen," n.d. [March? 1956] to Dr. Hans Globke, Federal Chancellery, BAStA B 136/1552/I Band 3/128, 133.

17. Ludwig Erhard to Adenauer, 4 April 1955, "Vertraulich," BAStA B 136/1551/I Band 2/322–26.

18. Hans-Christoph Seebohm to Adenauer, 8 March 1956, BAStA B 136/2775/Bd. 19; Cermakian, *Moselle,* 103; Vogel, "Ausbau der Mosel," 80.

19. The BDI was formed in August 1946 as a lobby to represent the interests of the country's industry and to shape policies affecting it.

20. John Gillingham, *Coal, Steel, and the Rebirth of Europe, 1945–1955: The Germans and French from Ruhr Conflict to Economic Community* (New York: Cambridge University Press, 1991), 193. WVESI united six major Ruhr firms and aggressively represented their interests.

21. Stein and Dr. Hay (BDI) and Paul Beyer (board of directors, DIHT) to Adenauer, 9 November 1953, BAStA B 136/1550/I Bd. 1/79–80; Hast (Wirtschaftsvereinigung Bergbau) and Sohl (WVESI) to Seebohm and Erhard, 10 January 1955, BAStA B 136/1551/I Bd. 3/270–73; E. Frohne (First President, DBB), "Exposé der Deutschen Bundesbahn über die Moselkanalisierung," 6 January 1955, BAStA B 136/1551/I Bd. 2/261; Keyser (Wirtschaftsvereinigung Bergbau) to Hans Globke, 13 January 1955, BAStA B 136/1551/I Bd. 2/295; WVESI, "Anlage zu dem Schreiben der Wirtschaftsvereinigung Eisen- und Stahlindustrie an den Herrn Bundeskanzler vom 21.4.55 betreffend Moselkanalisierung," BAStA B 136/1551/I Bd. 2/358–59.

22. WVESI, "Anlage zu dem Schreiben vom 21.4.55," BAStA B 136/1551/I Bd. 2/360; Dr. Schroeder (chairman, WVESI) to Adenauer, "Vertraulich," 7 March 1956, Politisches Archiv, Auswärtiges Amt, Bonn, Abteilung 2 (Politische Abteilung), Referat 217, Aktenzeichen 372-08 E, Band 2 (hereafter PA/AA/Abt. 2/Ref. 217/Az. 372-08 E/Bd.2).

23. Stein, Hay, and Beyer to Adenauer, 9 November 1953, BAStA B 136/1550/I Bd. 1/79–80; Frohne, "Exposé der Deutschen Bundesbahn über die Moselkanalisierung," 6 January 1955, BAStA B 136/1551/I Bd. 2/261.

24. Heinrich von Brentano to Adenauer, 25 February 1956, BAStA B 136/1552/I Bd. 3/88–89.

25. Federal Chancellery, "Niederschrift über die Besprechung beim Bundeskanzler über den Moselkanal am 5. März 1956, 10,30 Uhr," BAStA B 136/1552/I Bd. 3/112–19. See also Vogel, "Ausbau der Mosel," 86–87.

26. *Spiegel,* 28 March 1956, 11.

27. Robert Pferdemenges [CDU *Bundestag* deputy], "Zum französischen Plan der Moselkanalisierung," 6 January 1955, BAStA B 136/1551/I Bd. 2/263–64; file note of official in Federal Chancellery concerning an SPD Fraktion meeting, 12 May 1956, BAStA B 136/1552/I Bd. 3/328; "Die Bundesregierung zur Moselkanalisierung," *Staatszeitung* [Rheinland-Pfalz], 18 May 1956, 4; Beutler, internal memo to Haenlein, Federal Chancellery, 1 June 1956, BAStA B 136/1552/I Bd. 3/358–358a; Vogel, "Ausbau der Mosel," 88.

28. Cermakian, *Moselle,* 103.

29. "Altmeier ohne Klare Stellungnahme," *Freiheit,* 25 May 1956, clipping in Rheinland-Pfalz Landeshauptarchiv Koblenz (LH K), Ministerium des Innern (880)/1231 (hereafter LH K 880/1231); "'Saarinteressen werden berücksichtigt.' Abstimmungssieg Altmeiers," *Rhein-Zeitung,* 24 May 1956, clipping in LH K 880/1231; Peter Altmeier to Adenauer, 19 February 1959, BAStA B 136/2755/Bd. 19.

30. Dr. Friedrich von Poll (business manager, Industry- and Chamber of Commerce of Koblenz) to Paul Beyer, 21 October 1953, BAStA B 136/1551/I Bd. 2/11–13; Poll to DIHT, 2 November 1953, BAStA B 136/1551/I Bd. 2/8–10; Industrie- und Handelskammer von Koblenz und Trier, *Der Moselausbau. Seine wirtschaftliche Problematik in der Sicht der deutschen Moselbezirke* (Trier: Volksfreund-Druckerei, 1953), in BAStA B 136/1551/I Band 2/76; Bussche, "Auszug aus dem Vortrag 'Technische Probleme des Moselausbaues' von Herrn Oberbaurat von dem Bussche, gehalten vor der Interessengemeinschaft zur Förderung der Kanalisierung von Mosel und Saar am 2.04.52 in Bernkastel," BAStA B 136/1550/I Bd. 1/154–56.

31. Dazert to Presidents of Administrative Districts, Rhineland-Palatinate, "Mitteilung der Ansichten einzelner von der sogen. Moselkanalisierung betroffenen Landkreise u. Städte," 25 September 1955, LH K 880/1231; Dr. Flecken (Min. a.D.) chairman, Rheinischer Verein für Denkmalpflege und Heimatschutz to Federal Chancellery, 24 April 1956, PA/AA/Abt. 2/Ref. 217/Az. 372-08 E/Bd. 3.

32. Heinrich Menke, "Die Schiffbarmachung der Mosel in landschaftlicher Sicht," *N & L* 31, no. 6 (1956): 88.

33. Alwin Seifert, "Der Landschaftsanwalt zum Mosel-Kanal," *Süddeutsche Zeitung,* 12 May 1956, clipping in LH K 880/1231.

34. Alwin Seifert, "Die Schiffbarmachung der Mosel," *N & L* 34, no. 4 (1959): 54–55. See also Seifert, *Ein Leben für die Landschaft* (Düsseldorf: Diederichs, 1962), 171.

35. Wolfram Pflug, "Die Landespflege beim Ausbau der Mosel," in DRL, *Landschaft und Moselausbau*, 23; Ernst Bittmann, "Auszug aus dem Gutachten über 'Die Grundlagen und Methoden der Uferbepflanzung beim Moselausbau,'" in DRL, *Landschaft und Moselausbau*, 36.

36. Seifert, "Die Schiffbarmachung der Mosel," *N & L* 34, no. 4 (1959): 54; Bittmann, "Uferbepflanzung beim Moselausbau," in DRL, *Landschaft und Moselausbau, 38.*

37. Pflug, "Die Landespflege beim Ausbau der Mosel," in DRL, *Landschaft und Moselausbau,* 23–24.

38. See Thomsen, "Aufzeichnung," 19 April 1956, PA/AA/Abt. 2/Ref. 217/Az. 372-08 E/4316/56/Bd. 2. Among the few letters critical of Adenauer see Fritz Hofmann to Adenauer, 19 March 1956; August Gratenau to Foreign Office, 4 June 1956; Henry Brockhahne to [unspecified], 14 May 1956; and Dr. Hans Makulik to [unspecified], 5 May 1956, all in PA/AA/Abt. 2/Ref. 217/Az. 372-08 E/Bd. 3. Unless otherwise noted, all letters and postcards from citizens are found in PA/AA/Abt. 2/Ref. 217/Az. 372-08 E/Bd. 3

39. Hans Krieg to Federal Chancellery, 26 March 1956, PA/AA/ Abt. 2/ Ref. 217/Az. 372-08 E/Bd. 2.

40. Thomsen to Hans Krieg, 6 April 1956.

41. Liese-Lott Mergert to Federal Chancellery, 4 May 1956.

42. See Friedrich Schnoor to Federal Chancellery, 26 April 1956; Dr. jur. Ernst Waag to Federal Chancellery, 26 March 1956; Walter Schumacher to Adenauer, 18 April 1956; Friedrich Enkemann to Federal Chancellery, 4 April 1956; Ilse Friedhoff to Federal Chancellery, 21 April 1956; Kurt Schaefer (for Bundesführung der Freikörperkultur Jugend, Bund der Lichtscharen) to Adenauer, 8 April 1956; Westfälischer Naturschutztag, telegram to Federal Chancellery, 5–6 May 1956.

43. Among the many letters and postcards that spurned "sacrificing" the Mosel to accommodate France's economic interests see Ilse Friedhoff to Federal Chancellery, 21 April 1956; Anita Lefeldt to Federal Chancellery, 7 April 1956; Jürgen [Tomm?] to Federal Chancellery, April 1956; Henry Brockhahne to [not specified], 14 May 1956.

44. Martin Höppner to [not specified], 5 May 1956.

45. E.A. Meyer to Adenauer, 3 April 1956.

46. A. Schneider to Foreign Office, 13 May 1956.

47. Georg Fahrbach (for the League of German Mountaineering and Hiking Societies) to Federal Chancellery, 16 April 1956.

48. Junge Adler, Deutsche Jugendbewegung (Düsseldorf) to Federal Chancellery, 6 April 1956. On youth in the Knechtsand conflict see Engels, *Naturpolitik,* 185–89.

49. See Margot Heesch to Federal Chancellery, 2 May 1956; Seeman to Federal Chancellery, 20 April 1956; Kurt Schaefer (national chapter, Freikörperkultur Jugend) to Adenauer, 8 April 1956; Klasse 13 der Mädchenoberschule, Cuxhaven, to Federal Chancellery, 10 April 1956.

50. Rosemarie Eggers to Federal Chancellery, 30 April 1956; Liese-Lott Mergert to Federal Chancellery, 4 May 1956. See also Peter Eggers to Federal Chancellery, 25 April 1956; Ful. Caesar, Dr. Jur., Regierungsrat to Federal Chancellery, 20 April 1956; Verband naturwissenschaftlich-heimatkundlicher Vereine (Prof. Dr. Dr. E Martini, president) to Federal President Dr. Theodor Heuss and Adenauer, 2 May 1956; Margot Heesch to Federal Chancellery, 2 May 1956; Paul Großmann to Federal Chancellor, 27 March 1956.

51. Karl Arnold to Federal Chancellery, 9 April 1956, PA/AA/Abt. 2/Ref. 217/Az. 372-08 E/Bd. 2. See also Alfred Toepfer to Foreign Office, 11 April 1956.

52. Maria Cadmus to Federal Chancellor, 22 April 1956.

53. Else Feise to Adenauer, 20 April 1956.

54. Henry Koehn to Federal Chancellery, 29 April 1956.

55. Franz Giller to Federal Chancellery, 22 April 1956. See also Heinrich Messenburg to Federal Chancellery, 2 May 1956; Martin Höppner to Federal Chancellery, 5 May 1956.

56. Herbert Frank to Federal Chancellery, 8 May 1956. See also Verband naturwissenschaftlich-heimatkundlicher Vereine to Heuss and Adenauer, 2 May 1956; Lake Constance branch of the Vegetarischer-Union Deutschland to Federal Chancellor, 4 April 1956; Erika Borleis to Federal Chancellor, 2 April 1956; Rheinischer Verein für Denkmalpflege und Heimatschutz (Neuss) to Federal Chancellery, 24 April 1956; Paul Großmann, 27 March 1956; Rosemarie Eggers to Federal Chancellery, 30 April 1956; Verein Naturschutz Insel Sylt (Knud Ahlborn) to Adenauer, n.d.; Dr. Hans Makulik to [unspecified], 5 May 1956; Steigerthal and Dencker (second and first chairmen of Naturwacht e.V. Hamburg-Ohlstedt) to Foreign Office, 9 April 1956; P. Meesenburg (for a 36-member youth group) to Federal Chancellery, 2 May 1956.

57. Floristisch-Soziologische Arbeitsgemeinschaft (Dr. Erich Oberdorfer) to Foreign Office, 6 April 1956; Arbeitsgemeinschaft Rheinisch-Westfälischer Lepidopterologen e.V., Celle (Dr. Max Cretschmar) to Federal Chancellery, 26 April 1956; Arbeitsgemeinschaft der Westdeutschen Vogelschutzwarten (W. Hahn) to Foreign Office, 12 April 1956; Anita Lefeldt to Federal Chancellery, 7 April 1956.

58. Friedrich Schnoor to Federal Chancellery, 26 April 1956. See also Dr. Dietrich König [biologist in Schleswig-Holstein Ministry of Agriculture] to Federal Chancellery, 9 May 1956.

59. See Barbara Pless to Federal Chancellery, 28 April 1956; Höppner to Federal Chancellery, 5 May 1956.

60. Resolution of Landesfischereiverband Rheinland-Rheinhessen e.V. (Hillesheim, Chairman), n.d. [late June? 1956].

61. Thomsen to Federal Minister of Transport, 29 June 1956.

62. Cermakian, *Moselle*, 121; Willis, *France, Germany, and the New Europe*, 223–24.

63. The executive body of the International Mosel Corporation had fourteen members, with Germany and France each having six representatives and Luxembourg having two. West Germany's members included two representatives from the Federal Ministry of Transportation, and one representative each from the Federal Ministries of Finance and Economics, the Foreign Office, and the state of Rhineland-Palatinate.

64. Karl Ohem, "Teure Moselkanalisierung," *Deutsche Zeitung-Wirtschaftszeitung*, 24 May 1961; "Moselkanal teurer als erwartet," *Frankfurter Allgemeine Zeitung*, 28 April 1961, clippings in BAStA B 136/2755/Bd. 19; Willis, *France, Germany, and the New Europe*, 224; Federal Minister of Transportation to President, *Bundestag*, "Bericht über den Fortgang der Arbeiten zur Schiffbarmachung der Mosel in den Jahren 1957 und 1958," 14 January 1959, Drucksache 789, 2–3, in BAStA B 136/2755; K. Fraaz, "Der Ausbau der Mosel," in DRL, *Landschaft und Moselausbau*, 14–16.

65. A. Meinen, "Rheinland-Pfalz und der Ausbau der Mosel zur Großschiffahrtsstraße," in DRL, *Landschaft und Moselausbau*, 10–11; "Regierungspräsident: Enteignung und Entschädigung bei der Moselkanalisierung mit aller Gründlichkeit," *Trierische Landeszeitung*, 5 February 1959, clipping in LH K 880/6774.

66. Pflug, "Landespflege beim Ausbau der Mosel," in DRL, *Landschaft und Moselausbau*, 33.

67. Seifert, "Die Schiffbarmachung der Mosel," *N & L* 34, no. 4 (1959): 55.

68. Wolfram Pflug, "Landespflege beim Ausbau der Mosel—Erfolge und Probleme," in *Landespflege und Raumordnung. Forschungs- und Sitzungsberichte der Akademie für Raumforschung und Landesplanung*, ed. Akademie für Raumforschung und Landesplanung, no. 43 (Hanover: Gebrüder Jänecke, 1968): 33–36. See also Pflug, "Landespflege beim Ausbau der Mosel," 26–27; Meinen, "Rheinland-Pfalz und der Ausbau der Mosel," 10–11, both in DRL, *Landschaft und Moselausbau*. Participating in canalization were the Federal Boating and Navigation Administration in Mainz, the Federal Institute for Hydrology in Koblenz,

Rhineland Palatinate's Ministry of Agriculture, Viniculture and Forestry, and the water management offices of Koblenz and Trier.

69. Pflug, "Landespflege beim Ausbau der Mosel—Erfolge und Probleme," 34.

70. Meinen, "Rheinland-Pfalz und der Ausbau der Mosel," 10; Pflug, "Landespflege beim Ausbau der Mosel," 25–26, 30, both in DRL, *Landschaft und Moselausbau.*

71. Pflug, "Die Landespflege beim Ausbau der Mosel," in DRL, *Landschaft und Moselausbau,* 31.

72. Ohem, "Teure Moselkanalisierung," *Deutsche Zeitung-Wirtschaftszeitung,* 24 May 1961, clipping in BAStA B 136/2755/Bd. 19; Meinen, "Rheinland-Pfalz und der Ausbau der Mosel," in DRL, *Landschaft und Moselausbau,* 12.

73. For an overview of canalization's effects on the water supply see Ministry of Agriculture, Rhineland-Palatinate to Minister of Economics and Transportation, Rhineland-Palatinate, 9 February 1959, copy in LH K, Sozialministerium (930)/5496 (hereafter LH K 930/5496); Federal Minister of Transportation to President of *Bundestag,* "Bericht über den Fortgang der Arbeiten zur Schiffbarmachung der Mosel im Jahre 1961," 2 February 1962, 5, BAStA B 136/2755. On the conflict between federal and state government officials see Minister-President Peter Altmeier, Rhineland-Palatinate to Adenauer, 19 February 1959 and Altmeier to Federal Minister of Finance, Etzel, 29 December 1959, both in BAStA B 136/2755. Concerns of local government officials are evident in *Bezirksregierung* Koblenz to Ministry of Agriculture, Rhineland-Palatinate, 3 December 1958, LH K 880/6774; [n.a.], "Niederschrift über die Versammlung der Bürgermeister und Amtsbürgermeister der Städte und Gemeinden an der Mosel am 21 März 1959 in Merl an der Mosel," LH K, Stadt Bernkastel Kues (615)/822 (hereafter LH K 615/822); Landtag Rheinland-Pfalz, III Wahlperiode. Ausgegeben am 10 Dezember 1958, Nr. 477, Kleine Anfrage des Abg. Simonis (CDU), Zell, re: Schiffbarmachung der Mosel; Landtag Rheinland-Pfalz, III Wahlperiode. Ausgegeben am 3 Dezember 1958, Nr. 499, Große Anfrage der Fraktion der SPD betr. Moselkanalisierung und Wasserbauwirtschaftsplanungen der Ufergemeinden, both in LH K 880/6774.

74. Meinen, "Rheinland-Pfalz und der Ausbau der Mosel," in DRL, *Landschaft und Moselausbau,* 11; Friedel Thörnig, "Moselgemeinden stehen durch die Schiffbarmachung des Flusses vor ernsten Problemen," *Trierische Landeszeitung,* 17/18 January 1959; "Traben-Trarbach nach der Moselkanalisierung. Pressegespräch mit Bürgermeister Spalink," *Rheinische Zeitung,* 22 October 1959, clippings in LH K 880/6774.

75. "Traben-Trarbach nach der Moselkanalisierung," *Rheinische Zeitung,* 22 October 1959, clipping in LH K 880/6774; Amtsverwaltung Zeltingen to state Ministry of Agriculture, 16 October 1959, LH K 880/6774.

76. "Schiffbarmachung der Mosel bereit Mehring große Sorgen," *Trierische Landeszeitung,* 11 December 1958, clipping in LH K 880/6774; Meinen, "Rheinland-Pfalz und der Ausbau der Mosel," in DRL, *Landschaft und Moselausbau,* 12–13.

77. Pflug, "Die Landespflege beim Ausbau der Mosel," in DRL, *Landschaft und Moselausbau,* 31; Wasserwirtschaftsamt Trier to Ministry of Agriculture, Rhineland-Palatinate, 17 May 1965, copy in LH K 930/5515.

78. Pflug, "Die Landespflege beim Ausbau der Mosel," 29–31, 33; Graf Lennart Bernadotte to Federal Minister of Transportation, Georg Leber, 5 December 1966, 5–7, both in DRL, *Landschaft und Moselausbau.* See also District Government, Trier to Ministry of Agriculture, Rhineland-Palatinate, September 1967, copy in LH K 930/5507; Bittmann, "Uferbepflanzung beim Moselausbau," in DRL, *Landschaft und Moselausbau,* 36–43.

79. Pflug, "Die landschaftsökologischen und landschaftsgestalterischen Auswirkungen des Moselausbaues," in *Probleme der Nutzung und Erhaltung der Biosphäre. Bericht über ein internationales Colloquium der Deutschen UNESCO-Kommission veranstaltet mit finanzieller Unterstützung der UNESCO vom 17. bis 18. April 1968 in Berchtesgaden,* ed. Deutsche

UNESCO-Kommission (Cologne: Deutsche UNESCO-Kommission, 1969), 97, 99; Fraaz, "Der Ausbau der Mosel," in DRL, *Landschaft und Moselausbau*, 17.

80. Günter Jens, "Die Moselfischerei vor und nach dem Ausbau des Stromes," in DRL, *Landschaft und Moselausbau*, 44; Meinen, "Rheinland-Pfalz und der Ausbau der Mosel," in DRL, *Landschaft und Moselausbau* 12; Cioc, *The Rhine*, 189.

81. Pflug, "Die Landespflege beim Ausbau der Mosel," in DRL, *Landschaft und Moselausbau*, 28–29; Pflug, "Die landschaftsökologischen und landschaftsgestalterischen Auswirkungen des Moselausbaues," 101.

82. Seifert, *Ein Leben für die Landschaft*, 171.

83. Pflug, "Landespflege beim Ausbau der Mosel—Erfolge und Probleme," 30–31; Pflug, "Landespflege beim Ausbau der Mosel, in DRL, *Landschaft und Moselausbau*, 33–34; "Einigung in der Moselufer-Gestaltung," *Rhein-Zeitung Mittelmosel*, 16 October 1963, clipping in LH K 930/5510.

84. Bernadotte to Leber, 5 December 1966, in DRL, *Landschaft und Moselausbau*, 6–7.

85. Bernadotte to Leber, 5 December 1966, 6–7, 8; Pflug, "Die Landespflege beim Ausbau der Mosel," 35, both in DRL, *Landschaft und Moselausbau*.

86. Cermakian, *Moselle*, 126–40; Jens, "Die Moselfischerei vor und nach dem Ausbau des Stromes," in DRL, *Landschaft und Moselausbau*, 44; Pflug, "Die landschaftsökologischen und landschaftsgestalterischen Auswirkungen des Moselausbaues," 100–101.

87. Cermakian, *Moselle*, 126. To ensure cooperation in administering the canal, France, West Germany, and Luxembourg formed the Moselle Commission in 1956 in Trier. It went into operation in 1962. The six member commission (two members from each of the three states) determines tolls and oversees their collection among other responsibilities.

88. Pflug, "Die Landespflege beim Ausbau der Mosel," in DRL, *Landschaft und Moselausbau*, 35.

Chapter 6

INVENTING THE ENVIRONMENT AND
REDISCOVERING NATURE, 1967–1975

In 1970, conservationists declared that they had arrived at a "great turning point" as European Conservation Year (ECY) exposed the "perilous situation of humans and their environment" "five minutes before twelve." While some announced that year that "Grandpa's *Naturschutz*" was dead, others insisted the concept "*Naturschutz*" should be "completely reformulated" so that the public recognized it to be a political issue concerned with nothing less than protecting people in their increasingly imperiled surroundings.[1] What conservationists did not foresee, however, was that the "turning point" for *Naturschutz* occurred when it was swept up in, and subordinated to, state-sponsored environmental protection. Halfway through ECY, Chancellor Willy Brandt's coalition government of Social Democrats and the liberal, pro-business Free Democratic Party (FDP) announced an Action Program on the Environment, inventing "the environment" as a tangible and legitimate sphere for political activity.[2] Media coverage of the government's Action Program and of its more substantive Environmental Program of 1971 contributed significantly to making the public conscious of the existence of the environment and the multiple threats to it.

The coalition government, and more specifically, officials in the Federal Ministry of the Interior (BMI), imported the concept of "*Umwelt*" late in 1969 directly from the United States to bring together several competencies, which previously had been dealt with as public health or regional planning issues. At first, some prominent West Germans expressed misgivings about the term. *Bundestag* President Kai-Uwe von Hassel (CDU) editorialized in 1972 that even

---

Notes for this chapter begin on page 204.

though the older concept *Naturschutz* clearly had come to mean "the protection of humanity in nature," it had been displaced by "*Umweltschutz,*" in his estimation a "downright unfortunate and vague word formation!"[3] By then, however, *Umweltschutz* had become a catchy political slogan and was a major reform program with growing public support.

Of course, the environment was not merely a government invention. "Environmental conscience and environmental consciousness," one ecologist explained in 1971, were "modern concepts born out of a distressing experience" and were capable of expressing what people heretofore had experienced, but thought very little about, namely their surroundings.[4] The public's sensitivity was heightened by media coverage openly critical of environmental accidents abroad and at home, from major oil spills in southern England (*Torrey Canyon,* 1967) and Santa Barbara (1969), to massive fish kills, such as the one in June 1969 caused when the insecticide Thiodan leaked into the Rhine. A steady stream of images in print and on television of sea birds cloaked in tar and of fish floating belly up provided potent symbols of an affluent consumer society urgently needing reform.[5]

Reinforcing this view was a vocal minority of educated middle class students across Europe who, in the late 1960s, rebelled against the affluence and materialism that modern industrialism had made possible. Why, they wanted to know, would individuals with the freedom of choice opt to live in such a society? In addition, though they rarely expressed concern to protect nature or curb pollution, their confrontational style of protest, and their demand during the Grand Coalition (1966–1969) for an "extraparliamentary opposition" (APO) to express dissent outside of the political establishment, gradually made grassroots opposition by "ordinary" citizens more acceptable.[6]

Against the backdrop of student radicalism, Chancellor Willy Brandt's challenge to citizens in 1969 to "risk more democracy" through greater involvement in the political process seemed a timely, conciliatory gesture. But Brandt's appeal for cooperation also reflected a general trend in modern industrialized nations of the government seeing itself as a neutral force standing above partisan struggles. Using planning, objective science, and technical expertise, officials assumed they could shape society for the welfare of citizens. Among the SPD, there were some who insisted that citizens should play a key part in shaping the government's domestic reform program, which aimed to expand the welfare system, continue improving education and transportation, and strengthen employees' rights in the workplace.[7] Only when pressed to do so did the coalition government also prioritize environmental protection.

Initially, it was officials in the FDP-led Federal Ministry of the Interior (BMI) who expressed the most concern to promote *Umweltschutz.* They conceived of environmental protection as a state planning project that could be managed with better laws, the latest technologies, and professional expertise, and sustained with broad public support. But as such it was only partially successful.[8] While conservationists applauded the government's attention to environmental clean up, they faulted the program for emphasizing pollution control and underestimating the need to protect the health of ecological systems. Their critique of the program's "ecological deficit" was an appeal to formulate solutions not only with technology's possibilities in mind, but also with nature's (measurable) limits in clear view. It also was the latest expression of their bid for more influence in planning decisions.

In addition, however, concern about an "ecological deficit" revealed the importance that the science of ecology had attained during the 1960s and hinted at its use toward diverse ends in the 1970s. Some, like the landscape planners discussed in chapter 4, relied on ecology to undergird a presumably more objective approach to managing ecosystems. But others, among them Bernhard Grzimek and Hubert Weinzierl, formed what historian Jens Ivo Engels has described as a "new conservation elite," and used a popularized version of ecology to provide a quasi-scientific basis for their familiar cultural criticism and their increasingly apocalyptic vision of the future, one they shared with citizens' initiatives. Influenced by the tactics of student radicals, these more confrontational conservationists projected an image of rebels fighting for a noble cause, revitalizing *Naturschutz* by associating it with criticism of the government on the one hand, and visions of a healed environment (*heile Umwelt*), on the other. Viewed as oppositional, protecting nature in a threatened environment attracted a younger generation from the political left, though without losing its traditional base of support among conservatives.[9]

In the new arena of environmental politics, however, conservationists had to share space and sometimes compete with concerned citizens wanting more direct involvement in decisions that affected their daily lives. Around 1970, but noticeably already under the Grand Coalition of the late 1960s, hundreds of West German citizens formed grassroots initiatives against local planning decisions that compromised the quality of life in their communities. Initially supportive of the government's program on the environment, citizens' initiatives (CIs) grew impatient with what they perceived to be its technocratic emphasis and underestimation of an environmental crisis. Influenced by the 1972 United Nations Conference on the Human Environment in Stockholm, international predictions about "limits to growth," and domestic discussions about "quality of life," citizens' initiatives began to coordinate their activism at the national level, hoping thereby to force the state to make deep social changes and better protect an individual's right to a healthy environment.

As the environment came to be perceived as something tangible (because it had become unsafe for its human occupants), citizens and some politicians renewed appeals made a decade earlier for constitutional guarantees of an individual's right to live in a dignified environment (*menschenwürdige Umwelt*). This demand underscored the defining characteristics of environmental protection as it came to be popularly understood: looking to the state to protect the individual against stresses experienced subjectively, irrespective of residency. By making the individual the point of reference, people of diverse walks of life and political persuasion could personalize the challenge to protect any of the many environments they inhabited. But what were the implications of this for nature? Initially it was not clear. Over time, however, the invention of the environment in West Germany and elsewhere led to "the reinvention of nature as a fragile and finite space" warranting protection.[10]

Prelude to Environmental Protection: Managing the Biosphere

Some of the concerns that eventually were united under the concept "environmental protection" were first brought together as a set of issues to be resolved through spatial planning. In response to the federal government's disconcerting Spatial Planning Report of 1966, the *Bundestag* called for an assessment of the stress capacity of the "household of nature" and an estimate of the cost of conserving "the natural bases of life." For its part in answering parliamentarians, the Federal Ministry of Agriculture commissioned the BAVNL in 1967 to conduct a study that, with hindsight, might be described as an attempt to report on the state of the environment, though with emphasis on land use. The BAVNL's findings, published in 1969 under the title, "Strains on the Landscape," expanded on earlier reports in examining how agriculture, construction, mining, military training, pollution, and waste disposal altered climates, reduced species diversity, and compromised the productivity and "stress capacity" of soil, water, and forests.[11] Because the study appeared at the end of the legislative period, it had limited impact on political debates, and with its highly technical language, failed to capture public notice. Yet the report shows how nature and landscapes had been reconfigured into ecosystems with "capacities" that experts could quantify and then manage to maximize long term use.[12]

As West German landscape planners and others in related fields relied on ecology to scientifically manage land and resources in the 1960s, they came to view their work in highly technical, abstract terms. It was their job to assess the land's ecological limits, to measure the productive capacity (*Leistungspotential*) of natural ecosystems, and to estimate the tolerance level (*Belastungspotential* or *Belastbarkeit*) for stress of a particular area of land. With their technical expertise, they were confident that they could manage the "ecological systems" in nature, preserving or restoring them to health, with the goal of maximizing their use over the long term. This scientification of landscape planning assured practitioners a place within the bureaucracy, yet simultaneously created a communication gap between themselves and lay persons who lacked their expertise and technical vocabulary, and who were more inclined to express concerns in cultural, moral, and emotional arguments (which experts often dismissed as subjective). Leading conservationists' more scientific and managerial approach was influenced by their participation in international conferences sponsored by the IUCN, NATO, and the United Nations Educational, Scientific and Cultural Organization (UNESCO), among other organizations. Indeed, their membership in a global network of experts that met more frequently in the 1960s facilitated the ongoing integration of international practices into West German conservation.[13]

Among the most important gatherings of the decade was the 1968 conference in Paris on the biosphere sponsored by UNESCO. This meeting brought together over 300 people representing sixty-three governments and almost thirty international organizations, such as the World Health Organization and the IUCN. West Germany's eleven delegates included Konrad Buchwald, Herbert Offner, BAVNL director Gerhard Olschowy, and the directors of several public research institutes.[14] The Biosphere Conference was organized in response to scientists who had become more overtly political in the 1960s in their shared concern about harm to nature caused by the rapid increase in global population and the accelerated pace of urbanization and industrialization. Indicative of a more abstract view of nature, and one that transcended national boundaries and cultural traditions, the "biosphere" meeting discussed the history of the human impact on all parts of the earth inhabited by living organisms, with an emphasis on the "terrestrial part of the biosphere."

In part the culmination of collaborative research through the International Biological Program in operation between 1964 and 1974 to monitor ecosystems and their use, the conference provided a forum for sharing research on managing soil, water, vegetation, and wildlife, and on the dynamics of ecosystems.[15] Despite acknowledging the limits of current research, participants expressed an unmistakable confidence that more study and international cooperation would enable them to develop the "scientific foundations for the rational use and preservation of the potential of the biosphere."[16] Neither species and their habitats nor scenic landscapes were the primary object of rational management; the "energy potential" of the living world was. Delegates insisted on "vigorous steps to preserve genetic resources," which, if lost, would constitute "an irreparable loss, considering their economic, scientific, educational and aesthetic values for man." While reducing plants, animals, and other organisms to "genetic resources" having value because of their importance to people, the conference simultaneously elevated conservation to a matter vitally important for human well being.[17] Underscoring that "man is a key factor in the biosphere," yet conceding how little was known about the effects of human activities on ecosystems, delegates demanded more research on the interaction between human and natural "systems" and of the consequences for both of this reciprocal relationship. This agenda led to the establishment of the Man and the Biosphere Program and determined the focus of the UN Stockholm Conference slated for 1972.[18]

Yet the final report of the Biosphere Conference proposed few new strategies to confront environmental deterioration. "[T]o a large degree," the report concluded with cautious optimism, "*man now has the capability and responsibility to determine and guide the future course of his environment*," and to implement "national and international corrective actions." Emphasis has been added to highlight the report's view that humans had become the architects of their environment and thus were responsible for managing their "ecological relations with nature." They could do so, according to the report, with more effective regional planning and by putting ecological considerations on equal footing with economic ones in political decisions.[19]

Although the Biosphere Conference challenged participants to envision new ways of protecting the biosphere, it did not result in significant changes in strategy in the Federal Republic or elsewhere. While some delegates returned home convinced that "land cultivation" (*Landespflege*) was the German equivalent of "sustainable use" of the "biosphere," others grasped that something more was involved than what land cultivation conveyed, proposing "environmental hygiene" (*Umwelthygiene*) to communicate the daunting task of "preserv[ing] . . . healthy living conditions on the planet."[20]

The scientific deliberations of the Biosphere Conference went little noticed by the West German public, but with upcoming elections in 1969, some private groups hoped to put conservation on candidates' political radar. As DNR executive committee member Hubert Weinzierl announced, it was time to stop talking about conservation "only in hiking clubs and pubs" and start making it of consequence in political elections.[21] The DNR, now under Wolfgang Engelhardt's presidency, claimed to represent two million people through its member organizations, making it the third largest organization in the country behind the German Trade Union Congress (*Deutscher Gewerkschaftsbund*) and the German Sports League. Hoping to be viewed as an assertive national alliance defending nature and citizens' rights, the DNR dispatched letters to party chairmen, scolding them for platforms that ignored the "vitally necessary task of preserving an environment that serves human dignity and that is biologically able to function for our generation and those that follow." The executive committee also polled federal and state parliamentarians and candidates for office about their stance on conservation. But only 164 politicians replied—far fewer than the 1002 contacted. Although responses were vaguely supportive, the poll indicated that most politicians failed to grasp that "modern conservation"—in the DNR's words—involved nothing less than "securing a healthy living space in which people could fulfill their human potential."[22] In addition, some politicians had other priorities.

This certainly was the case with Chancellor Willy Brandt. After narrowly securing the chancellorship in 1969, Brandt was most concerned with normalizing relations with Eastern Europe, especially East Germany. But his policy of *Ostpolitik* was unpopular with conservatives, who claimed it was "soft" on communism. Brandt also hoped to implement a broad domestic reform program, but he did not initially emphasize nature or environmental protection. Under pressure from the new federal president, Gustav Heinemann (SPD), and letters from the public, Brandt mentioned *"Naturschutz"* in his government declaration in October 1969, viewing it as narrow preservation. He followed up words with deeds by creating the post of federal conservation commissioner within the chancellery. The man he named for the job was the popular television figure and Frankfurt Zoo Director, Bernhard Grzimek.[23]

Even before Grzimek's name was announced, officials in the Federal Ministry of Agriculture (BML) raised objections. They predicted that the *Länder* would resent the new position as a potential source of competition and complained justifiably that it would duplicate efforts by the BAVNL and the German Council for Land Cultivation. But the choice of Grzimek was more objectionable to BML officials than the new post. They respected Grzimek's work as the director of a first rate zoo with over 5,000 animals, and appreciated his efforts to promote wildlife conservation in Africa through his personal initiatives, his popular journal, *Das Tier,* and his long running television show, "A Place for Animals," which captivated twenty million viewers each week. But they doubted that the keeper of a zoological garden was the person best suited to promote conservation in Germany. They were thinking about Grzimek's much derided Taunus project from the mid 1960s that never got off the ground and his controversial role in establishing the country's first national park in Bavaria on forest service land. His involvement in the latter undertaking divided the DNR and was partly responsible for limiting his presidency to one term. When Grzimek announced that he would not run for the top DNR office again, he remarked that he no longer wanted his advocacy to be constrained by deference to any organization. How, some officials wondered, would this go-it-alone attitude be an asset in a job requiring cooperation? But Grzimek had broader public appeal than most conservationists whose influence was based on ties to officials. By effectively using the media to cultivate an image as a professor, rebel, and animal friend, Grzimek won popular support well beyond conservation circles and raised impressive funds for species preservation around the world.[24]

The 61-year-old Grzimek took over the job in January 1970, but refused a salary so that he might remain unencumbered by restrictions associated with his official position.[25] From his federal post in Bonn, he called for DM 100 million to be set aside in 1970 to combat pollution and promote conservation—far more than the current outlay he estimated to be DM 6 million.[26] After three years of frustration and disappointment, however, Grzimek resigned. According to BML officials, Grzimek's difficulties stemmed from his "almost constant absence," the lack of clarity in his job description, and his "underhanded" maneuvers to shift responsibility for conservation from the agriculture to the interior ministry (which Grzimek claimed would be more neutral).[27] Grzimek explained that he was obstructed by the bureaucracy and by the "wholly inadequate material and financial provisions" for conservation in the BML where it remained subordinate to forestry and agriculture. In Grzimek's place, a new conservation advisory council was established in the BML, which included Wolfgang Engelhardt, Graf Lennart Bernadotte, and Theodor Sonnemann, a body with experienced people, but as Grzimek publicly complained, one comfortable with the establishment and unwilling to stand up to the agriculture lobby.

Grzimek stepped down also because he had grown impatient with politicians' apparent unwillingness to share his increasingly apocalyptic outlook. "The protection of life," he wrote Brandt shortly after resigning, "that is, rescuing human, animal and plant life on our earth—protecting it against poisoning, overpopulation, and too much technology, has become the . . . most urgent task for politicians." But this pressing political responsibility, he complained, continued to be parceled out to several ministries which lacked a unified perspective and prioritized "economic and class interests." Based upon his anti-establishment rhetoric, the liberal Hamburg based weekly newspaper *Die Zeit* described Grzimek as a champion of direct democracy. His support for the Green List in parliamentary elections in Hesse in 1978 reinforced his image as a non-conformist who eluded attempts at categorization.[28]

European "Conservation" Year: From "*Naturschutz*" to "*Umweltschutz*," 1970

More effective than one man in raising public awareness about the range of responsibilities that had come to be associated with conservation was the steady flow of information through the media during European Conservation Year (ECY) in 1970. ECY had been planned by the Council of Europe in the early 1960s when scientists became more overtly political in their conviction that international cooperation was essential to manage the continent's natural resources.[29] Each of the eighteen member states established national committees to organize a program of events for the year. West Germany's national committee was chaired by Herbert Offner, the officer responsible for conservation in the Federal Ministry of Agriculture, and included representatives of the BAVNL, conservation commissioners, the DNR, the Association for the Protection of the German Forest (SDW), Toepfer's VNP, the Interparliamentary Working Association for a Sustainable Economy (IPA), and the Alliance for the Protection of Germany's Waters. Since the 1950s, these groups had forged a cooperative alliance that contributed to their self-understanding as the core carriers of conservation in the country. Involvement in ECY gave them more influence than most had ever had—or would have in the future.

With federal and state funds, the national committee and a well-established network of conservation and hiking groups put together a full calendar of events.[30] In Bavaria, the League for Nature Protection under Hubert Weinzierl's energetic leadership organized ECY activities. In Baden-Württemberg, Georg Fahrbach and the Swabian Alb Society formed a coalition of around thirty organizations to do the job. Local chapters of the German Mountaineering and Hiking Society coordinated events in Hesse, while the SDW had oversight in most other states.[31] The DNR assumed overall responsibility for ECY and emerged from the challenge invigorated and hopeful about attracting new members. Near the end of the year, it added "Federal Association for Environmental Protection" to its name and began creating new working groups for wildlife conservation and "ecological" and "technical" environmental protection.[32]

In general, however, ECY looked at lot like business as usual. Relying on the familiar strategy of linking conservation events to public figures, the national committee secured Federal President Heinemann to serve as the official patron of the year long campaign and minister-presidents of the *Länder* to do so at the state level.[33] Most individuals available for speaking engagements were faces familiar mainly in conservation circles, with the exception of more widely known personalities like the anti-nuclear activist and medical doctor, Bodo Manstein, and the conservative animal behavioralist Konrad Lorenz.[34] Because public events were usually held in conjunction with the annual meetings of conservation groups, turn out by "average" citizens was disappointing.[35] Even the call to action aimed at local governments remained in the realm of the familiar, recommending the establishment of new reserves and recreation areas and the adoption of stricter ordinances to control pollution and manage garbage.[36]

But some ECY events had a more lasting impact. After a bitter three year debate over the country's first national park in the Bavarian Forest (1966–1969), Weinzierl and Engelhardt pushed ahead its official opening by several months to make it the "crowing event" of the year. They also initiated planning for a second national park in Königsee near Berchtesgaden, which opened in 1978.[37] One of ECY's largest initiatives was an anti-litter campaign, which Weinzierl spearheaded and packaging industries supported. Modeled after Anglo-American initiatives to "Keep Britain Tidy" and "Keep America Beautiful," the West German effort to "Keep the Countryside Clean" made people more conscious of the need to fight litter, though it did less to educate them about the importance of reducing consumer packaging.[38] There also is indication that participation was limited. Only four people from "the general public," for example, showed up for a trash pick up day in Wuppertal organized by the SDW and supported by 200 people from its youth chapters and city officials. But the anti-litter campaign was not a one year event. By the end of the decade, 50,000 trash pick up actions had been conducted, primarily by youth.[39]

It is difficult to assess the effectiveness of ECY because it occurred at the same time that the Brandt government introduced its Action Program on the Environment and the United States formulated a comprehensive environmental policy. As ECY, the Action Program, and US policy initiatives converged in media coverage, the public received a message that fluctuated between hope and alarm. This mixed message was evident in an award winning forty-minute film, "Alarm! Alarm!," produced at the request of the DNR with financial support from the BML and a DM 5,000 contribution from Grzimek. Premiered at a closing event for ECY, the film subsequently was made available to DNR member groups and schools.[40] The film's sensational title contrasted with its reasoned argument that progress was desirable, but not at any price. Scenes of idling cars stalled in traffic and of hedgeless machine-worked fields sprayed with pesticides reinforced the narrator's warning that there was poison in the air and in the landscape. Footage of a fish kill, an oil slick, and effluents pouring into a stream condemned those who polluted a shared resource with impunity. After depicting multiple causes for alarm, the film showed bucolic scenes of parks and reserves, offering the familiar and thus unremarkable assessment that such spaces were an integral part of any regional plan and vital to public health. Whoever helped protect nature, the narrator emphasized, was not a romantic dreamer, but "a realist!" Maneuvering between pragmatism and alarm, the film urged individuals to take constructive action to prevent society from becoming "suicidal."[41]

The combination of sobering facts, alarmist predictions, and a challenge for the state and the individual to do more was evident in the populist message of ECY's leading propagandist, Hubert Weinzierl (b. 1935). This rising star in conservation earned his degree in forestry from the University of Munich in 1958. He began publicity work for the DNR the following year and was elected to the executive committee in 1964. From 1965 until 1969, he also served as district conservation commissioner for Lower Bavaria. Weinzierl maintained ties to the state's conservative CSU party, but insisted that preventing the "sell out of the environment" was a cause that transcended party affiliation. Through his leadership positions as first chairman of the Bavarian League for Nature Protection and as the DNR's special commissioner for Conservation Year, Weinzierl made his debut as a passionate defender of nature and the environment. Unlike the emerging corps of professional conservationists who distanced themselves from emotional arguments in favor of presumably neutral, scientific ones, Weinzierl urged people to have "the courage to remain romantic and . . . to think modern and realistic." Echoing the anti-urban sentiments associated with traditional preservation, he warned that "the loneliness of big cities gives rise to . . . anxiety . . . and to an impoverishment of the soul." The city man, he insisted, needed "healing nature as much as he needs his daily bread." Inspired by the tactics, though not the radical message, of students in revolt, Weinzierl projected the image of a rebel fighting for a moral cause. Finally, he declared, a "militant opposition of responsible citizens (an APO of conservatives)" was making *Naturschutz* a matter of political consequence. By combining cultural criticism, an apocalyptic tone, and a message of social protest that appealed to a disgruntled younger generation, Weinzierl gave conservation a new, more powerful voice.[42]

The explosive potential of the student generation was one of several factors motivating US President Richard Nixon to identify environmental clean up as "the big problem of the Seventies" in his State of the Union Address to Congress in January 1970. Nixon's call for expensive measures to reduce pollution and preserve nature played an important part in generating support for conservation and environmental protection in West Germany. According to conservationists, it had more impact than ECY's official opening in Strasbourg a month later. These orderly proceedings featuring speeches by Prince Philip, Duke of Edinburgh, and World Wildlife Fund activist, Prince Bernhard of the Netherlands, contrasted sharply with spectacular events across the Atlantic a few months later on Earth Day when twenty million Americans took part in teach-ins and demonstrations across the country.[43]

The elevation of environmental protection to a "political matter of the highest order" in the US compelled the SPD/FDP coalition government to develop its own policy to catch up with international trends. In addition, the Brandt administration was under pressure from NATO, especially its dominant member, the US, to help make the military alliance an influential organization for environmental protection through sharing innovative technologies. In a time of loosening Cold War tensions, some NATO members viewed the transfer of environmental technology as a legitimate way to encourage cooperation with the communist bloc.[44]

Responding to these international pressures, the federal chancellery urged West German officials to develop a coherent environmental policy. Hans-Dietrich Genscher and Walther Scheel, left wing members of the FDP who had gained the upper hand in the party, accepted the challenge, claiming for Genscher's interior ministry responsibility for several competencies, which BMI officials labeled "environmental protection," a concept they imported directly from the US. In assuming responsibility for *Umweltschutz*, the FDP strengthened its role in the government, snared needed voters from the educated middle classes, and deflected criticism from the coalition's controversial *Ostpolitik*.[45] The FDP also put environmental protection on the agenda because it seemed to be an ideal example of state planning that relied on citizens' participation and attracted broad public support. Indeed, between 1970 and 1972, there was general consensus on the need for environmental protection, from the *Bundestag* to state parliaments, from labor unions to industry (until demand for "limits to growth" grew louder). Despite widespread support, the BMI struggled to implement reforms smoothly, hindered by competency struggles among ministries and with state governments.[46]

The government's Action Program, announced in September 1970, posited three principles that continue to hold relevance in European environmental policy: polluters must pay for harm to the environment (*Verursacherprinzip*); preventive measures must be taken to prevent damage before it occurs (*Vorsorgeprinzip*); and protecting the environment requires cooperation among officials at all levels of government as well as the involvement of citizens (*Kooperationsprinzip*).[47] Conceived of as a prelude to the more substantive environmental policy of 1971, the Action Program introduced little that was new. Many of the laws it called for were under consideration, such as legislation to control emissions, reduce noise pollution, regulate waste disposal, update the water maintenance law, and ban DDT.[48]

Conservationists applauded the government's efforts to lay out a clear plan to clean up the environment. But they were disappointed that the program focused primarily on "technical environmental protection" and ignored the equally vital activities associated with "ecological environmental protection," which included protecting habitats and restoring ecological "health" to areas compromised by development.[49] The Action Program did reflect officials' prioritization of technological measures. "Environmental protection," a BMI statement explained, "is the active design of technical processes that . . . influence environmental factors . . . [and] is closely connected with, and has a reciprocal effect on, public health, regional planning, urban construction, and policies for science, the economy, and transport."[50]

Little mention in this working definition was made of protecting ecosystems. This lack of attention reflected in part the limited interest in ecology or conservation among BMI officials, but it was somewhat surprising in light of the fascination with cybernetics (systems theory) and futurology of the program's primary designer, Peter Menke-Glückert. In addition, however, the limited attention to ecology revealed the continued weakness of this science relative to more established fields. Partly in response to this marginalization, ecologists formed the German Society for Ecology in 1970. This international professional organization based in Gießen aimed to protect the professional integrity of the field against "pretenders," strengthen the study of ecology in higher education, and increase ecologists' leverage in political discussions. Precisely the lack of attention to ecology in the government's action program, and ecologists' limited participation in its more comprehensive environmental program announced the following year, heightened demand for experts in the ecological sciences, especially human ecology.[51]

Another weakness of the Action Program was its failure to integrate conservation into environmental protection administratively, despite Genscher's efforts to add *Naturschutz* to the BMI's responsibilities.[52] He was blocked from doing so by Federal Minister of Agriculture Josef Ertl, who refused to renounce control over it. Revealing the BML's outdated understanding of conservation and its refusal to acknowledge industrialized agriculture's role in generating pollution and causing species decline, BML officials claimed they ought to continue having authority over conservation because 86 percent of the country's territory was used either for forestry or farming, uses that shaped the "appearance of the cultural landscape."[53] The competency struggle between the BML and BMI stymied efforts to incorporate *Naturschutz* more fully into *Umweltschutz,* a move that would have strengthened both. The continued separation of these responsibilities also reflects their origins as two distinct traditions: the public health tradition with its pragmatism, professionalism, and emphasis on protecting property, body, and life, and the nature and homeland preservation tradition with its idealism, volunteerism, and educational priorities.[54]

The Action Program generated considerable media attention, not all of it favorable. The magazine that took the lead in publicizing concern about the environment, the respected weekly magazine *Spiegel,* published an exposé in October 1970 on the "poisoned environment," criticizing Bonn for providing only "half-hearted" measures to alleviate the problem. While newspaper reports hinted that billions of marks would be set aside to fight pollution, the cover story declared, no such figure was found in Genscher's program. Its greatest expense—DM 45 million to be spent until 1974—involved the development of new technologies, such as lead free gasoline, biodegradable packaging materials, and better techniques to purify air and water.[55]

The bleak cover story prompted responses from readers that ranged from alarm to cautious optimism. A letter writer from Baden-Württemberg warned against placing too much faith in science and technology, arguing that both had a "boomerang effect on humanity." A doctor from Fürth expressed the opposite sentiment. Science and technology had gotten people into an environmental morass, he reasoned, and it would help get them out of it. A West Berlin resident viewed the alarming ecological changes as nothing more than evidence of the laws of nature operating for the benefit of the species. Humanity, he wrote, had long needed a rod of iron.[56] The dozen letters that were printed do not offer solid evidence that the nation had become environmentally conscious, but they illustrate a range of opinions about environmental problems and the shared expectation that the government should do more to combat them.

More indicative of public consciousness about the environment are the fourteen binders of correspondence from citizens sent in increasing numbers between 1970 and 1972 to the BMI. The majority of letters from 1970 contain requests for information about the new program for educational purposes. But many also express impatience with the pace of reform. After studying the October cover story in *Spiegel,* one angry reader blamed Genscher for further environmental decline because of his "mini-environmental protection program." A more heartening letter from a Lutheran pastorate near Stuttgart, signed by over seventy church-goers, thanked the BMI for its efforts to protect the environment but urged officials to resolve competency struggles quickly. Other correspondence indicated that citizens were responding to the government's challenge to "risk more democracy," such as the letter from a Karlsruhe resident noting the formation of a local initiative, "Action Clean Environment," which was collecting signatures as part of a public awareness campaign. A homemaker from Giessen reported that she had gathered over 350 signatures in support of her letter, which regretted that "European Conservation Year is over without our environment being better protected." The time for talking was over, she wrote, the time for action had begun. Among several recommendations, the former teacher urged the government to pass a federal law for environmental protection and to establish a federal research institute to objectively assess pollution, "even if [findings] offend certain interest groups."[57]

This evidence indicates that in 1970, media coverage of the Action Program, ECY, and events in the US heightened public awareness of an imperiled environment while simultaneously raising people's expectations for the government to develop immediate solutions. Over the next two years, a vocal minority of citizens would become deeply concerned about an "environmental crisis" and frustrated by what they perceived to be the government's underestimation of the problem. In contrast to BMI officials' hope that its environmental policy would demonstrate the effectiveness of state planning and consensus building, these citizens came to associate environmental protection with government incompetence. Participating in efforts to save the environment allowed them to express disappointment with "the system."[58] But in 1970, citizens' concern had not yet given way to frustration.

As 1970 came to a close, organizers of European Conservation Year concluded that the biggest success had been the media's handling of environmental issues. With satisfaction Engelhardt announced that frequently, "environmental protection pushed politics, cars, and sex from the headlines." According to a news clipping service, nearly 11,000 accounts about the environment appeared in print media between January and November, twelve times the publicity generated the previous year. Another study conducted several years after ECY, however, tentatively concluded that coverage in some major daily newspapers in 1970 differed little from the previous year.[59] Neither of these assessments evaluates radio and television, but by the end of ECY, it was apparent that TV was the medium to exploit to reach the most people. Indeed, more than 90 percent of all West German households owned a television in 1970 and people spent approximately 20 percent of their free time watching it. That year there were seventeen televised programs devoted to environmental issues, a number that increased over the decade, reaching one-hundred forty by the mid 1980s.[60]

Despite extensive media coverage, at the end of the ECY the public remained confused about the definition of *"Umweltschutz."* According to a survey conducted by the Institute for Applied Social Sciences in Bad Godesberg in the autumn of 1970, 59 percent of the people polled had not heard of the concept. Of the 41 percent who had, 17 percent thought that it involved "protection against theft and crime." Still others associated *Umweltschutz* with civil defense or external security. One could hardly speak of an environmental consciousness, Wolfgang Erz commented, only "a trickling down of awareness" (*Umweltberiese-lung*). A year later, however, over 90 percent of West Germans polled associated *Umweltschutz* with environmental clean up or conservation.[61]

Part of public uncertainty in 1970 stemmed from conflicting interpretations of the relationship between *Umweltschutz* and *Naturschutz*. According to Grzimek, "'*Umweltschutz*' is nothing other than '*Naturschutz* for mankind.'" Although those involved with ECY referred facetiously to conservation year as "conversation year," all of the talk and publicity about *"Umweltschutz,"* Grzimek argued, had provided "effective advertising" for *Naturschutz*.[62] Engelhardt agreed, remarking that viewing the two terms as distinct was merely "juggling with concepts." The person who protected "air, water, soil, the plant and animal world, the foundations of human life that make up man's natural environment," and did so for humanity's sake, "pursues *Naturschutz*, and thus also *Umweltschutz*."[63] Grzimek's aide, Wolfgang Erz, disagreed. He understood that no matter how broadly conservationists had come to define *Naturschutz* by 1970, it still did not involve all that was associated with *Umweltschutz*. "Grandpa's *Naturschutz* is dead," he declared, replaced by a "form of 'environmental welfare'" concerned with nothing less than protecting people from harm and ensuring their well being.[64]

At the end of 1970, *Naturschutz* was elevated to a level of importance that it had never known previously, yet in the process, it became an ill-defined component of *Umweltschutz*. Chancellor Brandt contended that *Naturschutz* was "an important part of our complex of environmental problems," but only a part. The task ahead, he stated, involved preventing the degradation of nature while "actively shaping our environment."[65] Some critics were uneasy about the displacement of "nature" by the "environment," wondering what the view of nature was that guided those entrusted with designing the environment (*Umweltgestaltung*). According to one observer, "environment" and "environmental design" had a certain "rhetorical flair," yet compared with words like "nature, life, growth," sounded "somewhat sallow." As a sociological concept, *"Umwelt"* referred to everything that surrounded people, including household furniture and workplace facilities. Yet it was apparent, she concluded, that people recognized something needed to happen "to preserve the vital nature in our environment."[66] This commentary implies that by 1970 some West Germans had come to view "nature" not so much as an idealized landscape external to their daily lives, but as an integral part of their surroundings, something finite, but essential to healthy living. What that something—nature—was and how it ought to be protected or shaped, restored or removed from "the environment," remained ill defined and thus contested. But the new slogan *Umweltschutz* placed the individual at the center of concern, making it possible for people of diverse backgrounds to personalize the challenge to protect the world (*Welt*) around (*um*) them. The boundaries of *Umwelt* were fluid, constantly shifting between home and work, from local to global, but the individual remained the fixed point of reference.

As "the environment" came to be perceived as a tangible space—discernable because its harmful condition threatened individuals—some political leaders argued that the state had an obligation to protect the right of citizens to live in a healthy environment. But it was a legal challenge without clear precedent, as Bavarian *Landtag* President Rudolf Hanauer (CSU) made clear in an ECY address to parliamentarians. Now that a "healed environment" (*heile Umwelt*) appeared to be the exception rather than the rule, he observed, the need to protect an individual's "inherent right" to a safe and sound one had "entered legal consciousness," requiring foundations in the law. Such a right, he explained, was related to the constitutionally guaranteed rights of the individual, namely the inviolability of individual dignity, the freedom of self-development, and the protection against bodily harm. Yet because the environment existed outside of the person, it could be protected on the same grounds that private property was. Unlike private property, however, the environment was something that everyone had and could not do without. Thus, although the right to a healthy environment was related to individual and property rights, and like both, it involved certain social constraints, it remained distinct. And efforts to define what constituted a "healthy environment" would always be incomplete.[67]

Legislating *Umweltschutz*

Despite the near impossibility of guaranteeing an individual's right to a healthy environment, the federal government took on the challenge of legislating environmental clean up with its Environmental Program, introduced in September 1971. West Germany's program did not have the same "statutory significance" as the US's National Environmental Policy Act of 1969, but it had comparable influence in initiating a period of unprecedented legislative activity. Between 1970 and 1976, over fifty laws and ordinances were implemented to address problems from solid waste removal to controlling pesticides.[68] The BMI supervised the program's development with help from several ministries that oversaw a dozen project groups (e.g., for clean air maintenance and environmentally friendly technologies), which were divided further into forty-eight smaller committees involving over 500 experts from industry and the sciences. The government also held regular meetings with journalists to educate the public and generate positive publicity that was essential for broad, popular support.[69]

Conservationists—both professionals and leaders of private groups—appreciated the program's attention to managing environmental media individually, but again regretted that it lacked a vision for combating these interrelated problems collectively. Some scholars view this complaint as landscape planners' final bid for total planning competency, yet that seems dismissive of their legitimate critique of an "ecological deficit."[70] The program referred to the "ecological capacity" of nature's household and maintained that it could be "repaired" (*wiederhergestellt*) and used with more research and data on its stress limits (*Belastungsgrenzen*), but there was little indication that ecology was used to guide economic development (to be sure something that few industrialized nations addressed until the 1990s). Plans for highway construction into the mid 1980s, for example, projected using 180,000 hectares of land, but outlined no plans for restoring ecological health to the areas affected by the massive project. In general, the BMI did not view ecology as the scientific basis for its program, but as a field of research warranting financial support.[71] An exasperated Grzimek complained in 1973 that Genscher had fifteen officers for technical environmental protection, while Ertl had one for conservation.[72]

Genscher defended his emphasis, and insisted that "whoever develops the most modern environmental technologies will win the markets of the future." He was right. By the 1990s, Germany and Japan led the world in exporting environmental technology.[73] The effectiveness of technology in ameliorating problems justified the government's emphasis and the public's apparent confidence. A new Research and Technology Ministry, erected in 1972, encouraged further innovation. The government constructed incinerators and central waste dumps to manage garbage and prioritized cleaning up the Rhine and Lake Constance. Between 1972 and 1976, DM 5.09 billion was spent on water treatment facilities alone, and led to improvements in water quality. Air, too, was cleaner because of a reduction in particulate matter, heavy metals, lead, cadmium, sulfur dioxide, and carbon monoxide.[74]

In this period of technological environmental reform, conservation remained peripheral. Competency struggles among federal ministries and state governments frustrated efforts to strengthen federal authority over conservation. Conservationists lobbied hard for the change, hoping it would enable the federal government to protect ecosystems with the same force it already had in regulating areas potentially harmful to the environment, namely commerce, industry, transportation, real estate transactions, and nuclear power.[75] A constitutional amendment in 1972 gave Bonn more control over air and noise pollution and waste disposal, but the states retained primary jurisdiction for conservation and water management. Conservationists had to settle for federal guideline legislation that went into effect in 1976. The law required land-use plans in developing and renaturing rural and urban areas and stressed the need to protect or restore "viable ecological conditions" to the land. But it did not acknowledge exploitative practices associated with forestry and agriculture. Instead, it made generous concessions to them, thanks to their powerful lobbies. Nor did the law grant organizations the coveted right to file suit when officials "bent" conservation laws, because doing so, it was argued, would stretch the resources of administrative offices. Furthermore, it would be difficult to decide which groups should have this right.[76]

Noticeable successes in the government's environmental program failed to calm the fears of a vocal minority of citizens who, by 1972, were alarmed by an apparent environmental crisis of global proportions. Shaping the mindset of this segment of the population were gloomy predictions about "limits to growth" published by the Club of Rome in March 1972.[77] The Club of Rome's report, completed by MIT scientists, was the most influential study of the era to rely on futurology, a science that developed in the West in the 1960s and early 1970s and relied on cybernetics, a field that shared with ecology a focus on interconnections and energy cycles. Using computer models to process available data, the MIT team made long range predictions about the cumulative effects of interrelated problems of acute concern, from global population to the use of non-renewable natural resources. In contrast to the earlier predictions of futurologists that tended to be optimistic, the Club of Rome report described a less hopeful scenario. In striving to provide more people with a better standard of living, the computer models predicted, societies in the very near future would confront "changes in the world system [that] might lead society to collision with . . . the limits to growth in a finite world." According to the report's famous conclusions, "If the present . . . trends . . . continue unchanged, the limits to growth on this planet will be reached sometime within the next one hundred years."[78]

These alarming predictions, and those made by a host of other authors around the same time, revitalized longstanding cultural pessimism by giving it a scientific framework with the potential to captivate a broad audience. Unlike conservationists in the 1950s who had issued warnings based mainly on moral conviction and intuition, the "prophets of doom" of the late 1960s and 1970s conveyed their concerns with references to scientific data that, when processed using computer models, predicted the cumulative effects of interrelated problems. And according to these calculations, reform was not optional, but essential.[79] But Brandt and other political leaders and officials, and pragmatic conservationists like Engelhardt, cautioned that doomsday predictions only contributed to hysteria and resignation.[80]

Publicity about limits to growth coincided with the UN Stockholm Conference on the Human Environment, which brought together 113 countries and 400 intergovernmental and non-governmental organizations, and challenged nations around the world to make sustainability the goal in economic development. A term that gained currency only in the 1990s, sustainability assumes that economic development can be supported over the long term only by protecting ecological processes of which humans are an integral part. In preparation for Stockholm, the BMI, with assistance from several federal ministries, agencies, and state governments, produced a 159-page assessment of the country's environmental problems and of steps planned or underway to address them.[81] The section prepared by the BAVNL explained that conservation was less concerned with preserving a static order than with protecting the ecological health of landscapes to ensure biological diversity and efficient use of land and natural resources. To illustrate the possibilities for restoring a "more natural" order to an engineered landscape, West Germany spotlighted its successful re-cultivation of the Rhenish lignite coal field near Cologne.[82] But the planning, design, and technology used in this grand ecological reconstruction project were limited in their ability to respond to a problem with broader dimensions and a human face.

The international debate about "limits to growth" and Stockholm's critique of the "economic-growth-equals-progress" mindset coincided with public discussions in West Germany about "quality of life" issues. Since the days of Ernst Rudorff, conservationists had emphasized the centrality of moderation and non-material values in their definition of well-being, but without arousing widespread notice. During Brandt's successful reelection campaign in 1972, however, SPD Minister for Economic Cooperation, Erhard Eppler, popularized the concept "quality of life" in an attempt to link environmental protection to his party's other domestic reforms, which included improvements in education and social welfare. In a well publicized address before the Industrial Metal Trade Unions in April, Eppler called for "more humane standards" in defining economic productivity. Policies, technologies, and consumer goods, he maintained, needed to be evaluated not just in terms of their economic benefits, but also in terms of their ecological impact. In this statement and other writings, Eppler claimed that the SPD, with its ecological sensitivity that served the common good, was stronger in defending the environment than the opposition (which was allegedly preoccupied with economic growth and closely aligned with special interests). But neither Eppler nor his party intended to restrict economic growth, which might reduce material goods. When the recession hit during the 1973 oil crisis, the government had little choice but to promote economic stability and growth. Doing so meant that the SPD failed to emerge as the leader in environmental reform and did little to enhance the state's image as the provider of environmental protection. Yet public opinion polls indicated that people supported the government's partially green compromise, which protected the standard of living to which they had grown accustomed.[83]

The Environment as a Sphere for Citizen Activism

After making "the environment" a legitimate sphere for political action between 1970 and 1971, officials were keenly aware that the success of their program depended upon broad public support. Between 1972 and 1974, the BMI actively cultivated, and partially tried to control, citizen involvement in reform.[84] Hoping to increase its political leverage, the German Conservation Ring sought federal support from and influence with the FDP-led BMI. Officials recommended dialogue with the DNR because of its large membership, its involvement in environmental protection, and its intention to publicize candidates' record on environmental reform. But officials cautioned that the executive committee was "oriented toward the CSU/CDU [Weinzierl, Engelhardt, and Sonnemann]."[85]

A more comfortable alliance for the BMI appeared to be the coalition of citizens' initiatives that formed in 1972, the Federal Alliance of Citizens' Initiatives for Environmental Protection (*Bundesverband Bürgerinitiativen Umweltschutz,* or BBU). BMI officials were pleased by the "coup d'état-like revolutionary act" that landed FDP members in the alliance's leadership positions.[86] Although the FDP, BMI, and Protestant Church contributed to the start up of the BBU, they could not claim sole credit for its existence, nor could any of them control its eventual development into a vocal critic of state policy. The BBU's establishment coincided with the UN Stockholm Conference and debates about "limits to growth," which convinced some citizens that cleaning up the environment was merely fighting the symptoms of a problem that could be remedied only with deep societal changes.

CIs were the harvest of left-wing dissent during the 1960s and contributed to a new political culture in West Germany and elsewhere in Western Europe, one favorably disposed to participatory, not just representative, democracy.[87] Citizens' initiatives emerged in the mid 1960s, particularly in the Ruhr region, with their numbers increasing under the Grand Coalition. They tended to be spontaneous, informal alliances formed locally by an average of thirty people to target specific problems, often planning decisions that called for expanding industry, housing, and transportation. By the mid 1970s, there existed between 3,000 and 4,000 CIs, involving anywhere from 60,000 to 120,000 citizens, with a majority of these initiatives focusing on environmental concerns, especially energy and transportation issues and care of the countryside. At the end of the decade, roughly 115,000 citizens were organized in environmental initiatives.[88]

Initially, conservation organizations viewed CIs as allies in a shared cause.[89] As initiatives began to coordinate their efforts on the regional and national levels in 1972, the DNR, in particular, regarded them as potential rivals. At the time, the DNR was at a critical juncture. Under Grzimek's controversial leadership in the 1960s the organization had adopted a more offensive strategy that politicized conservation and occasionally broke ranks with officials.[90] When Engelhardt took over as president in 1968 the DNR's influence continued to rise, and the organization took center stage during ECY. But it was difficult to sustain that level of activity. In addition, not all member groups or executive committee members supported Engelhardt's attempt to go beyond conservation and take on environmental issues.[91] The alliance also lacked funds. When raising membership dues proved inadequate (because some groups did not pay the amount assessed them based on the size), the DNR turned to the federal government, receiving a subsidy of DM 100,000 from the BML in 1972, support that in subsequent years restricted its freedom of action.[92]

In April 1972, Engelhardt wrote fellow executive committee member Georg Fahrbach expressing concern that the CIs appeared to be veering off on a track "that we cannot approve of." He was referring to rumblings of a united front of initiatives with more aggressive tactics and "red" leanings, which he feared would give environmental protection a bad name and compete with the DNR for government support and dues paying members. In Fahrbach he found a sympathetic listener because of competition in Baden-Württemberg between Fahrbach's coalition of hiking groups and a more confrontational alliance recently formed by the ornithologist Gerhard Thielcke. To probe the intentions of the initiatives, Fahrbach met with the two men who had emerged as leaders among the CIs, Kurt Oeser and Horst Zilleßen, both associated with the Protestant Church (Oeser was a pastor) and active in local and regional initiatives.[93] After their two hour conversation in mid June, Fahrbach (an FDP member who had worked with the Protestant Church to organize conservation events in the 1960s) was satisfied by their promise to remain non-partisan, despite their FDP leanings, and convinced of their desire to avoid competition with the DNR should initiatives form a federal union.[94]

The DNR must have been disappointed when, later that month, fifteen citizens' initiatives, many of them based in the Rhine-Ruhr region, formed the BBU to work for environmental issues nationwide.[95] Within eight months of the BBU's founding, member CIs increased from fifteen to fifty-eight. By 1975, it had a membership of 100 regional and local initiatives. This number is much lower than the 1,000 the BBU claimed (because it ignored the entangled alliances among the CIs and thus counted member initiatives more than once). Despite BBU's real and imagined growth, internal disputes in the first year distracted the alliance from developing a coherent strategy and action plan.[96] Indicative of the conservative, paternalistic mindset that prevailed among old-guard conservationists, DNR Vice President Sonnemann reacted to BBU's founding by warning BMI officials that the sudden increase in the number of citizens anxious about the environment could generate demands for reforms that "contradict the views of lawmakers and the government." It was essential, he contended, for the BMI to "coordinate" (i.e., control) the activities and opinions of environmental groups and develop an official position on what was realistic in terms of reform.[97]

Despite the BBU's claim to be non-partisan, in its early years the leadership leaned toward the FDP, making it a more natural political ally for the BMI than the Conservation Ring with its CDU/CSU-oriented executive committee. The founding meeting of the BBU was made possible in part through financial support from the Protestant Church and the FDP-linked Friedrich Naumann Foundation.[98] The BBU's charismatic, yet abrasive first chairman from 1973 until 1977, the industrial chemist and environmental activist Hans-Helmuth Wüstenhagen (b. 1923), belonged to the FDP, as did two of the twelve executive committee members.[99]

The BBU and the BMI had a complex, symbiotic relationship, though government support should not be overemphasized. BMI officials wanted to have a lobby outside of the bureaucracy and parliament that could serve as a counterweight to powerful economic interests which might oppose controversial environmental policies. The BMI hoped that by representing citizens' initiatives across the country, the BBU would become a "competent partner in discussions."[100] Like traditional conservation groups, the BBU depended on the state as a source of funding for public events and as the primary institution to appeal to with grievances and reform proposals. In return, the BMI relied on the BBU to decipher public attitudes about environmental protection, for example by surveying CIs for their views on the "ecological deficit" in the government's environmental program. The BBU also functioned as an environmental lobby whose experts presented recommendations to parliamentary committees.[101]

In its rhetoric, however, the BBU projected the image of an anti-establishment, grassroots organization. In a formal statement in November 1972 to the recently reelected Brandt government and the *Bundestag,* the BBU demanded that "[e]cology and environmental politics must be given a central position" and industrial growth should be subordinate to a constitutionally guaranteed right to a healthy environment. Advocating an alternative lifestyle less preoccupied with material consumption, the BBU called for the expansion of public transportation, a reduction in private automobile use in cities, stronger food safety laws, support for organic farming, and careful study of energy issues, especially nuclear power. The alliance wanted more citizen involvement in local planning decisions and echoed conservation groups in insisting that environmental organizations should have the right to file lawsuits.[102]

Although increasingly critical of "the establishment," the BBU, and CIs in general, would not have been taken seriously by policymakers had it not been for their leaders and members with technical expertise. (The same held true for conservation groups.) This professionalization within the CIs helped institutionalize their alternative agenda, as the founding of the BBU's Environmental Science Institute in 1975 indicates. In two years, it had evolved into the Freiburg-based Eco Institute with fulltime employees who prepared studies and provided the public with scientific information on environmental problems and advice for alternative living according to ecological principles (e.g., decentralized economies, grassroots participatory democracy, and non-violence). The institute's politically diverse board of trustees included CDU *Bundestag* deputy, Herbert Gruhl, Grzimek, and Eppler. In addition, some BBU leaders went on to have careers in politics, Green Party member Petra Kelly among the most well known.[103]

Simultaneously with this institutionalization and professionalization, the BBU grew more radical in the face of the government's controversial energy policy. When the oil crisis hit in the fall of 1973, West Germans became more conscious of debates about limits to growth as the government instituted car-free Sundays and speed limits to conserve fuel.[104] In September 1973, just prior to the oil crisis, the Brandt government announced that it would reduce oil imports by expanding the use of nuclear power. By 1985, nuclear power plants were to supply 15 percent of the country's energy needs, up from one percent in 1973. Meeting this goal required the construction of an estimated fifty nuclear facilities. A minority of West Germans had protested the use and testing of nuclear weapons since the 1950s, but not until the 1970s, when the government proposed a significant increase in commercial use of nuclear power, was there any large scale, organized opposition to it.[105]

One of West Germany's first nuclear showdowns occurred between 1973 and 1976 at Wyhl, a small rural community in Baden-Württemberg. But Wyhl was not the origin of the anti-nuclear movement that locals and sympathetic journalists remembered it to be. Nor was the nine month occupation of the construction site in 1975 decisive in blocking the nuclear facility. More critical was the court ordered delay in construction (issued in response to lawsuits filed by individuals and communities) and the decision by a Freiburg administrative court to revoke *Badenwerk*'s construction license in March 1977 because of inadequate safety features. (Only in 1994 were plans for the project dropped.)

Although popular memory exaggerated the significance of the sustained protest at Wyhl, the event illustrated that the nuclear cause in particular, and environmental protection more generally, was capable of uniting diverse groups in broad unlikely alliances. In the case of Wyhl, local farmers and vintners found support from leftist university groups based in Freiburg, over a dozen CIs in the region, area CDU representatives, and Protestant and Catholic church leaders. Protestors relied on petitions and rallies as in the Wutach protest of the 1950s, but they went further, boycotting businesses of facility supporters, filing lawsuits, and most radical of all, occupying the construction site illegally in 1975. Paranoid that left-wing extremists were responsible, Minister-President Hans Filbinger (CDU) ordered 650 police armed with water hoses, truncheons, and dogs to force the non-violent occupants from the site, an overreaction that generated sympathy for protestors and immediate reoccupation of the site for the next several months. In this politicized space, locals and outside activists created an alternative culture in which protest became a part of the daily routine. For the state and the utility company, the most unsettling aspect of the resistance was that respected local leaders remained central to the opposition, normalizing protest at a time when it was associated with radicals.[106]

After Wyhl, citizens' initiatives joined the BBU in increasing numbers, making the alliance the leading voice in the anti-nuclear movement and an influential force outside of traditional politics. Armed with ecologized rhetoric, the alliance led the offensive against the status quo, becoming the main organization of the diffuse ecology movement that sought to advance its minority vision for an alternative society. By adopting sensational, non-violent tactics to protest nuclear power, the BBU helped to make what had been perceived as a predominantly middle class movement more appealing to West Germany's "New Left," which included radical "K-groups" that tended to follow Maoist ideology, and "spontis" who advocated alternative living and "spontaneous" political activity (anarchy).

But increased involvement between 1975 and 1977 of the New Left espousing radical tactics that invited violent responses from authorities divided the BBU. During anti-nuclear protests at Brokdorf on the Elbe River in 1976 and Grohnde in Lower Saxony in 1977, locals retreated into the background, overshadowed by outsiders who led the occupation of construction sites, only to be repulsed by police. The radical tactics of "spontis" and K-groups discredited anti-nuclear protests, linking them all too closely to left-wing terrorism, which peaked in West Germany in 1977. Yet the BBU remained the leading voice of the ecology and anti-nuclear movement until 1980 when the Green Party largely took over this role.[107]

When the BBU pushed the nuclear issue to the forefront, conservation organizations were forced to take a stance on it. In 1974, the DNR committee on technical environmental protection concluded that "massive economic interests" were at odds with security and public health concerns, but then only urged authorities to make energy generation more efficient and limit the number of nuclear reactors, not to halt their construction.[108] This response illustrates why some thought the DNR was too conciliatory toward officials to develop an activist strategy that could garner results in the current political climate.

Partly for this reason, some of the members of traditional conservation groups helped found a new national organization with a more confrontational message and style, the League for Environmental and Nature Protection in Germany (*Bund für Umwelt- und Naturschutz in Deutschland,* or BUND). Established in 1975 by Weinzierl, Grzimek, Konrad Lorenz, Gerhard Thielcke, and Bodo Manstein (elected first chairman), among others, BUND overcame internal difficulties early on to become one of the most influential environmental organizations in the country, a distinction it still holds. According to one recent study, BUND's emergence marked the waning influence of the old conservation elite that was homogeneous in age, politics, and socioeconomic background, and its replacement by a new, loosely united elite sharing a conviction about the seriousness of environmental problems, something that linked them with many CIs.[109]

Several of the founding members of BUND had joined forces around 1970 out of frustration with the technocratic, dispassionate solutions promised by experts and bureaucrats, and with the non-confrontational strategies of established conservation groups. These leaders had connections, financial means, and diverse professional experience (several earned a living in conservation related jobs as scientists, journalists, or politicians). Although established by an elite from above, BUND drew support from below by incorporating existing organizations as state and local chapters, allowing them to keep their structure and political tactics. BUND functioned as an umbrella organization with group members, but also operated as a typical association in permitting individual memberships, a move that encouraged direct participation and gave BUND an advantage over the DNR and the BBU, neither of which allowed personal memberships. By the mid 1980s, BUND was a network of state, local, and youth chapters with 145,000 members, 32,000 of whom held individual memberships. The largest, most influential chapter with 40 percent of all BUND members, the Bavarian League for Nature Protection, remained rather traditional in its approach, while Baden-Württemberg's Alliance for Nature and Environmental Protection established by Thielcke in 1973 operated more like a citizen initiative. BUND exhibited flexibility in preserving ties to other major environmental groups. Some chapters of BUND, for example, also held membership in the BBU. In addition, the national organization of BUND belonged to the DNR until the early 1980s. DNR President Wolfgang Engelhardt was a member of BUND's advisory board, and when he retired from the DNR leadership in 2000, Weinzierl succeeded him.

Under Thielcke's leadership (1976–1983), BUND launched a successful public relations campaign, marketing itself to the youth as an activist, ecologically conscious, nature loving, anti-nuclear, environmental organization. To guard against projecting too radical of an image when left-wing terrorism was at its peak and environmental activism often was associated with subversive activity, BUND approved a new constitution that pledged the organization's support for the Basic Law. While maintaining an image of a passionate and sometimes rebellious force (which political leaders had grown accustomed to), BUND also made itself a legitimate participant in political dialogue through its experienced leaders.

BUND revitalized critiques of progress by relying on a politicized and popularized view of ecology that emphasized stability, harmony, and balance in nature. By adopting a non-exploitative lifestyle that conformed to nature's biological limits, so the argument went, the individual, society, and nature would be restored to a healthier, more harmonious state. But this popularized understanding of ecology contrasted sharply with the view that scientists had adopted, which emphasized constant flux in ecosystems rather than harmony and balance.[110] Nonetheless, conservation as promoted by BUND was intentionally adapted to West Germany's urban society. While continuing to protect alpine lakes, fragile sand dunes, and endangered species, BUND cultivated an appreciation for the ecological processes at work in the country's diverse engineered landscapes, from canalized rivers to abandoned quarries. Its literature still assumed that unhealthy landscapes were indicators of an unhealthy society, but abandoned the view that had prevailed into the 1960s that restoring health to landscapes would automatically restore health to society. Similar to the ecology movement, BUND taught that society, especially its economic order, needed reforming first.[111]

By 1970, worsening pollution, urban sprawl, well-publicized accidents at home and abroad, and international pressures contributed to the invention of the "the environment" as a tangible space requiring urgent attention. Technocrats, bureaucrats, conservation and environmental groups, and citizens' initiatives all vied for a part in shaping it according to their values and ideals for society—but often only indirectly according to their views of nature and the relationship that humans should have with it. The SPD-FDP coalition government set environmental reforms in motion, some of them already underway as public health and regional planning measures. But in doing so, the government ignited a small revolution that, once begun, it could not control. The initial successes of *Umweltschutz* heightened public expectations for the state to do even more. Yet the pace of reform slowed by 1973 because of the challenge of implementing environmental protection in the midst of a global energy crisis.[112] When the Brandt government responded to oil shortages by increasing West Germany's nuclear program, *Umweltschutz* came to be viewed as oppositional to the status quo.

For some, like those involved with the BBU and the diffuse ecology movement, environmental protection became a rallying cry for changing the very nature of society. In the late 1970s and early 1980s, an estimated 80,000 activists established alternative grocery stores, cafes, theaters, and newspapers to support significant lifestyle changes. Inspired not by duty, as conservationists were in former times, but by the principle of "engagement," activists viewed their participation in the ecology movement as an opportunity both for self-development and for social reform. By walking instead of driving, or by toting a jute bag handmade in the Third World instead of a plastic one, participants transformed personal choices into political acts that protected the environment and helped the oppressed.[113]

What emerged from the challenge of protecting the environment in a democracy, however, was a commingling of diverse understandings of *Umweltschutz* and the acceleration of what historian Michael Bess has described as the "partial greening" of the mainstream of society. This greening process was evident in citizens' heightened expectation for the state to protect their right to live in healthy surroundings and in the expansion of the environmental bureaucracy at all levels of government committed partly to that end. The invention of the environment as an object of reform in West Germany and elsewhere meant more power in the hands of government, not less. Implementing *Umweltschutz* involved the passage of state and federal laws, the enforcement of new regulations for industry and trade, and the approval of a constitutional amendment in 1972 which strengthened federal authority over controlling pollution and managing solid waste. It led to the establishment of research institutes and state environment ministries, and the development of environmental education programs—all supported with tax money. Few people remained untouched by these legal and administrative reforms aimed at creating a healthier, "greener" society.

Broad public acceptance of the need for environmental protection contributed to the formation of new organizations such as the BBU and BUND, as well as the revitalization of existing ones, most notably Bavaria's League for Nature Protection, the DNR, and the German League for Bird Protection. The long term success of BUND, in particular, illustrates the successful commingling of diverse understandings of environmental protection. During the 1970s, when the BBU veered sharply to the left on its anti-nuclear crusade and the DNR remained handicapped by internal disagreements and its conciliatory stance toward officials, BUND steered a moderate course through the political landscape. It integrated people representing diverse political views and degrees of involvement, and blended the hierarchical structure and lobbying activities of traditional organizations with the confrontational stance of citizens' initiatives.[114]

The fortunes of the BBU illustrate the compromises that more radical groups, too, made in promoting their vision for a society that was "deep green" (i.e., exhibiting a commitment to decentralized economies, ecologically sustainable uses of natural resources, environmentally friendly technologies, grassroots participatory democracy, peace, and social justice). In the latter 1970s, the BBU emerged as the leading voice in the anti-nuclear movement and presented itself as a radical, anti-establishment organization dedicated to sweeping societal reforms. Yet even the radicalized BBU appealed to the state to implement its reform proposals. The alliance also understood that having political leverage required experienced leadership, professional expertise, and financial and institutional support. Partly because of its institutionalization, the BBU still exists. Already at the end of the 1970s, however, its influence was eclipsed by the Green Party. The presence of the Greens in parliament helped force the major political parties to make good their promise to protect the environment, if only in a "light green" way.

The partial greening of government, politics, and society succeeded because of the shared belief among the diverse supporters of *Umweltschutz* that a healthy environment was fundamental to an improved standard of living. But neither federal and state governments nor a majority of citizens was willing to give ecological considerations the same weight as economic ones to create a "deep green" society because doing so, it was feared, would mean more restrictions on individual and economic freedoms. Nor did governments or a majority of the population abandon their faith in economic growth because of the belief that doing so would compromise the material comforts society had come to expect and enjoy.

Beginning in the 1970s, the Federal Republic was little different from other industrial democracies in having a public that was ecologically conscious and generally supportive of environmental reforms, yet equally in favor of economic growth, mass consumption, and technological modernization. The coexistence of these dual, often competing priorities are characteristic of what Michael Bess has called the "light-green" society. As Bess explains:

> [F]aced with a tough choice between technological modernity and a green vision of the future, [people in industrial democracies] . . . hedged, and in effect chose both. Through a long, incremental process of improvisation and give-and-take, they pieced together a new kind of social order—an increasingly pervasive overlay of ecological ideas and environmental constraints upon the growth-driven, consumer-oriented system inherited from mid-century.[115]

One of the material benefits associated with living in a partially green society included access to landscapes displaying varying degrees of naturalness. The invention of the environment contributed to the rediscovery of nature as something finite, yet vital to life. Accordingly, *Naturschutz* experienced a renaissance.[116] Beginning in the 1970s, conservation in theory and in practice tended to be defined narrowly, as stringent preservation, with preference assigned to species that had adapted to, and biotopes that had evolved along with, historical uses of the land. After ecologists criticized this approach for its cultural prejudices, experts devised a strategy in the 1980s which aimed to protect the "ecological processes" at work in a particular area. The goal here is to preserve the dynamic at work in nature, which experts describe as a "mosaic-like ensemble of diverse stages of succession." But even this attempt to make preservation reflect nature's "natural" operation is artificial because it is confined to a specific area and requires human intervention to protect the continuation of a particular dynamic.[117] Thus, although *Naturschutz* experienced a revival, not even experts agreed on what to protect, how, or why.

The adoption of the concept *Umweltschutz* in West Germany and elsewhere conveyed the understanding that humans were the primary architects of the world they inhabited and were responsible for restoring it to a more healthy order. While the boundaries of the environment constantly shifted, the individual remained the fixed point of reference. As the microbiologist René Dubos commented, however, "[t]he word environment does not convey the quality of the relationships that humankind can ideally establish with the Earth. Its widespread use points . . . to the present poverty of these relationships." In order for the environment to become a place that satisfied people's spiritual and emotional needs—a place that provided more "than conditions suitable for our health, resources to run the economic machine, and whatever is meant by good ecological conditions," the environment needed to have "the fusion of the natural and the human order."[118]

For this very reason, Hubert Weinzierl urged a "return to the protection of nature" in 1972. Within the context of *Umweltschutz*, he argued, *Naturschutz* acquired new significance as a cultural duty guided by idealism. Protecting nature was not just a scientific or economic undertaking. It also involved protecting things of beauty that could inspire awe in people living now and in the future. A "healed environment," he wrote, required pollution control, species diversity, and ecologically healthy landscapes, but also places of natural beauty.[119] Unlike an older generation of conservationists that was often ignored for this sort of moralizing idealism, Weinzierl attracted support with his appeal because of a perceived loss of nature and the natural world. The following chapter—a case study on establishing West Germany's first national park in the Bavarian Forest—examines conservation when it had reached "a turning point," when a new conservation elite had begun to believe that they had no alternative but to constantly manage "the environment" to keep parts of it "more natural" and less engineered. Yet there was fierce debate over the shape that nature ought to take in the new park, reflecting the priorities of diverse social groups. While some viewed the national park as a favorable solution to an economic and regional planning challenge, others like Weinzierl understood it as a cultural endeavor above all, one that revealed how finite nature seemed to have become.

Notes

1. Hubert Weinzierl, *Die große Wende im Naturschutz* (Munich: BLV Verlagsgesellschaft, 1970), 7, 9; Wolfgang Erz, "Opas Naturschutz ist tot," *Das Parlament* 20, no. 34 (22 August 1970).

2. On the federal government's influence on initiating environmental protection see Küppers, Lundgreen, and Weingart, *Umweltforschung;* Hans-Peter Vierhaus, *Umweltbewußtsein von oben. Zum Verfassungsgebot demokratischer Willensbildung* (Berlin: Duncker & Humblot, 1994); Edda Müller, *Innenwelt der Umweltpolitik: Sozial-liberale Umweltpolitik—(Ohn)macht durch Organisation* (Opladen: Westdeutscher Verlag, 1986); Wolfgang

Rüdig, "Eco-Socialism: Left Environmentalism in West Germany," *New Political Science* 14 (1986): 3–37.

3. Kai-Uwe von Hassel, "Naturschutz in der Entscheidung," *N & L* 47, no. 10 (1972): 271.
4. G. Helmut Schwabe, "Umweltkrise und Umweltpolitik," *N & L* 46, no. 4 (1971): 88.
5. McCormick, *Reclaiming Paradise*, 57–60; Russell J. Dalton, *The Green Rainbow: Environmental Groups in Western Europe* (New Haven: Yale University Press, 1994), 35–36; Bess, *Light-Green Society*, 81. For an analysis of print and television reporting on environmental scandals in the late 1960s and 1970s see Engels, *Naturpolitik*, 222–26.
6. Bess, *Light-Green Society*, 79–81.
7. Süß, "'Wer aber denkt für das Ganze?'" in Frese, Paulus, and Teppe, *Demokratisierung*, 362–63.
8. Engels, *Naturpolitik*, 282–84.
9. Körner, *Theorie*, 121; Engels, *Naturpolitik*, chap. 7, esp. pp. 309–10.
10. Bess, *Light-Green Society*," 5; Max Oelschlaeger, *The Idea of Wilderness: From Prehistory to the Age of Ecology* (New Haven: Yale University Press, 1991).
11. Gerhard Olschowy, "Zur Belastung der Biosphäre," *N & L* 44, no. 1 (1969): 3–6; Konrad Buchwald, "Behörden und Fachstellen für Landschaftspflege und Naturschutz in der Bundesrepublik Deutschland," *Landschaft & Stadt* 1, no. 1 (1969): 8. See also Küppers, Lundgreen, and Weingart, *Umweltforschung*, 104–6.
12. Werner Trautmann and Walter Mrass, "Der Aufbau der Bundesforschungsanstalt für Naturschutz und Landschaftsökologie von 1964 bis 1978," *N & L* 53, no. 2 (1978): 43; Küppers, Lundgreen, and Weingart, *Umweltforschung*, 104–6; Wey, *Umweltpolitik*, 200.
13. Among the many examples of scientification see the reports in the Deutsche UNESCO-Kommission, "Probleme der Nutzung und Erhaltung der Biosphäre" (Cologne: Deutsche UNESCO-Kommission, 1969). See also Körner, "Entwicklung des Naturschutzes," in Brüggemeier and Engels, *Natur- und Umweltschutz*, 92–96. On the global network of experts see Kai F. Hünemörder's "Vom Expertennetzwerk zur Umweltpolitik. Frühe Umweltkonferenzen und die Ausweitung der öffentlichen Aufmerksamkeit für Umweltfragen in Europa (1959–1972)," *Archiv für Sozialgeschichte* 43 (2003): 275–96; more extensively Hünemörder, *Frühgeschichte*.
14. Rainer Piest, "Die wissenschaftlichen Grundlagen für eine rationale Nutzung und Erhaltung des Potentials der Biosphäre," *N & L* 44, no. 4 (1969): 94.
15. UNESCO, *Use and Conservation of the Biosphere. Proceedings of the Intergovernmental Conference of Experts on the Scientific Basis for Rational Use and Conservation of the Resources of the Biosphere* (Paris: UNESCO, 1970), foreword, 256; McCormick, *Reclaiming Paradise*, 60–61, 88–90, 189–90.
16. Piest, "Die wissenschaftlichen Grundlagen," *N & L* 44, no. 4 (1969): 94–95.
17. UNESCO, *Biosphere*, 212–22, quotes from pp. 216 and 228.
18. UNESCO, *Biosphere*, 196–97, 205–6, 209–12; McCormick, *Reclaiming Paradise*, 89–90.
19. UNESCO, *Biosphere*, 235.
20. Compare Piest, "Die wissenschaftlichen Grundlagen," *N & L* 44, no. 4 (1969): 95; Kurt Petrich (BML official and leader of the German delegation), "Die UNESCO-Biosphärenkonferenz 1968—ein Auftakt," *N & L* 44, no. 9 (1969): 215; and Konrad Buchwald, "Zusammenfassung des Seminars," *N & L* 44, no. 9 (1969): 264; with the broader conception expressed in Wolfgang Erz, "Was heißt heute Naturschutz? Zum Europäischen Naturschutzjahr 1970," *Nord Friesland Zeitschrift für Kultur, Politik, Wirtschaft*, no. 1–2 (May 1970): 53.
21. "Antrittsrede des neuen Bundesleiters Dipl.-Forstwirt Hubert Weinzierl," *Blätter für Naturschutz* 49, no. 3 (August 1969): 38; Hoplitschek, "Der Bund Naturschutz in Bayern," 144.

22. Engelhardt to parliamentarians, 18 April 1969, DNR Archive, "DNR Rundschreiben 1967–1969"; DNR, "Forderungen des Deutschen Naturschutzringes," to candidates in the *Bundestag* election, 22 April 1969, DNR Archive, "DNR Rundschreiben, Aufsätze, Protokolle, Tagungen, 1968–1969"; DNR *Rundschreiben Neue Folge,* Sonderrundschreiben zur Bundestagswahl 1969, no. 22 (16 September 1969): 1–6.

23. "Regierungserklärung. Den rasier' ich," *Spiegel,* 3 November 1969, 31.

24. See esp. Abteilung V, Federal Ministry of Agriculture, "Entwurf," "Persönlich," to Professor Dr. Ehmke, Federal Chancellery, 11 December 1969, BAK B 116/10843; and Federal Ministry of Agriculture, "Vermerk der Abteilungen II und V," 16 December 1969, BAK B 116/10843. On the popularity of Grzimek's television show see Dominick, *Environmental Movement,* 197; and more extensively, Engels, *Naturpolitik,* 242–51. Grzimek's decision not to run again is found in DNR *Rundschreiben Neue Folge,* no. 18. (20 September 1968). According to Ditt, "Umweltpolitik," 309, Grzimek did not run again after DNR member groups opposed his confrontational challenge to Minister of Health, Elisabeth Schwarzhaupt (CDU), to unite responsibility for environmental media in one ministry. But the national park controversy was most critical because it broke conservationists' traditional alliance with hunters and foresters. See chap. 7.

25. "Nichts zu tun," *Spiegel,* 29 June 1970, 31.

26. "Natur-Schmutz," *Spiegel,* 4 May 1970, 22; "Nichts zu tun," *Spiegel,* 29 June 1970, 31.

27. Abteilungsleiter V, Federal Ministry of Agriculture to Federal Minister of Agriculture [Ertl], 16 February 1973, BAK B 116/ 32387.

28. Bernhard Grzimek to Chancellor Willy Brandt, 23 January 1973; quote in Grzimek to Brandt, 28 January 1973, both in BAK B 116/ 32387. See also Engels, *Naturpolitik,* 267–69.

29. Herbert Offner, "Auch der Europarat befaßt sich mit Naturschutz," *N & L* 39, no. 6 (1964): 94–95; McCormick, *Reclaiming Paradise,* 179–80; Dominick, *Environmental Movement,* 146–47.

30. DNR *Rundschreiben Neue Folge,* no. 20 (30 April 1969): 1; "Protokoll über die Sitzung des nationalen Komitees der BRD am 23. September 1969 in Bad Godesberg, Heerstraße 110," 1–2, DNR Archive, "DNR Rundschreiben, Aufsätze, Protokolle, Tagungen, 1968–1969"; Wolfgang Engelhardt, "Der Beitrag des Deutschen Naturschutzringes e.V.—Bundesverband für Umweltschutz—zum Europäischen Naturschutzjahr 1970," *N & L* 45, no. 12 (1970): 414; Dominick, *Environmental Movement,* 146, 253, n. 104.

31. DNR *Rundschreiben Neue Folge,* no. 20 (30 April 1969): 3; "Protokoll über die Sitzung des nationalen Komitees der BRD am 20. November 1969 in Bad Godesberg," DNR Archive, "DNR Rundschreiben, Aufsätze, Protokolle, Tagungen, 1968–1969"; DNR *Rundschreiben Neue Folge,* no. 23 (30 December 1969): 1; Georg Fahrbach, ed., *Der Mensch in seiner Umwelt* (Stuttgart: Fink, 1970), 7.

32. "Protokolle über die Präsidialsitzung vom 10. Oktober 1970 in Wilsede/Lüneburger Heide," 20 October 1970, DNR Archive, "DNR Korrespondenz 1970 bis April/Mai 1971"; DNR *Rundschreiben Neue Folge,* no. 27 (10 August 1971): 3–4. On changes to Bavaria's League for Nature Protection see Hoplitschek, "Der Bund Naturschutz in Bayern," 143, 163–65, 178–81, 286.

33. Wolfgang Engelhardt to *Bundestag* President Kai-Uwe von Hassel, 21 November 1969; "Protokoll über die Sitzung des Nationalen Komitees der BRD am 23. September 1969," 2, both in DNR Archive, "DNR Rundschreiben, Aufsätze, Protokolle, Tagungen 1968–1969."

34. DNR *Rundschreiben Neue Folge,* no. 23 (30 December 1969): 2; "Liste von Persönlichkeiten, die sich als Redner für das Europäische Naturschutzjahr 1970 zur Verfügung gestellt haben," DNR Archive, "DNR Rundschreiben, Aufsätze, Protokolle, Tagungen, 1968–1969."

35. Per-Halby Tempel, "Wie läßt sich die Bevölkerung einer Stadt für Naturschutz und Landschaftspflege interessieren?" *N & L* 45, no. 12 (1970): 424–25.

36. DNR *Rundschreiben Neue Folge,* no. 23 (30 December 1969): 2–3; "Programm für Landschaftspflege und Naturschutz, ein Aufruf . . . an die Landkreise, Städte und Gemeinden," n.d. [early 1970] to all county governments, DNR Archive, "DNR Korrespondenz, 1970 bis April/Mai 1971." On activities in Bavaria see Hubert Weinzierl, "Initiativen des Bundes Naturschutz in Bayern im Europäischen Naturschutzjahr," *N & L* 45, no. 12 (1970): 422–23; DNR *Rundschreiben Neue Folge,* no. 27 (August 10, 1971): 2–3; Bergmeier, *Umweltgeschichte,* 92–111.

37. See below chap. 7; Hubert Weinzierl to the Bavarian government, *Landtag,* and Senate, 5 May 1970; Wolfgang Engelhardt to Alfons Goppel, 17 April 1970, both in Bayerisches Hauptstaatsarchiv (BHStA), Munich, Staatsministerium für Unterricht und Kultus (MK)/51186 (hereafter BHStA MK/51186).

38. "Protokoll über die Sitzung des Nationalen Komitees der BRD am 20. November 1969," DNR Archive, "DNR Rundschreiben, Aufsätze, Protokolle, Tagungen, 1968–1969"; DNR *Rundschreiben Neue Folge,* no. 24 (25 March 1970): 4; "Sei kein Dreckspatz!" *N & L* 45, no. 3 (1970): 73.

39. Tempel, "Bevölkerung," *N & L* 45, no. 12 (1970): 424–25; Engels, *Naturpolitik,* 306, n. 359.

40. DNR *Rundschreiben Neue Folge,* no. 20 (30 April 1969): 1; "Protokoll über die Präsidialsitzung vom 10. Oktober 1970," DNR Archive, "DNR Korrespondenz 1970 bis April/Mai 1971"; DNR *Rundschreiben Neue Folge,* no. 28 (5 June 1972): 5. The film received first price in the category of conservation in Padua in 1971.

41. *Alarm! Alarm,* film # 8149, AID Film Archiv.

42. Weinzierl, *große Wende,* 7, 32, 43, 54, 55, 103; Weinzierl, "Gegen den Ausverkauf der Umwelt," *Kosmos* 66, no. 9 (1970): *282–*86; Weinzierl, "Rebellieren gegen den Ausverkauf der Umwelt," in *Mitteilungen Deutscher Heimatbund, Sonderheft* (August 1970), 32, in BAK, Bundesministerium des Innern (B 106)/25522 (hereafter BAK B 106/25522); Engels, *Naturpolitik,* 306.

43. Wolfgang Erz, "Europäisches Naturschutzjahr 1970—und was wurde erreicht?" *N & L* 45, no. 12 (1970): 409–10; Gerhard Olschowy, "Internationale Konferenz zur Eröffnung des Europäischen Naturschutzjahres 1970," *N & L* 45, no. 5 (1970): 143–44. On the perceived importance of Nixon's address for West Germany see "Aide Memoire über das Gespräch des Herrn Bundespräsident mit dem Präsidium des Deutschen Naturschutzringes am 19. Februar 1970," DNR Archive, "DNR Korrespondenz 1970 bis April/Mai 1971"; Herbert Offner, "Europäisches Naturschutzjahr 1970 aus der Sicht des dafür eingesetzten Komitees," *N & L* 45, no. 12 (1970): 412. See also Ditt, "Umweltpolitik," 314–19.

44. German Embassy, Washington, DC to German Foreign Office, 13 February 1970, BAK B 106/25521; Hünemörder, *Frühgeschichte,* 141–45; Ditt, "Umweltpolitik," 324–26.

45. Horst Bieber, "Langsam stirbt der Umweltschutz. Von deutscher Naturromantik zur politischen Macht—doch der alte Schwung ist hin," *Zeit,* 20 October 1978, 8; Küppers, Lundgreen, and Weingart, *Umweltforschung,* 128–29; Michael Kloepfer, ed., *Schübe des Umweltbewußtseins und der Umweltrechtsentwicklung* (Bonn: Economica, 1995), 104; Wey, *Umweltpolitik,* 201.

46. Bergmeier, *Umweltgeschichte,* 92–111, 138–53; Ditt, "Umweltpolitik," 337–42; Engels, *Naturpolitik,* 284–86. On anticipated competency struggles see the draft of a statement from Referat U I 6 [Spezielle Rechtsfragen und Investitionsangelegenheiten], Federal Ministry of the Interior to Chancellor Brandt, spring 1970, BAK B 106/25500.

47. Lothar Finke, "Ecology and Environmental Problems," in Schöller, Puls, and Buchholz, *Spatial Development,* 54–55.

48. Küppers, Lundgreen, and Weingart, *Umweltforschung,* 127–32; Dominick, *Environmental Movement,* 147, 192; Wey, *Umweltpolitik,* 201–2; Bocking, *Nature's Experts,* 191.

49. Gerhard Olschowy, "Stellungnahme zum Sofortprogramm für Umweltschutz der Bundesregierung," *N & L* 46, no. 4 (1971): 103–5.

50. Federal Ministry of the Interior, "Grundlinien eines Umweltschutzprogramms," Anlage 1, September 1970, copy in BAK B 116/15290.

51. Küppers, Lundgreen, and Weingart, *Umweltforschung,* 117–20, 128–32; Engels, *Naturpolitik,* 286–88; Hünemörder, "1972—Epochenschwelle der Umweltgeschichte?" in Brüggemeier and Engels, *Natur- und Umweltschutz,* 129.

52. Referat U I 6, Federal Ministry of the Interior to Chancellor Brandt, 1970, BAK B 106/25500; Wey, *Umweltpolitik,* 202–3.

53. Hans Dieter Griesau, "Naturschutz und Landschaftspflege im Sofortprogramm der Bundesregierung für den Umweltschutz," *N & L* 45, no. 12 (1970): 418–19. On the competency struggle between the BMI and BML see Hans-Dietrich Genscher to Josef Ertl, 3 February 1970, BAK B 116/10843 and numerous internal BML memos in the same file.

54. Edda Müller, "Die Beziehung von Umwelt- und Naturschutz in den 1970er Jahren," in Stiftung Naturschutzgeschichte, *Natur im Sinn,* 32–34; Engels, *Naturpolitik,* 276.

55. "Morgen kam gestern," *Spiegel,* 5 October 1970, 74–96. On *Spiegel*'s coverage see Küppers, Lundgreen, and Weingart, *Umweltforschung,* 114–15.

56. Letters to the editor, *Spiegel,* 26 October 1970, 13–14, 17–18.

57. Erich Schöndorf to Hans-Dietrich Genscher, 8 October 1970; photocopy of public letter, Evangelisches Pfarramt, Stuttgart-Riedenberg, 4 October 1970; Kurt Erzinger to Dr. Gustav Heinemann, Federal President, 6 April 1970, all in BAK B 106/25521; Brigitte Kranz to Interior Minister [Genscher], 12 December 1970, BAK B 106/25526.

58. Engels, *Naturpolitik,* 290–94.

59. Erz, "Europäisches Naturschutzjahr 1970," *N & L* 45, no. 12 (1970): 410; Engelhardt, "Der Beitrag des Deutschen Naturschutzringes," *N & L* 45, no. 12 (1970): 414. Dominick, *Environmental Movement,* 183–87, corroborates Engelhardt's claims based on a survey of the *Frankfurter Allgemeine Zeitung* and *Zeit.* Compare with Küppers, Lundgreen, and Weingart, *Umweltforschung,* 112–15, who surveyed *Spiegel* and the science section of the *Süddeutsche Zeitung* between 1968 and 1974.

60. Tempel, "Bevölkerung," *N & L* 45, no. 12 (1970): 425; Engels, *Naturpolitik,* 218, 225.

61. Erz, "Europäisches Naturschutzjahr," *N & L* 45, no. 12 (1970): 410; Axel R. Bunz, *Umweltpolitisches Bewußtsein 1972* (Berlin: Erich Schmidt, 1973), 4; "Nur 8% der Bevölkerung wissen nichts vom Umweltschutz," *N & L* 47, no. 7 (1972): 192.

62. Bernhard Grzimek in *Das Parlament,* 22 August 1970, 1; Grzimek, "Europäisches Naturschutzjahr 1970—ein Anfang," *N & L* 45, no. 12 (1970): 408.

63. Wolfgang Engelhardt, "Beginn und Verpflichtung für die 70er Jahre," *N & L* 46, no. 1 (1971): 8–9.

64. Erz, "Opas Naturschutz ist Todt," *Das Parlament* 20, no. 34 (22 August 1970); Erz, "Was heißt heute Naturschutz?" 58.

65. Willy Brandt, quoted in "Gesellschaftspolitische Bedeutung eines wirksamen Umweltschutzes," *N & L* 46, no. 1 (1970): 3–5.

66. Dr. Inge Feuchtmayr, "Umweltgestaltung, eine Lebensnotwendigkeit für die Gesellschaft," *Landschaft & Stadt* 2, no. 2 (1970): 78–81, quotes on pp. 78 and 79.

67. Rudolf Hanauer, address excerpted in "Zum Grundrecht auf eine heile Umwelt," *N & L* 45, no. 12 (1970): 427–28.

68. Federal Republic of Germany, *Umweltpolitik. Das Umweltprogramm der Bundesregierung,* 5 ed. (Stuttgart: Kohlhammer, 1976); Mangun, *Administration of Environmental Policy,* 31;

Ditt, "Umweltpolitik," 331–34; Engels, *Naturpolitik,* 275–76; Vierhaus, *Umweltbewußtsein,* 110–14.

69. Engels, *Naturpolitik,* 287; Hünemörder, "Epochenschwelle," in Brüggemeier and Engels, *Natur- und Umweltschutz,* 130; Küppers, Lundgreen, and Weingart, *Umweltforschung,* 116.

70. Körner, *Theorie,* 121.

71. Wolfram Pflug, "Kommt der ökologische Umweltschutz im Umweltprogramm der Bundesregierung zu kurz?" *N & L* 47, no. 7 (1972): 186–89; Hermann Josef Bauer and Gerhard Olschowy, "Zum Umweltprogramm der Bundesregierung," *JfNL* (1972): 98; Müller, *Innenwelt,* 423–24. For similar complaints in France see Bess, *Light-Green Society,* 222.

72. Bernhard Grzimek, "Naturschutz erhält die Lebensqualität," *Kosmos* 69, no. 11 (1973): 447–49.

73. Hans-Dietrich Genscher in *Das Parlament* 20, no. 34 (August 22, 1970): 2; Genscher, *Erinnerungen* (Berlin: Siedler, 1995), 126; Curtis Moore and Alan Miller, *Green Gold: Japan, Germany, and the United States and the Race for Environmental Technology* (Boston: Beacon Press, 1994), chap. 1.

74. Bunz, *Umweltpolitisches Bewußtsein,* 33–34; Fulbrook, *Divided Nation,* 199; Wey, *Umweltpolitik,* 217; Cioc, *The Rhine,* chap. 7; Ditt, "Umweltpolitik," 343; Brüggemeier, *Tschernobyl,* 198.

75. Werner Hoffmann, "Warum konkurrierende Gesetzgebung für Naturschutz und Landschaftspflege?" *JfNL* (1970): 82–87; ABN, "Stellungnahme zur Vorrangsgesetzgebung des Bundes für Naturschutz und Landschaftspflege," *N & L* 46, no. 3 (1971): 77; Wolfgang Erz, "Entwurf für ein Bundesgesetz für Landschaftspflege und Naturschutz vorgelegt," *N & L* 46, no. 8 (1971): 223.

76. Müller, *Innenwelt,* 335–97; Günter Zwanzig, "50 Jahre Reichsnaturschutzgesetz (RNG)," *N & L* 60, no. 7/8 (1985): 276. On conservation groups' attempts to get the right to file lawsuits see DNR *Rundschreiben Neue Folge,* no. 23 (30 December 1969): 2–3 and no. 24 (25 March 1970): 3.

77. The Club of Rome was founded in 1968 by the industrialist Dr. Aurelio Peccei when he convened thirty people from science, industry, economics, the humanities, and education in Rome to discuss environmental decline, changes in values, urbanization, and waning support for institutions. By 1970, the group had seventy-five members representing twenty-five nations.

78. Donella H. Meadows, Dennis L. Meadows, Jørgen Randers and William W. Behrens III, *The Limits to Growth. A Report for the Club of Rome's Project on the Predicament of Mankind* (New York: Signet, 1972), 94, 29, 178–79. On weaknesses of the report see McCormick, *Reclaiming Paradise,* 80–84; Ronald Inglehart, *The Silent Revolution. Changing Values and Political Styles Among Western Publics* (Princeton: Princeton University Press, 1977), 379–89.

79. See for example Paul Ehrlich, *The Population Bomb* (New York: Ballantine, 1968); Barry Commoner, *The Closing Circle. Nature, Man, and Technology* (New York: Bantam, 1974). On reception in West Germany of alarmist predictions see Küppers, Lundgreen, and Weingart, *Umweltforschung,* 113–14, 123; Hermand, *Grüne Utopien,* 131–33; Engels, *Naturpolitik,* 280–82; Hünemörder, "Expertennetzwerk," 291; and in Europe more generally, Dalton, *Green Rainbow,* 35–36.

80. Willy Brandt, "Notizen des Bundeskanzlers zur Umweltpolitik. 9. Juli 1972," Document #70, *Berliner Ausgabe,* vol. 7, *Mehr Demokratie wagen. Innen- und Gesellschaftspolitik 1966–1974,* ed. Wolther von Kieseritzky (Bonn: Dietz, 2001), 338; Eberhard Eppler, *Ende oder Wende. Von der Machbarkeit des Notwendigen,* 6th rev. ed. (Munich: Deutscher Taschenbuch Verlag, 1976); Wolfgang Engelhardt, "Das Primat der natürlichen Umwelt," *JfNL* (1972), 48–49; Engels, *Naturpolitik,* 290.

81. Federal Republic of Germany, *Report of the Federal Republic of Germany on the Human Environment Prepared for the United Nations Conference on the Human Environment June 1972, Stockholm, Sweden* (Bonn: Federal Ministry of the Interior, 1972).

82. Federal Republic of Germany, *Report on the Human Environment*, 115–33.

83. Excerpts from Eppler's speech in *Kosmos* 69, no. 12 (1973): 492–94. The ideas are discussed more fully in Eppler, *Ende oder Wende*, 46–56. On the SPD and "quality of life," see Engels, *Naturpolitik*, 292–94. For indication of the public's tendency to define "quality of life" as material well being see the 1973 poll conducted by the Tübingen-based Wickert Institute in *Kosmos*, 69, no. 12 (1973): 493.

84. Referat U A I 2 [Umweltprogramm der Bundesregierung, Angelegenheiten der Raumordnung], Federal Ministry of the Interior, "Vermerk. Betr.: Studie zur Informationspolitik des BMI auf dem Gebiet des Umweltschutzes," 26 September 1973, BAK B 106/63670; Kloepfer, *Schübe des Umweltbewußtseins*, 108-9.

85. Referat U I 1 [Wasserrecht], Federal Ministry of the Interior, "Betr.: DNR, hier: Gesprächsunterlage für den Herrn Minister für die Besprechung mit dem Präsidiumsmitglied des DNR, Dipl. Forstwirt Hubert Weinzierl, am 20 Juni 1972"; DNR circular letter, 7 August 1972, both in BAK B 106/29457.

86. Ministerial Referat Dr. Stahl, Federal Ministry of the Interior to Unterabteilungsleiter U A I [Umweltgrundsatzangelegenheiten], Abteilungsleiter U A [Umweltpolitik, Reaktorsicherheit und Strahlenschutz], State Secretary Hartkopf and Hans-Dietrich Genscher, 2 December 1974, BAK B 106/63670.

87. Scholarship on CIs is vast. Among the most influential older studies are Inglehart, *Silent Revolution;* Karl-Werner Brand, *Neue soziale Bewegungen. Entstehung, Funktion und Perspektive neuer Protestpotentiale. Eine Zwischenbilanz* (Opladen: Westdeutscher Verlag, 1982); Brand, Detlef Büsser, and Dieter Rucht, eds., *Aufbruch in eine andere Gesellschaft. Neue soziale Bewegungen in der Bundesrepublik* (Frankfurt am Main: Campus, 1983); Bernd Guggenberger and Udo Kempf, eds., *Bürgerinitiativen und repräsentatives System*, 2d rev. ed. (Opladen: Westdeutscher Verlag, 1984); Roland Roth and Dieter Rucht, eds. *Neue Soziale Bewegungen in der Bundesrepublik Deutschland* (Frankfurt am Main: Campus, 1987). Studies that challenge or modify older interpretations include Joseph Huber, "Fortschritt und Entfremdung. Ein Entwicklungsmodell des ökologischen Diskurses," in *Industrialismus und Ökoromantik. Geschichte und Perspektiven der Ökologisierung*, ed. Dieter Hassenpflug (Wiesbaden: Deutscher Universitätsverlag, 1991), 19–42; Steven Brechin and Willett Kempton, "Global Environmentalism. A Challenge to the Postmaterialism Thesis?" *Social Science Quarterly* 74 (1994): 245–69; Roland Roth, "'Patch-Work.' Kollektive Identitäten neuer sozialer Bewegungen," in *Paradigmen der Bewegungsforschung*, ed. Kai-Uwe Hellmann and Ruud Koopmanns (Opladen: Westdeutscher Verlag, 1998), 51–68. Engels, *Naturpolitik*, 324–26, provides an instructive overview of changes in scholarly interpretations.

88. Wolfgang Rüdig, "Bürgerinitiativen und Umweltschutz. Eine Bestandsaufnahme der empirischen Befunde," in *Bürgerinitiativen in der Gesellschaft: politische Dimensionen und Reaktionen*, ed. Volker Hauff (Villingen-Schwenningen: Neckar-Verlag, 1980), 119–84; Bernd Guggenberger, "Umweltpolitik und Ökologiebewegung," in *Die Geschichte der Bundesrepublik Deutschland*, vol. 2, *Wirtschaft*, ed. Wolfgang Benz (Frankfurt am Main: Fischer, 1989), 398; Engels, *Naturpolitik*, 322–27.

89. Henry Makowski, "Bürgerinitiativen und Naturschutz," *N & L* 47, no. 4 (1972): 99; DNR *Rundschreiben Neue Folge*, no. 28 (5 June 1972): 4.

90. DNR *Informationsbrief* (September 1965), 59–65; and (August/September 1966), back cover; Ditt, "Umweltpolitik," 309.

91. Alfred Toepfer to Wolfgang Engelhardt, 21 January 1972, DNR Archive, "Organisation, Präsidium, Protokolle, Rundschreiben 1972."

92. "Protokoll über die Präsidialsitzung vom 10. Oktober 1970," DNR Archive, "DNR Korrespondenz 1970 bis April/Mai 1971"; Rucht, "Von der Bewegung zur Institution?" in Roth and Rucht, *Neue soziale Bewegungen,* 248, indicates that in the early 1980s, federal support constituted 50 to 65 percent of the DNR's annual budget.

93. Wolfgang Engelhardt to Georg Fahrbach, 27 April 1972, DNR Archive, "Organisation, Präsidium, Protokolle, Rundschreiben 1972"; Engels, *Naturpolitik,* 334; Reichelt, *Wach sein,* 211–13.

94. Georg Fahrbach to Wolfgang Engelhardt, 21 June 1972, DNR Archive, "Organisation, Präsidium, Protokolle, Rundschreiben 1972."

95. Udo Kempf, "Der Bundesverband Bürgerinitiativen Umweltschutz (BBU)," in Guggenberger and Kempf, *Bürgerinitiativen und repräsentatives System,* 404ff.; Martin Leonhard, *Umweltverbände: zur Organisation von Umweltschutzinteressen in der Bundesrepublik Deutschland* (Opladen: Westdeutscher Verlag, 1986), 131–32.

96. On the conflict between Hans-Helmuth Wüstenhagen and two member organizations with right-wing tendencies, the World Federation for the Protection of Life and the German Federation for the Protection of Life, see the correspondence in BAK B 106/63670. These two groups left the BBU in October 1973 to form another alliance. See also Kempf, "Der Bundesverband Bürgerinitiativen Umweltschutz," in Guggenberger and Kempf, *"Bürgerinitiativen und repräsentatives System,"* 408; Rucht, "Von der Bewegung zur Institution?" in Roth and Rucht, *Neue soziale Bewegungen,* 252–53. On the World Federation see Jonathan Olsen, *Nature and Nationalism. Right-Wing Ecology and the Politics of Identity in Contemporary Germany* (New York: St. Martin's, 1999), 18–19, 82–83.

97. Theodor Sonnemann to State Secretary Dr. Günter Hartkopf, Federal Ministry of the Interior, 14 July 1972, DNR Archive, "Organisation, Präsidium, Protokolle, Rundschreiben 1972." See also Sonnemann, *Jahrgang 1900. Auf und ab im Strom der Zeit* (Würzburg: Johann Wilhelm Naumann, 1980), 386–88.

98. Referent für Öffentlichkeitsarbeit [Verheugen], Federal Ministry of the Interior, "Betr.: Zusammenarbeit mit dem Bundesverband BBU," 10 July 1972; Horst Zilleßen, BBU to Referent für Öffentlichkeitsarbeit [Verheugen], Federal Ministry of the Interior, 13 December 1972, both in BAK B 106/63670.

99. Hans-Helmuth Wüstenhagen to Peter Menke-Glückert, 18 November 1973; Wüstenhagen to Menke-Glückert, 30 January 1974, both in BAK B 106/63670. On Wüstenhagen see Kempf, "Der Bundesverband Bürgerinitiativen Umweltschutz," in Guggenberger and Kempf, *Bürgerinitiativen und repräsentatives System,* 406–13; Engels, *Naturpolitik,* 336–37.

100. Peter Menke-Glückert [?], Federal Ministry of the Interior to Hans-Helmuth Wüstenhagen, 25 March 1974, BAK B 106/63670. See also Referat U A I 2, Federal Ministry of the Interior, "Betr. Studie zur Informationspolitik des BMI auf dem Gebiet des Umweltschutzes," 26 September 1973, BAK B 106/63670; Joachim Raschke, *Soziale Bewegungen. Ein historisch-systematischer Grundriß* (Frankfurt am Main: Campus, 1985), 205, 213.

101. Peter Menke-Glückert, Federal Ministry of the Interior to Hans-Helmuth Wüstenhagen, 3 September 1973; Verheugen, Federal Ministry of the Interior to BBU [Wüstenhagen], 21 September 1973, both in BAK B 106/63670.

102. Horst Zilleßen, First Chairman, BBU, to the Federal Government, SPD, CDU/CSU, and FDP, 24 November 1972, BAK B 106/63670.

103. Engels, *Naturpolitik,* 332–38, 377–78.

104. Brand, Büsser, and Rucht, *Aufbruch,* 79–80; Michael T. Hatch, *Politics and Nuclear Power. Energy Policy in Western Europe* (Lexington: University Press of Kentucky, 1986), 69.

105. Dieter Rucht, *Von Wyhl nach Gorleben. Bürger gegen Atomprogramm und nukleare Entsorgung* (Munich: C.H. Beck, 1980), 17–30; Hatch, *Nuclear Power,* 70. For an extensive account

of nuclear energy in West Germany see Joachim Radkau, *Aufstieg und Krise der deutschen Atomwirtschaft 1945–1975. Verdrängte Alternativen in der Kerntechnik und der Ursprung der nuklearen Kontroverse* (Reinbek: Rowohlt, 1983).

106. Engels, *Naturpolitik*, 344–76; Rucht, *Wyhl*, 74–85, 87; Rucht, "Wyhl: Der Aufbruch der Anti-Atomkraftbewegung," in Linse, Falter, Rucht, and Kretschmer, *Bittschrift*, 128–64.

107. Rucht, *Wyhl*, 85–98; Dominick, *Environmental Movement*, 217–18; Kempf, "Der Bundesverband Bürgerinitiativen Umweltschutz (BBU)," in Guggenberger and Kempf, *Bürgerinitiativen und repräsentatives System*, 412; Engels, *Naturpolitik*, 404.

108. DNR circular letter, 29 October 1974, "Stellungnahme 'Bericht über die Umweltbelastung infolge der Energieversorgung durch Kernkraftwerke in der BRD,'" DNR Archive, "Rundschreiben 1974."

109. Engels, *Naturpolitik*, 309–10.

110. Bocking, *Nature's Experts*, 67–69; Schulze Hannöver and Becker, "Natur im Sinn," 16–19.

111. The discussion of BUND and of its uses of ecology draws on Engels, *Naturpolitik*, 311–22. Refer also to Hoplitschek, "Der Bund Naturschutz in Bayern," 51, 88, 98–99, 117–19, 166, 178–79, 213; Rucht, "Von der Bewegung zur Institution?" 247, 249–50.

112. Horst Bieber, "Langsam stirbt der Umweltschutz. Von deutscher Naturromantik zur politischen Macht—doch der alte Schwung ist hin," *Zeit*, 20 October 1978, 7–9.

113. Engels, *Naturpolitik*, chap. 10.

114. Engels, *Naturpolitik*, chap. 7.

115. Bess, *Light-Green Society*, 241.

116. A revival is evident in *N & L*. Refer also to Uekötter, *Naturschutz im Aufbruch*, chaps. 6–7.

117. Körner, "Entwicklung des Naturschutzes," in Brüggemeier and Engels, *Natur- und Umweltschutz*, 97–99, 101–2; more extensively, Potthast, *Evolution und der Naturschutz*.

118. René Dubos, *The Wooing of Earth. New Perspectives on Man's Use of Nature* (New York: Scribner's, 1980), 109–10.

119. Hubert Weinzierl, "Zurück zum Naturschutz!" *Unser Wald* 5 (October 1972): 154–55.

Chapter 7

DESIGNING THE BAVARIAN FOREST NATIONAL PARK, 1966–1975

Locals called it "Bavarian Siberia." For seven months out of the year, the coldest and remotest areas of the Bavarian Forest above 1,150 meters lay beneath one to three meters of densely packed snow. Here between the peaks of Rachel and Lusen, not far from the former Iron Curtain, forests almost exclusively of spruce, some of them 300 to 400 years old, have adapted to a climate that is more severe than other alpine regions of the same altitude. On more protected southern slopes spruce, white fir, and beech thrive, while ferns, lilies, and birch trees settle in the cool shaded valleys. Spruce are found here as well, but in the marshy ground their roots grow close to the surface, making them vulnerable to violent windstorms that occasionally sweep through forest as they did in 1925, 1929, 1930, and again in 1983, each time clearing large patches of woodland while contributing to a natural rejuvenation. Because of the long, cold winters and snow that covers the ground from mid autumn until June, relatively few animals inhabit the area, although woodpeckers, owls, and a variety of other birds adapt easily to the forest environment. Red and roe deer can be found at lower elevations where there is less snow and more vegetation.[1] But it was the remotest part of the Bavaria Forest, where old-growth forest remained well preserved, that a vocal minority of conservationists singled out in the late 1960s to be the centerpiece of West Germany's first national park.

The Bavarian Forest, together with the neighboring Bohemian (Šumava) Forest, makes up the largest continuous woodland in Central Europe. It is not pristine wilderness, but a hybrid landscape sculpted over centuries by the interplay of natural processes and human use. In the Middle Ages, settlers

Notes for this chapter begin on page 236.

came to the area to farm, mine, or tap into the lucrative salt trade between Bohemia, Berchtesgaden, and Salzburg. The development of glassworks in the fifteenth century brought more people, who carved out settlements like Altschönau, Riedlhütte, and Spiegelau, and operated thriving local industries that exploited the surrounding woodlands for charcoal and potash. As nearby stands of trees dwindled, settlements crept deeper into the forest. By the eighteenth century, more trees were harvested for lumber and larger streams were straightened and widened to facilitate the transport of timber down to sawmills in the growing towns. As entire areas were clear-cut, mixed forests of trees of diverse ages gave way to young woods. Old-growth forest dwindled further during the two world wars. By 1949, little more than 20 percent of the Bavarian Forest was old-growth, compared with 50 percent a century earlier. During the 1950s, however, foresters began to return parts of it to a mixed forest of beech, spruce, and fir.[2] By introducing evergreens into areas with primarily deciduous trees and the reverse, foresters produced a landscape with a diversity of species and color. They guarded "their" cultivated woodland proudly, and resisted the idea of converting it into a national park where forestry would be restricted, if not prohibited.[3]

The national park idea prevailed, not because it resonated with a more environmentally aware public, but because it promised to breathe new life into the troubled economy of the Bavarian Forest. For local and state government leaders, the Inner Bavarian Forest was a regional planning problem in search of a solution. It had the highest rate of unemployment and lowest income per capita in the country. Its unusually harsh climate, dense forests, and location in the border zone along the Iron Curtain contributed to the region's underdeveloped economy. Like other rural areas across Europe in the 1960s, it was hit hard by the out-migration to cities as the agricultural sector shrank. The national recession of 1966–1967 dealt another blow to the region. Attempts to attract industry had had limited success, so state planners and local government leaders pinned their hopes on expanding tourism.[4] While some advocated another nature park to add to the eight then in existence or in the final planning stages in Bavaria, a minority proposed a national park, an option untested in West Germany.

In 1969, the Bavarian *Landtag* approved the plan to transform a professionally managed forest into a national park. But the decision was preceded by three years of acrimonious debate that at its core involved a struggle to define the cultural significance of nature for an advanced industrial urban nation. As scholars emphasize, national parks are not pristine spaces, but landscapes that have been designed according to a particular aesthetic of nature and then made available for public consumption. International standards bar traditional economic uses of land and resources in national parks, making it possible for a specific vision of nature to be protected and showcased to the public. National parks do indeed protect nature, but they also protect cultural views of what nature is to be like; they seek to naturalize what is deeply cultural.[5]

As the debate over West Germany's national park illustrates, images of what nature is and how it ought to appear differ depending upon people's occupation, class, and residence, among other factors. In this particular case, national park proponents were led by an elite group of conservationists who were worried about vanishing cultural opportunities for experiencing "wild" nature.[6] Leading the opposition to a national park was the state forest service, which owned nearly all of the land in question. The majority of people associated with traditional conservation lined up on the side of the forest service, preferring yet another nature park where visitors could relax in manicured woods. Local government officials emerged on the other side, eager to use the national park designation to boost tourism and revitalize the troubled economies of their communities.

With good reason, historians emphasize that national parks mean increased state control over land at the expense of locals. But in Bavaria, erecting a national park also involved making a unique landscape more accessible to the public at the expense of groups traditionally associated with elitism and exclusive use: foresters and hunters. The nature aesthetic that initially shaped the design of the national park reflected the state government's attempt to make concessions to all parties involved in the debate, leading some to dub the Bavarian Forest the "compromise park." After being transformed into a national park, however, this new landscape—the product of physical geography, local economic realities, political decisions, and cultural values—eventually became a space where a new aesthetic of nature emerged. In a remote corner of this densely populated, urban, industrial country, nature could be protected "for its own sake" and natural processes could take their own course to the degree that was possible.

The Failure of an Idea: National Park Plans in Germany Before the 1960s

Since the early twentieth century, Germans had considered establishing national parks, but most believed that only countries with vast "uninhabited" space could support such use of land, most notably the United States where the world's first national parks were erected in the late nineteenth century. In the US, protecting "wilderness" in the form of national parks found support from federal and state governments, the public, and railroad companies. But creating these new "pleasure grounds" for tourists often involved dispossessing Native Americans of some of their tribal land.[7] In Germany, the idea of "wilderness" had a somewhat different history. Because Germans associated "wilderness" with "wasteland" ("*Ödland*" or "*Unland*"), they made a concerted effort to transform "unproductive" "wild" land into fertile "cultural landscapes."[8] During the Third Reich,

"wilderness" came to be associated with the "degraded" landscapes of the conquered "wild" East. Simultaneously, however, preservationists like Schoenichen
advocated the preservation of areas viewed as "*Ödland*" in the Old Reich, stressing their value for scientific research and for protecting soil fertility and the
water supply.[9]

These debates in Germany took place in a time of growing international cooperation in preservation, especially among imperial powers wanting to manage
the landscapes and wildlife of their colonial possessions. Since the late 1800s,
Britain led the way in establishing national parks and game reserves in its African colonies, imposing its vision of nature on foreign landscapes, and in the
process, redefining who possessed the land and its resources. By the 1930s, the
extermination of some wildlife species by colonial authorities, white settlers, and
hunting parties prompted the British government to sponsor the 1933 London
Convention on the preservation of plants and animals in Africa. At this international gathering, colonial powers agreed to safeguard animal populations
by establishing large reserves and national parks. Guiding their vision for future national parks was the "Yellowstone model," which prohibited traditional
uses of the land, including hunting by indigenous populations. The Yellowstone
model ignored humans' role in shaping nature, yet, paradoxically, required human intervention to shape landscapes into places perceived to be "wild," and
to maintain them in that condition. According to the London Convention, areas designated as national parks had to have clear boundaries, be overseen by
the state, and be set aside for public enjoyment and the preservation of nature.
Economic use of land and natural resources was prohibited, as was hunting or
gathering plants, except under supervision of park authorities. These guidelines
remained in place until 1969 when the IUCN made the standards stricter. After
the London Convention, nations from the Netherlands to Japan erected national parks within their borders.[10]

Influenced by these international trends, some Nazi elites and preservationists took steps to establish several national parks in Germany. Because of the
dictatorship that concentrated power at the center, they now had the means
to confiscate property (and seize foreign territory) for large reserves. In the late
1930s, the Reich Forest Office and the Reich Agency for Nature Protection
drafted plans for national parks in the Lüneburg Heath, the Kurische Neh-
rung (Curonian Spit) in East Prussia, the Bavarian and Austrian Alps, and the
Bavarian-Bohemian forests. But none of these proposals was implemented, un-
dermined by the war that was to have helped make them a reality. Lutz Heck,
the Berlin Zoo director and head of preservation in the Reich Forest Office,
had proposed designating these areas "national parks" rather than "Reich nature
reserves" to protect them from the Reich Forest Master's greedy reach. As Reich
Forest Master, Göring had abused the latter legal category from the RNG when
he seized several Reich nature reserves for private hunting, among them former

royal game reserves such as the Schorfheide near Berlin, the Rominten in East Prussia, and the Darß in West Pomerania.[11]

In the 1950s, conservationists in both Germanys renewed their attempts to establish national parks, but without success. Ignoring international criteria for national parks that still were not accepted universally, Hans Klose proposed designating the Lüneburg Heath a national park to prevent the British from practicing military maneuvers there. DNR President Hans Krieg tried to erect a national park in the Ammergebirge north of Garmisch-Partenkirchen, but the project ran aground amid opposition from property owners. His attempt to revive plans for a national park around Königsee nature reserve was blocked by foresters who feared limits on hunting in this former royal game reserve.[12] The Federal Republic's failed efforts stood in sharp contrast to an international trend at the time. During the 1950s, Great Britain opened ten of its eleven, and Japan four of its twenty-eight, national parks. Even the densely populated Netherlands set up one national park to add to the two in existence since the 1930s.[13]

West Germans, including some conservationists, were skeptical of national parks for several reasons. There was the opposition for reasons of space already mentioned, but reluctance also because of worry (not unique to Germany) that increased visitor traffic would harm the very areas the parks were to protect. Financial considerations also came into play, especially in the 1950s when few state governments could afford to compensate property owners, much less erect and then maintain a national park. Furthermore, spatial planning, a policy tool that could integrate national parks into a state's existing economic structure, was not well developed until the 1960s (though this consideration had not held back other nations). But more effective planning was needed to overcome the strong opposition to national parks from foresters, hunters, and industrialists—groups enjoying exclusive access to some areas for hunting. The success of the nature park program points to another reason for the failure of the national park idea, and underscores officials' reluctance to restrict traditional economic uses of nature.

For some of the same reasons, East Germans did not erect national parks either. In the most organized campaign of the 1950s, advocates failed to convince the regime to designate as a national park the sandstone cliffs along the Elbe River near Dresden. To make this cultural landscape popularly know as Saxon Switzerland (*Sächsische Schweiz*) a national park, clear cutting would have to end in the spectacular Bastei reserve, pure stands of pine and spruce would have to be returned to a mixed forest, and the polluted Elbe would have to be cleaned up. Officials also worried about unwanted pressures on the still closed border with Czechoslovakia. The East German regime also objected to national parks as an expression of American capitalist ideology, a concern its communist neighbors apparently did not share: between 1950 and 1970, Poland opened eight national parks, and Czechoslovakia established three. Although socialism was compatible with the national park goal of making unique landscapes accessible to the public, the GDR regime feared the oppositional potential of the idea, especially after the *Sächsische Schweiz* campaign attracted broad support. Nor did the state want tourists in several other prized landscapes where hunting privileges of the regime's elite were protected more than nature was.[14]

The two Germanys were unique in Europe in not having national parks. Their absence in both countries can be attributed only partly to the high cost involved in establishing and maintaining them, and to officials' concern to use nature efficiently and productively, not to "waste" it through stringent preservation. Also at issue during the Cold War was the highly political "national park" label, especially in the 1950s when most Germans considered their countries' boundaries temporary. In West Germany, where the Hallstein Doctrine (1955–1972) refused diplomatic relations with nations recognizing the GDR, the national park designation could have been used to reinforce Bonn's claim to be the only legitimate Germany. But such a move might have been unpopular with West Germans who held out hopes for reunification. West Germany's European allies might have been even more critical of the designation, viewing it as overly nationalistic.

A Divisive Beginning: The National Park Debate, 1966–1967

When West German conservationists revived the national park idea in the mid 1960s, they did so partly in reaction to regional plans for the Bavarian Forest that seemed eager to promote mass tourism by exploiting the area's natural beauty. One plan, for example, called for a cable car on Mt. Rachel and a chair lift to Mt. Lusen. It was the newly appointed conservation commissioner for the district of Lower Bavaria, Hubert Weinzierl, who proposed a national park to strengthen the economy without compromising the forest.[15] Past experience in the region had shown that piecemeal preservation offered no comprehensive protection for nature, though it had resulted in several reserves of varying sizes. In the mid 1930s, local preservationists had failed to get the Bavarian Forest declared a Reich nature reserve to shield it from exploitative forestry. Only in 1939, when the military tried to seize Arber, Lusen, and Rachel, three peaks in the heart of the forest, did Göring's office intervene—and then not to aid local preservationists, but to pursue imperialistic plans to create the "Bohemian Forest National Park," a 1,000 square-kilometer area (100,000 hectares), over half of which would lie in German controlled Czechoslovakia.[16] Nothing came of the plan, though ten reserves (ranging in size from 2.5 hectares to 309 hectares) encompassing 630 hectares were established in the Bavarian Forest between 1938 and 1941. Nine more reserves covering 514 hectares were set aside in the 1950s.[17] Efforts to protect these islands of nature more effectively by including them in a much larger landscape reserve (75,000 hectares) that stretched across five rural districts along the Czech border succeeded only in 1967, a delay caused by opposition from property owners who feared restrictions on land use, and local governments that anticipated more obstacles for economic development.[18]

But a landscape reserve (*Landschaftsschutzgebiet*) did not bar forestry or farming and offered less protection for nature than was possible in a national park. While reviewing files in his office in Landshut, Weinzierl found the plans from the 1930s for the Bohemian Forest National Park and worked doggedly over the next three years to implement a scaled-back version of them. After exploring the forest around Falkenstein in the spring of 1966 with DNR President Bernhard Grzimek, Weinzierl dispelled the latter's initial doubts about a national park for West Germany and gained a politically savvy ally, though a controversial one.[19]

In mid July 1966, Grzimek and Weinzierl initiated discussions with the Bavarian government over the national park. Grzimek presumptuously billed the idea as a "serious desire of the DNR . . . [and] probably one of the most fervent wishes of the entire German conservation movement." In July, Grzimek, Weinzierl, Engelhardt, *Landtag* deputy Max Streibl (CSU), and representatives of the district government of Lower Bavaria and the League for Nature Protection met with Minister-President Alfons Goppel (CSU) to outline the plan, working behind the scenes as conservationists tended to do. Grzimek informed Goppel that the park would need to be at least 50 square kilometers (5,000 hectares) to comply with international standards. Compared with other national parks in neighboring countries, this was on the small side. (Poland's Bialowieza National Park was 47 square kilometers, Switzerland's Engadin National Park was 160 square kilometers, and Czechoslovakia's Tatra National Park was 511 square kilometers). To minimize conflicts with property owners, the plan recommended situating the park between Rachel and Ferdinand's Valley north of Falkenstein, on land owned almost exclusively by the state forest service.[20]

After hearing the vague proposal with a price tag of between DM 5 million and DM 10 million over several years, Goppel turned the matter over to several ministries for a critical appraisal by the end of summer.[21] For the next three years, they remained gridlocked. The Ministry of the Interior (as the state's highest conservation office) favored the national park in principle. Precisely because the proposal promised to enliven tourism in a remote underdeveloped area, planners in the economics ministry, Bavaria's highest planning authority, favored it. But their superior, State Secretary Sackmann, announced that his office would "not give one Pfennig for the national park," arguing that the future lay in nature parks. Officials in the Ministry of Finance flinched at the expense of the project and predicted that it would eliminate locals' jobs in the timber industry.[22] Minister of Agriculture Alois Hundhammer[23] (CSU) was less hostile, but still opposed, despite Grzimek's attempts to win him over and even after a tour of Sweden's national parks, which left him impressed.[24] The Ministry of Agriculture's forestry division and the forest service office in Regensburg launched the most determined attack against the park, arguing predictably that the restrictions on forest management would reduce their revenues and eliminate an estimated fifty badly needed jobs. More distressing for them was that a national park would rule out forestry, "threatening" the landscape they had sculpted over decades.[25]

The most troubling aspect of the plan, and not only for foresters, was Grzimek's insistence on reintroducing wildlife that "once had lived in *German forests*" [emphasis added], a proposal that paid little attention to the physical geography of the Bavarian Forest or its ability to support species that might never have been native. Grzimek's primary concern was to create a mosaic of forest habitats in one location that just happened to be Lower Bavaria. As the plan evolved, however, it focused on recreating a landscape that might have existed in the area a thousand years earlier when buffalo, chamois, moose, lynx, beaver, and wild boar inhabited the region. Although reintroducing wildlife had the potential to preserve species that had become rare or extinct in the region, it implied a lack of appreciation for the forest and the animals that existed there, including elk, red deer, otter, hazel hen, owls, and other birds of prey. Grzimek's vision to reproduce a medieval forest in Bavaria was shaped by the assumption that a "natural state" of nature was one showing limited human use. Paradoxically, recreating and then maintaining the landscape in a static state would require constant upkeep by park employees. Grzimek admitted that the area in its current condition could not sustain more wildlife. He therefore suggested clearing patches of forest to create open meadows for grazing, a measure, he argued, that would make wildlife more visible to tourists and diversify and enrich the scenery. Even foresters, he noted, had artificially kept areas that had been used for livestock grazing in the Middle Ages free of trees to support red deer populations, which they then hunted.[26]

Forestry officials raised a number of concerns that warranted careful responses. They doubted that clearing woods for grazing would provide wildlife with sufficient food. And feeding the animals in the harsh winter months as was done in other national parks hardly seemed to be a "natural" solution. In "Grzimek's animal park," some predicted, the forest would be "sacrificed to wildlife." People who wanted to view wildlife under zoo-like conditions, a few snidely suggested, could visit Munich-Hellabrunn or any other zoological garden.[27] Their frequent references to animal parks recalled Grzimek's failed initiative from the early 1960s to take pressure off the crowded Frankfurt Zoo by constructing a large reserve for African wildlife in the state-owned Taunus Forest. The Hessen government had intended to appropriate DM 12 million to build the park, which might reduce the forest service's deficit. But the SDW, hunting clubs, and wildlife protection groups blocked the project that, according to Engelhardt, had caused "so much headache" for many. Grzimek recalled the outcome differently, attributing the plan's failure to opposition primarily from industrialists who had hunting rights to the land in question.[28] Regardless of why the proposal was scrapped, it generated enough publicity to be recalled a few years later, especially by foresters who assumed the zoo director was pursuing a similar scheme in their territory.

Grzimek deserves credit for keeping the national park plan alive in its infancy and for using the media to sell the idea to the public, including skeptical locals. His vast experience campaigning to save wildlife in Africa, in particular, added to his credibility.[29] But he alienated the people whose support he needed most. In the fierce competition that developed between the two sides—each claiming superior professional experience and scientific expertise—Grzimek railed against the "very exclusive," "authoritarian," and territorial forest service. Foresters had increased the country's forested land, he conceded, but only by producing "timber plantations" that bore no resemblance to the "German Forest" praised by nineteenth century writers like Joseph von Eichendorff and Adalbert Stifter and that failed to provide favorable habitats for native plants and animals.[30] He irritated foresters by referring to them as "non-specialists" on national park issues, a jab that elicited an emotional response from one who feared the "rape" of "one of the most beautiful, original and valuable forested areas of Germany" by "professional" conservationists whose "supreme representative" was "Professor Dr. Grzimek."[31]

Grzimek also was partly responsible for a rift among conservationists that rendered the DNR, the largest umbrella organization for protecting nature, mute in the national park debate. When Grzimek, Weinzierl, and Engelhardt met with Goppel to introduce the national park idea, they did so clearly as representatives of the DNR, though they denied this to other members of the executive committee. Thus, when the private meeting with Goppel was covered in the press and the conservation ring was credited with the proposal, other members of the DNR executive committee were miffed that they had not been consulted. Within days of the 15 July meeting, Georg Fahrbach, the dominant personality at the helm of German hiking clubs, and Professor Dr. Hasselbach, a leading figure in the national hunting association, joined the opposition.[32]

But among the DNR leadership, VNP chairman Alfred Toepfer emerged as the most vocal and active opponent of a national park. Reintroducing wildlife into a park the size of the one proposed, he argued, would result in a crowded "amusement park," and allowing the forest to evolve without the managing hand of foresters would produce an unkempt woodland sure to disappoint visitors. In general, Toepfer stated with confidence, "Germans love the tended forest." Grzimek responded in a personal letter to Toepfer, accusing the VNP chairman of weakening conservation by going public with his opposition and by championing a program that promoted recreation using public funds intended for preservation.[33]

This disagreement among DNR executive committee members reflected the different priorities of nature preservers and nature users and the opposing strategies of those such as Grzimek and Weinzierl, who intended to politicize conservation and be openly confrontational, if necessary, and those like Toepfer who preferred to keep negotiations congenial and conflict free. The rift also stemmed from the constant blurring of DNR leaders' multiple professional and private responsibilities. As a popular television figure, Grzimek could do as he pleased, despite holding the office of DNR president. But he was unique in this regard. When Weinzierl publicly advocated the national park as district conservation commissioner, and when Engelhardt promoted the project as an independent expert and civil servant, Toepfer reproached them for doing so without the DNR's endorsement.[34]

Disagreements within the DNR went beyond the executive committee. If Grzimek, Weinzierl, and Engelhardt presumed that their leadership roles in the organization would give them leverage with Goppel, enabling them to claim to speak for an estimated one million people, or if they hoped that member groups would support their actions after the fact, they miscalculated. Not long after the DNR was cited in the press as the author of the national park idea, the SDW, the German Hunting League, and the Alliance for the Protection of Germany's Waters wired telegrams to Goppel, urging him to hold off on reaching a decision about the park until all DNR member organizations had debated the plan.[35] Their resentment toward Grzimek for his arrogance and undemocratic exclusion of them is understandable. Yet their reluctance to consider alternatives to the status quo must have frustrated national park proponents enough to risk criticism in pursuit of a goal that seemed morally and ecologically superior.

The National Park Plan Wins Local Government Support

After conservationists went public with the national park proposal, its fate was determined by federal, state, and local governments, all of them guided by the conflicting opinions of scientific experts, who, by the 1960s, had emerged as important players in political decision making. The federal government had a limited role in the debate until the final stage, as will be seen. Even though the issue at hand was a national park, it fell under the purview of officials responsible for conservation and regional planning, two areas over which the *Länder* had primary jurisdiction. Thus, the Bavarian government decided the outcome of the debate. Here at the state level, however, inter-ministerial conflicts produced three years of gridlock that parliamentarians only slowly overcame.

Initially, it was local authorities' organized support for a national park keeping the idea alive after such an unpromising beginning. Community leaders were desperate to find ways to revitalize the economy of the region, which had the highest rate of unemployment and lowest income per capita in the country. State planners had attempted to lure small industries to the remote area, but these had had limited success in strengthening the sagging rural economy, employing women primarily and leaving men to commute elsewhere for work, much as before. For this reason, local leaders concluded that tourism offered the "only real chance" for improving the livelihood of area residents. They were hopeful, for example, about planners' efforts to promote vacationing on farms (*Urlaub auf dem Bauernhof*), and were considering the establishment of a nature park. But rather than settle for another nature park, some local leaders in the Inner Bavarian Forest supported a national park, hoping it would give their communities a competitive advantage in the region's emerging tourist industry.[36]

In January 1967, the city council of Grafenau led the way in announcing unanimous support for the national park, describing it as an asset to local tourism. By the end of the month, all twenty-two communities in the district of Lower Bavaria had followed suit.[37] But CSU *Landtag* deputies representing the area backed local leaders cautiously. Their resolution, passed by parliament in mid May, called upon the state government only to report on the feasibility of the national park.[38] Unfortunately, only the far-right NPD supported the national park. The major parties held off for another eight months, concerned about job losses for locals.[39]

Meanwhile, local leaders organized a single purpose organization to promote the park. Established in August 1967, the League for the Promotion of the Bavarian Forest National Park Project (*Zweckverband zur Förderung des Projekts eines Nationalparks Bayerischer Wald*) included the counties (*Landkreise*) of Grafenau, Wolfstein, and Wegscheid, the towns of Grafenau and Freyung, six municipalities (*Gemeinde*) near the proposed national park, the League for Nature Protection in Bavaria, and Grzimek's Frankfurt-based Zoological Society. Led by Karl Bayer, the pragmatic mayor of Grafenau, former chief forester for Spiegelau, and critic of the state forest service, the league lobbied legislators and officials and continued to cultivate the support of locals through regular press releases, public meetings, and rallies. It also drafted a detailed plan for the national park. Among the members of the league's nine-member advisory board were Grzimek, Weinzierl, and Engelhardt, individuals self-appointed to retain some control over the project.[40] When Engelhardt tried to recruit Konrad Buchwald, now a professor at Hanover's Technical University and supporter of the nature park program, Toepfer accused him of resorting to "unpleasant" tactics.[41] A few months later, in November 1967, the DNR executive committee recused the country's largest conservation organization from the national park debate.[42] Grzimek, Weinzierl, and Engelhardt continued to work on the project, but not as DNR representatives. Largely because of this rift, Grzimek did not run for another term as president. Engelhardt replaced him, serving in the post from 1968 until 2000.

Weinzierl, Grzimek, and Grafenau mayor Karl Bayer completed the league's comprehensive plan for the national park and submitted it to the *Landtag* in December 1967. They timed the release of the proposal to coincide with the publication of results from a public opinion poll, which was conducted by the Munich-based Infratest at the league's request. Although few respondents could describe a national park accurately—an indication of the lack of clarity in the debate thus far and of Germany's inexperience with national parks—the poll results allowed the league to assert that nine out of ten Germans supported its vision in principle.[43]

Among the most noteworthy changes to the alliance's proposal from when it was first presented to Goppel over a year before were increases in the size of the park from 5,000 to 9,000 hectares and in the estimated cost for establishing and operating it, now set at DM 6.5 million, with an annual maintenance cost of DM 800,000. The league insisted that forestry should be restricted to measures essential for maintaining the park, yet recommended invasive changes to accommodate wildlife. The plan repeated Grzimek's suggestion to clear patches of forest to create at least 100 hectares of meadow for animal grazing. To reduce damage to new forest growth by red deer, the proposal favored fencing off some sections that were particularly vulnerable and providing an alternative source of food by planting 800 hectares with softwoods. To control the deer population, the league did not rule out regulated hunting. While red and roe deer would be free to roam about, moose, buffalo, boar, chamois, and beaver would be held in five large pens of 100 to 200 hectares each. On the national park designation, the league refused to negotiate.[44] But by remaining committed to the introduction of animals, and to the intrusive management that this part of their proposal would require, advocates played into the hands of those who advocated another nature park as a more appropriate alternative.

Searching for Common Ground: The Experts Weigh In

Between 1967 and 1968, efforts were underway on several fronts to strengthen arguments for and against the national park. Proponents needed to provide evidence of cooperation on the other side of the Iron Curtain from neighboring Czechoslovakia, which was in the midst of liberalizing political reforms though it did not have formal relations with West Germany because of the Hallstein Doctrine. From the outset, Grzimek had assured Goppel that Czechoslovakia would administer the area along the border with West Germany as if it were a national park, though he conceded a one way flow of visitors from the Federal Republic to Czechoslovakia. Grzimek reported that the electric fences, barbed wire, and land mines began some distance away from the actual border. The area that would neighbor the national park was a 1,000-hectacre "no-man's-land" with moors and open space where park animals could find refuge.[45] Based on two visits to Czechoslovakia in May and August 1967, Weinzierl reported that the regime intended to create a national park in the core of the recently established Šumava Forest landscape reserve, across the border from Lusen (a plan realized only in 1991). But it is difficult to know how the regime of Antonín Novotny reacted to a national park in West Germany because potentially relevant files in the central government ministry of culture have yet to be cataloged.[46]

To build a case against the introduction of wildlife, forestry officials consulted several specialists who concluded that even a 9,000 hectare park would be too small to support large animal populations. Under natural conditions, internationally known Austrian wildlife biologist Dr. Peter Krott explained, lynx needed a minimum of 20,000 hectares to roam about. Other experts warned that lynx, owls, and other animals of prey would not have adequate food in winter because the species they hunted would retreat to lower elevations.[47]

Of all the studies and opinions in government hands by the beginning of 1968, the one that proved to be the most influential was prepared by Wolfgang Haber, landscape ecologist and director of the Institute for Landscape Care at the Technical University of Munich-Weihenstephan at the request of the German Council for Land Cultivation (DRL). It was logical that the DRL would weigh in on this land use planning issue of regional and national significance, but the council's involvement was spurred on by two of its members, Alfred Toepfer, who opposed the national park, and Bavarian *Landtag* President Rudolf Hanauer (CSU), who favored it, and possibly at the request of Bavaria's agriculture minister, Alois Hundhammer.[48] Haber's non-binding, forty-two page report, completed late in 1967, attests to the influence that ecologists had come to have as "neutral" experts in political decision making. Haber's study was a welcome addition to the many opinions vying for the attention of officials and parliamentarians because of its breadth, its reasoned arguments, and its presentation of a compromise solution that made concessions to all parties involved.

Although Haber remained remarkably objective, he did scold national park advocates for using "demagogic half truths and one-sided arguments" in promoting their goal. He criticized Grzimek specifically for antagonizing the forest service, the very people who had done so much to shape the landscape and whose support would be needed to implement any land use plan for the area.[49] Haber applauded the idea of promoting tourism in an economically poor region while also setting aside an area where nature received fuller protection than in most of the country's nature and landscape reserves.[50] But "[a]s soon as a nature reserve is made accessible for tourism . . . ," he cautioned, "a fully protected reserve is neither practicable nor sensible." In contrast to those who insisted that the reintroduction of animals would set the area apart from nature parks and make it worthy of being called a national park, Haber believed that "the largest continuous German forested area" could be elevated to that status with little difficulty and without the introduction of animals. In his opinion, the constant upkeep necessitated by Grzimek's proposal made it more like a nature park than a national park.[51]

Haber concluded that national park proponents had not taken the forest vegetation and climate adequately into account, despite their claims to the contrary. The highly acidic, sandy, and loamy soil of large parts of the forest could support only a limited diversity of plant and animal species. On a recent tour of the Šumava landscape reserve (one arranged by Bavarian foresters), Haber had seen the damage that red deer could cause, trampling young seedlings and making trees less resistant to wind storms and snow by eating their bark. He thus recommended temporarily fencing off new-growth forest, a measure also found in the league's proposal. Haber concurred with wildlife experts who believed that animals would struggle under the severe conditions that prevailed between Lusen and Mauth. To provide wildlife with more feeding places in winter, Haber recommended doubling the size of the park, extending the boundaries farther north and west, and building a dozen feeding stations in the south for the wildlife that would roam about freely.[52] These measures were less intrusive than the league's recommendation to plant non-native softwoods and create meadows requiring constant tending.

Haber doubted that a national park would have a noticeable impact on the region's economy. He cautioned that people might be disappointed when they discovered that their expectations for a national park—tame bears along the road as in Yellowstone, or large herds of animals as on the open steppes of Africa—could not be realized in the Bavarian Forest. As park proponents acknowledged, the vegetation in the Bavarian Forest could not support large numbers of wildlife and the dense forest would hide them from view. To fulfill potentially conflicting goals—meeting visitors' expectations to see wildlife, bringing people in closer contact with animals, and steering large numbers of people through nature with minimum impact—Haber recommended keeping larger animals in five natural-looking enclosed areas near the park entrance in the south. By making these enclosures between six and fifteen hectares, much smaller than those proposed by the league, they would be large enough so that animals noticed tourists little, but small enough so that visitors could see them. The "true nature friend," Haber wrote, could venture away from the crowds, deeper into the forest.[53]

Despite a number of reservations about the proposal as it stood, Haber recommended several compromises to help realize the national park, some of which the league also advocated. One already mentioned called for confining larger animals in enclosed areas to not obstruct "the essential tending of the forest." Other animals such as deer and chamois would live throughout the park, but to control their populations and ensure that they did not exceed a combined total of 230 head, Haber did not rule out hunting.[54] Neither did he oppose some timber production to generate revenue to help pay for the cost of maintaining the park and to make an entrance fee unnecessary, an arrangement used successfully in De Hoge Veluwe National Park in the Netherlands [a questionable model because this park did not implement stringent preservation]. Haber regretted the plan's emphasis on reintroducing wildlife, but did not call for abandoning this part of the plan.[55] Even though he considered the woodland important enough in its own right to be preserved, possibly as a national park, he agreed with proponents and opponents alike that the public was more interested in seeing rare animals than in exploring dense forest.

Even though Haber did not discourage the designation "national park" explicitly in this study,[56] the DRL did, disappointing the league and giving opponents a slight edge.[57] Consistent with its procedures, the DRL presented its views in late January and early February to the Bavarian *Landtag* and Senate and to Minister-President Goppel. After studying Haber's report, the DRL concluded that the climate, soil, and vegetation of the Bavarian Forest could not support the reintroduction of wildlife. (One wonders how the DRL would have responded had national park promoters dropped this part of their plan.) As an alternative to a national park, the DRL recommended the creation of a European nature park in the area, one that would encompass an existing nature park to the north and eventually, the landscape reserve in Czechoslovakia. A more suitable location for a national park, the DRL proposed, would be the Bavarian Alps, an idea that had been around for decades and one that Toepfer supported. Within two years, Toepfer joined with Engelhardt and Weinzierl to lobby for the creation of Berchtesgaden National Park, a plan realized in 1978.[58]

Ending Government Paralysis and Reaching a Compromise

By January 1968, government officials and political leaders possessed more than enough material to assess the feasibility of a national park. But another year and a half passed before the matter was resolved, a delay that reflected the paralysis of the government and legislators' indecisiveness. The state ministries remained divided over the issue, but Goppel was reluctant to use the cabinet council to force through a decision on an issue that had begun to win the support of deputies in the *Landtag,* irrespective of party. Until the beginning of 1968, however, neither the governing CSU faction nor the opposition SPD pursued the question aggressively, waiting first for the government's response to their demand in May 1967 for a feasibility study. Only in mid January 1968, after lengthy debate within the party and persuasive arguments by representatives from Lower Bavaria, did the CSU force the administration's hand, introducing a resolution that called on the government to develop plans to establish a national park and to secure federal financial support. The SPD followed suit with a resolution that same day.[59]

This tactical move by the *Landtag* prompted forestry officials in the Ministry of Agriculture to push through the government impasse. In late January 1968, Agriculture Minister Hundhammer presented parliamentarians with the forestry division's negative evaluation of the league's plan. The forestry division's well-known views did not represent the government's official position (it still did not have one), but they acquired added weight with the timely arrival of the DRL's negative recommendations. National park proponents needed a powerful advocate in the state government, but the most logical choice—the interior ministry as the supreme conservation office—had produced nothing to counter the nay-sayers.[60]

Ultimately, it was developments at the federal level that helped break through the state government logjam. In late June, the Federal Ministry of Agriculture (BML) announced its intentions to fund efforts by the *Länder* to develop model recreation centers in areas economically weakened by the decline in agriculture. The BML's initiative was prompted by reforms within the European Economic Community (EEC). In 1968, the EEC's commissioner for agriculture, Sicco Mansholt of the Netherlands, introduced a controversial plan to address Western Europe's surpluses in agricultural production that had resulted from the Common Agricultural Policy (CAP), introduced in 1962. As intended, CAP had successfully protected European farmers from price fluctuations on the world market and had made their production more efficient with larger farms and up-to-date technology. But a negative consequence of the plan was overproduction. To address the surplus, the Mansholt Plan sought to accelerate a trend already underway, creating larger, more efficient farms while closing down smaller, less productive ones. Experts estimated, however, that 5 million European farmers would be removed from the agricultural sector. Radical in its consequences, the plan was eventually scaled back.[61]

When the Mansholt Plan was announced, however, the West German government responded by offering federal aid to state governments for developing regional plans that would integrate people squeezed out of farming into other sectors of the economy. Enticed by the prospect of federal aid, some Bavarian officials argued that a regional plan featuring a national park would be a novel and winning proposition. In late August, officials representing several ministries agreed that their proposal for a recreation area would focus on the Inner Bavarian Forest. But they could not move forward without a consensus on the national park question.[62]

The proposed compromise—drafted in consultation with local and district governments and under severe time constraints—would have been a national park in name only, one with the same boundaries as the Inner Bavarian Forest Landscape Reserve established a year earlier and sharing its weak provisions for protecting nature. When the forestry division understandably objected to the national park designation, the interior ministry urged Goppel to end the gridlock in a meeting of the cabinet council. Forestry officials cried foul, accusing the interior ministry of trying to resolve the issue administratively and present it as a done deal to parliament after its summer recess.[63] This indeed was the strategy in order to comply with the federal agriculture ministry's timetable, but it stirred up deputies, especially those in the opposition SPD who warned that such a move would be viewed as "an unfriendly act against the *Landtag.*"[64]

Federal officials in Bonn made it clear that a national park would receive no federal funds through the agriculture policy.[65] Federal Minister of Agriculture Hermann Höcherl, a Bavarian from the area near the proposed national park, wanted to help his homeland with federal aid. But he considered a national park inappropriate because it would restrict forestry and elevate preservation above recreation, a view influenced by Herbert Offner, the BML's conservation officer and champion of nature parks.[66] In a display of particularism for which Bavarians are well known, the state parliament refused to bow to pressure from Bonn. At a joint meeting of the committees on agriculture and borderland issues in January 1969, deputies debated whether or not to "roll over" the state leadership. An alarmed Höcherl in Bonn ordered Minister-President Goppel to submit Bavaria's model plan immediately so that it would not compromised by a "hasty declaration of a national park in the Bavarian Forest."[67]

But state parliamentarians and locals were resolute. When the *Landtag* committee on agriculture convened on 30 January 1969, a crowd of people, most of them from the Bavarian Forest, filled the conference room beyond capacity, forcing the meeting to be relocated. The committee unanimously endorsed the plan to establish a national park in the area around Rachel and Lusen, based on Haber's study.[68] When the Budget and Finance Committee took up the issue in May, several hundred spectators, again bussed to Munich from the Bavarian Forest, were at the meeting. More critical was the presence of Hans Eisenmann (CSU), former chairman of the finance committee and the new agriculture minister who had replaced Hundhammer in March.

More than any other official, Eisenmann helped to make the national park a reality. Only weeks earlier he had asserted Bavaria's autonomy from Bonn when he publicly announced that a national park was not dependent on federal funding (then, however, it would be called the *Bavarian* National Park). He also overcame foresters' opposition by insisting that the park administration should be placed directly under the Ministry of Agriculture, but not within the forestry division, a compromise that ensured a measure of autonomy for the park administration while encouraging its cooperation with forestry officials. Eisenmann also secured promises of financial support from the BML toward the DM 1.5 million now estimated for annual maintenance of the park. His adroit handling of this divisive issue reflected his genuine support for the project, but also the pressure he was under to prove his environmental credentials. In negotiations for a new environment ministry to be established during European Conservation Year, Goppel had promised the new minister, Max Streibl, responsibility over state-owned forests. Eisenmann worked quickly on the national park to not lose control over it or state forests.[69]

On 11 June 1969, in a lively exchange in the *Landtag*, parliamentarians unanimously approved a resolution to use the Haber study to transform forested land between Rachel and Lusen and south to Mauth into West Germany's first national park. They adopted Haber's report because of its thoroughness and broad scope (other reports focused only on certain aspects of the plan, such as suitable wildlife) and its compromise proposal that allowed all parties involved to gain at least something. Noteworthy for its absence in the resolution was the word "*Naturschutz*," an omission that underscored parliamentarians' primary concern to foster economic development through tourism.[70] To get the project underway, deputies appropriated DM 1.5 million in start-up money. But it took over a decade and a half, and well over DM 50 million (with roughly 90 percent coming from Bavaria and 10 percent from the federal government), to shape this landscape into a national park conforming to international standards. On 22 July, the Ministry of Agriculture issued an ordinance creating a national park office in Spiegelau (in 1976 it was moved to its current site in Grafenau) and forming a broadly inclusive advisory board that brought together groups and individuals who had been on both sides of the debate, including Weinzierl and Engelhardt, forestry officials, experts such as Haber, local authorities, and tourist associations. Two young foresters were appointed director and deputy director of the park, Dr. Hans Bibelriether and Dr. Georg Sperber, respectively. Only thirty-six when he took the post, Bibelriether recalls that he got the job because few other foresters wanted it. The other leading candidate was Sperber, Bibelriether's friend since their university years in Munich. Bibelriether remained the director until his retirement in 1997.[71]

Designing the National Park

West Germany's first national park officially opened on 7 October 1970, hailed as the "crowing" event of European Conservation Year. But much had been done weeks and months earlier to ready the area for public consumption. The painstaking work of transforming the area into a national park began in 1969, with landscape ecologists preparing detailed land use plans and scientists assessing the "biological potential" of the area. In keeping with the Haber report, and borrowing from the structure of nature parks, planners divided the national park into three zones which were the physical manifestations of the multiple purposes this landscape was expected to fulfill and of the variety of nature experiences tourists could enjoy. The first zone, designed to educate the public and absorb the heaviest impact of visitors, included the large enclosed animal reserves, nature trails, youth hostels, and a visitors' center (completed in 1982). The second and largest zone was designed for more solitary relaxation and hiking. Here intensive forestry had resulted in a landscape of woodlands broken up by open vistas, enabling hikers to take in the landscape as scenery. In the third zone, the core of the park, fragile ecosystems and very old and relatively untouched spruce forests in the highest elevations in the northern most part of the park were stringently protected, accessible only along well-marked paths for researchers and hikers wanting a more "authentic" nature experience.[72]

While planners determined the strict zoning of the park, other specialists collected data on climate, bodies of water, and seasonal growth of vegetation, and began the involved process of inventorying flora and fauna. Researchers analyzed the vegetation and soils to provide an ecological map of the region and to reconstruct the "original" distribution of trees, vegetation, and the wildlife it supported. Although the kinds of trees growing in the park area had changed little over the centuries, the structure of the stands had (i.e., the distribution of age and height). Other specialists bored into the ground every fifty meters, studying the layers of soil they collected with each drive into the earth to find clues for interpreting the ecological history of the park. When the soil inventory had been completed, 48,000 pits had been dug—each 1.2 meters deep, two meters long and a meter wide—to use as sites for reconstructing the natural and human forces that shaped the forest's evolution.[73] This research was essential for developing a long range plan for managing the park and for returning the entire landscape to a healthier forest, one that presumably resembled its condition before being altered by human hands. Whether or not this state is "more natural" continues to inspire debate.

To provide favorable conditions for the animals that had been approved for reintroduction, dams were constructed to create wetlands, straightened streams were returned to a less linear course, and forests stocked primarily for timber production were converted into meadows for grazing. In the middle and core zones of the park, new hiking trails and paths were laid, and existing ones redirected to minimize visitors' impact on protected biotopes.[74] A year before the park opened, the League for Nature Protection in Bavaria under Weinzierl's leadership, together with the DNR, used the media, including television, to attract a diverse group of sponsors of wildlife. The cost of animals to be reintroduced reflected their size and rarity, ranging from DM 6,000 for moose to DM 300 for an owl. The city of Biberach (appropriately) sponsored a beaver (*der Biber*), as did the cabaret star, Hanne Wieder. Siemens signed on to sponsor a chamois, while a 13-year-old boy used his DM 600 savings to sponsor two owls. The recently retired Minister of Agriculture, Alois Hundhammer, an opponent of the national park, had a change of heart: he sponsored a wild boar. Over the next several months, the first enclosed areas in the southern part of the park were readied for buffalo, elk, and lynx. Two pair of lynx came from Finland and the Tatra Mountains, while four buffalo (one bull and three cows) were purchased from Sweden by the League for Nature Protection for DM 36,000.[75]

A week before the park opened, an estimated 2,000 people appeared at the enclosed reserves to catch a glimpse of the new inhabitants. While animals explored their new surroundings, curious onlookers trampled newly planted vegetation and let their children climb around the reserves, to the dismay of park employees. Though Bibelriether emphasized that the centerpiece of the national park was not the carefully planned reserves for animals but the forest itself, for the majority of park visitors—between 50 and 60 percent of the park's one million visitors recorded in 1973—the enclosed animal reserves were the main attraction. The area where wildlife are currently enclosed is laid out in a seven-kilometer circular route encompassing 200 hectares. Although this part of the national park is primarily a concession to tourism, it serves educational goals long associated with preservation, informing the public about animals and their habitats. The area is home to over thirty species of animals, some of which have become rare or locally extinct, including buffalo, lynx, bear, wolf, otter, wild boar, badger, eagles, and owls.[76]

Already in the park's early years, officials could boast of preservation efforts that not only protected but also increased the populations of endangered species, such as wildcats, hazel hen, and certain owl species. Buffalo reproduced in the enclosed reserves so successfully that some had to be given away. Not long after the park opened, lynx again roamed freely in the park, though some remained in pens.[77] Only once did animals break out of their enclosures. When eight wolves escaped in 1976, conservation officials initially decided to let them roam freely. The following spring, however, a young boy was bitten by a wolf while trying to play with it, giving the park publicity it did not need (the sensationalist *Bild Zeitung* reported that a "Wolf had ripped apart a child (*zerfleischt*)"). Officials then ordered the eight wolves hunted down. Eleven were found; all were shot dead.[78]

The park also had to grapple with damage to six square kilometers of forest caused by an unusually large population of red deer, estimated at 500 head in 1970. Not wanting bad press, the state government barred the weak park administration and concerned foresters from publicizing the problem. To circumvent the censure, park officials turned to Grzimek and the journalist Horst Stern who exposed the controversy in a prime time television program on Christmas Eve in 1971. Stern also spotlighted the longstanding, mutually beneficial alliance between some foresters and hunters who ignored ecological harm to forests caused by overly large deer populations in order to guard what was for them an almost mystical experience of hunting trophy animals. Eisenmann defended park officials who were criticized for defying orders and backed their plan to reduce the deer population. By permitting hunting temporarily and scaling back feedings, they brought down the number of red deer to 150 in 1976.[79]

The large deer population in this transition period was but one of many controversial issues that drew fire from Grzimek and Weinzierl, who wanted the country's only national park to conform to new guidelines adopted by the IUCN in 1969 and agreed to by West Germany.[80] They complained that the national park urgently needed a detailed ordinance for protecting nature. Only the areas around Lusen and Rachel had the legal status of nature reserves (*Naturschutzgebiete*).[81] Because of the administration's clear goals for protecting nature, however, the national park was recognized by the IUCN in 1972.

This approval came even though timber production in the park continued at an estimated 55,000 fest meters annually throughout the 1970s. Eisenmann defended the policy, asserting that it helped to fulfill IUCN guidelines recommending immediate measures to protect a park's unique features. "Our national park is a model for protecting nature through shaping it (*gestaltender Naturschutz*)," he stated, and "goes well beyond the possibilities of traditional preservation." But Eisenmann was more worried that ending timber production would hurt locals employed in the industry, generating resentment against the park. In general, timber was cut from young stands, sparing areas that contained old growth. By 1984, production was scaled back to 28,000 fest meters per year and ceased altogether in the 1990s. Today, only a 500 meter band around the perimeter is carefully managed.

While timber production decreased, the park and the area within it under stringent protection increased. Within a few years of the park's opening, the original 9,000 hectare area was expanded to 13,000 hectares. Another expansion in 1997, opposed by locals, nearly doubled the size to 24,250 hectares and enabled the national park to form a unity with the Czech Republic's Šumava National Park. In this period, the area stringently protected increased from 700 hectares [the pre-existing nature preserves around Rachel and Lusen] to around 8,000 hectares in early 1990. These areas, designated "reserve zones" (*Reservatzonen*), are more stringently protected than nature reserves and are accessible to researchers and tourists.[82]

The establishment of the national park helped introduce alternative ways of understanding and interacting with nature. According to Bavaria's new conservation law of 1973, a "national park" was a special category for protecting nature, one that sought to balance recreation, preservation, and research, and helped correct the assumption that stringent preservation meant protecting nature from people. That same law stated that a national park "serves no specific economic use," providing the legal means to manage the park according to international criteria that barred traditional economic uses. When the park first opened, the administration emphasized actively changing and managing nature, reflecting the technocratic style that prevailed among professional conservationists, as well as the population's preference for well-kempt forests, something Toepfer understood. In the 1980s, Bibelriether instituted a less interventionist policy. Influenced by the German Catholic Bishops' declaration of 1980, which decreed that plants and animals had a right to life that existed independently of human uses, Bibelriether responded by trying to make the national park one of the few places in the country where nature had that right and could operate according to its own dynamic. People benefited as well, he believed, by being able to observe natural processes at work (a definition that implied humans were outside of "natural processes").[83]

This policy was seriously tested in August 1983, when a storm with hurricane force winds ripped through the Bavarian Forest, pounding down trees in an area covering 90 hectares. While foresters and many locals expected the park management to salvage timber from the "catastrophe," Bibelriether argued that nature knew no "catastrophes." He persuaded officials to leave 23,000 cubic meters of timber to rot on the forest floor in the core of the park. According to many locals, the decaying trees were a waste of an estimated DM 3 million. In the eyes of others, they were nutrients essential for the new growth of plants and animals. When the population of bark beetle increased over the next few seasons in areas hit by the storm, the park administration did not fight the insect in the core of the park, explaining that its presence was part of a natural process. In near natural or old-growth forests, Bibelriether instructed, these insects would not spread to healthy forests and rarely would kill large numbers of trees. Germans' preference for well-tended "green" forests, he contended, implied an ignorance of how nature worked. But many of the locals, whose families had lived in the area for generations, considered the decision morally wrong. They did not like the ideal of "wild" nature imposed upon them by the park administration in *their Heimat*. (For this same reason, locals opposed the park's expansion in 1997.) Offering a different interpretation of the morally correct course, Bibelriether noted that 98 percent of the country's forested land was used for timber production. At least in a few areas, the forest could be left alone to evolve on its own. The national park—a space open to and belonging to all visitors (on terms established by the administration)—was an appropriate place to "let nature be nature," protecting and respecting it "for its own sake."[84]

This approach to protecting nature continues to stir up controversy. After a decade of hotter, drier weather, the bark beetle population increased in the late 1990s, gnawing away at weakened old-growth spruce forests, particularly between Rachel and Lusen. Where locals and many tourists saw ugly infested brown forest, park officials saw nature's constant evolution: the beetle worked to renew the forests and the human influenced warmer climate enabled beech trees to grow at higher elevations. Park officials did not combat the beetle along the Czech border, though their Czech counterparts did, felling infected trees and replanting, but producing less resilient uniform stands as a result.[85]

The establishment of the Bavarian Forest National Park succeeded after a long process of consensus building, an approach to politics typical in West Germany. The initial proponents of the park, a new elite group of conservationists, were concerned primarily with protecting a presumably more authentic nature experience than was possible in the country's many nature parks. They did as the leaders of private conservation groups had done in the past, turning to public officials with their idea but without adequately considering the views of those they claimed to represent. Unlike in the past, however, these leaders did not hesitate to politicize their cause, a strategy that divided the DNR and revealed weaknesses that had limited the effectiveness of the organization since its founding. After going public with their idea, these advocates garnered the support of local authorities, pooling their experience and expertise to develop a plan that would protect nature and the economy in the region and preserve a specific image of natural beauty in the nation. But the proposal was blocked by forestry officials whose near exclusive influence over the area would be most directly affected by the national park. To sort through conflicting arguments in the debate, all sides sought expert opinions, including that of the presumably neutral DRL. Interministerial conflicts prolonged deliberations until pressure from the *Landtag,* foresters, and in this particular case, also the federal government, spurred the state government into action. The compromise that resulted was evident in the park's administration and its broadly representative advisory council.

The national park's administration bears the stamp of the Federal Republic's decentralized approach to conservation. In a country where the *Länder* have primary jurisdiction over *Naturschutz,* even national parks are administered by state governments. Because the Bavarian Forest is roughly 95 percent forested land owned by the state, its administration was under the state Ministry of Agriculture until 2003, when it was placed under the state Ministry for the Environment (established as the nation's first in 1970). Despite the controversy that surrounded its creation, the Bavarian Forest National Park anchored the national park idea in public consciousness and provided useful lessons for other *Länder* in establishing fourteen additional national parks between 1978 and 2004.[86]

Partly because the states administered conservation—not the federal government—the effort to establish the Bavarian Forest National Park was not an overtly nationalistic undertaking, reminders aside that West Germany lacked what many other nations had. The absence of a national park reflected the Cold War context (which received surprisingly little attention in the debate) and Germans' belief that they lacked adequate space to stringently protect large areas where economic use was restricted. It also revealed the continued influence of foresters and hunters in decisions about land use in some of the country's more remote areas. The Bavarian Forest was singled out for protection, not because it was seen as hallowed ground symbolizing a mythical national character—or a uniquely Bavarian one—or because it had grassroots support from "the people" (documents record the vocal support of local CSU leaders, but offer fewer clues about the opinions of ordinary folk). Rather, the Bavarian Forest became the site of West Germany's first national park because it was a unique, sparsely populated landscape situated in a region in economic trouble. Bavarian officials and politicians endorsed the national park plan because it offered a solution to a regional economic problem. Indeed, in the 1980s, tourism in the area generated over DM 25 million annually, much of it from the national park that attracted over one million visitors each year.[87]

Initially, the intersection of conservation and regional planning in creating the national park subordinated preservation to economic development. Within a generation, however, the national park became a place where preservation acquired almost the same status as tourism and recreation. This was made possible by the development of a new aesthetic of nature that departed from the clean, orderly model prevailing during the Miracle Years. At the beginning of the national park debate, both proponents and opponents shared a preference for nature that was shaped and organized through human intervention. Foresters who opposed the national park believed that constant management was required to maintain a healthy mixed forest that was economically productive and accessible to visitors. Promoters of another nature park envisioned a manicured forest the focal point of tourists' nature experience. Intervening in nature's transformation also was central to Grzimek's original plan to recreate a medieval German forest that would cater to public fascination with wildlife, though under conditions resembling a zoo.

The park's current strategy of "letting nature be nature" is also a "cultural task," Bibelriether admits, but one that requires humans to intervene in nature's processes as little as possible. This particular approach to preservation is informed by an understanding of nature as disorderly and unpredictable. It is a strategy that reflects the belief held by some like Bibelriether that cultures "have the duty to preserve the natural inheritance of our land . . . not only in view of what is beautiful and pleases us, but also with respect to that which is not beautiful and does not please us."[88] Such convictions indicate the diminishing influence of the view that a people's character is shaped by nature. In its place is the belief that people shape nature by the images they have of it and by the choices they make about its treatment. Yet there persists the idea that civilization needs and is indeed influenced by the existence of "natural" nature—that part of the world which is at once a reflection of culture and yet beyond human control.

Notes

1. Bayerisches Staatsministerium für Ernährung, Landwirtschaft und Forsten (hereafter BStL), ed., *Nationalpark Bayerischer Wald,* 2d ed. (Munich: Bayerisches Staatsministerium für Ernährung, Landwirtschaft und Forsten, 1988), 11–33.
2. BStL, *Nationalpark Bayerischer Wald,* 34–40; Reinhard Strobl, "Die Geschichte des Waldes und seiner Besiedlung," in *Eine Landschaft wird Nationalpark,* ed. BStL, Schriftenreihe des

Bayerischen Staatsministeriums für Ernährung, Landwirtschaft und Forsten, vol. 11 (Grafenau: Morsak, 1983), 8–31.

3. Dr. Hermann von Unold (*Regierungsforstdirektor,* Regensburg), "Ein Nationalpark im Bayerischen Wald?" *Allgemeine Forstzeitschrift,* no. 36 (1967), in Bayerisches Hauptstaatsarchiv (BHStA), Munich, Staatskanzlei (StK)/17031 (hereafter BHStA StK/17031); and Konrad Klotz (*Oberregierungsforstrat,* Zwiesel, Niederbayern) to Weinzierl, 3 January 1967, DNR Archive, "NPBW, 1966–67."

4. Kluczka, "Raumordnung," in Schöller, Puls, and Buchholz, *Spatial Development,* 11–17; Thomas Schlemmer, Stefan Grüner, and Jaromir Balcar, "'Entwicklungshilfe im eigenen Lande'—Landesplanung in Bayern nach 1945," in Frese, Paulus, and Teppe, *Demokratisierung,* 379–450.

5. See esp. Roderick P. Neumann, *Imposing Wilderness. Struggles over Livelihood and Nature Preservation in Africa* (Berkeley: University of California Press, 1998); White, "From Wilderness to Hybrid Landscapes," 557–64; and Denis Cosgrove, "Landscape and Landschaft," *Bulletin of the German Historical Institute,* no. 35 (Fall 2004): 57–71.

6. White, "From Wilderness to Hybrid Landscapes," 557–64; Franz Handlos, "Grzimek: letzte Möglichkeit für Nationalpark," *Münchner Merkur,* 28 July 1966, 8, clipping in BHStA StK/17030.

7. Mark David Spence, *Dispossessing the Wilderness. Indian Removal and the Making of the National Parks* (New York: Oxford University Press, 1999); Richard W. Sellars, *Preserving Nature in the National Parks: A History* (New Haven: Yale University Press, 1997).

8. Kraus, *Zerstörung der Natur,* 94–96.

9. Wolschke-Bulmahn, "All of Germany a Garden?" in Mauch, *Nature in German History,* 74–92; Blackbourn, *Conquest,* chap. 5; Schoenichen, "Ödlandaufforstung?—Jawohl! aber mit Bedacht," *Naturschutz* 15, no. 4 (1934): 78–82.

10. Michael Haug, "Entstehungsgeschichte des Nationalparks Bayerischer Wald und die Entwicklung seit 1969," in BStL, *Eine Landschaft wird Nationalpark,* 38; Neumann, *Imposing Wilderness,* chap. 1; McCormick, *Reclaiming Paradise,* 17–24.

11. Heinrich Eberts [former official in the Reich Ministry of Agriculture] to Egon Selchow, 16 July 1958, VDN Archiv, binder entitled "Schriftwechsel 1958/59 A-G"; Georg Sperber, "Entstehungsgeschichte eines ersten deutschen Nationalparks im Bayerischen Wald," in Stiftung Naturschutzgeschichte, *Natur im Sinn,* 65–70; Uekötter, *Green and the Brown,* 6, 72–73, 99–109.

12. On Hans Klose's suggestions see "Zur Frage der Nationalparke in der Bundesrepublik," *Verhandlungen* (1954): 27–32. On Hans Krieg's efforts see Richard Scheid (Alpenverein) to Herbert Ecke, 26 March 1952; and "Keine Wachtposten für die bayerischen Berge aber einen Naturschutzpark zwischen Ettal und dem Ammergebirge," clipping from unidentified newspaper, n.d. [March 1952?], both in BAK B 245/254. On foresters' resistance see Wolfgang Engelhardt to Alfred Toepfer, 10 April 1967 and 20 July 1967, both in DNR Archive, "NPBW, 1966–67"; Hubert Weinzierl, *Die Krönung des Naturschutzgedankens: Deutschlands Nationalpark im Bayerischen Wald soll Wirklichkeit werden* (Grafenau: Morsak, 1983), 42–43.

13. See the UN list of protected areas available at http://www.unep-wcmc.org.

14. Chaney, "Divided Nation," in Lekan and Zeller, *Germany's Nature,* 228; Volker Schurig, "Politischer Naturschutz: Warum wurde in der DDR kein Nationalpark gegründet?" *N & L* 66, no. 7/8 (1991): 363–71; Kurt Wiedemann, "Landschaftsschutz für die Sächsische Schweiz," *Natur & Heimat,* no. 5 (1958): 152–55.

15. Haug, "Entstehungsgeschichte," 40–41.

16. On developments in the 1930s and 1940s see BAK B 245/241; Haug, "Entstehungsgeschichte," 37–39; Sperber, "Entstehungsgeschichte," 65–70.

17. Haug, "Entstehungsgeschichte," 40–41; "Übersicht der bestehenden Naturschutzgebiete im Inneren Bayerischen Wald im Jahr 1967" (doc. 1.2), in BStL, *Eine Landschaft wird Nationalpark,* 83.

18. Haug, "Entstehungsgeschichte," 40. On opposition to a landscape reserve see BHStA, Ministry of Economics and Transportation (MWi)/22062 (hereafter BHStA MWi/22062).

19. Hubert Weinzierl, "Der Bayerische Wald—Erholungsgebiet der Zukunft!" *Blätter für Naturschutz,* no. 4 (1965): 81–83; Weinzierl, *Krönung,* 43.

20. Bernhard Grzimek to Minister-President Alfons Goppel, "Denkschrift des Deutschen Naturschutzringes über die Errichtung eines Bayerischen Nationalparks," 15 July 1966, BHStA StK/17030.

21. *Ministerialdirektor* Dr. Bayer [Director, State Chancellery] to Bavarian ministries of the interior, agriculture, and economics, 19 July 1966, BHStA StK/17030. For cost estimates see *Regierungsdirektor* Dr. Landseder, "Vormerkung über ein Gespräch in der Bayerischen Staatskanzlei. Betreff: Errichtung eines Bayer. Nationalparks im Bayerischen Wald," 19 July 1966, BHStA StK/17030.

22. Dr. Mayer, Bavarian Ministry of the Interior to Bavarian Chancellery, 16 September 1966; Dr. Mayer, State Planning Agency, Bavarian Ministry of Economics to Bavarian Chancellery, 12 October 1966; Dr. Pöhner, *Staatsminister,* Bavarian Ministry of Finance to Bavarian Chancellery, 14 October 1966, all in BHStA StK/17030; Franz Sackmann, "Naturpark ohne Nationalpark," *Bayerische Staatszeitung,* 4 April 1969, clipping in former SDW Archiv, photocopy in author's possession. Note: When the Bavarian chapter of SDW turned over its records to the state archive in the 1990s, some newspaper clippings previously available to researchers in the chapter archive were discarded. Notes will reference those clippings no longer available in the state archives as "photocopy in author's possession."

23. Alois Hundhammer (1900–1974), an historian and economist, served as state minister of culture (1946–1950) and *Landtag* president (1951–1954).

24. Weinzierl, *Krönung,* 50; Alois Hundhammer, "Freigehege und Ansiedlung von Industriebetrieben," *Münchner Merkur,* 21 May 1968, 21; Erich Seydel, "Ist der Nationalpark schon abgeschrieben?" *Bayerische Staatszeitung,* 15 March 1968, 3, photocopy in author's possession. On lobbying Hundhammer see Bernhard Grzimek, *Auf den Mensch gekommen. Erfahrungen mit Leuten* (Munich: Bertelsmann, 1974), 457–58.

25. Dr. Max Woelfle, *Ministerialdirektor, Forstabteilung,* Bavarian Ministry of Agriculture to Bavarian Chancellery, 31 August 1966, BHStA StK/17030; Unold, "Ein Nationalpark im Bayerischen Wald?"; Klotz, "Soll der Bayerische Wald ein Nationalpark werden? *Holz-Zentralblatt* 93, no. 19 (13 February 1967): 297–98, both available in BHStA StK/17031; Ursula Peters, "Zwischen Staatsforst und Nationalpark," *Süddeutsche Zeitung,* 11 January 1967, 17.

26. Bernhard Grzimek to Alfons Goppel, 15 July 1966 and 12 September 1966, both in BHStA StK/17030.

27. Woelfle to Bavarian Chancellery, 31 August 1966, 8, BHStA StK/17030.

28. On the failed Taunus animal park see Vitus Dröscher, "Letzte Chance für Elche: Gefahr für Nationalparkplan im Bayerischen Wald," *Zeit,* 7 October 1966, clipping in BHStA StK/17030; Wolfgang Engelhardt to Alfred Toepfer, 22 July 1966, DNR Archive, "NPBW, 1966–67." Compare SDW, national chapter to Bernhard Grzimek, 4 August 1965, BAK B 116/10843 with Grzimek, *Auf den Mensch gekommen,* 369–70.

29. Bernhard Grzimek and Michael Grzimek, *Serengeti Shall Not Die,* trans. E. and D. Rewald (New York: Dutton, 1960).

30. Grzimek to Goppel, 12 September 1966; Grzimek to Baer [*Ministerialdirektor,* Bavarian Chancellery], 10 October 1966, both in BHStA StK/17030; Grzimek to Eugen Gerstenmaier, 5 December 1967, DNR Archive, "NPBW, 1966–67."

31. Klotz, "Soll der Bayerische Wald ein Nationalpark werden?" 298, BHStA StK/17031.

32. Wolfgang Engelhardt to Alfred Toepfer, 22 July 1966 and 26 September 1966; Georg Fahrbach to Engelhardt, 19 September 1966 and 21 September 1966, all in DNR Archive, "NPBW, 1966–67"; Hasselbach, "Niedersachsen und der 'Deutsche Nationalpark,'" *Niedersächsischer Jäger*, no. 7 (April 5, 1968), 131–33, in BHStA StK/17033.

33. Bernhard Grzimek to Alfred Toepfer, 17 April 1967, DNR Archive, "NPBW, 1966–67."

34. Alfred Toepfer to Hubert Weinzierl, 1 March 1967; implied in Wolfgang Engelhardt to Toepfer, 10 April 1967, both in DNR Archive, "NPBW, 1966–67."

35. These organizations' telegrams to Goppel in August 1966 are available in BHStA StK/17030.

36. *Stadtverwaltung* Grafenau, "Nationalpark Bayerischer Wald Resolution," 24 January 1967, BHStA StK/17031; Schlemmer, Grüner, and Balcar, "Entwicklungshilfe," in Frese, Paulus, and Teppe, *Demokratisierung*, 403–6, 412–16; Wengert, "Land Use Planning," 519–21. On support for nature parks in the context of territorial planning see BHStA MWi/22058.

37. *Stadtverwaltung* Grafenau, "Nationalpark Bayerischer Wald Resolution," 24 January 1967; "Gemeinsamer Beschluß der Kreistage Wolfstein, Grafenau und Wegscheid in der Sitzung am 14.2.1967," both in BHStA StK/17031; Haug, "Entstehungsgeschichte," 42–43.

38. *Verhandlungen des Bayerischen Landtags,* VI. Wahlperiode, 1966–1970, 6. Legislaturperiode, Bd. I, Beilage 210, 20 April 1967 and Beilage 294, 11 May 1967; *Verhandlungen des Bayerischen Landtags,* VI. Wahlperiode, 1966–1970, 6. Legislaturperiode, Bd. I, Beilage 383, 22 June 1967.

39. Oskar Hatz, excerpt from his weekly column "Blick hinter die Kulissen," *Passauer Neue Presse,* 13 January 1968, in BStL, *Eine Landschaft wird Nationalpark,* 104–5; Volkmar Gabert (SPD state party chairman and *Landtag* deputy) to Wolfgang Engelhardt, 9 November 1966, DNR Archive, "NPBW, 1966–67"; Sperber, "Entstehungsgeschichte," 84.

40. Johann Riederer, District Government, Lower Bavaria to *Zweckverband,* 12 September 1967, BHStA StK/17031; Weinzierl, *Krönung,* 50, 54; Haug, "Entstehungsgeschichte," 43–44; Professor Dr. K. Ullrich, "Für und wider die Nationalpark-Idee," *Münchner Merkur,* 2 March 1968, photocopy in author's possession.

41. Alfred Toepfer to Wolfgang Engelhardt, 12 September 1967; Engelhardt to Toepfer, 13 October 1967, both in DNR Archive, "NPBW, 1966–67."

42. Weinzierl, *Krönung,* 57.

43. "Von zehn Deutschen wollen neun den ersten Nationalpark," DNR Archive, "NPBW, 1966-67," also available in BHStA StK/17031.

44. The *Zweckverband*'s sixteen-page proposal, dated 18 October 1967, and its 18 December 1967 resolution to the *Landtag* are available in BHStA StK/17031.

45. Woelfle to Bernhard Grzimek, 27 July 1966, DNR Archive, "NPBW, 1966–1967"; Grzimek to Goppel, 12 September 1966, 2, BHStA StK/17030.

46. Hubert Weinzierl, "Traumziel—ein deutsch-tschechischer Nationalpark," 28 August 1967, BHStA, Abteilung V. Nachlässe und Sammlungen, Schutzgemeinschaft Deutscher Wald, Altarchiv/20 (hereafter BHStA Abt. V, SDW, A/20); Weinzierl, *Krönung,* 51–54. The author thanks Mrs. Vlasta Mestankova of the Czech National Archives for her efforts to locate relevant files and for translating documents on the Šumava landscape reserve.

47. *Ministerialdirigent* Haagen, *Forstabteilung,* Bavarian Ministry of Agriculture to Bavarian Ministry of Culture, 12 January 1968, BHStA MK/51185; *Forstabteilung,* Bavarian Ministry of Agriculture, "Äußerungen maßgeblicher Wildbiologen zum Exposé des Zweckverbandes," "Beilage 2" to Bavarian Ministry of Culture, BHStA MK/51185; Sperber, "Entstehungsgeschichte," 80.

48. Graf Lennart Bernadotte, DRL to Dr. Ludwig Huber, Bavarian Ministry of Culture, 6 December 1967, BHStA MK/51185; Weinzierl, *Krönung*, 52.

49. Wolfgang Haber, "Gutachten zum Plan eines Nationalparkes im Bayerischen Wald," n.d. [1967], 36–37, 40, BHStA StK/17032. The report also is published in *Landschaft und Erholung*, Schriftenreihe des Deutschen Rates für Landespflege, ed. Deutscher Rat für Landespflege, no. 11 (Bonn: Buch- und Verlagsdruckerei Ludwig Leopold, 1969).

50. Wolfgang Haber, interview by author, 20 June 1992, Freising.

51. Haber, "Gutachten," 3–8, 37, 42, quotes on pp. 37 and 8 respectively.

52. Haber, "Gutachten," 17–30, 31–32.

53. Haber, "Gutachten," 12–17, 30–31.

54. Haber, "Gutachten," 32, 38–39, 41, 42, quote on p. 41.

55. Haber, "Gutachten," 32, 38–42.

56. Haber later recommended against the designation. See "Professor Haber lehnt den Nationalpark ab," *Passauer Neue Presse*, 15 October 1968, photocopy in author's possession.

57. Karl Bayer (for the *Zweckverband*) to Alfons Goppel, 27 March 1968, BHStA StK/17033.

58. Graf Lennart Bernadotte to the *Landtag* and to Alfons Goppel, both in DRL, *Landschaft und Erholung*, 24–26; Bernadotte to the Bavarian Senate, 8 February 1968, BHStA StK/17033. On Alfred Toepfer's promotion of an alpine national park see his letter to the editor, *Grafenauer Anzeiger*, n.d. [January 1968?], in *Naturschutz- und Naturparke*, no. 48 (First Quarter, 1968): 61. On Berchtesgaden National Park see Toepfer to Goppel, 26 March 1970; Wolfgang Engelhardt to Goppel, 17 April 1970, both in BHStA StK/17035; Hubert Weinzierl to the Bavarian Government, *Landtag* and Senate, 5 May 1970, BHStA MK/51186.

59. *Verhandlungen des Bayerischen Landtags*, VI. Wahlperiode, 1966–1970, 6. Legislaturperiode, Bd. II, 17 January 1968, Beilage 720 (CSU) and Beilage 721 (SPD). On the delayed responses by the SPD and CSU see Oskar Hatz, "Leidiger Nationalpark-Streit," *Passauer Neue Presse*, 13 January 1968, in BStL, *Eine Landschaft wird Nationalpark*, 104–5.

60. "Stellungnahme der Ministerialforstabteilung zum Antwortschreiben des Zweckverbands vom 18.10.1967," BHStA StK/17032.

61. On the Mansholt Plan see <http://www.europe.eu/scadplus/leg/en/lvb/104000.htm> (accessed 10 July 2006).

62. Dr. Mayer, State Planning Agency, Bavarian Ministry of Economics to Bavarian ministries of agriculture and the interior, and Bavarian Chancellery, 20 August 1968; Dr. Brugger, Bavarian Chancellery, "Betreff: Agrarprogramm der Bundesregierung; hier Modell eines Erholungszentrums in einem agrarpolitischen Problemgebiet," n.d. [August 1968?], both in BHStA StK/17033.

63. Bavarian Ministry of the Interior to Alfons Goppel, 27 August 1968; *Forstabteilung*, Bavarian Ministry of Agriculture to Bavarian Ministry of the Interior, 9 September 1968, both in BHStA StK/17033.

64. Siegfried Hännl, "Fragen nach dem Nationalpark. SPD befürchtet eigenmächtige Entscheidung der Regierung," *Süddeutsche Zeitung*, 30 September 1968, clipping in BHStA StK/17034; Deputies Fuchs, Schuster, Wösner (CSU) to Alfons Goppel, 3 September 1968, BHStA StK/17033.

65. Federal Ministry of Agriculture to Bavarian Chancellery, 21 August 1968, BHStA StK/17033.

66. "Interview mit Bundesminister Hermann Höcherl," *Allgemeine Forstzeitschrift* 47 (1968): 810; Herbert Offner, "Nationalpark oder Naturpark?" *Der Forst und Holzwirt* 24, no. 2 (23 January 1969): 39–41; Sperber, "Entstehungsgeschichte," 89.

67. Hermann Höcherl to Alfons Goppel, January 1969, BHStA StK/17034.

68. Karl Köbelin, "Vorentscheidung für den Nationalpark," *Süddeutsche Zeitung*, 31 January 1969, 19, photocopy in author's possession.

69. Excerpts from the budget committee meeting of 22 May 1969, in Haug, "Entstehungsge-schichte," 50–52; "Dr. Eisenmann: wir machen eigene nationalpark-verwaltung, n.d. [April 1969?]; "Eisenmann will Nationalpark im Bayerischen Wald verwirklichen," n.d. [April 1969?], press releases in BHStA StK/17034; Sperber, "Entstehungsgeschichte," 89–92.

70. *Verhandlungen des Bayerischen Landtags,* VI. Wahlperiode, 1966–1970, Stenographische Berichte, Bd. IV, 73. Sitzung, Mittwoch, 11. Juni 1969, 3598–600.

71. Sperber, "Entstehungsgeschichte," 95–96; Bayerischer Rundfunk, "Dr. Hans Bibelriether, Ehe-maliger Leiter des Nationalparks Bayerischer Wald im Gespräch mit Reinhold Gruber, Sendetag: 20.01.1999, 20.15 Uhr," <http://www.br–online.de/alpha/forum/vor9901/19990120_i.shtml> (accessed 31 July 2004).

72. Erik Spemann, "Nationalpark: Es geht nicht nur um wilde Tiere," *Münchner Merkur,* 14 April 1970, 15, photocopy in author's possession.

73. Spemann, "Es geht nicht nur um wilde Tiere," *Münchner Merkur,* 14 April 1970, photocopy in author's possession; Michael Haug, "Wozu ein Nationalpark in Deutschland?" *N & L* 47, no. 5 (1972): 131.

74. Haug, "Wozu ein Nationalpark?" *N & L* 47, no. 5 (1972): 131; Haug, "Entstehungsge-schichte," 61–64; BStL, *Nationalpark Bayerischer Wald,* 42–48; Hans Eisenmann, "Natio-nalpark Bayerischer Wald—Chance und Aufgabe," *Allgemeine Forst Zeitschrift* 28, no. 17 (28 April 1973): 391.

75. "Aufruf des Bundes Naturschutz in Bayern zur Übernahme von Patenschaften für National-park–Tiere" (doc. 2.4), in BStL, *Eine Landschaft wird Nationalpark,* 114–15; Spemann, "Es geht nicht nur um wilde Tiere," *Münchner Merkur,* 14 April 1970, photocopy in author's possession.

76. Erik Spemann, "Nationalpark Bayerischer Wald: Die große Schau der Natur," *Münchner Merkur,* 7 October 1970, 6, photocopy in author's possession; "Sitzung des Fachbeirates des Nationalparks Bayerischer Wald, 7.10.1974," *Nationalpark,* no. 4 (1974): 38.

77. Haug, "Entstehungsgeschichte," 61–64; BStL, *Nationalpark Bayerischer Wald,* 42–48; Georg Sperber, "Ein Porträt des Nationalparks Bayerischer Wald," *Blätter für Naturschutz,* Sonderdruck, "Eröffnung des Nationalparks Bayerischer Wald" (1970): 13.

78. Bayerischer Rundfunk, interview with Bibelriether (1999), see note 71.

79. Sperber, "Entstehungsgeschichte," 101–6, 110–14; Hans Eisenmann to Rudolf Hanauer, President, Bavarian *Landtag,* 26 May 1977, BHStA, Abt. V, SDW Archiv, B100.

80. Haug, "Wozu ein Nationalpark?" *N & L* 47, no. 5 (1972): 131–32; Haug, "Entstehungsge-schichte," 60–61.

81. Criticisms of the national park are documented in BHStA Abt. V, SDW Archiv, B100 and B101. See also Klaus Hermann, "Der Kompromiß-Park," *Passauer Neue Presse,* 9 October 1975, photocopy in author's possession.

82. Quotes from Hans Eisenmann, "Der Nationalpark Bayerischer Wald," *Bayerische Gemeinde-Zeitung,* 18 September 1972, photocopy in author's possession. On timber production, park expansion, and protected areas see Eisenmann to Hanauer, 26 May 1977, 7; Haug, "Entste-hungsgeschichte," 61–64, 73; Hans Bibelriether, "Das größte Naturwaldreservat Mitteleu-ropas," *Nationalpark,* no. 71 (February 1991): 49; Hans-Heinrich Vangerow, "Nationalpark Bayerischer Wald," *N & L* 49, no. 4 (1974): 98; "Dr. Bibelriether: Weinzierls Presserklärung ist unfair und verletzend," *Grafenauer Anzeiger,* 6 September 1980, clipping in BHStA, Abt. V, SDW Archiv, B101; Joachim Hofer, "The Bavarian Forest National Park," *Kulturchronik,* no. 6 (1996), 48–50.

83. Bibelriether, "Naturwaldreservat," 48–51. On trends in managing the park see Vangerow, "Nationalpark Bayerischer Wald," *N & L* 49, no. 4 (1974): 98, 100; Haug, "Entstehungsge-schichte," 53–54, 57–59, 76, 84–85.

84. Horst Stern, "Bayerisches und Allzubayerisches," *Natur,* no. 2 (1984): 74–77; Hans Kie-ner, "Neuer Wald nach Windwürfen und Borkenkäferbefall," *Nationalpark,* no. 68 (March

1990): 49–53; Hans Bibelriether, interview by author, 22 June 1992, Grafenau; quotes from Bayerischer Rundfunk, interview with Bibelriether (1999), see note 71. On locals' criticisms of the nature ideal in national parks see Körner, "Entwicklung des Naturschutzes," in Brüggemeier and Engels, *Natur– und Umweltschutz*, 86.

85. Hans Bibelriether, "Natur im Nationalpark schützen. Welche? Für wen? Wozu?" *Nationalpark*, no. 68 (March 1990): 29–31; Bibelriether, "Naturwaldreservat," 48, 50.

86. Germany's other national parks include Berchtesgaden, Schleswig-Holstein Wattenmeer, Lower Saxony Wattenmeer, Hamburg Wattenmeer, Jasmund, Vorpommersche Boddenlandschaft, Müritz, Sächsische Schweiz, Hochharz, Harz, Unteres Odertal, Hainich, Eifel, and Kellerwald-Edersee.

87. Eisenmann, "Chance und Aufgabe," *Allgemeine Forst Zeitschrift* 28, no. 17 (28 April 1973): 392; Haug, "Entstehungsgeschichte," 76.

88. Bayerischer Rundfunk, interview with Bibelriether (1999), see note 71.

CONCLUSIONS

In the history of Germany's long tradition of caring for nature, the period between 1945 and 1975 exhibited striking continuities with the past, yet also displayed incremental, noteworthy changes. When the war was over, conservationists used the legal and administrative framework of the RNG and the message and tactics of traditional nature and homeland preservation to anchor their work in uncertain times. They could do so in part because *Naturschutz* was not any more tainted than other endeavors that had been unevenly coordinated under National Socialism. Old and newly formed private organizations continued to rely on prominent public figures as patrons and leaders, and worked behind the scenes lobbying officials to achieve typically narrow goals that did little to slow the march of industrialism. With their steady refrain to defend "pristine" nature against unnecessary intrusions by technology and industry, they echoed their turn of the century predecessors. And yet their warnings captured a sense of loss that others registered only later as they noticed their hybrid landscapes becoming increasingly engineered.

The Miracle Years witnessed the rapid transformation of West Germany's urban and rural landscapes in far reaching ways that forced conservationists to distance themselves from homeland preservation in favor of professional landscape planning, which depended on "rigorous scientific form." Yet their scientific, presumably more objective approach to caring for nature continued to be informed by social conservatism, one that emphasized conservationists' ideals of healthy landscapes and of healthy living. This social conservatism was evident in Alfred Toepfer's initial vision for promoting constructive use of leisure time in clean, orderly nature parks, in Konrad Buchwald's effort to create a new class of professionals to design healthier landscapes for the urban masses, and in the German Council for Land Cultivation's exclusivity in evaluating development projects.

Yet the modernization and scientification of conservation during the 1960s enabled practitioners to emerge as political actors who shaped decisions about land use, albeit rarely to the extent they desired. Influenced by their participation

Notes for this chapter begin on page 249.

in international conferences, an expanding corps of professional conservationists relied increasingly on ecology to manage land and resources to maximize their use over the long term. This professionalization sealed the fate of honorary conservation advisors who were phased out in the 1970s and replaced by experts occupying fulltime positions within the bureaucracy. But the dispassionate and managerial approach of professionals representing increasingly narrow, specialized fields set them apart from "ordinary" lay activists who looked for leadership in men like Grzimek, Weinzierl, and the journalist Horst Stern, who had a more confrontational message and style and who appreciated the moral justifications traditionally associated with preservation.[1]

Through conservationists' steady, often conservative presence within the mainstream of West German society, they ensured that by 1970, the map of the country was dotted with hundreds of reserves, dozens of nature parks, and the first of several new national parks. Their cautious resolutions and behind the scenes lobbying contributed to the adoption of state and federal laws that integrated conservation into agricultural reforms and spatial planning. Yet such measures proved inadequate to prevent people's surroundings from becoming perceptibly degraded and unhealthy. Around 1970, conservationists participated in, and were simultaneously transformed by, the shift to left-leaning environmental protection. Initially enthused about growing popular concern to protect the environment, longstanding conservation groups like the DNR soon competed with citizens' initiatives, which preached a more radical message and used more sensational tactics. The BBU quickly distinguished itself from existing conservation groups by relying on grassroots activism, campaigning against nuclear power, and demanding non-exploitative lifestyles.

But existing groups did not collapse under the weight of competition. They survived by modifying their goals, strategies, and activism, and retained a niche in the sphere of environmental politics. Citizens' initiatives, which prided themselves on their spontaneous grassroots activism, recognized early on that they had to become more institutionalized to remain influential. During the 1980s, however, BBU's influence was eclipsed by the West German Green Party, which took over as the leading voice of the ecology and anti-nuclear movement. Once the Greens became a part of the parliamentary process, mass member groups like BUND increased their leverage in the political arena as lobbies for environmental issues.[2] To have influence today, all of the major environmental organizations depend on leaders with professional expertise and fundraising skills and employ modern marketing strategies. The DNR continues to be criticized for relying on government subsidies which restrict its activism. Yet mass member organizations are constrained by their dependence on dues and donations from members whose commitment to environmental causes can fluctuate.[3]

Traditional conservation organizations differed in striking ways from environmental groups formed in the 1970s, yet similarities between the two exist.[4]

Most members of nature and environmental groups belonged to the educated middle classes and looked to the state for financial support and answers to their grievances. Even citizens' initiatives of the late 1970s expected the state to implement their reform proposals. Supporters of conservation and environmentalism also were alike in using a range of measures to achieve their goals, though environmentalists formed alliances broader than those of conservationists and relied on confrontational public protests more frequently. Whether defending nature-as-*Heimat* in the 1950s or fighting for a healthy environment in the 1970s, citizens tended to view themselves as a misunderstood minority fighting for a noble cause. Recent scholarship emphasizes, however, that over three decades the image activists had of themselves shifted from that of a proud elite defending innocent nature to that of an oppressed group committed to social justice and resistance.[5] Although conservationists and environmentalists claimed their fight was in the interest of the common good, their activism was inspired by a range of motives, including, but not limited to, self-interest. Members of both groups also presupposed supporters' conformity to specific understandings of "the good life." In the 1950s that involved becoming self-disciplined, introspective individuals through solitary walks in nature. Two decades later that required the adoption of an alternative lifestyle which demonstrated a commitment to social justice, including the consumption of environmentally acceptable products.[6]

This study has resisted the easy separation between "old" conservation and "new" environmentalism, however noteworthy some of the differences. It has argued instead that conservationists and other citizens concerned about the future development of their communities during the Miracle Years contributed in some measure to the partial greening of society. Had they kept silent and remained inactive, West Germany's landscapes probably would have become more engineered than they were by 1970. The work of West German conservationists during the 1950s and 1960s deserves to be seen as part of a lengthy process, one that created a society increasingly committed to protecting nature and the environment on the one hand, yet still attached to economic growth and technological progress on the other.

Each of the case studies in this book illustrates some of the many compromises that resulted in partial gains and losses for defenders of nature and for advocates of technology and economic growth. (Admittedly, the two sides were not always so clearly divided.) Because of the activism of citizens living in South Baden, there is no dam today at the headwaters of the Wutach River. Yet this small, noteworthy gain for proponents of preservation was only a minor defeat for those who championed economic growth. SSW's partial loss in the Wutach conflict ensured its profitable expansion elsewhere, which in turn enabled it to generate more electricity to meet upward spiraling demand by industry and households. In the debate over canalizing the Mosel, supporters of economic growth, western integration, and technological modernization (excluding Ruhr industrialists, in this case) scored a significant win once Chancellor Adenauer agreed to France's demand to build the shipping lane. Despite ending up on the "losing" side, conservationists claimed partial gains when the treaty over the canal addressed their concerns to protect water quality and the scenery of the river valley. In addition, the involvement of conservationists and landscape planners at various stages of construction ensured that at least some stretches of the Mosel looked more natural than engineered. The establishment of the Bavarian Forest National Park appeared to result in wins for nearly all parties involved, especially those concerned about resuscitating the sagging local economy and those eager to protect nature in an environment that seemed increasingly artificial. Only foresters and locals came away with a sense of loss that reflected their opposition to the image of "wild" nature eventually imposed upon them. Yet foresters had to acknowledge that nearly all of the country's forested land was used for timber production. Seen from this perspective, foresters made only a small concession to preservationists in letting the forest evolve largely on its own in a remote corner of the country. The nature park program epitomizes the partially green compromises made during the Miracle Years. Local communities benefited from the revenue generated through tourism in nature parks, but these green spaces did more to protect a variety of recreational opportunities than to protect nature. Moreover, the popularity of the program reflected the assumption that steps were being taken to protect nature, without slowing economic growth.

The greening of society accelerated in the early 1970s with the emergence of the environment as an object of reform and an arena for political action. The federal government adopted a managerial approach to *Umweltschutz* in prioritizing the passage of environmental legislation and the development of technologies to reduce pollution and manage waste. Yet it also elicited citizens' involvement in planning decisions and promoted public discussion about "quality of life" concerns. Professional conservationists joined other scientists in managing ecosystems to create healthier environmental conditions, while revitalized conservation groups like the DNR and the new BUND stepped up efforts to support environmental clean up and to protect species and biotopes. Yet none of these measures challenged economic growth. By contrast, the BBU called for a range of reforms that would lead to less exploitative lifestyles, including the development of alternative energy sources, increased public transportation, support for organic farming, and more citizen involvement in local planning decisions. On the other end of the spectrum, Herbert Gruhl, Bundestag Deputy (CDU) and early Green Party member, proposed nothing short of an ecological authoritarian system in his bestselling book, *A Planet is Plundered* (1975). According to Gruhl, only strict measures by the state would force people to cut consumption and guarantee the West's military security and access to natural resources.[7]

West Germans in the diffuse ecology movement, some of them members of the BBU, proposed the most far-reaching changes in their effort to create a green society. These activists promoted an alternative culture based on an understanding of nature as organic, pristine, and representative of "all that humans have lost." Those who later joined the West German Greens shaped the party's view of nature as harmonious, and influenced theorists' belief that a lifestyle which conformed to nature's limits would heal the wounds in society and build a better world in which the individual could participate fully in all aspects of life.[8] After conservatives like Gruhl left the Greens in its difficult early years, the leftists who came to dominate the party expanded its agenda to include feminism, civil rights, social justice, and peace.

But political ecology remained central to the Greens' identity. The party's critique of "economic growth equals progress" and its emphasis on non-material values were not entirely new. Expressed under different political and economic conditions, however, they carried more weight than when similar assertions had been made by conservationists during the Miracle Years. But the Greens called for significant changes in lifestyle which traditional conservationists rarely would have considered. Supporters of the Greens, who tended to be urban, young, middle class, well educated people, advocated a thirty-five-hour work week, expansion of the welfare state, environmental protection, alternative energy, gender equality, minority rights, a nuclear-free Europe, and support for less economically developed nations. They also favored small scale technology and a decentralized economy as alternatives to exploitative and environmentally destructive large scale industrial production.[9] In the 1980s, the Greens made *Umweltschutz* an issue of ongoing importance to the wider public, and forced the major political parties to keep their promise to protect the environment. Unlike previously when conservationists adjusted their goals and arguments to conform to dominant political, social, and economic considerations, the Greens forced the debate about ecology and the environment to become one to which other issues had to adjust.

The 1980s witnessed a greening not only of politics, but also of industry and the marketplace. Responding to demands by ecological consumers concerned about their impact on nature, businesses marketed an array of items, from organically grown foods to environmentally friendly batteries. Purchasing products took on political significance, down to the means of transportation one used to get to the store and the kind of bag one used to carry items back home. Well-organized centers for recycling paper, glass, plastics, and oil reduced volumes of trash while creating a demand for new technologies to salvage materials for some later use. Nature, it seemed, had invaded people's daily life, shaping even the most mundane decisions in unanticipated ways. In making choices about consumption and disposal, the individual could make a political statement and fashion a lifestyle that was presumably more natural, though often without having to cut consumption or limit economic growth.[10]

As the end of the twentieth century approached, the Federal Republic was like other industrial democracies in showing all of the "paradoxical features associated . . . with the light-green society," to borrow from Bess again. It had:

> the presence of a vibrant and influential green movement, side-by-side with a tenacious popular faith in economic growth and technological progress; a consumer economy that incorporates many elements of ecological thinking, while continuing to offer shoppers an explosively proliferating gamut of products and services; widespread practices of recycling and other forms of nature conservation, coexisting with rampant increases in energy consumption, the volume of trash, and the use of cars and planes; environmentalist ideas playing a regular role in political discourse, but then very often taking a back seat to other priorities; the systematic institutionalization of environmental protection within the laws and apparatus of government, while at the same time key green initiatives languish for lack of funding or support; the business world scrambling to incorporate ecological measures into everyday practices of production and selling, while still focusing primarily on short-term competitiveness and the bottom line.[11]

The partial greening of the mainstream of society contributed to a new appreciation for protecting nature, though primarily the protection of nature on a small scale. With its predominantly urban population, its small agriculture sector, its tiny patches of restored "wild" nature, and its preponderance of hybrid landscapes displaying varying combinations of naturalness and human engineering, the Federal Republic of Germany, like other nations of Western Europe, serves as an indicator of what the future might hold for nature in an environment designed primarily by people.[12] As the principle architects of the environment, humans shoulder the responsibility for determining how, why, where, and for whom parts of the environment will retain varying degrees of naturalness. Sometimes these decisions might involve restoring ecosystems to a more natural state to protect some human settlements, although at the expense of others. This is the case, for example, along stretches of the "rectified" Oder River in eastern Germany. Here measures to control inundations will require flooding a few sparsely populated areas (after relocating residents) to provide a retention basin offering safer conditions for the majority of people who make their home along the river.[13] Other times those choices will involve leaving ecosystems alone to a large degree so that they show limited evidence of humans, such as in designated areas of national parks. There also is merit in protecting the Lüneburg Heath as a cultural landscape. To leave the area alone would mean allowing the heath to evolve into forest. Protecting it in a particular state, at least in places, provides a way to preserve the history and traditions that shaped the heath as well as the plants and animals that thrive in it. So, too, is it necessary to protect public parks and gardens, and even smaller spaces that form part of the natural habitat of plants, animals, and people making the urban environment their home.

These illustrations are meant to invite people to find beauty in places that might at first glance seem unnatural, perhaps even artificial.[14] But they are not meant to imply that all forms of nature are equally valuable.[15] In the absence of a universal norm for nature and what counts as "natural," people must thoughtfully reflect on, and openly debate, their understandings of both. And because nature is something deeply unlike us and beyond our absolute control, people must be constantly vigilant, knowing that the choices they make about what to protect, how, and for whom will influence their environment for generations to come, in ways both intended and unforeseen. In the age of global warming, nanotechnology, and germline genetic engineering, that is a troubling realization indeed.[16]

Notes

1. Horst Stern, "Mut zur Emotion," *Kosmos*, 70, no. 12 (1974): *366–72; Stern, "Was muß der Naturschutz vom Bürger erwarten?" *JfNL* (1974): 45–58; Engels, *Naturpolitik*, chap. 5.

2. Dominick, *Environmental Movement*, 215–16; Engels, *Naturpolitik*, chap. 7; Jürgen Hoffmann, "From Cooperation to Confrontation: The Greens and the Ecology Movement in Germany," in Goodbody, *Culture of German Environmentalism*, 66–80.

3. Rucht, "Von der Bewegung zur Institution?" in Roth and Rucht, *Neue soziale Bewegungen in der Bundesrepublik Deutschland*, 248. On the relationship between environmental groups' professionalized staff and fund-raising efforts see Dalton, *Green Rainbow*.

4. This summary relies on Engels, *Naturpolitik*, as well as Sandra Chaney, review of Engels, *Naturpolitik*, H–German, H–Net Reviews, September 2007, available at http://www.h–net .org/reviews/.

5. Engels, *Naturpolitik*, chap. 10.

6. Engels, *Naturpolitik*, chap. 10

7. Herbert Gruhl, *Ein Planet wird geplündert. Die Schreckensbilanz unserer Politik* (Frankfurt am Main: Fischer, 1975), 226, 320–25.

8. Sabine Von Dirke, *"All Power to the Imagination." The West German Counterculture from the Student Movement to the Greens* (Lincoln: University of Nebraska Press, 1997), 189–92, quote on pp. 191–92.

9. Herbert Kitschelt, *The Logics of Party Formation. Ecological Politics in Belgium and West Germany* (Ithaca: Cornell University Press, 1989), 95; Horst Mewes, "The West German Green Party," *New German Critique*, no. 28 (Winter 1983): 61–62; Werner Hülsberg, *The German Greens. A Social and Political Profile*, trans. Gus Fagan (London and New York: Verso, 1988), 107–18, 180–87; Hülsberg, "The Greens at the Crossroads," *New Left Review* (July/August 1985): 10–17.

10. Bess, *Light-Green Society*, chap. 15; Engels, *Naturpolitik*, chap. 10.

11. Bess, *Light-Green Society*, 240–41.

12. Bess, *Light-Green Society*, 291–95.

13. Blackbourn, *Conquest*, 363.

14. Compare Bill McKibben, *End of Nature* (New York: Random House, 1989) with Cronon, *Uncommon Ground;* and White, *Organic Machine*. See also Bess, *Light-Green Society*, chap. 13.

15. Albert Borgmann, "The Nature of Reality and the Reality of Nature," in *Reinventing Nature?: Responses to Postmodern Deconstruction,* ed. Michale E. Soulé and Gary Lease (Washington, DC: Island Press, 1995), 36, 38, 39.

16. Bill McKibben, *Enough. Staying Human in an Engineered Age* (New York: Henry Holt, 2003); Michael Bess, "Artificialization and its Discontents," *Environmental History* 10, no. 1 (January 2005): 32–33.

MAPS

MAP 1 Germany under Allied Occupation and Postwar Territorial Losses

MAP 2 Federal Republic of Germany (1949-1990), including West Berlin

MAP 3 *Schluchseewerk Aktiengesellschaft* and the Wutach-Gauchach Nature Reserve (ca. 1952)

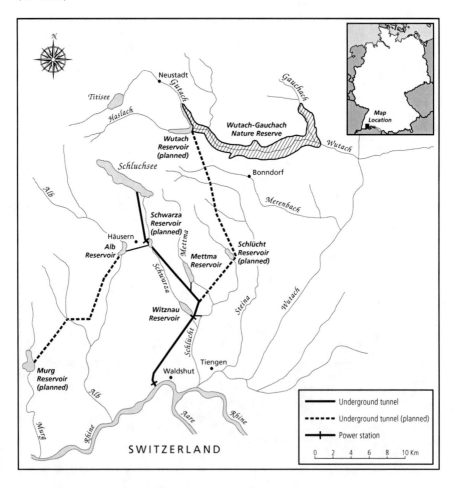

Map 4 West Germany's Nature Parks (in hectares) and the Bavarian Forest National
Park (ca. 1975)

MAP 5   The Canalized Mosel River

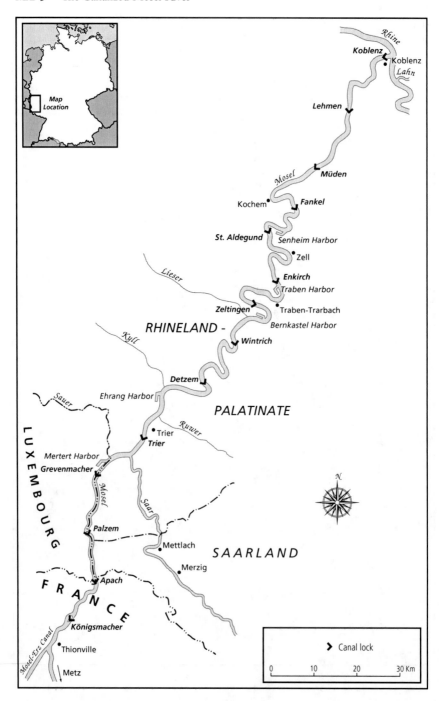

Map 6 The Bavarian Forest National Park, the Inner Bavarian Forest Landscape Reserve (ca. 1970), and the Proposed (1942) Bohemian Forest National Park

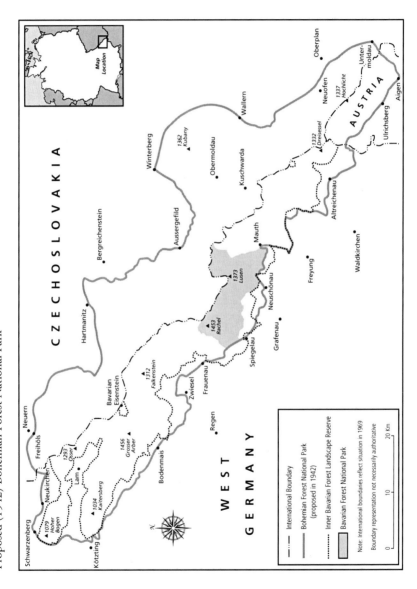

BIBLIOGRAPHY

Archival Sources

Auswärtiges Amt, Politisches Archiv, Bonn.
 Politische Abteilung, Referat 217 (Bundeswasserstraßen)
Auswertungs- und Informationsdienst für Ernährung, Landwirtschaft und Forsten, Film Archiv, Bonn-Bad Godesberg.
Bayerisches Hauptstaatsarchiv, Munich.
 Abteilung V. SDW Archiv
 Staatskanzlei
 Staatsministerium des Innern
 Staatsministerium für Unterricht und Kultus
 Staatsministerium für Wirtschaft und Verkehr
Bundesamt für Naturschutz, Naturschutzarchiv, Bonn-Bad Godesberg.
 Wutach (0831513)
Bundesarchiv, Koblenz.
 Bundesamt für Naturschutz (B 245)
 Bundesministerium des Innern (B 106)
 Bundesministerium für Ernährung, Landwirtschaft und Forsten (B 116)
Bundesarchiv-Zwischenarchiv, St. Augustin-Hangelar.
 Bundeskanzleramt (B 136)
  Moselkanalisierung
Deutscher Naturschutzring Archive, Bonn.
Landesarchiv Baden-Württemberg, Hauptstaatsarchiv Stuttgart.
 Innenministerium (EA 2/006)
 Kultusministerium (EA 3/102)
Rheinland-Pfalz, Landeshauptarchiv Koblenz.
 Stadt Bernkastel Kues (615)
 Ministerium des Innern (880)
 Sozialministerium (930)
Schwarzwaldverein Archive. Records in possession of Mr. Friedbert Zapf, First Chairman of the Black Forest Society, Bonndorf Chapter.
Verband Deutscher Naturparkträger Archive, Niederhaverbeck, Lüneburg Heath.
Verein Naturschutzpark Archive, Niederhaverbeck, Lüneburg Heath.

Periodicals

Blätter für Naturschutz. 1960–1970.
Der Grüne Kreis. 1960–1973.
DNR *Informationsbrief.* 1960–1966.
DNR *Rundschreiben.* 1951–1959.
DNR *Rundschreiben Neue Folge.* 1967–1972.
Grünes Blatt. 1948–1949.
Jahrbuch für Naturschutz und Landschaftspflege. 1967–1975.
Kosmos. 1948–1975.
Natur und Landschaft. 1953–1975.
Naturschutz. 1933–1943.
Naturschutz und Landschaftspflege. 1951–1952.
Naturschutzparke. 1930–1965.
Naturschutz- und Naturparke. 1966–1975.
Spiegel. 1947–1975.
Unser Wald. 1950–1959.
Verhandlungen Deutscher Beauftragter für Naturschutz und Landschaftspflege. 1947–1967.

Published Primary Sources

Adenauer, Konrad. *Briefe 1953–1955.* Adenauer Rhöndorfer Ausgabe. Edited by Hans Peter Mensing. Berlin: Siedler, 1995.
———. *Briefe 1955–1957.* Adenauer Rhöndorfer Ausgabe. Edited by Hans Peter Mensing. Berlin: Siedler, 1998.
———. *Teegespräche 1955–1958.* Adenauer Rhöndorfer Ausgabe. Edited by Rudolf Morsey and Hans-Peter Schwarz. Berlin: Siedler, 1986.
Arbeitsgemeinschaft "Heimatschutz Schwarzwald," ed. *Wutach-Brevier.* Freiburg: [Karl Schillinger?], 1955. Available in BAN Naturschutzarchiv 0831513.
Bieber, Horst. "Langsam stirbt der Umweltschutz. Von deutscher Naturromantik zur politischen Macht—doch der alte Schwung ist hin." *Zeit,* 20 October 1978, 7–9.
Bodamer, Joachim. *Gesundheit und technische Welt.* 2d ed. Stuttgart: Ernst Klett, 1960 [1955].
Borchers, Kurt. *Der Wald als deutsches Volksgut.* Lüneburg: Im Kinau, 1948.
Brandt, Willy. *Berliner Ausgabe.* Vol. 7, *Mehr Demokratie wagen. Innen–und Gesellschaftspolitik 1966–1974.* Edited by Wolther von Kieseritzky. Bonn: Dietz, 2001.
Buchwald, Konrad. *Die Zukunft des Menschen in der industriellen Gesellschaft und die Landschaft.* Braunschweig: Hans August–Stolle, 1965.
Bundesarchiv and Institut für Zeitgeschichte, ed. *Akten zur Vorgeschichte der Bundesrepublik Deutschland 1945–1949.* Vol. 1, *September 1945–Dezember 1946.* Edited by Walter Vogel and Christoph Weisz. Munich: Oldenbourg, 1976.
———, ed. *Akten zur Vorgeschichte der Bundesrepublik Deutschland 1945–1949.* Vol. 2, *Januar 1947–Juni 1947.* Edited by Wolfram Werner. Munich: Oldenbourg, 1982.
Bunz, Axel R. *Umweltpolitisches Bewußtsein 1972.* Berlin: Erich Schmidt, 1973.
Byrnes, James F. *Speaking Frankly.* New York: Harper, 1947.
Clay, Lucius D. *Decision in Germany.* New York: Doubleday, 1950.
Commoner, Barry. *The Closing Circle. Nature, Man, and Technology.* New York: Bantam, 1974.
Demoll, Reinhard. *Ketten für Prometheus: gegen die Natur oder mit ihr?* Munich: Bruchmann, 1954.
Deutsche Gartenbau-Gesellschaft, ed. *Grüner Lebensraum um des Menschen willen, 4. Mainauer Rundgespräche, April 24, 1960.* Schriftenreihe der Deutschen Gartenbau-Gesellschaft, no. 8. Privately published, 1960.
Deutscher Naturschutzring. *25 Jahre Deutscher Naturschutzring.* Siegburg: Buch- und Offsetdruckerei Daemisch-Mohr, 1976.

Deutscher Rat für Landespflege, ed. *Bodenseelandschaft und Hochrheinschiffahrt.* Schriftenreihe des Deutschen Rates für Landespflege, no. 3. Bonn: Buch- und Verlagsdruckerei Ludwig Leopold, 1965.

———, ed. *Landschaft und Erholung.* Schriftenreihe des Deutschen Rates für Landespflege, no. 11. Bonn: Buch–und Verlagsdruckerei Ludwig Leopold, 1969.

———, ed. *Landschaft und Moselausbau.* Schriftenreihe des Deutschen Rates für Landespflege, no. 7. Bonn: Buch- und Verlagsdruckerei Ludwig Leopold, 1966.

———, ed. *Probleme der Abfallbehandlung.* Schriftenreihe des Deutschen Rates für Landespflege, no. 13. Bonn: Buch–und Verlagsdruckerei Ludwig Leopold, 1970.

Ehrlich, Paul. *The Population Bomb.* New York: Ballantine, 1968.

Engelhardt, Wolfgang. *Naturschutz: seine wichtigsten Grundlagen und Forderungen.* Munich: Bayerischer Schulbuch Verlag, 1954.

———. *Umweltschutz. Gefährdung und Schutz der natürlichen Umwelt des Menschen.* Munich: Bayerischer Schulbuch Verlag, 1973.

Enzensberger, Hans Magnus. "A Critique of Political Ecology." Translated by Stuart Hood. *New Left Review* 84 (March/April 1974): 3–31.

Eppler, Erhard. *Ende oder Wende: Von der Machbarkeit des Notwendigen.* 6th rev. ed. Munich: Deutscher Taschenbuch Verlag, 1976.

Erz, Wolfgang. "Was heißt heute Naturschutz? Zum Europäischen Naturschutzjahr 1970." *Nord Friesland Zeitschrift für Kultur, Politik, Wirtschaft* (May 1970): 52–58.

Fahrbach, Georg, ed. *Der Mensch in seiner Umwelt.* Stuttgart: Fink, 1970.

———, ed. *Naturschutz—eine politische Aufgabe?* Stuttgart: Fink, 1965.

Federal Republic of Germany, Bundesregierung. *Report of the Federal Republic of Germany on the Human Environment Prepared for the United Nations Conference on the Human Environment June 1972, Stockholm, Sweden, by the Federal Government with the Assistance of the Länder.* Bonn: Federal Ministry of the Interior, 1972.

———. *Umweltpolitik. Das Umweltprogramm der Bundesregierung.* 5th ed. Berlin, Cologne: Kohlhammer, 1976.

Feuchtmayr, Inge. "Umweltgestaltung, eine Lebensnotwendigkeit für die Gesellschaft." *Landschaft & Stadt* 2, no. 2 (1970): 78–81.

Fries, Walter. *Muss die Wutach abgeleitet werden? Wirtschaftliche Betrachtungen zum Plan der Wutachableitung durch die Schluchseewerk AG.* Freiburg: Karl Schillinger, 1955. Available in BAN Naturschutzarchiv 0831513.

———. *Rettet die Wutachschlucht! Eine Antwort auf die Pläne der Schluchseewerk AG.* Freiburg: Karl Schillinger, 1954. Available in BAN Naturschutzarchiv 0831513.

Genscher, Hans-Dietrich. *Erinnerungen.* Berlin: Siedler, 1995.

Gruhl, Herbert. *Ein Planet wird geplundert. Die Schreckensbilanz unserer Politik.* Frankfurt am Main: Fischer, 1975.

Grzimek, Bernhard. *Auf den Mensch gekommen. Erfahrungen mit Leuten.* Munich: Bertelsmann, 1974.

Grzimek, Bernhard and Michael Grzimek. *Serengeti Shall Not Die.* Translated by E. and D. Rewald. New York: Dutton, 1960.

Haber, Wolfgang. "Conservation and Landscape Maintenance in Germany: Past, Present, and Future." *Biological Conservation* 5, no. 4 (October 1973): 258–64.

Hanstein, Udo. *Entwicklung, Stand und Möglichkeiten des Naturparkprograms in der Bundesrepublik Deutschland—ein Beitrag zur Raumordnungspolitik.* Beiheft 7, *Landschaft + Stadt.* Stuttgart: Eugen Ulmer, 1972.

Hard, Gerhard. "'Landschaft'—Folgerungen aus einigen Ergebnissen einer semantischen Analyse." *Landschaft + Stadt* 4, no. 2 (1972): 77–89.

Heintze, Gottfried. "Landschaftsplanung—Grundlage für die Entwicklung der Naturparke zu Vorbildslandschaften." *Garten und Landschaft,* no. 1 (1968): 4–7

Hellmich, Walter. *Natur- und Heimatschutz.* Stuttgart: Franckh'sche, 1953.

Hockenjos, Fritz. "Wutachschlucht Erinnerungen." *Der Schwarzwald,* no. 2 (1979): 61–65.

Hornsmann, Erich. *Innere Kolonisation oder Man Made Desert.* Stuttgart: Verlag der Pflanzenwerke im Verlag Oscar Angerer, 1948.

———. *... sonst Untergang. Die Antwort der Erde auf die Mißachtung ihrer Gesetze.* Reinhausen: Verlagsanstalt Rheinhausen, 1951.

Institut für Besatzungsfragen. *Einwirkung der Besatzungsmächte auf die Westdeutsche Wirtschaft.* Tübingen: Institut für Besatzungsfragen, 1949.

Kindleberger, Charles. *The German Economy, 1945–1947: Charles P. Kindleberger's Letters from the Field.* Westport, CT: Meckler, 1989.

Klose, Hans. *Fünfzig Jahre Staatlicher Naturschutz.* Giessen: Brühlscher, 1954.

Kraus, Otto. *Bis zum letzten Wildwasser? Gedanken über Wasserkraftnutzung und Naturschutz im Atomzeitalter.* Aachen: Georgi, 1960.

————. *Über den bayerischen Naturschutz. Eine Rückschau.* Munich: Öko–Markt, 1979.

————. *Zerstörung der Natur. Unser Schicksal von Morgen? Der Naturschutz in dem Streit der Interessen.* Nuremberg: Glock und Lutz, 1966.

Leopold, Aldo. *A Sand County Almanac.* New York: Oxford University Press, 1949; Ballantine, 1966.

Lienenkämper, Wilhelm. *Grüne Welt zu treuen Händen. Naturschutz und Landschaftspflege im Industriezeitalter.* Stuttgart: Franckh'sche, 1963.

Lorch, Walter and Wolfgang Burhenne. *Die Natur im Atomzeitalter. Versuch einer Prognose.* Bonn: Selbstverlag Schutzgemeinschaft Deutsches Wild, 1957.

Mäding, Erhard. *Landespflege. Die Gestaltung der Landschaft als Hoheitsrecht und Hoheitspflicht.* 2d ed. Berlin: Deutsche Landesbuchhandlung, 1943.

Meadows, Dennis, Donella Meadows, Jørgen Randers, and William Behrens III. *The Limits to Growth.* New York: Universe Books, 1972. Reprint, New York: Signet, 1972.

Metternich, Adolph. *Die Wüste droht. Die gefährdete Nahrungsgrundlage menschlichen Gesellschaft.* Bremen: Friedrich Trüjen, 1947.

Noelle, Elisabeth and Erich Peter Neumann. *The Germans. Public Opinion Polls, 1947–1966.* Translated by Gerard Finan. Allensbach and Bonn: Verlag für Demoskopie, 1967. Reprint, Westport, CT: Greenwood Press, 1981.

Osborn, Fairfield. *Our Plundered Planet.* Boston: Little, Brown and Company, 1948.

Pflug, Wolfram. "Die landschaftsökologischen und landschaftsgestalterischen Auswirkungen des Moselausbaues." In *Probleme der Nutzung und Erhaltung der Biosphäre. Bericht über ein internationales Colloquium der Deutschen UNESCO-Kommission veranstaltet mit finanzieller Unterstützung der UNESCO vom 17. bis 18. April 1968 in Berchtesgaden,* ed. Deutsche UNESCO–Kommission, 97–102. Cologne: Deutsche UNESCO-Kommission, 1969.

————. "Landespflege beim Ausbau der Mosel—Erfolge und Probleme." In *Landespflege und Raumordnung. Forschungs- und Sitzungsberichte der Akademie für Raumforschung und Landesplanung,* ed. Akademie für Raumforschung und Landesplanung, no. 43, 27–39. Hanover: Gebrüder Jänecke, 1968.

Schluchseewerk Aktiengesellschaft. *Ist die Wutach-Schlucht wirklich gefährdet?* Freiburg: [privately published?], 1953. Available in BAN Naturschutzarchiv 0831513.

————. *Schluchseewerk Aktiengesellschaft.* 2d ed. Freiburg: 1952. Available in BAN Naturschutzarchiv 0831513.

Schoenichen, Walther. *Natur als Volksgut und Menschheitsgut.* Stuttgart: Eugen Ulmer, 1950.

————. *Naturschutz, Heimatschutz. Ihre Begründung durch Ernst Rudorff, Hugo Conwentz und ihre Vorläufer.* Stuttgart: Wissenschaftliche Verlagsgesellschaft, 1954.

Schütze, Christian. "Schon möglich, daß die Erde sterben muß. Anfänge öffentlicher Meinung zum Thema Umweltschutz." *Merkur* 25 (1971): 470–85.

Schutzgemeinschaft Deutscher Wald. *Uns ruft der Wald. Ein Buch deutscher Dichter und Waldfreunde.* Rheinhausen: Verlagsanstalt Rheinhausen, 1949.

Schutzgemeinschaft Deutsches Wild. *Leitsätze, Geschäftsordnung, Satzung der Schutzgemeinschaft Deutsches Wild.* Munich: Selbstverlag Schutzgemeinschaft Deutsches Wild, 1952.

Schwenkel, Hans. *Die Landschaft als Natur und Menschenwerk.* Stuttgart: Franckh'sche, 1957.

Seifert, Alwin. *Ein Leben für die Landschaft.* Düsseldorf: Diederichs, 1962.

Siebold, Werner. *Geschützte Natur.* Mannheim: Bibliographisches Institut AG, 1958.

Smith, Jean Edward, ed. *The Papers of General Lucius D. Clay.* Vol. 1, *Germany 1945–1949.* Bloomington: Indiana University Press, 1974.

Sonnemann, Theodor. *Jahrgang 1900. Auf und ab im Strom der Zeit.* Würzburg: Johann Wilhelm Naumann, 1980.

Sturm, Vilma. "Verantwortung der Bürger für ihre grüne Umwelt." *Der grüne Kreis* (July 1966): 11-16.

Toepfer Alfred. *Erinnerungen aus meinem Leben 1894–1991*. Hamburg: Christians, 1991.

UNESCO. *Use and Conservation of the Biosphere. Proceedings of the Intergovernmental Conference of Experts on the Scientific Basis for Rational Use and Conservation of the Resources of the Biosphere, Paris, 4–13 September 1968*. Paris: United Nations Educational, Scientific and Cultural Organization, 1970.

United States Department of State, ed. *Germany 1947–1949. The Story in Documents*. Washington, DC: U.S. Government Printing Office, 1950.

United States Office of Military Government for Germany. Special Report of the Military Governor. *The German Forest Resources Survey*, no. 40 (1 October 1948).

———. *A Year of Potsdam: the German Economy since the Surrender*. Prepared by Brigadier General William H. Draper, Jr. Washington, DC: U. S. Government Printing Office, 1946.

Utley, Freda. *The High Cost of Vengeance*. Chicago: Henry Regnery, 1949.

Verein Naturschutzpark e.V., ed. *Das Naturpark-Programm und seine Probleme*. Schriftenreihe des Vereins Naturschutzpark e.V. Stuttgart and Hamburg: privately printed, n.d. [1962?].

———, ed. *Naturparke in technischer, medizinischer und organisatorischer Sicht*. Schriftenreihe des Vereins Naturschutzpark. Stuttgart and Hamburg: privately printed, n.d. [1963?].

———, ed. *Vorträge über Naturparke II*. Schriftenreihe des Vereins Naturschutzpark e.V. Stuttgart and Hamburg: privately printed, 1962.

———, ed. *Wiedergabe von Vorträge, 3/4 Oktober 1969, Mitgliederversammlung des Verbandes Deutscher Naturparke*. Schriftenreihe des Vereins Naturschutzpark e.V. Stuttgart and Hamburg: privately printed, 1969.

Vogt, William. *The Road to Survival*. New York: William Sloane, 1948.

Ward, Barbara and René Dubos. *Only One Earth. The Care and Maintenance of a Small Planet*. New York: Norton, 1972.

Weinzierl, Hubert. *Die große Wende im Naturschutz*. Munich: BLV, 1970.

———. *Die Krönung des Naturschutzgedankens: Deutschlands Nationalpark im Bayerischen Wald soll Wirklichkeit werden*. Grafenau: Morsak, 1983.

Secondary Sources

Abelshauser, Werner, *Die langen Fünfziger Jahre. Wirtschaft und Gesellschaft der Bundesrepublik Deutschland 1945–1966*. Düsseldorf: Schwann, 1987.

———. ed. *Umweltgeschichte: Umweltverträgliches Wirtschaften in historisher Perspektive*. Göttingen: Vandenhoeck & Ruprecht, 1994.

Abrams, Meyer Howard. *Natural Supernaturalism: Tradition and Revolution in Romantic Literature*. New York: Norton, 1971.

Andersen, Arne. "Das 50er-Jahre-Syndrom. Umweltfragen in der Demokratisierung des Technikkonsums." *Technikgeschichte* 65, no. 4 (1998): 329–44.

———. *Der Traum vom guten Leben. Alltags- und Konsumgeschichte vom Wirtschaftswunder bis heute*. Frankfurt am Main: Campus, 1997.

———. "Mentalitätenwechsel und ökologische Konsequenzen des Konsumismus. Die Durchsetzung der Konsumgesellschaft in den fünfziger Jahren." In *Europäische Konsumgeschichte: Zur Gesellschafts- und Kulturgeschichte des Konsums (18. bis 20. Jahrhundert)*, ed. Hannes Siegrist, Hartmut Kaelble, and Jürgen Kocka, 763–91. Frankfurt am Main: Campus, 1997.

Applegate, Celia. "Localism and the German Bourgeoisie: the 'Heimat' Movement in the Rhenish Palatinate before 1914." In *The German Bourgeoisie: Essays on the Social History of the German Middle Class from the Late Eighteenth to the Early Twentieth Century*, ed. David Blackbourn and Richard J. Evans, 224–54. New York: Routledge, 1991.

———. *Nation of Provincials: The German Idea of Heimat*. Berkeley: University of California Press, 1990.

Barthelmeß, Alfred. *Landschaft—Lebensraum des Menschen. Probleme von Landschaftsschutz und Landschaftspflege*. Freiburg im Breisgau: Alber, 1988.

————. *Wald—Umwelt des Menschen. Dokumente zu einer Problemgeschichte von Naturschutz, Landschaftspflege und Humanökologie.* Freiburg im Breisgau: Alber, 1972.

Bayerisches Staatsministerium für Ernährung, Landwirtschaft und Forsten, ed. *Eine Landschaft wird Nationalpark.* Schriftenreihe des Bayerischen Staatsministeriums für Ernährung, Landwirtschaft und Forsten, no. 11. Grafenau: Morsak, 1983.

————, ed. *Nationalpark Bayerischer Wald.* 2d ed. Munich: Bayerisches Staatsministerium für Ernährung, Landwirtschaft und Forsten, 1988.

Berghahn, Volker. *Modern Germany: Society, Economy and Politics in the Twentieth Century.* 2d ed. Cambridge: Cambridge University Press, 1982.

Bergmann, Klaus. *Agrarromantik und Grossstadtfeindschaft.* Meisenheim am Glan: Anton Hain, 1970.

Bergmeier, Monika. *Umweltgeschichte der Boomjahre 1949–1973. Das Beispiel Bayern.* Münster: Waxmann, 2002.

Bess, Michael. "Artificialization and its Discontents." *Environmental History* 10, no. 1 (January 2005): 32–33.

————. *The Light–Green Society. Ecology and Technological Modernity in France, 1960–2000.* Chicago: University of Chicago Press, 2003.

Bibelriether, Hans. "Das größte Naturwaldreservat Mitteleuropas." *Nationalpark,* no. 71 (February 1991): 49–51.

————. "Natur im Nationalpark schützen. Welche? Für wen? Wozu?" *Nationalpark,* no. 68 (March 1990): 29–31.

Bird, Elizabeth Ann R. "Social Construction of Nature: Theoretical Approaches to the History of Environmental Problems." *Environmental Review* (Winter 1987): 255–64.

Blackbourn, David. *The Conquest of Nature. Water, Landscape, and the Making of Modern Germany.* New York: Norton, 2006.

Bocking, Stephen, *Ecologists and Environmental Politics: A History of Contemporary Ecology.* New Haven: Yale University Press, 1997.

————. *Nature's Experts. Science, Politics, and the Environment.* New Brunswick: Rutgers University Press, 2004.

Böhme, Gernot. *Natürlich Natur. Über Natur im Zeitalter ihrer technischen Reproduzierbarkeit.* Frankfurt am Main: Suhrkamp, 1992.

Bölsche, Jochen, ed. *Die deutsche Landschaft stirbt: zerschnitten—zersiedelt—zerstört.* Reinbek: Rowohlt, 1983.

Bramwell, Anna. *Blood and Soil. Walther Darré and Hitler's Green Party.* Buckinghamshire: Kensal, 1985.

————. *Ecology in the 20th Century.* New Haven: Yale University Press, 1989.

Brand, Karl-Werner. *Neue soziale Bewegungen. Entstehung, Funktion und Perspektive neuer Protestpotentiale. Eine Zwischenbilanz.* Opladen: Westdeutscher Verlag, 1982.

————, ed. *Neue soziale Bewegungen in Westeuropa und den USA: ein internationaler Vergleich.* Frankfurt am Main: Campus, 1985.

Brand, Karl-Werner, Detlef Büsser, and Dieter Rucht. *Aufbruch in eine andere Gesellschaft. Neue soziale Bewegungen in der Bundesrepublik Deutschland.* Frankfurt am Main: Campus, 1983.

Brechin, Steven and Willett Kempton. "Global Environmentalism. A Challenge to the Postmaterialism Thesis?" *Social Science Quarterly* 74 (1994): 245–69.

Brüggemeier, Franz-Josef. *Tschernobyl, 26. April 1986. Die Ökologische Herausforderung.* München: Deutscher Taschenbuch Verlag, 1998.

Brüggemeier, Franz-Josef, Mark Cioc, and Thomas Zeller, eds. *How Green Were the Nazis?: Nature, Environment, and Nation in the Third Reich.* Athens: Ohio University Press, 2005.

Brüggemeier, Franz-Josef and Jens Ivo Engels, eds. *Natur- und Umweltschutz nach 1945. Konzepte, Konflikte, Kompetenzen.* Frankfurt am Main: Campus, 2005.

Brüggemeier, Franz-Josef and Thomas Rommelspacher, eds. *Besiegte Natur. Geschichte der Umwelt im 19. und 20. Jahrhundert.* Munich: C.H. Beck, 1989.

Brüggemeier, Franz-Josef and Thomas Rommelspacher. *Blauer Himmel über der Ruhr. Geschichte der Umwelt im Ruhrgebiet 1840–1990.* Essen: Klartext-Verlag, 1992.

Brun, Rudolf, ed. *Der grüne Protest.* Frankfurt am Main: Fischer, 1978.

Brunnengräber, Richard. *Deutschland—Deine Landschaften. Ein Geographiebuch zum Thema Umweltzerstörung.* 2d rev. ed. Munich: Deutscher Taschenbuch Verlag, 1985.

Bryson, Bill. "Main-Danube Canal." *National Geographic* 182, no. 2 (August 1992): 3–31.
Buchwald, Konrad and Wolfgang Engelhardt, eds. *Handbuch für Landschaftspflege und Natur-schutz. Schutz, Pflege und Entwicklung unserer Wirtschafts- und Erholungslandschaften auf öko-logischer Grundlage*. Vol. 4, *Planung und Ausführung*. Munich: BLV Verlagsgesellschaft, 1969.
Bullock, Alan. *Ernst Bevin*. Vol. 3, *Foreign Secretary, 1945–1951*. New York: Norton, 1983.
Cairncross, Sir Alec. *The Price of War: British Policy on German Reparations, 1941–1949*. New York: Blackwell, 1986.
Cermakian, Jean. *The Moselle: River and Canal from the Roman Empire to the European Economic Community*. Toronto: University of Toronto Press, 1975.
Chaney, Sandra. "Visions and Revisions of Nature: From the Protection of Nature to the Invention of the Environment in the Federal Republic of Germany, 1945–1975." PhD diss., University of North Carolina at Chapel Hill, 1996.
Childs, David. *Germany in the Twentieth Century*. New York: Harper Collins, 1991.
Cioc, Mark. "The Impact of the Coal Age on the German Environment: A Review of the Historical Literature." *Environment and History* 4, no. 1 (1998): 105–24.
———. *The Rhine: An Eco-Biography, 1815–2000*. Seattle: University of Washington Press, 2002.
Confino, Alon. "The Nation as a Local Metaphor: Heimat, National Memory and the German Empire, 1871–1918." *History and Memory* 5, no. 1 (Spring/Summer, 1993): 42–86.
———. *The Nation as a Local Metaphor: Württemberg, Imperial Germany, and National Memory*. Chapel Hill: University of North Carolina Press, 1997.
Cosgrove, Denis and Stephen Daniels, eds., *The Iconography of Landscape: Essays on the Symbolic Representation, Design and Use of Past Environments*. Cambridge: Cambridge University Press, 1988.
Cosgrove, Denis and Geoff Petts, eds. *Water, Engineering and Landscape. Water Control and Landscape Transformation in the Modern Period*. London: Belhaven, 1990.
Cronon, William, ed. *Uncommon Ground. Toward Reinventing Nature*. New York: Norton, 1995.
Dalton, Russell J. *The Green Rainbow: Environmental Groups in Western Europe*. New Haven: Yale University Press, 1994.
Daniels, Stephen. *Fields of Vision: Landscape Imagery and National Identity in England and the United States*. Princeton: Princeton University Press, 1993.
Diebold, William. *Schuman Plan: A Study in Economic Cooperation*. New York: Frederick A. Praeger, 1959.
Diefendorf, Jeffry M., Axel Frohn, and Hermann-Josef Rupieper, eds. *American Policy and the Reconstruction of West Germany, 1945–1955*. New York: Cambridge University Press, 1993.
Ditt, Karl, "Die Anfänge der Umweltpolitik in der Bundesrepublik Deutschland während der 1960er und frühen 1970er Jahre. In *Demokratisierung und gesellschaftlicher Aufbruch. Die sechziger Jahre als Wendezeit der Bundesrepublik*, ed. Matthias Frese, Julia Paulus, and Karl Teppe, 305–48. Paderborn: Schöningh, 2003.
———. "Nature Conservation in England and Germany 1900–70: Forerunner of Environmental Protection?" Translated by Jane Rafferty. *Contemporary European History* 5, no. 1 (1996): 1–28.
———. "Naturschutz und Tourismus in England und in der Bundesrepublik Deutschland 1949–1980." *Archiv für Sozialgeschichte* 43 (2003): 29–49.
Dominick, Raymond H. *Environmental Movement in Germany. Prophets & Pioneers, 1871–1971*. Bloomington: Indiana University Press, 1992.
Dubos, René. *Wooing of Earth. New Perspectives on Man's Use of Nature*. New York: Scribner's, 1980.
Eisenberg, Carolyn. *Drawing the Line. The American Decision to Divide Germany, 1944–1949*. New York: Cambridge University Press, 1996.
Engels, Jens Ivo. *Naturpolitik in der Bundesrepublik. Ideenwelt und politische Verhaltensstile in Naturschutz und Umweltbewegung 1950–1980*. Paderborn: Schöningh, 2006.
———. "Von der Sorge um die Tiere zur Sorge um die Umwelt. Tiersendungen als Umweltpolitik in Westdeutschland zwischen 1950 und 1980." *Archiv für Sozialgeschichte* 43 (2003): 297–323.
Eser, Uta. *Der Naturschutz und das Fremde. Ökologische und normative Grundlagen der Umweltethik*. Frankfurt am Main: Campus, 1999.

Evernden, Neil. *Social Creation of Nature*. Baltimore: The Johns Hopkins University Press, 1992.

Fehrenbach, Heide. *Cinema in Democratizing Germany: Reconstructing National Identity after Hitler*. Chapel Hill: University of North Carolina Press, 1995.

Fischer, Norbert. "Der neue Blick auf die Landschaft: Die Geschichte der Landschaft im Schnittpunkt von Sozial-, Geistes- und Umweltgeschichte." *Archiv für Sozialgeschichte* 36 (1996): 434–42.

Fischer, Per. *Die Saar zwischen Deutschland und Frankreich. Politische Entwicklung von 1945– 1959*. Frankfurt am Main: Metzner, 1959.

Frese, Matthias, Julia Paulus, and Karl Teppe, eds. *Demokratisierung und gesellschaftlicher Aufbruch. Die sechziger Jahre als Wendezeit der Bundesrepublik*. Paderborn: Schöningh, 2003.

Freymond, Jacques. *The Saar Conflict, 1945–1955*. New York: Praeger, 1960.

Frohn, Hans-Werner and Friedemann Schmoll, eds. *Natur und Staat. Staatlicher Naturschutz in Deutschland 1906–2006*. Bonn: Bundesamt für Naturschutz, 2006.

Frost, Robert L. "The Flood of 'Progress': Technocrats and Peasants at Tignes (Savoy), 1946– 1952." *French Historical Studies* 14, no. 1 (Spring 1985): 117–40.

Fulbrook, Mary. *The Divided Nation. A History of Germany 1918–1990*. New York: Oxford University Press, 1992.

Gillingham, John, *Coal, Steel, and the Rebirth of Europe, 1945–1955. The Germans and French from Ruhr Conflict to Economic Community*. Cambridge: Cambridge University Press, 1991.

Glaser, Hermann. *Kleine Kulturgeschichte der Bundesrepublik Deutschland 1945–1989*. Munich: Carl Hanser, 1991; Bonn: Bundeszentrale für politische Bildung, 1991.

Goodbody Axel, ed. *The Culture of German Environmentalism: Anxieties, Visions, Realities*. New York: Berghahn, 2002.

Granieri, Ronald J. *The Ambivalent Alliance. Konrad Adenauer, the CDU/CSU, and the West, 1949–1966*. New York: Berghahn, 2003.

Gröning, Gert and Joachim Wolschke. "Die Landespflege als Instrument Nationalsozialistischer Eroberungspolitik." *Arch + 81* (August 1985): 46–59.

Gröning, Gert and Joachim Wolschke-Bulmahn. *Die Liebe zur Landschaft*. Vol. 1, *Natur in Bewegung. Zur Bedeutung natur- und freiraumorientierter Bewegungen der ersten Hälfte der 20. Jahrhunderts für die Entwicklung der Freiraumplanung*. Munich: Minerva, 1986.

———. *Die Liebe zur Landschaft*. Vol. 3, *Der Drang nach Osten. Zur Entwicklung der Landespflege im Nationalsozialismus in den 'eingegliederten Ostgebieten' während des Zweiten Weltkriegs*. Munich: Minerva, 1987.

———. "Naturschutz und Ökologie im Nationalsozialismus." *Die Alte Stadt* 10 (1983): 1–17.

Großklaus, Götz and Ernst Oldemeyer, eds. *Natur als Gegenwelt. Beiträge zur Kulturgeschichte der Natur*. Karlsruhe: Loeper, 1983.

Gudermann, Rita. *Morastwelt und Paradies: Ökonomie und Ökologie in der Landwirtschaft am Beispiel der Meliorationen in Westfalen und Brandenburg (1830–1880)*. Paderborn: Schöningh, 2000.

Guggenberger, Bernd. "Umweltpolitik und Ökologiebewegung." In *Die Geschichte der Bundesrepublik Deutschland*. Vol. 3, *Wirtschaft*, ed. Wolfgang Benz, 393–427. Frankfurt am Main: Fischer, 1989.

Guggenberger, Bernd and Udo Kempf, eds. *Bürgerinitiativen und repräsentatives System*. 2d rev. ed. Opladen: Westdeutscher Verlag, 1984.

Häberle, Manfred. "Environmental Protection—The German Experience." *Chemistry and Industry* (6 January 1986): 12–16.

Hatch, Michael T. *Politics and Nuclear Power. Energy Policy in Western Europe*. Lexington: University Press of Kentucky, 1986.

Hauff, Volker, ed. *Bürgerinitiativen in der Gesellschaft: politische Dimensionen und Reaktionen*. Villingen-Schwenningen: Neckar-Verlag, 1980.

Haug, Michael. "Die Entstehungsgeschichte des Nationalparks Bayerischer Wald und die Entwicklung seit 1969." In *Eine Landschaft wird Nationalpark*. Schriftenreihe des Bayerischen Staatsministeriums für Ernährung, Landwirtschaft und Forsten, ed. Bayerisches Staatsministerium für Ernährung, Landwirtschaft und Forsten, no. 11, 35–76. Grafenau: Morsak, 1983.

Hays, Samuel P. *Beauty, Health and Permanence. Environmental Politics in the United States, 1955–1985*. New York: Cambridge University Press, 1987.

———. *A History of Environmental Politics Since 1945.* Pittsburgh: Pittsburgh University Press, 2000.

Heineman, Elizabeth. "The Hour of the Woman: Memories of Germany's 'Crisis Years' and West German National Identity." *American Historical Review* 101, no. 2 (April 1996): 354–95.

Herf, Jeffrey. *Divided Memory. The Nazi Past in the Two Germanys.* Cambridge: Harvard University Press, 1997.

Hermand, Jost. *Grüne Utopien in Deutschland. Zur Geschichte des ökologischen Bewußtseins.* Frankfurt am Main: Fischer, 1991.

———, ed. *Mit den Bäumen sterben die Menschen. Zur Kulturgeschichte der Ökologie.* Cologne: Böhlau 1993.

Herndl, Carl G. and Stuart C. Brown, eds. *Green Culture. Environmental Rhetoric in Contemporary America.* Madison: University of Wisconsin Press, 1996.

Hoplitschek, Ernst. "Der Bund Naturschutz in Bayern. Traditioneller Naturschutzverband oder Teil der neuen sozialen Bewegungen?" PhD diss., Free University of Berlin, 1984.

Huber, Joseph. "Fortschritt und Entfremdung. Ein Entwicklungsmodell des ökologischen Diskurses." In *Industrialismus und Ökoromantik. Geschichte und Perspektiven der Ökologisierung,* ed. Dieter Hassenpflug, 19–42. Wiesbaden: Deutscher Universitätsverlag, 1991.

Hülsberg, Werner. *The German Greens. A Social and Political Profile.* Translated by Gus Fagan. London and New York: Verso, 1988.

———. "The Greens at the Crossroads." *New Left Review* 152 (July/August 1985): 5–29.

Hünemörder, Kai F. *Die Frühgeschichte der globalen Umweltkrise und die Formierung der deutschen Umweltpolitik (1950–1973).* Stuttgart: Steiner, 2004.

———. "Vom Expertennetzwerk zur Umweltpolitik. Frühe Umweltkonferenzen und die Ausweitung der öffentlichen Aufmerksamkeit für Umweltfragen in Europa (1959–1972)." *Archiv für Sozialgeschichte* 43 (2003): 275–96.

Inglehart, Ronald. "Post-Materialism in an Environment of Insecurity." *American Political Science Review* 75 (1981): 880–900.

———. *The Silent Revolution. Changing Values and Political Styles among Western Publics.* Princeton: Princeton University Press, 1977.

Jarausch, Konrad H. *After Hitler: Recivilizing Germans, 1945–1995.* Translated by Brandon Hunziker. New York: Oxford University Press, 2006.

———. ed. *After Unity: Reconfiguring German Identities.* Providence: Berghahn, 1997.

Judt, Tony. *Postwar. A History of Europe Since 1945.* New York: Penguin, 2005.

Kiener, Hans. "Neuer Wald nach Windwürfen und Borkenkäferbefall." *Nationalpark,* no. 68 (March 1990): 49–53.

Kitschelt, Herbert. *The Logics of Party Formation. Ecological Politics in Belgium and West Germany.* Ithaca: Cornell University Press, 1989.

Kleßmann, Christoph. *Die doppelte Staatsgründung: Deutsche Geschichte 1945–1955.* 5th ed. Göttingen: Vandenhoeck & Ruprecht, 1982; Bonn: Bundeszentrale für politische Bildung, 1991.

———. *Zwei Staaten, eine Nation. Deutsche Geschichte 1955–1970.* Göttingen: Vandenhoeck & Ruprecht, 1988; Bonn: Bundeszentrale für politische Bildung, 1988.

Kloepfer, Michael, ed. *Schübe des Umweltbewußtseins und der Umweltrechtsentwicklung.* Bonn: Economica, 1995.

Kluge, Thomas and Engelbert Schramm. *Wassernöte: Sozial- und Umweltgeschichte des Trinkwassers.* Aachen: Alano-Verlag, 1986.

Knaut, Andreas. "Die Anfänge des staatlichen Naturschutzes. Die frühe regierungsamtliche Organisation des Natur- und Landschaftsschutzes in Preußen, Bayern und Württemberg." In *Umweltgeschichte: Umweltverträgliches Wirtschaften in historischer Perspektive,* ed. Werner Abelshauser, 143–62. Göttingen: Vandenhoeck & Ruprecht, 1994.

———. *Zurück zur Natur! Die Wurzeln der Ökologiebewegung.* Greven: Kilda-Verlag, 1993.

Körner, Stefan. *Theorie und Methodologie der Landschaftsplanung, Landschaftsarchitektur und sozialwissenschaftlichen Freiraumplanung vom Nationalsozialismus bis zur Gegenwart.* Berlin: Technische Universität Berlin, 2002.

Koshar, Rudy. *Germany's Transient Pasts. Preservation and National Memory in the Twentieth Century.* Chapel Hill: University of North Carolina Press, 1998.

Kramer, Dieter. *Der sanfte Tourismus. Umwelt und sozialverträglicher Tourismus in den Alpen.* Vienna: Österreichischer Bundesverlag, 1983.

Kreis, Georg, Gerd Krumeich, Henri Ménudier, Hans Mommsen, and Arnold Sywottek, eds. *Alfred Toepfer: Stifter und Kaufman; Bausteine einer Biographie—Kritische Bestandsaufnahme.* Hamburg: Christians, 2000.

Küppers, Günter, Peter Lundgreen, and Peter Weingart. *Umweltforschung—die gesteuerte Wissenschaft? Eine empirische Studie zum Verhältnis von Wissenschaftsentwicklung und Wissenschaftspolitik.* Frankfurt am Main: Suhrkamp, 1978.

Küster, Hansjörg. *Geschichte des Waldes. Von der Urzeit bis zur Gegenwart.* Munich: C.H. Beck, 1998.

Lekan, Thomas. *Imagining the Nation in Nature. Landscape Preservation and German Identity, 1885–1945.* Cambridge: Harvard University Press, 2004.

———. "Regionalism and the Politics of Landscape Preservation in the Third Reich." *Environmental History* 4, no. 3 (July 1999): 384–404.

Lekan, Thomas and Thomas Zeller, eds. *Germany's Nature. Cultural Landscapes and Environmental History.* New Brunswick: Rutgers University Press, 2005.

Lenger, Friedrich, ed. *Towards an Urban Nation. Germany since 1780.* Oxford: Berg, 2000.

Leonhard, Martin. *Umweltverbände. Zur Organisation von Umwelschutzinteressen in der Bundesrepublik Deutschland.* Opladen: Westdeutscher Verlag, 1986.

Linse, Ulrich. *Ökopax und Anarchie. Eine Geschichte der ökologischen Bewegung in Deutschland.* Munich: Deutscher Taschenbuch Verlag, 1986.

Linse, Ulrich, Reinhard Falter, Dieter Rucht, and Winfried Kretschmer, ed. *Von der Bittschrift zur Platzbesetzung. Konflikte um technische Großprojekte.* Bonn: Dietz, 1988.

Lister, Louis. *Europe's Coal and Steel Community: An Experiment in Economic Union.* New York: Twentieth Century Fund, 1960.

Lütkepohl, Manfred and Jens Tönnießen. *Naturschutzpark Lüneburger Heide.* Hamburg: Ellert & Richter, 1992.

Mangun, William Russell. *Public Administration of Environmental Policy: A Comparative Analysis of the United States and West Germany.* Bloomington: Institute of German Studies, 1977.

Marshall, Barbara. "German Attitudes to British Military Government 1945–47." *Journal of Contemporary History* 15 (1980): 655–84.

Mauch, Christof, ed. *Nature in German History.* New York: Berghahn, 2004.

McCormick, John. *Reclaiming Paradise. The Global Environmental Movement.* Bloomington: Indiana University Press, 1989.

McKibben, Bill. *End of Nature.* New York: Random House, 1989.

———. *Enough. Staying Human in an Engineered Age.* New York: Henry Holt, 2003.

McNeill, John R. *Something New Under the Sun. An Environmental History of the Twentieth Century World.* New York: Norton, 2000.

Meine, Curt. *Aldo Leopold: His Life and Work.* Madison: University of Wisconsin Press, 1988.

Mewes, Horst. "The West German Green Party." *New German Critique,* no. 28 (Winter 1983): 51–85.

Mitchell, W. J. T. *Landscape and Power.* 2d ed. Chicago: University of Chicago Press, 2002.

Mitman, Gregg, "In Search of Health: Landscape and Disease in American Environmental History." *Environmental History* 10, no. 2 (April 2005): 184–210.

Moeller, Robert G. *War Stories: The Search for a Usable Past in the Federal Republic of Germany.* Berkeley: University of California Press, 2001.

———, ed. *West Germany under Construction. Politics, Society, and Culture in the Adenauer Era.* Ann Arbor: University of Michigan Press, 1997.

Moore, Curtis and Alan Miller. *Green Gold: Japan, Germany, and the United States and the Race for Environmental Technology.* Boston: Beacon Press, 1994.

Morton, Timothy. *Ecology Without Nature: Rethinking Environmental Aesthetics.* Cambridge: Harvard University Press, 2007.

Mosse, George L. *Crisis of German Ideology: Intellectual Origins of the Third Reich.* New York: Grosset & Dunlap, 1964.

Mrass, Walter. *Die Organisation des staatlichen Naturschutzes und der Landschaftspflege im Deutschen Reich und in der BRD seit 1935 gemessen an der Aufgabenstellung in einer modernen Industriegesellschaft.* Beiheft 1, *Landschaft + Stadt.* Stuttgart: Eugen Ulmer, 1970.

Müller, Edda. "Die Beziehung von Umwelt- und Naturschutz in den 1970er Jahren." In *Natur im Sinn. Beiträge zur Geschichte des Naturschutzes,* ed. Stiftung Naturschutzgeschichte, 31–45. Essen: Klartext-Verlag, 2001.

———. *Innenwelt der Umweltpolitik: Sozial-liberale Umweltpolitik—(Ohn)macht durch Organisation.* Opladen: Westdeutscher Verlag, 1986.

Müller, Rolf-Dieter. *Hitlers Ostkrieg und die deutsche Siedlungspolitik.* Frankfurt am Main: Fischer, 1991.

Nehring, Dorothee. *Geschichte des Stadtgrüns. Stadtparkanlagen in der ersten Hälfte des 19. Jahrhunderts.* Hanover: Patzer, 1979.

Nelson, Arvid. *Cold War Ecology. Forests, Farms, & People in the East German Landscape, 1945– 1989.* New Haven: Yale University Press, 2005.

Neumann, Roderick P. *Imposing Wilderness. Struggles over Livelihood and Nature Preservation in Africa.* Berkeley: University of California Press, 1998.

Oberkrome, Willi. *"Deutsche Heimat." Nationale Konzeption und regionale Praxis von Naturschutz, Landschaftsgestaltung und Kulturpolitik in Westfalen-Lippe und Thüringen (1900–1960).* Paderborn: Schöningh, 2004.

Oelschlaeger, Max. *The Idea of Wilderness: From Prehistory to the Age of Ecology.* New Haven: Yale University Press, 1991.

Olschowy, Gerhard, ed. *Natur- und Umweltschutz in der BRD.* Hamburg: Paul Parey, 1978.

Olsen, Jonathan. *Nature and Nationalism. Right-Wing Ecology and the Politics of Identity in Contemporary Germany.* New York: St. Martin's, 1999.

Palmowski, Jan. "Building an East German Nation: The Construction of a Socialist *Heimat,* 1945–1961." *Central European History* 37, no. 3 (September 2004): 365–99.

Patel, Kiran Klaus. "Neuerfindung des Westens—Aufbruch nach Osten. Naturschutz und Landschaftsgestaltung in den Vereinigten Staaten von Amerika und in Deutschland, 1900–1945." *Archiv für Sozialgeschichte* 43 (2003): 191–223.

Pfister, Christian, ed. *Das 1950er Syndrom. Der Weg in die Konsumgesellschaft.* Bern: Paul Haupt, 1995.

Pfizer, Theodor, ed. *Baden-Württemberg. Staat, Wirtschaft, Kultur.* Stuttgart: Deutsche Verlags-Anstalt, 1963.

Pflug, Wolfram. "200 Jahre Landespflege in Deutschland. Eine Übersicht." In *Stadt und Landschaft, Raum und Zeit. Festschrift für Erich Kühn zur Vollendung seines 65. Lebensjahres,* ed. Alfred C. Boettger and Pflug, 237–89. Cologne: Deutscher Verband für Wohnungswesen, Städtebau und Raumplanung, 1969.

Poblotzki, Ursula. *Menschenbilder in der Landespflege 1945–1970.* Munich: Minerva, 1992.

Poiger, Ute. *Jazz, Rock, and Rebels: Cold War Politics and American Culture in a Divided Germany.* Berkeley: University of California Press, 2000.

Pois, Robert A. *National Socialism and the Religion of Nature.* London: Croom Helm, 1986.

Potthast, Thomas. *Die Evolution und der Naturschutz. Zum Verhältnis von Evolutionsbiologie, Ökologie und Naturethik.* Frankfurt am Main: Campus, 1999.

Proctor, Robert N. *The Nazi War on Cancer.* Princeton: Princeton University Press, 1999.

Radkau, Joachim. *Aufstieg und Krise der deutschen Atomwirtschaft 1945–1975. Verdrängte Alternativen in der Kerntechnik und der Ursprung der nuklearen Kontroverse.* Reinbek: Rowohlt, 1983.

———. *Natur und Macht. Eine Weltgeschichte der Umwelt.* Munich: C.H. Beck, 2000.

Radkau, Joachim and Frank Uekötter, eds. *Naturschutz und Nationalsozialismus.* Frankfurt am Main: Campus, 2003.

Raschke, Joachim. *Soziale Bewegungen. Ein historisch-systematischer Grundriß.* Frankfurt am Main: Campus, 1985.

Reichelt, Günther. *Wach sein für Morgen. 40 Jahre Bürger für Natur- und Umweltschutz in Baden-Württemberg.* Stuttgart: Theiss, 1992.

Riechers, Burkhardt. "Nature Protection during National Socialism," *Historical Social Research* 29, no. 3 (1996): 34-56.

Riordan, Colin, ed. *Green Thought in German Culture: Historical and Contemporary Perspectives.* Cardiff: University of Wales Press, 1997.

Rohkrämer, Thomas. *Eine andere Moderne? Zivilisationskritik, Natur und Technik in Deutschland 1880–1933.* Paderborn: Schöningh, 1999.

Rollins, William. *A Greener Vision of Home. Cultural Politics and Environmental Reform in the German Heimatschutz Movement, 1904–1918.* Ann Arbor: University of Michigan Press, 1997.
———. "Whose Landscape? Technology, Fascism, and Environmentalism on the National Socialist Autobahn. *Annals of the Association of American Geographers* 85, no. 3 (September 1995): 494–520.
Rommelspacher, Thomas. "Zwischen Heimatschutz und Umweltprotest. Konflikte um Natur, Umwelt und Technik in der BRD 1945–1965." In *Soziologie als Krisenwissenschaft,* ed. Hans Uske, Hermann Völlings, Jochen Zimmer, and Christof Stracke, 74–95. Münster: Lit, 1998.
Rössler, Mechtild. "'Area Research' and 'Spatial Planning' from the Weimar Republic to the German Federal Republic: Creating a Society with a Spatial Order under National Socialism." In *Science, Technology and National Socialism,* ed. Monika Renneberg and Mark Walker, 126–38. Cambridge: Cambridge University Press, 1994.
———. "Die Institutionalisierung einer neuen Wissenschaft: Raumforschung und Raumordnung 1935–1945." *Geographische Zeitschrift* 75 (1987): 177–94.
Rössler, Mechtild and Sabine Schleiermacher, eds. *Der 'Generalplan Ost': Hauptlinien der nationalsozialistischen Planungs- und Vernichtungspolitik.* Berlin: Akademie Verlag, 1993.
Roth, Roland. "'Patch-Work.' Kollektive Identitäten neuer sozialer Bewegungen." In *Paradigmen der Bewegungsforschung,* ed. Kai-Uwe Hellmann and Ruud Koopmanns, 51–68. Opladen: Westdeutscher Verlag, 1998.
Roth, Roland and Dieter Rucht, eds. *Neue Soziale Bewegungen in der Bundesrepublik Deutschland.* Frankfurt am Main: Campus, 1987.
Rubner, Heinrich. "Naturschutz, Forstwirtschaft und Umwelt in ihren Wechselbeziehungen, besonders im NS-Staat." In *Wirtschaftsentwicklung und Umweltbeeinflussung,* ed. Hermann Kellenbenz, 105–23. Wiesbaden: Steiner, 1982.
Rucht, Dieter, ed. *Flughafenprojekte als Politikum. Die Konflikte in Stuttgart, München, und Frankfurt.* Frankfurt am Main: Campus, 1984.
———. "The Impact of Environmental Movements in Western Societies." In *How Social Movements Matter,* ed. Marco Giugni, Doug McAdam, and Charles Tilly, 204–24. Minneapolis: University of Minnesota Press, 1999.
———. *Von Wyhl nach Gorleben. Bürger gegen Atomprogramm und nukleare Entsorgung.* Munich: C.H. Beck, 1980.
Ruck, Michael. "Ein kurzer Sommer der konkreten Utopie—Zur westdeutschen Planungsgeschichte der langen 60er Jahre." In *Dynamische Zeiten. Die 60er Jahre in den beiden deutschen Gesellschaften,* ed. Axel Schildt, Detlef Siegfried, and Karl Christian Lammers, 362–401. Hamburg: Christians, 2000.
Rüdig, Wolfgang, "Eco-Socialism: Left Environmentalism in West Germany." *New Political Science,* no. 1 (Winter 1985/1986): 3–37.
———. "The Greening of Germany." *The Ecologist* 13, no. 1 (1983): 35–39.
Schäfer, Wolf. *Neue Soziale Bewegungen: Konservativer Aufbruch im bunten Gewand?* Frankfurt am Main: Fischer, 1983.
Schama, Simon. *Landscape and Memory.* New York: Knopf, 1995.
Schildt, Axel. "From Reconstruction to 'Leisure Society': Free Time, Recreational Behaviour and the Discourse on Leisure Time in the West German Recovery Society of the 1950s." *Contemporary European History* 5, no. 2 (1996): 191–222.
———. "'Mach mal Pause!' Freie Zeit, Freizeitverhalten und Freizeit-Diskurs in der westdeutschen Wiederaufbau–Gesellschaft der 1950er Jahre." *Archiv für Sozialgeschichte* 33 (1993): 357–406.
Schildt, Axel, Detlef Siegfried, and Karl Christian Lammers, eds. *Dynamische Zeiten. Die 60er Jahre in den beiden deutschen Gesellschaften.* Hamburg: Christians, 2000.
Schildt, Axel and Arnold Sywottek, eds. *Modernisierung im Wiederaufbau: Die westdeutsche Gesellschaft der 50er Jahre.* Bonn: Dietz, 1998.
Schissler, Hanna, ed. *The Miracle Years: A Cultural History of West Germany, 1945–1968.* Princeton: Princeton University Press, 2001.
Schmoll, Friedemann. *Erinnerungen an die Natur. Die Geschichte des Naturschutzes im deutschen Kaiserreich.* Frankfurt am Main: Campus, 2004.
Schöller, Peter, Willi Walter Puls, and Hanns J. Buchholz, eds. *Federal Republic of Germany. Spatial Development and Problems.* Paderborn: Schöningh, 1980.

Schroeder, Gregory F. "Ties of Urban Heimat: West German Cities and Their Wartime Evacuees in the 1950s." *German Studies Review* 27, no. 2 (May 2004): 307–24.

Schulze Hannöver, Sandra and Martin Becker. "Natur im Sinn." In *Natur im Sinn. Beiträge zur Geschichte des Naturschutzes,* ed. Stiftung Naturschutzgeschichte, 9–30. Essen: Klartext- Verlag, 2001.

Schumacher, Winfried. "Konrad Adenauer und die Saar." In *Die Saar 1945–1955: Ein Problem der europäischen Geschichte,* ed. Rainer Hudermann and Raymond Poidevin, 49–74. Munich: Oldenbourg, 1992.

Schurig, Volker. "Politischer Naturschutz: Warum wurde in der DDR (1949–1989) kein Nationalpark gegründet?" *N & L* 66, no. 7/8 (July/August 1991): 363–71.

Scott, James C. *Seeing Like a State. How Certain Schemes to Improve the Human Condition Have Failed.* New Haven: Yale University Press, 1998.

Sellars, Richard W. *Preserving Nature in the National Parks: A History.* New Haven: Yale University Press, 1997.

Sheail, John. *Nature in Trust. The History of Nature Conservation in Britain.* Glasgow: Blackie, 1976.

Sieferle, Rolf Peter. *Fortschrittsfeinde? Opposition gegen Technik und Industrie von der Romantik bis zur Gegenwart.* Munich: C.H. Beck, 1984.

———. "Heimatschutz und das Ende der Romantischen Utopie." *Arch +,* no. 81 (August 1985): 38–42.

Siegrist, Hannes, Hartmut Kaelble, and Jürgen Kocka, eds. *Europäische Konsumgeschichte: zur Gesellschafts- und Kulturgeschichte des Konsums (18. bis 20. Jahrhundert).* Frankfurt am Main: Campus, 1997.

Simmons, Ian G. *Interpreting Nature. Cultural Constructions of the Environment.* London: Routledge, 1993.

Smith, Woodruff D. *Politics and the Sciences of Culture in Germany, 1840–1920.* New York: Oxford University Press, 1991.

Soulé, Michale E. and Gary Lease, eds. *Reinventing Nature?: Responses to Postmodern Deconstruction.* Washington, DC: Island Press, 1995.

Spelsberg, Gerd. *Rauchplage: Hundert Jahre Saurer Regen.* Aachen: Alano-Verlag, 1984.

Spence, Mark David. *Dispossessing the Wilderness. Indian Removal and the Making of the National Parks.* New York: Oxford University Press, 1999.

Sperber, Georg. "Entstehungsgeschichte eines ersten deutschen Nationalparks im Bayerischen Wald." In *Natur im Sinn. Beiträge zur Geschichte des Naturschutzes,* ed. Stiftung Naturschutzgeschichte, 63–115. Essen: Klartext-Verlag, 2001.

Spirn, Anne Whiston. *The Language of Landscape.* New Haven: Yale University Press, 2000.

Stern, Fritz. *Politics of Cultural Despair. A Study in the Rise of the Germanic Ideology.* Berkeley: University of California Press, 1974 [1961].

Strobl, Reinhard. "Die Geschichte des Waldes und seiner Besiedlung." In *Eine Landschaft wird Nationalpark.* Schriftenreihe des Bayerischen Staatsministeriums für Ernährung, Landwirtschaft und Forsten, ed. Bayerisches Staatsministerium für Ernährung, Landwirtschaft und Forsten, no. 11, 8–31. Grafenau: Morsak, 1983.

Tönnießen, Jens and Gottfried Vauk. "Heide statt Kanonendonner." *Nationalpark,* no. 74 (January 1992): 19–23.

Trepl, Ludwig. *Geschichte der Ökologie. Vom 17. Jahrhundert bis zur Gegenwart.* Frankfurt am Main: Atheneum, 1987.

———. "Ökologie—eine grüne Leitwissenschaft? Über Grenzen und Perspektiven einer modischen Disziplin." *Kursbuch,* no. 74 (December 1983): 6–27.

Uekötter, Frank. *The Green and the Brown. A History of Conservation in Nazi Germany.* New York: Cambridge University Press, 2006.

———. "Green Nazis? Reassessing the Environmental History of Nazi Germany." *German Studies Review* 30, no. 2 (May 2007): 267–87.

———. *Naturschutz im Aufbruch. Eine Geschichte des Naturschutzes in Nordrhein-Westfalen 1945–1980.* Frankfurt am Main: Campus, 2004.

———. "Umweltbewegung zwischen dem Ende der nationalsozialistischen Herrschaft und der 'ökologischen Wende': Ein Literaturbericht." *Historical Social Research* 28 (2003): 270–89.

———. *Von der Rauchplage zur ökologischen Revolution. Eine Geschichte der Luftverschmutzung in Deutschland und den USA 1880–1970.* Essen: Klartext-Verlag, 2003.

Vierhaus, Hans-Peter. *Umweltbewußtsein von oben. Zum Verfassungsgebot demokratischer Willensbildung.* Berlin: Duncker & Humblot, 1994.

Vogel, Ludwig. "Der Ausbau der Mosel zur Gross–Schiffahrtsstraße 1945–1957." *Geschichte im Westen* 11 (1996): 72–90.

Von Dirke, Sabine. *"All Power to the Imagination." The West German Counterculture from the Student Movement to the Greens.* Lincoln: University of Nebraska Press, 1997.

Weiner, Douglas. "A Death-defying Attempt to Articulate a Coherent Definition of Environmental History." *Environmental History* 10, no. 3 (July 2005): 404–20.

Wengert, Norman. "Land Use Planning and Control in the German Federal Republic." *Natural Resources Journal* 15 (July 1975): 511–28.

Wettengel, Michael. "Staat und Naturschutz 1906–1945: Zur Geschichte der Staatlichen Stelle für Naturdenkmalpflege in Preußen und der Reichsstelle für Naturschutz." *Historische Zeitschrift* 257, no. 2 (October 1993): 355–99.

Wey, Klaus-Georg. *Umweltpolitik in Deutschland: kurze Geschichte des Umweltschutzes in Deutschland seit 1900.* Opladen: Westdeutscher Verlag, 1982.

Weyergraf, Bernd. *Waldungen. Die Deutschen und Ihr Wald.* Berlin: Nicolaische Verlagsbuchhandlung, 1987.

White, Richard. "From Wilderness to Hybrid Landscapes: The Cultural Turn in Environmental History." *The Historian* 66, no. 3 (Fall 2004): 557–64.

———. *The Organic Machine. The Remaking of the Columbia River.* New York: Hill and Wang, 1995.

Williams, John Alexander. "'The Chords of the German Soul are Tuned to Nature': The Movement to Preserve the Natural *Heimat* from the Kaiserreich to the Third Reich." *Central European History* 29, no. 3 (1996): 339–84.

Williams, Raymond. *The Country and the City.* New York: Oxford University Press, 1975.

Willis, Frank Roy. *France, Germany, and the New Europe, 1945–1963.* Stanford: Stanford University Press, 1965.

———. *The French in Germany.* Stanford: Stanford University Press, 1962.

Wolschke-Bulmahn, Joachim. *Auf der Suche nach Arkadien: Zu Landschaftsidealen und Formen der Naturaneignung in der Jugendbewegung und ihrer Bedeutung für die Landespflege.* Munich: Minerva, 1990.

Worster, Donald. *Nature's Economy: A History of Ecological Ideas.* Sierra Club Books, 1977. Reprint, New York: Cambridge University Press, 1985.

———. *The Wealth of Nature: Environmental History and the Ecological Imagination.* New York: Oxford University Press, 1993.

Zeller, Thomas. *Straße, Bahn, Panorama. Verkehrswege und Landschaftsveränderung in Deutschland von 1930 bis 1990.* Frankfurt am Main: Campus, 2002.

INDEX

and modernization of conservation,
4–5, 10, 11, 126–28, 132–33,
136–37, 138–39
and nature parks, 117, 122–26
and postwar goals of, 115–16
See also Federal Institute for Spatial
Planning; Federal Spatial
Planning Act
Speer, Albert, 88–89
Sperber, Georg, 230
State Agency for the Care of Natural
Monuments (Prussia) (*Staatliche
Stelle für Naturdenkmalpflege*), 23,
29, 31, 49
Stern, Horst, 232, 244
Stifter, Adalbert, 221
Stockholm Conference. *See* United Na-
tions, Conference on the Human
Environment
Storm, Theodor, 21
Strasbourg, 93, 186
Stuttgart, 24, 59, 64, 86, 94, 95, 102, 104,
107, 131, 189
Šumava National Park, 233. *See also* national
parks
sustainability, 194
Swabian Alb Society, 92, 96, 119, 184
Sweden, 123, 154, 219, 232
Switzerland, 91, 219

T
Tatra National Park (Czechoslovakia), 219.
See also national parks
Taunus Club, 25
Taunus Forest, 220
territorial planning. *See* spatial planning
terrorism, 199, 200
Thielcke, Gerhard, 196, 199, 200
Third Reich. *See* National Socialism
Titisee, 121
Todt, Fritz, 33, 34
Toepfer, Alfred, 62–64, 72, 223
and the Bavarian Forest National Park,
221–22, 223, 225, 227
and the nature park program, 117, 118–24
tourism. *See* nature and tourism; nature
parks; outdoor recreation
Tüxen, Reinhold, 34, 51

U
Umwelt, 7, 130, 133, 137, 176, 178–79. *See
also* environment
Umweltschutz, 2, 5
concept adopted, 176–78, 186
and democratic ideals, 137, 178, 191
ecological vs. technological, 178,
187–89
and the "light-green" society, 201–3,
248
vs. *Naturschutz,* 187–88, 190–91, 192–93
public reaction to, 188–89, 193, 194–99,
201
and rediscovery of nature, 203–4,
246–47, 248–49
See also environment; Action Program
on the Environment; Federal
Environmental Program
United Nations,
Conference on the Biosphere (Paris,
1968), 180–81
Conference on the Human Environment (Stockholm, 1972), 178,
181, 193–95
Educational, Scientific and Cultural
Organization (UNESCO),
180, 181
Food and Agriculture Organization
(FAO), 46, 69
United States, 4, 68, 114, 115, 130, 132, 154
and environmental protection, 178, 185,
186, 189, 191
and national parks, 21, 22, 61, 215
and Progressive Era conservation, 22, 29
Upper Silesia, 28, 37
urbanization, 21, 114–15, 132, 159, 180

V
Versailles treaty, 87, 93
Volk, 19, 20, 29, 32, 33, 36, 37, 68–69,
136
Volksgemeinschaft, 30, 35, 58
Vortisch, Friedrich, 102, 105

W
Walchensee, 24, 91
Wandervogel, 25, 62, 121
Wartheland (Poland), 34